RHYTHM
— AND —
SWING

Richard Hadlee

RHYTHM
— AND —
SWING

An Autobiography with
Richard Becht

SOUVENIR PRESS

ISBN 0 285 629603

© MOA Publications

Published in 1989 by
MOA Publications
P.O. Box 26092, Epsom, Auckland 3,
New Zealand.

First British edition published 1990
by Souvenir Press Ltd., 43 Great Russell Street,
London WC1B 3PA.

Typeset by
Typocrafters Ltd., Auckland

Printed through
Colorcraft Ltd., Hong Kong.

*To my family
and all those
who have supported me*

Contents

ACKNOWLEDGEMENTS

Thank you to the following people who have helped make this book possible —

My wife Karen for her support, recommendations and her chapter

Friends and family who have supported me throughout

All the cricketers for the memories — and the runs and wickets

Richard Becht who interpreted my screeds of notes to portray my life story

Peter Marriott for the compilation of the statistics

The photographers, whose names are acknowledged beside the illustrations

The many journalists and authors who have recorded my career and made researching my autobiography that much easier.

GLOSSARY

Nicknames and abbreviated names used

Mohinder Amarnath	Jimmy
Robert Anderson	Jumbo
Stephen Boock	Boocky
Ian Botham	Both, Beefy
Geoff Boycott	Boycs
John Bracewell	Braces
Lance Cairns	Lancer
Ewen Chatfield	Charlie, Chats
Jeremy Coney	Mantis
Bevan Congdon	Congo
Jeff Crowe	Chopper
Martin Crowe	Hogan
Joel Garner	Big Bird
Richard Hadlee	Paddles, Pads
Chris Kuggeleijn	Kuggs
David O'Sullivan	Daffy
Mark Plummer	Plums
Derek Randall	Arkle
Ken Rutherford	Ruds
Ian Smith	Smithy
Derek Stirling	Billy, Stirls
Gary Troup	Troupy
Glenn Turner	Turns
John Wright	Riggit, Shake, Wrighty

I·N·T·R·O·D·U·C·T·I·O·N

by Richard Becht

The word came back to the New Zealand dressing room within seconds. "We're bowling." John Wright had lost the toss, not the news the team wanted to hear. The whole battle plan revolved around batting first in the third test against Pakistan. The nature of the Eden Park pitch demanded it.

But one player wasn't so fazed about the gloomy tidings. It was 24 February, 1989, the first day of Richard Hadlee's 79th test; it could have been the opening morning of so many of his previous tests, or the 250-odd other first-class matches he'd played. Batting first made perfect cricket sense in this instance, but he wasn't averse, and never had been, to the idea of bowling first in any match — the pitch would never be more helpful for him, and it meant he could settle quickly into the rhythm of a game.

"We're bowling." It's some kind of music to Richard Hadlee's ears. It triggers off all manner of responses. It's the cue, the signal and the command to put on his battledress, right down to the trademark wrist bands — and those impressive size-11 boots. For Hadlee, it also represents an automatic invitation to make a ritualistic visit to the umpires' room so he can pore over the contents of a magical box, a receptacle containing a selection of new gleaming, red cricket balls . . . the tools of Hadlee's trade. Once he was the established lynchpin of the New Zealand attack, selection of the ball became his exclusive right (and the same applied in other first-class matches he played). He's always seen it as one of the perks of his job, an utterly vital function before mixing it with the opposition in the middle.

The cricket ball — it's a hard projectile weighing just five and a half ounces, encased in leather and stitched together by a pronounced seam. West Indian fast bowlers have transformed the ball into a feared weapon, sometimes using it with almost murderous intent. There's a brutish manner about the way they belt the object into the pitch intent on intimidation first, skill second . . . or so it seems.

But Hadlee's trip to the umpires' room and his studied selection of the ball he'll use, mirrors the man's attention to detail and his passion for making fast bowling an art form, not a crude expression of pace, strength and the ability to maim.

Usually there's a choice of a dozen balls, sometimes six; the master looks at them for colour. He tries each one in his hand. How does it feel? Does it sit comfortably in that lethal yet relaxed grip between the right thumb and fingers? How does the seam feel with the index and second fingers running down it? Is it a darker ball, giving it a better chance of swinging more? What about the shape? Then a closer study of the seam as he meticulously counts the number of stitches; he knows just how many stitches there should be in the ideal ball, depending on its make.

Then he finds the ball he wants. He puts a little mark on it, etched on with a fingernail, just so there's no chance of someone switching it on him before play starts. And that did happen once, if only as a bit of a lark. Hadlee was given the new ball to start a match, only to find something amiss. The ball was missing his fingernail inscription; it transpired later that Fred Titmus — according to reliable information — had indulged in a bit of a practical joke. Joke or not, Hadlee wasn't caught out. He knew instantly that he didn't have the ball he'd chosen.

It's the measure of the man's thirst for his job that he's so thorough and analytical before he even steps on to the ground. Nothing's left to chance — it's Hadlee's motto. And it's that kind of fanaticism which transformed him into undoubtedly the most valuable commodity New Zealand cricket's ever had.

After he'd taken his fabulous career-best nine for 52 against Australia in Brisbane in 1985–86, Hadlee swore the ball he had was a freak one, that it literally talked. The fact is, Hadlee, above all others of this age and perhaps any before him, has the innate gift to make the cricket ball obey his commands in all kinds of conditions. He's the one who makes it talk.

And through all the years of dragging his paddle-like feet up to the stumps and whirling down deliveries of metronomic precision, Hadlee's done an awful lot of talking with the ball throughout New Zealand cricket's most glorious phase. It's easy to label him the best cricketer New Zealand's produced, but such assessment's bound to be attacked as a subjective judgment. That's always the case as it has been whenever theories have been expounded about the greatest players in the game like Sir Donald Bradman or Sir Garfield Sobers. In the New Zealand case, Hadlee's detractors will say: "What about John (J.R.) Reid? Or Bert Sutcliffe?" Comparisons can be odious.

But statistics tell no lies, nor can they be influenced by subjective thinking. And the figures alone will always support theories he's the most valuable player this country's seen.

When he made his test debut in 1972–73, New Zealand had

experienced so little success since starting out in test cricket in 1929–30, that only seven of 102 matches had been won, and 46 had been lost. There were some gruesome details among the defeats as New Zealand laboured until 1955–56 for the first test win, and until 1969–70 for the first series triumph (against Pakistan). By 1972–73, New Zealand had still won only one series.

But the Hadlee years have coincided (and certainly not by accident) with this country's richest moments. By the end of that third test against Pakistan last summer — and it wasn't one of the more memorable ones for Richard Hadlee — there'd been a total of 92 tests during what might be called the Hadlee reign. He's missed only 13 of those matches, eight in the early years when he was trying to establish himself, three when he was unavailable for the 1984–85 tour to Pakistan and two through injury against England in 1987–88. During that time, New Zealand has had 20 wins, 33 losses and 39 draws; it's won nine series, and proven itself as a world force.

Better still is the record in the 1980s when 58 tests have provided 17 of those wins, 15 losses and 26 draws. All nine of the series victories have come in the '80s, when only six series have been lost. And last summer, the Kiwis rounded off the glorious decade with the proud record of not one series defeat at home — they'd won six, drawn four. Of the 28 tests played at home, 10 were won, 16 drawn and just two lost (to Australia in Christchurch in 1981–82 and the West Indies in Auckland in 1986–87). It's a marvellous record envied throughout the world (and one England can only dream about on its home form in the same decade).

That tells something of the era New Zealand cricket's enjoyed, without outlining why Richard Hadlee has meant so much. His 396 test wickets say plenty about the damage he's caused when in possession of the ball and, with almost 3000 runs as well, he's also proved the bat's a more than potent substitute weapon when he's not bowling. He's within reach of becoming only the fourth player to do the 3000–300 double in test cricket.

But digest some facts and figures and the enormity of Hadlee's contribution begins to hit home. Take the 1980s as an entity and, in the 53 tests Hadlee played, he scored 2040 runs at 30.90 and took 289 wickets at 19.28, emphasis of his glowing ranking as a quality all rounder at the highest level. And he's been most impressive in his overseas test appearances, the sure sign Richard Hadlee's a player who can perform in all conditions — of those 289 wickets in the '80s, he's taken 170 of them abroad at only 18.00 each. His career record shows nine bags of 10 wickets in a match — and six of those have been captured outside New Zealand and each of those in the 1980s.

Before leaving the statistics alone, there's another one which reinforces the contention New Zealand usually needs major contributions from Hadlee to manufacture test wins. In the 20 wins he's been involved in, he's taken 159 of his wickets at a minuscule average of 12.81 and scored 744 runs at 31.00!

The man who, in 1985–86, became only the sixth player to take more than 300 test wickets, has had his greatness measured with accolade upon accolade, including New Zealand Sportsman of the Year titles in 1980 and 1986. He also won the revised individual male sportsman of the year title in 1987. The crowning achievement was being named, with John Walker, as the co-winner of a special 25-year award made to commemorate the 25th Sportsman of the Year event in 1987, under the Murray Halberg Trust banner. There have been so many others, too.

There have been unofficial titles as well, like the one printed on bumper stickers by a fan after Hadlee's superb feats in Australia in 1985–86. It read: "Sir Richard Hadlee for Prime Minister". The first part appeals, the second not anywhere near so much. The New Zealanders knighted for services to sport have earned their honours off the field of play — Sir Ron Scott, Sir Lance Cross and Sir Murray Halberg. There would be something immediately appropriate if Hadlee was able to join the company of legendary figures like Don Bradman, Len Hutton, Gary Sobers and others who have been knighted for their deeds as cricketers.

Whenever the great fast bowlers are discussed today — or in the future — it's inevitable the names of Richard Hadlee and Dennis Lillee will be mentioned in the same breath, each player standing out as a wonderful technician. They form a mutual admiration society, Hadlee constantly acknowledging Lillee as the perfect model to follow. And Lillee, for his part, has always held Hadlee in the highest regard.

"On the field, it did not take much detective work for spectators to discover that Richard Hadlee and I faced each other fiercely but fairly, and, if a certain amount of needle was visible, then spectators were correct. But that did not diminish in the smallest way my high respect for him," said Lillee.

"We may have confronted each other on the field with hostile eyes, but off the field our relations were excellent. In fact, I can report with some pride that there were occasions when Richard sought my advice on bowling, particularly early in his career, and I was most happy to help whenever I could."

In latter years, Hadlee's been locked in battle for the mythical title of the world's best all rounder. There's been a four-way struggle involving Hadlee, Imran Khan, Kapil Dev and Ian Botham.

It's Imran whom Hadlee rates the outstanding all rounder of his time and Imran spares little in assessing Hadlee's attributes as a bowler: "He must be one of the best bowlers of all time. Over the years he has perfected his control to such an extent that he is probably the most dangerous bowler on a greentop that there has ever been. He has cut his run-up without losing much pace, and his outswinger can be almost unplayable. There can be no higher praise than to say Hadlee bears comparison with Dennis Lillee."

Former England batsman Derek Randall saw Richard Hadlee as both friend and foe. After 10 years at Nottinghamshire, Randall soon appreciated Hadlee's value as a team-mate but he also saw matters from the other side. "It's true of a lot of players that they are two different characters on and off the field, and that certainly applies to Richard. For the benefit of those people who wonder if he is capable of smiling, I can tell you he does have a tremendous sense of humour . . . when he's away

Richard Hadlee, the bowler . . .
Left: The raw express bowler in 1973.
Right: The refined version in the mid-1980s
Below: The appeal, a theatrical performance.

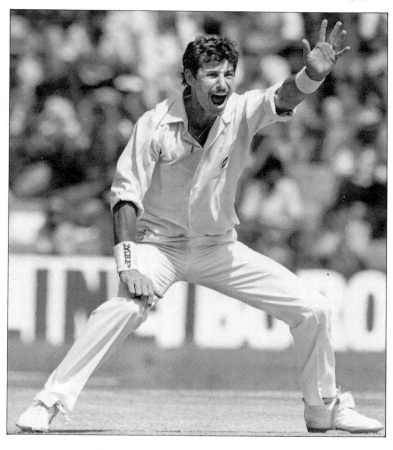

from the cricket field. Once he crosses that white rope, he is single-minded about his intentions and that's one of the prime reasons why he has established himself as one of the greatest all rounders in the world. As an opponent, he is one of the nastiest pieces of work I have come across." And well Randall might regard Hadlee as a "nasty", having lost his test wicket to the Kiwi nine times, making him Hadlee's most frequent test victim.

Hadlee and Sunil Gavaskar share something in common; when Hadlee took his world record 374th test wicket in Bangalore last year, he completed a nice double for the lesser lights of the cricketing world. The two most sought-after marks in test cricket — most runs and most wickets — both belonged to players from countries other than the traditional big two, England and Australia. Gavaskar, the first man to top 10,000 test runs, encountered Hadlee only in 1976–77 in India and in New Zealand in 1980–81 at the highest level. And he says of him: "No other cricketer has stirred the imagination of the sports-loving public of New Zealand more than Richard Hadlee. In sheer performance, charisma and crowd pulling ability, there's no one who has done as much for New Zealand as Richard Hadlee."

As one of New Zealand's long-time professionals who contributed so much to Kiwi cricket's arrival, John Wright has learned to admire what he calls the Hadlee Factor as a test team-mate and a county opponent. But it's at test level where Wright, Hadlee's most recent New Zealand captain, has marvelled at his ability. "I have been in a position (usually off-side saving one) to witness the Hadlee Factor and believe Richard to be the one truly great New Zealand cricketer of my test era. Paddles' bowling is like the medical kit he carries with his gear — fully stocked, clinical, exceptionally well organised and directed (a pilfering paradise for scrounging team-mates). His ability to bowl outswingers at pace with movement both ways off the seam is a great threat for any batsman."

When Richard Hadlee returned to Australia on the 1987–88 tour, he instantly slipped into lethal shape with 10 wickets at cheap cost as New Zealand demolished Western Australia in Perth. Now, Rod Marsh had never been anything but enormously impressed with his Australian team-mate Dennis Lillee during their long association at the top, but he was goggle-eyed about Hadlee's display in that game. "He's as good as anyone I've ever seen, including Dennis Lillee," he said. "The more he plays, the more you have to believe he's as good a bowler as Lillee. His control off the short run is really something to behold. It's fantastic. On a pitch that gives him any assistance at all, he is just sensational. He is more likely to get good batsmen out than anyone else I've seen in the last couple of years."

When New Zealand and England clashed in England in 1986, the first two tests were notable for the presence of Hadlee and the absence of England all rounder Ian Botham. Former England captain Mike Brearley made some comparisons between the two. "How changed the relative standing of the two men in 1986 (since the series between the two countries in England in 1978). Hadlee's cricket has matured in every department. His superbly fluid athleticism enables him to bowl with almost equal pace,

Richard Hadlee, the batsman . . .
Above: Doing what he likes best, crashing the wide delivery off the back foot.
Below: Not so pretty, but effective.

J.G. Blackwell

Richard Hadlee, the fieldsman . . .
Above: The former soccer goalkeeper, full of acrobatic athleticism.   Brooks-La-Touche
Opposite: Gleefully holding the ball aloft, Hadlee claims one of his most
memorable test catches . . . India's Kapil Dev taken at gully at Wellington's
Basin Reserve during the 1980–81 series.   P.G. Bush

greater control and more movement off a short run. As for his batting,
this has improved beyond recognition. Botham, five years his junior, has
in the meantime declined as a bowler as dramatically as Hadlee has
improved as a batsman. The difference in outcome comes down to personality. Hadlee, a stickler for detail, aims for perfection. Botham, on the
other hand, is all too rarely self-critical. He uses his failures to berate
others."

Two of Hadlee's county opponents during his 10-year stay at Nottinghamshire were Somerset's Peter Roebuck and Middlesex's Simon Hughes.
Roebuck writes extensively about the game and Hughes, during the
1988–89 season when he was in Auckland, contributed regularly to the *NZ
Herald.*

After seeing Hadlee take 10 wickets against Australia at the Melbourne Cricket Ground in late 1987 — but fail to capture the one wicket
he needed to give New Zealand another win — Roebuck wrote: "It's hard
to say whether a batsman about to face Richard Hadlee feels more like
a patient in a dentist's chair who is beginning to regret his penchant for
chocolate, or a pupil in a headmaster's study who's rueing his fondness
for cigarettes. Ian Botham may turn games into jousts, may buy wickets
when he's stuck. Hadlee disdains such loose living, and is quietly
menacing as he goes about his work. Hadlee is formidable because he's
disciplined."

Hughes looked at Hadlee from the bowler's mark, too. "Imagine
being enclosed in a small, brightly illuminated space where you are subjected to a barrage of searching questions by an indefatigable examiner.

Left: Richard Hadlee, the trainer . . . He adopts a professional attitude. And, when it comes to bowling in the nets, he definitely goes for quality. R.J. Hadlee Collection

Right: Richard Hadlee at leisure . . . An irregular but keen golfer, he plays the game with a difference. While he holds a cricket bat left-handed, the same man is a right-handed golfer! Robert Rathbone

Your responses are nervous gibberish. Facing Richard Hadlee is just like that. His bowling is like an interrogation."

But two of the most glowing tributes about New Zealand cricket's great man have come from arguably the two greatest names in the game.

The fabulous, the wonderful Sir Garfield Sobers was asked to pick a mythical world team from the players he had watched or played with or against since 1953. It was March, 1985, well before Hadlee's exceptional deeds against Australia later that year which provided the roller-coaster run of 130 wickets at test level. From November 1985 to February 1989 . . . 130 wickets in the space of 22 tests as he lifted his career tally from 266 wickets to 396. But even without the benefit of that evidence, Sobers unhesitatingly named Hadlee as one of his three quick bowlers alongside Dennis Lillee and Fred Trueman (and not a West Indian fast bowler in sight). "Richard Hadlee would be first change. The New Zealander is a real professional. His greatest assets are his knowledge — he quickly sums up a batsman's weak points — and his accuracy. Couple those qualities with pace, shrewd variation and the ability to get the ball to leap from the deadest pitches and Hadlee must play."

Perhaps the ultimate accolade comes from the man who has watched Richard Hadlee give new expression to fast bowling as an art. The words are from none other than Sir Donald Bradman: "Richard Hadlee . . . Richard doesn't have enough pace to be classified as genuinely fast, although he is certainly beyond medium pace. But no bowler I've seen had better control of seam and swing, and he is a wonderful model for young players to emulate in that he shows what can be done with a lovely action and proper body control without resorting to an exaggerated run."

C·H·A·P·T·E·R   O·N·E

World Record — At Last!

December 30, 1987 — 3.42 p.m.

The Melbourne Cricket Ground's buzzing; there's an air of optimism — Australian optimism anyway — as Allan Border and Mike Veletta walk off the ground for tea on the last day of the third test. No wonder. Border's 39, Veletta's on six and Australia is perfectly placed at 137 for three to go on to win.

We're not out of the contest, but Australia's winning target of 247 — with 40 overs still to be bowled — is looking ominously close, especially with Border still in. As the New Zealand players trudge off with Border, Veletta and the umpires, I'm in two minds. It's hot. The day's not going our way. How can we win from here? A crowd of about 24,000 looks tiny in this huge stadium, a venue which has known so much drama and controversy in Australia–New Zealand clashes. I glance up at the imposing electronic scoreboard, just catching the details before they're wiped for the inevitable commercials. The figures beside my name aren't anything special at all . . . 16–2–41–1.

We emerge after the break knowing our credibility's on the line. We've had a few minutes to collect our thoughts, to reassess our strategy. Obviously we need a big session — an extraordinary one — if we're to have any chance of winning the test to square the series and retain the Trans-Tasman Trophy. We have to believe it's possible, though. And it definitely is possible.

At 4.11 there's immediate hope. The third ball of my 18th over — my second since tea — beats Border off the pitch. He's barely forward, struck on the knee roll. There's no question he's in front. We go up for the appeal and umpire Tony Crafter has no hesitation. Up goes his finger. Border's out for 43 and Australia is 147 for four. He'd been my 300th test victim. Now he's my 370th, but I barely consider the fact.

There's cause for anxiety as Veletta and the new batsman Steve Waugh take Australia through to 176. They're both capable batsmen, if inexperienced under this sort of pressure. But then Ewen Chatfield strikes, Waugh clipping a ball off his pads to Dipak Patel at short leg — 176 for five. We've got a chance — provided we can pick up another wicket quickly.

The wait's agonising. By the time we reach the first hour after tea, Australia is 183 for five. After a brief rest, I return for my second, and ultimately last, spell of the session. The first over passes without incident. Veletta and Peter Sleep have become a problem as I begin my 22nd over. They're seemingly set and Australia, on 209 for five and with only 38 needed, is looking good again. But the fourth ball of the over skids through a little low, thudding into Sleep's pads. It has to be another leg before and the obliging Crafter agrees with my verdict. Sleep's gone for 20, Australia is 209 for six — and I begin to realise something else could happen here. Now I have 371 test wickets, just two away from the world record holder, Ian Botham, on 373. I'd never expected it to work out this way. If the record was to happen, I was sure it would be at home during the series against England. Suddenly the situation's changed. Will it be the MCG I remember for the most important moment of my career?

For the time being it doesn't really matter. We need four more wickets. Australia is close to victory but, with Veletta the only specialist batsman left, it might think about saving the match rather than winning. Australia's had such little test success in the 1980s . . . why throw it away now?

Only five minutes after Sleep's dismissal, they have to think draw rather than win. John Bracewell induces Veletta to sweep but the ball ricochets off his shoulder and Patel plucks the looping chance. From 209 for five, Australia has slumped to 209 for seven. It's all happening for us. Australia has plenty of time to make the runs — something like 18 overs — but it no longer has the batsmen.

Captain Jeff Crowe wants me to bowl through. I'm feeling the strain. As the clock climbs towards six o'clock, I've already bowled 25 overs in the day — and that's a hell of a lot of work, believe me. I have to drive myself, keep it going in the hope we can chip away and score a famous victory. But Greg Dyer and Tony Dodemaide continue to defy us. For 20 minutes they're together, then 25. There are only 10 overs left as the total inches up to 216.

I've plugged on, trying all I can think of. With the second ball of my 26th over, I manage to make the ball move away. Dyer comes forward, fails to cover the movement and the edge flies to Ian Smith. While he

Opposite: December 30, 1987. Admiration for Australian tailender Michael Whitney holding out for a draw — but disappointment, I couldn't take the one last wicket needed for victory . . . and for outright ownership of the world record.

John Knight

holds on to the catch, he doesn't know whether to jump for joy or cry because he's been operating with a broken finger. The catch is just so vital, though. Dyer departs for four, Australia is 216 for eight and I have wicket No. 372.

Jeff Crowe takes the new ball with seven overs left. There's time enough to capture the last two wickets, and there has to be some doubt now whether Australia can hang on. And when Tony Dodemaide falls leg before in my 29th over — and the 16th of the final 20 — the most unlikely win is tantalisingly close for us. At 227 for nine, Australia can now pray only for survival, nothing more. Crafter's bravely given me six lbws in the match, the sixth giving me a share of the world record. Amid such amazing scenes, such an unreal end to a test, I'm level with Botham on 373 wickets, just a step away from the ultimate achievement. But that's not important.

We have four overs and four balls left to take the last wicket. Craig McDermott or Michael Whitney? Who will it be? Whitney's a real rabbit but it's McDermott who's lucky to survive. Danny Morrison's leg before shout against him really couldn't have been any closer, but Dick French obviously doesn't have the same appreciation of the lbw rule as Tony Crafter. Constant replays on the big screen prove convincing. McDermott was surely out. Who'd be an umpire in this position to decide a test?

Somehow the two batsmen scrape through until I'm at the top of my mark at 6.49 to bowl the last over of the match. It's come down to six balls. Whitney's the batsman in strike, a player with no pretensions as a batsman. My mind's clogged up with thoughts. My body's crying out for rest. After bowling 30 overs, I have to make it just one more. I have to find the special delivery. It's up to me. It means so much. Just one ball and one wicket can give us the win, square the series, we'll retain the Trans-Tasman Trophy — and I'll be the outright holder of the world record for test wickets. So much riding on one delivery in this over! Mentally I'm ready for Whitney. "Bowl straight," I keep telling myself. "There's no point being too clever with this bloke. Just keep the ball up, and straight, and you should have him."

For the first three balls, I can't get it right. I'm bowling too wide and Whitney isn't in danger. I try a yorker. He digs it out and suddenly there's just one ball left. I have to rethink the whole business. What to do next?

I take my time. I talk to Jeff. We look at the field and still I come up with the same theory. Straight and full. I try it, but my bowling doesn't have quite the same zip it had earlier on. There's no spite in the delivery, Whitney puts a dead bat on it and pushes it away. The crowd's in a frenzy. They've just witnessed Australia's last pair holding out for 30 deliveries to save the test. They've seen a genuine No. 11 batsman thwarting Richard Hadlee despite the pressure of the world being on him. It's been one unreal afternoon, an amazing test. I'm disappointed, if not deflated, sorry I've failed to grab the one wicket wanted for the win. I was sure it was going to happen. But I'm full of admiration for what McDermott and Whitney have just achieved. You have to applaud that kind of effort so I walk up to Whitney, put my arm around his shoulders and congratulate him.

Minutes later I collapse in our dressing room, spent physically and mentally. In my last 11 overs I took three for 17, finishing with five for 67. For the 32nd time I've taken five wickets in a test innings. For the eighth time, 10 wickets in a match. It doesn't seem to matter much. We failed to win the test. The world record will have to wait until the first test against England!

February 12, 1988 — 10.58 a.m.

Lancaster Park, Christchurch — this is home for me. I lead the New Zealand team onto the park. It's a day set up to conquer, a hometown test against England. It's taken time, but now I'm well over the letdown at the MCG. I'm just hungry to get my world record business over and done with. There's extra appeal too, because England has my Nottinghamshire team-mates Chris Broad, Tim Robinson and Bruce French in its side. Will one of them become No. 374? It's a *fait accompli* the record will happen today . . . at least that's the way everyone sees it. I can't help but think the same. The build-up to the event has been unprecedented. Radio stations and newspapers have been running competitions asking readers and listeners to guess when the world record wicket will be taken, and who my victim will be. I don't mind the extra attention being concentrated on the bid to beat Botham. I actually feel quite relaxed about it all.

Quite a crowd is in at Lancaster Park. Expectant. Not quite as many people as the day in Wellington when I was chasing my 300th victim against Australia two years ago, but plenty in the members' area. And photographers everywhere, all hoping to capture the moment I want. There's even a television cameraman detailed to watch Dad and Karen looking for their reactions. I don't lack for support. The atmosphere's great, too.

And Jeff Crowe's done the perfect thing for me, by winning the toss and putting England in. It makes me feel even better. This is just the sort of pitch I want for the day, the ideal one to bowl on first. What a way for me to start as well . . . bowling to my Notts colleague Chris Broad. The first over's encouraging. Broad plays and misses at the second ball, twice I beat his stroke and thump into his pads, shouting for a leg before off the last ball of the over. In my second over I beat Martyn Moxon twice. It goes on much the same throughout my first seven overs, beating the bat but not quite finding the edge. I'm not disillusioned, though. "It's always the next ball the wicket will fall," I tell myself. The first spell ends with figures of 7-2-16-0.

Just before lunch, I have another burst and reach the break no better off with none for 28 off 10 overs and England 66 for one. Maybe the lunch break will change the pattern?

No chance. A spell of five overs has its share of useful deliveries but no real action before it's time for me to be rested again. By 3.22, I'm on again and the two players in — my Notts team-mates Broad and Tim Robinson — are well set. They've both come close to giving me a wicket, each of them edging towards slips but finding the edges landing just short of Martin Crowe and John Bracewell (unluckily). By now, though, they have England on course for a healthy total as they bring up their 150-run stand. I'm no less confident about success as I get through my 16th and 17th overs.

By 3.38 the record still hasn't fallen, though. I'm into my 18th over. But after bowling the first three balls comfortably, the unimaginable happens. Just as I move into the delivery stride for the fourth ball, there's an ache in my right calf muscle. Something's drastically wrong. I instantly know my dream's been shattered. All I can do is bowl the last two balls off a couple of paces and hobble off the field to tea. I sensed straight away that Operation No. 374 would have to be aborted, at least for the time being. On a day I thought would be mine, I'd failed — 18 overs and none for 50.

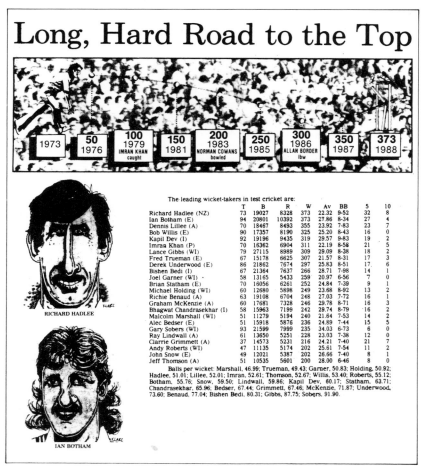

Long, Hard Road to the Top

| 1973 | **50** 1976 | **100** 1979 IMRAN KHAN caught | **150** 1981 | **200** 1983 NORMAN COWANS bowled | **250** 1985 | **300** 1986 ALLAN BORDER lbw | **350** 1987 | **373** 1988 |

RICHARD HADLEE

IAN BOTHAM

The leading wicket-takers in test cricket are:

	T	B	R	W	Av	BB	5	10
Richard Hadlee (NZ)	73	19027	8328	373	22.32	9-52	32	8
Ian Botham (E)	94	20801	10392	373	27.86	8-34	27	4
Dennis Lillee (A)	70	18467	8493	355	23.92	7-83	23	7
Bob Willis (E)	90	17357	8190	325	25.20	8-43	16	0
Kapil Dev (I)	92	19196	9435	319	29.57	9-83	19	2
Imran Khan (P)	70	16362	6904	311	22.19	8-58	21	5
Lance Gibbs (WI)	79	27115	8989	309	29.09	8-38	18	2
Fred Trueman (E)	67	15178	6625	307	21.57	8-31	17	3
Derek Underwood (E)	86	21862	7674	297	25.83	8-51	17.	6
Bishen Bedi (I)	67	21364	7637	266	28.71	7-98	14	1
Joel Garner (WI) ·	58	13165	5433	259	20.97	6-56	7	0
Brian Statham (E)	70	16056	6261	252	24.84	7-39	9	1
Michael Holding (WI)	60	12680	5898	249	23.68	8-92	13	2
Richie Benaud (A)	63	19108	6704	248	27.03	7-72	16	1
Graham McKenzie (A)	60	17681	7328	246	29.78	8-71	16	3
Bhagwat Chandrasekhar (I)	58	15963	7199	242	29.74	8-79	16	2
Malcolm Marshall (WI)	51	11279	5194	240	21.64	7-53	14	2
Alec Bedser (E)	51	15918	5876	236	24.89	7-44	15	5
Gary Sobers (WI)	93	21599	7999	235	34.03	6-73	6	0
Ray Lindwall (A)	61	13650	5251	228	23.03	7-38	12	0
Clarrie Grimmett (A)	37	14573	5231	216	24.21	7-40	21	7
Andy Roberts (WI)	47	11135	5174	202	25.61	7-54	11	2
John Snow (E)	49	12021	5387	202	26.66	7-40	8	1
Jeff Thomson (A)	51	10535	5601	200	28.00	6-46	8	0

Balls per wicket: Marshall, 46.99; Trueman, 49.43; Garner, 50.83; Holding, 50.92; Hadlee, 51.01; Lillee, 52.01; Imran, 52.61; Thomson, 52.67; Willis, 53.40; Roberts, 55.12; Botham, 55.76; Snow, 59.50; Lindwall, 59.86; Kapil Dev, 60.17; Statham, 63.71; Chandrasekhar, 65.96; Bedser, 67.44; Grimmett, 67.46; McKenzie, 71.87; Underwood, 73.60; Benaud, 77.04; Bishen Bedi, 80.31; Gibbs, 87.75; Sobers, 91.90.

February 12, 1988. Just a sample of the lengths the media went to in anticipation of the world record happening at Lancaster Park against England. It was all set up for me to conquer — until my calf muscle gave out on the opening day of the test.

Christchurch Star

My part in the series was over but I had to be philosophical about it. There had been so much expectation; what happened was out of my control. There really was nothing I could do about it. I still couldn't help indulging in some self-pity all the same, thinking about the dropped catches, the lbws not given, the near misses, turned down caught-behind appeals. Couldn't I have taken just one more wicket at some other stage?

I tried all sorts of treatment. Nothing worked quickly. This injury would take time and, when I returned for the fourth Rothmans Cup one-dayer against England — and then the Austral-Asia Cup tournament in Sharjah — it still wasn't 100 per cent. All sorts of theories were proffered as to why I'd failed. Some people were ready to list excuses for me. There were none, though. I'd failed to do the job on the day and that was it. I felt sorry for the people I'd let down . . . family, friends, supporters and my team-mates, not to mention the whole country. I was on the verge of achieving something unique for New Zealand. Now I was resigned; I didn't think I'd have the chance again to be the world recordholder. I figured Botham had a minimum of six tests during our winter — five against the West Indies and one against Sri Lanka — which would possibly take him to the 400 mark, or very close to it. I believed he'd become a cricketing version of Roger Bannister, going through the barrier. How could I ever catch him then?

Amid such gloom, news filtered through that Botham was having back trouble. In fact, it turned out he had a stress fracture which required an operation and put him out of action for the 1988 English season. I'd been given a reprieve. I now had another chance. It was an uncanny twist of fate.

So, my next opportunity could be November 12, 1988 — or somewhere around there — in Bangalore; the occasion, the first test between India and New Zealand. February 12 still lingered but now November 12 could be my day, if we bowl first.

The mere thought of returning to India must have seemed a little illogical given my attitude about touring that part of the world. I suffered on New Zealand's tour to Pakistan and India in 1976, having many health problems, and I was reluctant to savour the sub-continent's delights again. I declined the chance to go on the visit to Pakistan in late 1984 and to the 1987 World Cup in India; to be consistent, I shouldn't have considered the 1988 trip to India. But there was some pressure to change, to renege on my stance. Nothing's set in concrete and when Karen urged me to reconsider — motivated by the fact she also wanted to go to India — I began to weaken. Dad also said: "You'll have to go to India and do it."

This world record was too much to ignore. I was still reluctant but common sense prevailed. Not even India would stop me trying to make the record mine alone. How could I deny myself the opportunity? Even if it meant a little suffering and discomfort I knew I had to go to do the job everyone wanted to happen. I made my mind up, helped by the ruins I found myself in after the abortive attempt to create history for New Zealand cricket on February 12. The calf muscle was still a worry but nothing was going to stop me. I'd made private approaches to some members of the New Zealand Cricket Council about making myself available for India — now I confirmed my plans.

There was, of course, a counter-reaction to my scheme. Inevitably, pessimists said: "He won't go. He'll pull out." Or: "He'll go, get the wicket and then be on the next plane home." I was listening to talkback radio one night and one listener said: "Hadlee's going for only one reason — he's selfish. He should retire and let the youngsters have a chance."

My answer to these critics was simple. I felt I was on the verge of achieving something unique — and, if there were people who didn't want to be part of it, then I felt sad for them.

The assault on the world record had been held up by tailenders in Melbourne and blocked by injury in Christchurch, now there was plenty of time to prepare. If it all worked out, it would be nine months to the day between the Lancaster Park nightmare and success at last in Bangalore. It was never going to be easy, though. I had the calf injury to overcome for starters but I also had to face my first winter at home in 10 years; from 1978 through to 1987, county cricket had been a way of life for me. But now my connection with Nottinghamshire was over. How would I handle the prospect of such a lengthy break from playing the game? How would I maintain my fitness? Would my calf muscle continue to be an obstacle? I welcomed the thought of a break from the professional grind yet there were some self doubts just the same.

I need not have worried. The change in pace was a welcome relief from the monotony of year-round cricket, allowing me to relax and potter around at my own pace (with some real work popping up from time to time). I still had to be mindful about doing some training . . . but only after I'd given myself a two-month rest from fitness work of any type.

Jim Blair's something of a guru in the world of physical fitness and health, his efforts with the All Blacks plus the Canterbury and Auckland rugby teams being well known. Now he helped me, concocting a programme of exercises and routines to ensure I was on-stream for the big operation ahead. It meant using a gymnasium — the Canterbury Institute for Sport and Corporate Health — during the winter months and gradually progressing to cricket skills indoors by the time September arrived. Everything was fitting into place. I was tuned into the next wicket. Every run, every fitness work-out, every little bit of extra work counted towards the goal.

There were negative thoughts at times. The syndrome the long-distance runner suffers from is often one of unrelenting loneliness; I could empathise with that state of mind myself. It wasn't always easy training and working out on my own in Christchurch. I missed the contact of other players from the New Zealand team and would ask myself: "Why am I doing this? Why do I put myself through this?" It never took long to find the reason. All I had to do was tell myself: "It's one more wicket. It's the next ball. I want to be the best — so work for it!"

October arrived and, with it, the start of the club cricket season in Christchurch, but that didn't mean everything would be straightforward for me. Anything but. I was able to play only the second day of a two-day match which wasn't too convenient for my High School Old Boys senior side; it would have meant playing with 10 players on the first day to ensure a place was available for me a week later. I suggested trying the second grade side on the same basis but was told that was impossible because I'd be playing out of my grade! And yet I was eligible to mix it with players at fifth grade or in the president's competition. All I wanted was to have the best possible preparation for the tour to India. But, I didn't want to create too much of a scene, so I set myself for the president's side where the golden rule is: "If you turn up to practice, you're dropped."

It was an eye-opener for me. Through playing county cricket and having tour commitments, I've regrettably played precious few club matches over the years. If I needed any reminder about the conditions for players at that level, I soon discovered the reality. After the comforts of the best facilities at grounds around the world, I had to change behind some bushes! And our game had been transferred from one venue to another . . . at the last minute. You forget what goes on at the game's grass roots level.

I bowled my ten overs on the trot, off six paces, and found the two-piece ball swerving all over the place. Even if the cricket was low key, I needed the work with success only secondary to my aims. In fact, I finished with none for 12, when my team-mates and the opposition probably expected me to take five for eight or something like that. My eldest brother Barry, an accomplished batsman for Canterbury in his time, always fancied himself as a bit of a bowler — and he picked up two wickets for no cost in his first over, much to the delight of his team-mates . . . and to my dismay. And Martin, the next of we Hadlee brothers, also collected a couple of wickets with his off-spinners; the Hadlees had done well, except for RJ.

Eventually, I managed to play a senior club match before the build-up for India intensified, with a practice match against Northern Districts in Hamilton. The Northern batsmen were too frightened to hit the ball, exercised too much caution and got out with amazing regularity in making only 47 in their first innings. We won the match by 10 wickets but still derived some benefit from the exercise, even though there were a couple of points of concern.

Ian Smith, pulled up with a hamstring twinge when batting. Was this the first alarm? Had a vision of mine been destroyed? I'd thought about my next test victim —the magical 374th — and the way I saw him dismissed. The scorecard line read . . . Srikkanth c Smith b Hadlee . . . 8 (probably off the third ball of the match). If Ian was forced to withdraw from the tour so close to our departure, then Tony Blain would have to come into my plan. And, if it wasn't to be Kris Srikkanth, would it be Navjot Sidhu, Mohinder Amarnath, Dilip Vengsarkar or Kapil Dev — maybe even one of the Indian tailenders?

Lance Cairns played for Northern Districts in the practice match and the way he can change the course of a match has become legend. Some of the players had said to me: "We don't want him showing us how to do it because he retired from first-class cricket two years ago." When he batted in his side's second innings, I decided to bounce him, knowing he didn't fancy that and would probably flag his innings away. The bouncer was a good one. Lance flinched, ducked into it and the ball hit him on the jaw. The players more or less left me alone as if to say I shouldn't have done it, yet I knew deep down they enjoyed it. Lance wasn't too happy about it and was out soon after — and the chat we had later wasn't quite the same as usual because his jaw wasn't functioning so well!

Our preparation was complete. There wasn't anything else we could do. Our campaign in India would be an ordeal in trying conditions. I hoped for an improvement since my first visit there in 1976 but I accepted there'd be worries over the heat, humidity, food, the standard of grounds, accommodation and the travel all over the country. There'd be pills to take, the need to adhere to the "do's and don'ts" of eating in India, not to mention boredom. And how would the Indian umpires treat us after the troubles England and Australia experienced across the border in Pakistan? India also had a talented team with plenty of experience very difficult to beat there, remembering New Zealand had managed only one win in India in more than 30 years, at Nagpur in 1969–70 (a win in which my brother Dayle had taken part).

Being out of competitive cricket for so long, I needed to remind myself about my purpose in life and cricket, to give myself a refresher course on the standards I seek to attain. It's all written down on a card inside the lid of my cricket coffin, and is my philosophy on what playing cricket is all about:

- Desire is positive.
- Your mind is your brain — it's better than a computer.
- Attitude is a state of mind. Get your mind right.
- Simulate — put yourself in a position when you last achieved.
- Visualise — dream about the event.
- Confidence breeds success.
- Know your own ability, worth or value — self esteem.
- You must want to do it.
- Convert your mental thinking into physical action by doing it.
- Enjoy what you're doing.
- Record and replay the good things which have happened — erase the bad.
- Remember — you never get tired, just pleasantly weary.
- Beat your opponent — do the job better.
- Set your own goals but still be happy with your performance, even if someone else does it better.

And goals were what I started to set for the tour and for the season. There were tremendous opportunities to rewrite some records:

1. One more test wicket to become the greatest wicket taker.
2. I needed 27 wickets in a possible six tests to become the first man to reach 400.
3. Four bags of five wickets in an innings to reach 100 bags, the equivalent of the batting feat of 100 first-class hundreds.

4. Beat Stephen Boock's record of 66 wickets in a New Zealand first-class season (my best had been 62).

5. Score 230 test runs to complete the 3000 runs–300 wickets double.

6. Take 12 more wickets to head off Clarrie Grimmett as the most successful New Zealand-born bowler in first-class cricket (he'd taken 1424 wickets during his career).

7. Win back the Winsor Cup for the most meritorious bowling performances, which I'd lost after 11 consecutive seasons.

And still there was the dream. I couldn't shake Srikkanth from my thinking . . . it was the first morning of the match in Bangalore. There was a large crowd in. We lost the toss and bowled first (surprise, surprise). Srikkanth took strike. I had a field of three slips, gully, cover, mid-off, mid-on, bat-pad and fine leg. Srikkanth's unorthodox in his approach to batting and his technique. He likes to dominate, to play shots. His stance is unusual. Where most batsmen have their back foot behind the crease, Srikkanth has both feet behind the crease, so he never plays back because he's already in position. It means I have to pitch the ball up, to force him forward to grope for the ball. I desperately want to get this moment over — like everyone else — so we can get on with the game. It mustn't linger. I see the whites of his eyes, his blue helmet and his crouched stance as the ball leaves my hand, swinging in the air. It's an ideal length, he pushes at it, unable to cover it properly. The ball takes the edge. I jump for the skies even before the ball's reached Smithy. The catch is gloved comfortably . . . and I've still got two weeks to wait before I can attempt to make my dream reality. I told Smithy of my vision and he said: "I'd be quite happy to give Kris eight runs off the first two balls, and then get him out the next."

The trip to India gave me more time to contemplate. But I started to think about the itinerary, worrying about some of the places we would be going to and whether I'd again be haunted by illness which made my first tour so unforgettable in 1976. I didn't want to endure that again.

We'd settled in well in Bombay before our first tour match but suddenly, at two o'clock one morning, I had to make an unscheduled ablutions stop. My bowels moved rather rapidly and I started to vomit and dry retch. The tour hadn't started and I'd already picked up a bug! Luckily it was only a fleeting 24-hour visit from some Berty germ and I recovered — although you can never be too sure from one day to the next in India.

Our first tour match in Rajkot against West Zone wasn't expected to produce anything out of the ordinary, certainly not a result. But I came close to a career-best, taking nine for 55 and extracting four lbw decisions from one of the test umpires. Just like Brisbane in late 1985, I had a chance of taking all 10 wickets but John Bracewell prevented that. I was still delighted, though, mainly to see the new ball move appreciably in the air. Nothing happened off the pitch but the movement in the air further emphasised just how crucial it would be to use the new ball wisely.

I also watched the Indian batsmen closely, interested to see how they handled seam and swing bowling. Only a couple of them played with confidence by pushing forward at me; the rest floundered around the crease, giving me possible leg-before chances. That suited me. Rajkot also brought a new word into my mental armoury as I worked my way through the West Zone order — "destroy".

Whether I'd be able to "destroy" might rest largely on a niggle which had developed in my right achilles tendon. It became sore and, while I could still bowl comfortably, I had to have it sorted out with the first test in Bangalore only a week away. I was also worried when a bruise appeared for no reason on the back of my right calf . . . the same muscle which had gone on me at Lancaster Park nine months earlier. That concerned both me and our physiotherapist, Mark Plummer, but we never did work out why the bruise was there.

There were other worries in Rajkot, too. The game was delayed three hours on the first day because our bags didn't arrive. While we travelled by plane, our baggage was transported by truck. A supposedly 12-hour trip took 24 hours; evidently there was an accident which held up the driver for three hours but I never figured out why that lengthened the journey from 12 to 24 hours!

Our hotel was no better than one star but the locals tried hard, even if the chicken looked like sparrow and the standard of hygiene had to be questioned when a screwdriver was used to make an opening in a tin of orange juice.

But by now, the real focus of the tour — the test series —was becoming more apparent. The Indian media built up my confidence by giving me glowing ratings with headlines reading: "Hadlee: A Coach's Dream" or "Indian Batsmen Beware". The Indian batsmen were being constantly reminded of what I could do, which I read as a big advantage to me; one of them was going to make history and there'd be pressure on all of them until it was decided just who.

News of the Indian test squad caused some surprise, especially with Mohinder (Jimmy) Amarnath being omitted. I've always rated him and remember him for one frightening incident when I sconed him at Trent Bridge in 1979. His skull was fractured from that blow but he'd proved a capable player throughout the 1980s. Another name which hit me was Arun Lal. His name was new to me and he'd probably open the innings with Srikkanth, Sidhu coming in at No. 3.

After another lead-up game in Faridabad, the countdown for No. 374 began. We moved to Bangalore, India's garden city. I had a look at the Chinnaswamy Stadium, an impressive ground surrounded by tiered stands and one with a thatched roof. The dressing rooms were huge and the pitch — from a distance — looked agreeably green. My eyes lit up but my glee turned to dismay when closer inspection revealed the surface had been camouflaged with fresh grass clippings. There was no doubt at all this pitch would ultimately prove a haven for the spinners.

As we practised for two days before the match, I had doubts whether I'd be in perfect shape. The achilles was still irritating me. It wasn't just sore now. It was painful and uncomfortable.

Mark Plummer gave me no reassurance either. "It could get worse," he said, "and, if it gets worse, it would be the end of the season for you." With my ankle packed in ice, I sat in the dressing room and pondered

Dennis Lillee, my idol and the man who shaped my approach to fast bowling. What a gesture it was for him to come to Bangalore to wish me luck for another tilt at the world record. And, this time, I was sure it would happen. All-Sport, Simon Bruty

Mark's no-frills assessment. I'd have to pull out, wouldn't I? Plums worked around the clock, trying all he could to relieve the pain; he's thorough, professional. He did more than he ought to and finally reassured me: "I think you'll be okay Paddles." The test was less than a day away. I switched on again, toughened up mentally. What am I — a man or a mouse? John Wright asked me: "How are you, Pads?" "I'll get through, Riggit." And I knew I would.

All the goodwill in the world was behind me. On the eve of the match Dennis Lillee was at our practice session. The great Australian fast bowler's a man I respect, and a good friend; he was in India helping young fast bowlers through the MRF Pace Foundation (the equivalent of the pace bowling clinics he runs in New Zealand). He wanted to come to Bangalore to wish me well, giving me a bottle of champagne in anticipation of the magical wicket. "You deserve this — all the best," he told me. What a gesture from the great man.

Karen also arrived in Bangalore and, when I first saw her, she was suspicious something wasn't quite right. Maybe it was the strange look on my face and some vague comments I made. In the end I asked her: "What if I told you I'm not going to play tomorrow?"

"Why?" she asked. I explained the achilles tendon problem. She was unimpressed.

"You will play, otherwise you won't play again on tour. Your achilles won't come right in the next few weeks. If you don't play, you may as well go home." That was telling me.

I needed Karen there to help me through what could be a psychologically trying day or two. She was naturally aware of the intense pressures but found it difficult to relax me and so she virtually left me alone to meditate. The media also respected my wishes to sit this one out; I wanted the build-up to be as low-key as possible. Certainly I didn't want to be involved in any of the hype and everyone seemed to understand. Maybe I'd gone about it the wrong way in Christchurch; I needed a different tack this time as I counted down for the day I'd predicted everything would happen . . .

November 12, 1988 — 7.00 a.m.

The big day dawns at last. I had a lousy night's sleep but I'm still sharp. This will be the day, won't it? Or will I have to wait until the second or even third day? If we lose the toss, I'm sure it will be today.

At 8.24 we arrive at the ground. The Indians are doing their warm-ups, and they look shabby, dressed in 15 different training outfits. We go into our room. It's quiet as we prepare to go out for warm-ups.

Then the call. "Five minutes," Martin Snedden tells us.

We all amble onto the field to inspect the pitch. It's predictably one colour — brown, but firm with small cracks in it. Whoever wins the toss must bat first. I look around the stadium. It's an impressive venue, thousands of chairs being placed carefully for the throngs of spectators expected. The ground's surrounded by a fence with barbed wire running along the top to prevent fans running onto the field. Police and security guards are stationed in strategic places and already there must be 10,000 to 12,000 people in the arena.

As I stretch my limbs, muscles and joints I can't help thinking: "Wouldn't it be great if it happens today?" That, of course, would mean losing the toss, which would be contrary to the team's interests. After practice, the wait in the dressing room for the toss takes an eternity. Finally the word comes: "We're bowling." Not what the team wants but perhaps this is the start of what I've dreamed about months ago. To be honest, it always suits me to bowl first in any game, so I can immediately get involved in the match.

It's time for the last phase of preparation — on go the singlet, shirt, trousers, knee bandage, foot powder in the socks, socks on, ankle harness, then my boots, wrist bands, lip cream and the hat. Plums does some last-minute stretching exercises with me. The five-minute bell sounds. The lads wish me well. They want this as much as I do. "Please let it come quickly, say in the first two or three overs. Maybe the third ball, as I have dreamed." Wrighty gives his last-minute shot at us: "Come on guys — we're a team. We do it together, plenty of support for the bowlers. Let's make it happen."

It's 9.58. We step out into the cauldron. Polite applause ripples around the stadium, followed by a huge cheer as the Indian openers Arun Lal and Srikkanth follow. The skies are clear, a slight breeze blowing across the field which will help my outswinger if I bowl from the pavilion end. I feel encouraged to operate from that end for another reason. The umpire standing there is P.D. Reporter, who officiated at Rajkot when I took nine wickets (and he gave me four lbws). Wrighty asks me: "Which end?" "I'll take this one." The ball's tossed to me. An English-made Duke I had chosen from a box of six. It's quite a dark ball, which will help it swing. I'm much more comfortable with English cricket balls after playing with them for 10 years in county cricket.

Now the routine I've done so often I can't remember how many times, marking out my run-up. One, two, three . . . 15 paces I go before putting my marker down. Always the same since I cut the length of my run amid so much controversy in 1981. I better have a trial run to ensure everything's feeling all right. Not bad, but I know there'll be some pain from the achilles. A few practice balls to Ken Rutherford at mid-off. The seam's up. I'm ready to attack. Ready to try and destroy.

It's no surprise to find who has opted to take the strike — Srikkanth. The field set is three slips, gully, cover, mid-off, mid-on, bat-pad and fine-leg. I'd seen it in my vision. Srikkanth stands as I expect, crouched over his bat with both feet behind the crease and, under his white helmet (not blue as I'd anticipated), he looks more anxious than I feel. Does he think he'll go down in the history books for the wrong reasons? It's going to be my day. I know it now. I've done all the work over the years and feel I deserve the ultimate — to be No. 1, even though it might be for only a short time. Nine months of thought, of some doubts, of frustration and now utter determination is going to be tested.

There's chanting and clapping as I prepare for the first delivery of the match . . . I let it go. It's short of a length. Srikkanth plays safely. There's no four. The second's short outside the off stump and Srikkanth chases me. Again there's no boundary but I still like what I'm seeing. The third ball. This is the one I dreamed would take a wicket. It doesn't . . . it's short of a length, seaming away and Srikkanth fails to make contact. Then a no-ball, only just stepping over. The ball's too straight going down leg and Srikkanth works me to fine leg for a single. Now the new man Arun Lal. He gets a better length ball which swings away. With my sixth I dig it in a little. The ball seams and bounces but I know the pace and bounce I'm getting won't last. Another no-ball, again a marginal call but still annoying. The last ball I pitch much fuller and Arun Lal angles his bat to run the ball to the vacant third-man boundary. Not convincing. I've got a chance there! But the over's not a great one. Six runs and a couple of no-balls.

Charlie Chatfield produces some excitement in his first over. There's a shout for leg before, another for a bat-pad catch and, yes, it's a typical Chatfield maiden.

Over No. 2 for me begins. I've still got the same field. I have to work a little harder, sort out my rhythm. Arun Lal's in strike. The first ball's short of a length and outside off stump. He still plays at it, though. It's the same with the second. Still short of a length. He pushes it to cover off the back foot. Ball No. 3 is fuller, a little outside off stump and swinging away. Lal drives at it, fails to make contact. I sense I'm on to something. They're playing at me. There has to be a chance of an edge. My achilles is okay — just. The fourth ball. It's another no-ball. Well over this time.

I've got to sort it out otherwise it could be a long day. The next delivery Lal gets is short of a length outside off stump. He plays at it with an angled bat and runs it just wide of the slips for two runs. Keep tempting him. Something will happen. The next ball's fuller and he plays it straightish for no run. The test's almost two overs old for me. I've bowled three no-balls. One ball to go in this over. Again it's short of a length outside off, committing him to play but he fails to connect. It's not right yet. Smithy stops me. "Just looking at the red pitch marks, you're bowling at least two to three feet too short." Good advice. I look for any possible help from Smithy. He's in the best position to judge what's going on.

Charlie's the same as ever with his second over . . . another maiden. This guy just doesn't change. So reliable. Such a good foil to have at the other end.

Smithy's comments are in the back of my mind as I start over No. 3. I have to hit a fuller length. I move in to bowl to Arun Lal . . . only to pull up. There's a distraction. Someone walking in front of the sight-screen? Anyway, my rhythm temporarily thrown, I go back and start again. It's a better length, swinging away slightly. Arun Lal pushes at the ball, moving his feet a little across the crease. The bat's angled again — but this time the edge flies above the ground . . .

And Bryan Waddle tells Radio New Zealand listeners back home:

> "Out in the gully . . . he's caught at third slip! And there's the record-breaker for Hadlee. An emotion-charged moment for Richard Hadlee . . . he's finally achieved the record his efforts deserve. The team gathers around him and (the players) hug Richard Hadlee — and the Rolls Royce of fast bowlers opens a new page in cricket history with Arun Lal caught at third slip (by Chris Kuggeleijn) for six.
> "It's nine for one and Richard Hadlee breaks Ian Botham's shackles that for now makes Hadlee the greatest wicket taker in test history."

Waddle's comments man, and my former New Zealand captain, Jeremy Coney, then adds:

> "Well, that's a moment to savour, isn't it Bryan? For himself and for his wife Karen, who's sacrificed so much, and his family in Christchurch and his club, High School Old Boys . . . and his present team-mates and everybody who loves cricket. Even those who don't — they should just stop for a moment and they should just be generous and salute this man's long road to the summit.
> "And he's now the best in the world."

The catch went comfortably to Chris Kuggeleijn. He didn't look like missing it. At exactly 10.18, the first ball of my third over, my 16th of the match, makes history and, as Bryan Waddle and Jeremy Coney relay the moment to those back home, I rush towards Kuggs to slap him on the back. The lads surround me, offering congratulations. The big moment at last. In time I walk back towards my bowling mark to reflect. Kris Srikkanth congratulates me as I walk past him; it's strange because he's the batsman I'd wanted. P.D. Reporter also offers congratulations: "To complete my

World record day arrives at
last . . . November 12, 1988.
Right: Indian umpire P.D. Reporter
watches for the no ball (and there were a
few no balls early on) on the opening
morning of the first test in Bangalore. But
this was the magical delivery on a good
length and swinging away slightly . . .

J.G. Blackwell

Below: It found the edge and Indian opener
Arun Lal could only follow the flight to
Chris Kuggeleijn's safe hands at third slip.
Second slip John Bracewell, Mark
Greatbatch and wicketkeeper Ian Smith
move to congratulate Kuggeleijn and I'm
headed the same way. The record's now
mine!

Indian Express

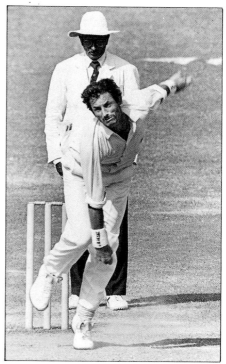

Time to celebrate . . . with champagne and ice — only the ice is for the injured right achilles tendon.   S. Utpal

cricket education I have to umpire in England, but today my education is complete." It's a lovely reaction. Strolling back to the top of my run, I look towards the No. 1 stand and gesture to Karen — and the non-playing team members — as if to say: "It's all over. Thanks for your support."

In the space of one delivery the tension and pressure have gone. There's a feeling of relief, not immediate satisfaction. In so many ways it happened quickly yet it was like slow motion watching the catch go to Kuggs. Now I can relax and get into the game we're playing. A dream's been fulfilled and I'm bursting with pride now just thinking about the significance of the occasion. I feel proud of myself, of my family, Mum and Dad, friends, all the players who have helped me — and proud to be a New Zealander creating this piece of history. But there's a test match going on here. There's more work to do. And only six deliveries later I have another wicket — this time it's Srikkanth!

As the day went by, I was inevitably in reflective mood away from the bowling crease. I'd beaten the best. It was like winning a gold medal — and no one can take it away from me. For so long I'd been just another bowler on the cricket stage who tried to do an honest day's work. Gradually I moved into the élite 300-wicket club, joining Dennis Lillee, Ian Botham, Bob Willis, Lance Gibbs and Fred Trueman. I topped Willis to assume the bronze medal position with 334 wickets at the end of the 1986 series against England. And then into the silver medal spot with Lillee on 355 during the only test in Sri Lanka in 1987. The 18 wickets in Australia in 1987–88 and I was with Botham — and now out on my own.

I reminded myself of the great fast bowlers who had graced the game all over the world. Names I'll always remember —Spofforth (The Demon), 'Typhoon' Tyson, 'Fiery Fred' (Trueman), Larwood and Voce, Rhodes, Statham, Lindwall, Miller, Bedser, Willis, Snow, Lillee, Davidson, Botham, Kapil, Imran and, of course, the West Indians from Hall and Griffith through to Roberts, Holding, Garner and Marshall. And perhaps now one R.J. Hadlee might join that sort of company. It's not for me to say who's the best fast bowler. It doesn't matter. We've all shown one thing — we've played this great game and demonstrated individual skills which people have seen and admired.

At the end of the day we celebrated in the dressing room. The whole team was there plus my good friend Roger Bhatnagar from New Zealand. An Indian, Roger loves the game and wanted to be in Bangalore to join in on the magical moment. He soon had me attired for the occasion in a Sound-Plus (his electronic company) T-shirt emblazoned with the words "The King". He had one, too, which he wore proudly in the stand the moment I'd taken No. 374.

Television cameras, photographers and journalists were all there, wanting to capture the moment at the end of the day. I had some difficulty getting the cork out of a magnum of Moet and, when I finally did, the celebrations could really start. By now I was also decked out like a maharajah, wearing a pure silk jacket and a turban Roger had given me to mark the event.

I was toasted, Wrighty and Bob Cunis saying a few words before I responded. I thanked Kuggs for holding the catch which mattered and all the other players who had contributed to my success over the years, Smithy (who'd gloved 37 catches off my bowling) and Braces among them. "It's a great moment for me," I said, "and I'm glad you've all shared it with me. There've been times when we've been involved in incidents and controversy but, at the end of the day, we've got out there and supported each other. Thanks for all your support."

Within hours there were congratulatory messages from all over the world, the most important being a written note Karen passed on to me:

Dear Richard,

This congratulatory note, per favour of Karen delivering it, is from your mother and me to say how much pleasure it has given us to see you enter new realms in the test arena. We are very proud of you and your achievements, and know that your brothers and their families are likewise delighted. Well done, indeed, and may you continue successfully towards the next goal, all of which will serve the interests of our national cricket.

I could not let the opportunity pass, and would have liked to be present, but that was not possible.

Best of good fortune.
Sincerely
Dad.

Stephen Boock, who had been celebrating and trying to contact us for two hours, was the first to phone from home, then Clive and Sue Rice from South Africa. Cables and telex messages came from the Leader of the Opposition, Jim Bolger, from the Minister of Recreation and Sport, Peter Tapsell, and from my brothers and friends. Now I knew I could also attack a favourite bottle of Beaujolais which had been gathering dust for nine months. On my return home Graham and Lynette, and friends, would be able to savour its delights since the bottle had been stowed away in February 1988 for this moment.

I also read in a local newspaper about Ian Botham's reaction to my success. "If I have my way, Paddles won't hold the record for long. For years he has carried the New Zealand attack and most of its recent successes have been due to him. He's shown how determined he is about the record by going back on his vow never to tour India again. Now he's done it, all I can say is good on him. He's a great fast bowler and deserves it."

The next day it was back to test match duty and on towards 400 test wickets. The Bangalore test helped me markedly in that respect. I went on to take five wickets in India's first innings to create more milestones — the five for 65 was my 33rd bag of five wickets in a test innings, it was also my 98th five-wicket haul in first-class cricket and I also captured my 1425th first-class wicket, so topping Clarrie Grimmett's record for the most wickets by a New Zealand player. Nothing could beat the world record, though.

Pakistan's Asif Iqbal was my first test victim, caught and bowled in Wellington in the first test of the 1972–73 series. But who would have believed, almost 16 years on, that Arun Lal c Kuggeleijn b Hadlee . . . 6 would create history in Bangalore, India, on November 12, 1988. I'd bowled more than 19,000 balls in test cricket to all sorts of batsmen in all types of conditions. There had been aches and pains, failures and disappointments but, with them, countless magical moments. This, though, had to be the ultimate — and it was.

As youngsters, most of us set out to achieve something special in our lives, sometimes without actually knowing what it might turn out to be. People have gone down in history as discoverers, inventors, scientists, artists and politicians. Perhaps my destiny was always going to be the cricket field — and later wanting the most test wickets in the history of the game.

Wicket 374 at last! November 12, 1988 — Chinnaswamy Stadium, Bangalore.
Above: Chris Kuggeleijn's collared by Mark Greatbatch seconds after catching
Indian opener Arun Lal to make the dream come true.
Below: Slapped, mobbed and mauled by the New Zealand players . . . a moment
to cherish, celebrating the magic of a world record.   J.G. Blackwell

The irony of it all — Kris Srikkanth offers his congratulations when, according to my constant dream, he should have been the record-breaking victim. Not that it mattered in the end. In any case, Srikkanth became No. 375 soon after.

Time for reflection and for a gesture to Karen in the stand. There's a sensation of relief the record's all over; it's an ordeal I no longer have to go through.

J.G. Blackwell

Time to celebrate. I momentarily assumed the status of a maharajah as the champagne flowed later on world record day. Wardrobe courtesy of Roger Bhatnagar.

S. Utpal

C·H·A·P·T·E·R   T·W·O

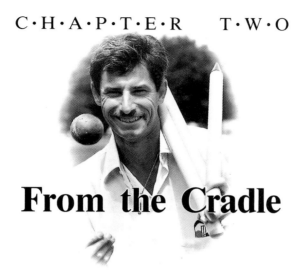

From the Cradle

When I was born Richard John Hadlee on 3 July, 1951, I guess I never had a chance . . . it was always going to be cricket, cricket and just a little more cricket for good measure. How could it be anything else really?

I suppose I should be thankful I provided Mum and Dad with their fourth son — and not their first daughter; there were certainly some people barracking for a change in gender of the Hadlee offspring. Dad recalls: "At the end of June 1951 we had three sons aged nine, four and three and our fourth child was about to be born. Well-wishing members of the family and friends hoped we would have a daughter but, happy with our three boys, we had no preference. On 3 July, the arrival of the fourth boy proved to be a great blessing." I've always said my greatest moment was being born, given life.

A blessing it was, too, for it ensured I'd be introduced to cricket at the earliest possible time; after all, I was living in what could be called the Hadlee cricket circus, surrounded by a cast of players starting with Dad, who'd captained New Zealand and played first-class cricket from 1933 to 1952, plus my elder brothers Barry, Dayle and Martin who all progressed to the High School Old Boys senior side and beyond.

As a wee bairn I would be bundled off to some venue or other for another day's cricket, but I was four before I really recall some obvious attachment to this strange game. My memory is reinforced by a photograph in the family album which shows a toddler doing everything wrong by the Hadlee cricket book. Standing on the concrete cricket pitch at our house in Wairarapa Terrace in Christchurch, I defied logic by picking the bat up left-handed — all the other Hadlees happened to be right-handed! No one, least of all Dad, suggested there was something amiss but, on reflection, it was rather against the odds that I should instantly announce myself as a leftie with the bat.

It wasn't so much a case of being pushed forcefully into cricket; in our household you had no option because you were effectively suffocated by all things cricket. Better still, I guess, I took to the game quickly. It never seemed a chore or a bore as certain sports can become when young kids are born into sporting families. No, I loved cricket and I very soon lived for it.

But there was a sadness about it in my formative years, and that was because I had been too young to see my father play first-class cricket. Between 1937 and 1950–51, he played a total of 11 tests, captaining New Zealand in eight of them, while his provincial career was spread between Canterbury and Otago in the Plunket Shield competition. It's a shame to have missed seeing him play at the highest level because all I have to go on is what I've read about him, what his contemporaries have told me and, of course, the record book which shows he scored 7421 runs at 40.11 at first-class level, including 543 at 30.16 in his 11 tests. Actually, I did see him in his final appearance for Canterbury, even though it was only a two-day match against Fiji. When he was out for a duck in the first innings I was mortified because I expected him to stroll out and take control of the attack; but when he made 30-odd not out in the second innings — and received a standing ovation — pride took over. When he was past 60 he filled in for the Old Boys senior side one day, emphasising yet again what a passion — and ability — he had for cricket.

Throughout all the years I can remember growing up, cricket was on the agenda, never more so than at the dinner table on Saturday nights when we'd discuss our exploits. During my Christchurch Boys' High School days, Dad, Barry, Martin and Dayle were all in the Old Boys senior team while my young brother Chris was in the top CBHS junior side. We didn't lack for cricket topics to talk about and we were forever playing the game in the backyard. The ritual of having "nets" at any time explains why Dayle and I became bowlers rather than batsmen, too. It was accepted practice that when Dad and Barry came home in the evening, Dayle and I would be the net bowlers; someone had to do it, we were the juniors and so we wore it. We had a useful set-up, too, because, on shifting to Fendalton Road, Dad went to great pains to lay down a grass pitch using Waikari soil. He made one mistake, though. There were 25 garage windows behind the pitch and, yes, you guessed it, not one of them survived.

All of us had some cricketing ability — and, with it, a fiercely competitive streak. In time that proved to be a good thing in terms of first-class careers which followed for Barry, Dayle and me. But the intensity of our backyard rivalry on Dad's carefully crafted pitch had its ugly side, too. Barry, Dayle and I all went on to national honours, and I'm sure Martin could have gone a long way as well; with lots of natural ability, he was a fast bowler at school but developed into a competent batsman, representing Canterbury at Brabin Cup level . . . but then finding his

Right: Wispy, curly locks and the air of innocence.　R.J. Hadlee Collection

Below: Early school days at Elmwood Primary School . . . well before I landed the nickname of Paddles. The six-year-old me is standing next to the teacher.

R.J. Hadlee Collection

cricket coming to a halt when accountancy studies and army training took over.

Of the five of us, Chris wasn't blessed with the same generous amount of talent for cricket but, because of the nature of the Hadlee cricketing beast, there was still some pressure — even if it was unintended — to succeed in this sport which dominated our family. The trouble is, Chris may have proved much better than we'll ever know. Being bigger and older boys — big bully brothers, I suppose — Dayle and I were, in hindsight, callous in the way we treated him in our games at home. He'd bat without any protective gear and Dayle and I pounded him both physically and mentally. He took some nasty knocks on the body and we both strove to do what was natural for young cricketers in the making. We wanted to beat his bat and get him out as much as possible. It must have been shattering for his confidence and I'll always feel guilty that I contributed significantly to his quitting cricket. When I look back now, I don't blame him one bit.

As I say, this is the sadder side of being part of such a cricket-mad family and Chris felt the need to measure up to the unwritten ideals. I remember one season he was having a dreadful run of scores but, one Saturday night, as we did our customary dinner table review of our cricketing deeds, Chris informed us he'd made 20. You can imagine the delight we felt for him — but we discovered the next day that he had, in fact, been out for a duck! We were all as guilty as each other. The expectations of a Hadlee were so high that Chris ultimately had to fabricate a story to try and compete on the same terms.

My hunger for the game became insatiable with each passing year. I used to relish the days when Mum took us to Lancaster Park to watch Barry playing for Canterbury in the old Plunket Shield days. For Chris, it was a bore. He'd occupy himself drawing pictures rather than watching the cricket (perhaps explaining why he later became an architect). I just wanted to be nearer the action, to be more involved, and stints selling programmes and working in the dark confines of the scoreboard gave me some experience of the real atmosphere.

While cricket was my big love, I enjoyed other sports and played the national game, rugby, among other things. There was never any danger I would excel as a rugby player; Dad remembers, vividly, my start in the oval ball game. He recalls I picked up the ball in my first game and, unlike William Webb Ellis, ran the wrong way! I did, however, play schoolboy representative rugby for Canterbury at 13 before switching to soccer. At the same age, I was playing schoolboy cricket for Canterbury, which opened up a world of fantasy for me.

I'd come home from school and bowl a golf ball at one stump, inventing an interesting list of rules — if I hit the stump, the "batsman" was out and, if the ball bounced back from the wall, I would dive forward on my follow-through to try and catch it. To me, it meant either a caught and bowled or that I had found the edge. Sometimes, I'd fish out another golf ball from Mum's golf bag . . . "taking the new ball" . . . and then I'd let my imagination run wild. For an over I'd be Dick Motz, for another Frank Cameron and then I'd be Garfield Sobers, bowling left-arm quicks. I threw in some left-arm spin and right-arm leggies, too. All ambitious stuff. The games boys will play!

My cricket dreams were much more involved when it rained. I'd go into the garage where I'd become immersed in fanciful games hitting a ball suspended from the rafters. This was cricket on the stage. Striving to give my solo matches an authentic edge, I'd dress up in Dad's old Canterbury cap and usually his gloves and pads as well. I devised run-scoring methods and, when I reached a half century or hundred, I'd raise my cap to acknowledge the crowd's cheers. Unbeknown to me, I sometimes had some very real "spectators" . . . Mum and Dad watching from behind the curtains upstairs in the house!

Collecting statistics also became an obsession, certainly more important than my homework at times, as I worked out averages of all sorts, but mainly for players who were involved in the Plunket Shield competition. This would occupy me in my bedroom, and so would other cricket games.

My favourite bedtime cricket game was having an empty scorebook, filling it in with the New Zealand players of the time, and then entering every detail of the matches my New Zealand team played; they never lost either. Hidden away, or so I thought, in the downstairs bedroom, I'd also indulge in imaginary commentaries . . . "Trueman comes in to bowl to Reid, it's slightly wide of off stump and Reid drives gloriously through the covers", and that sort of stuff. The games went on for hours and I listened to all the commentators carefully so I could imitate them. It seemed so genuine to me and I unashamedly revelled in this kind of absolute fantasy. Not until much later did I discover Dad used to sneak downstairs and listen to me outside my door as I tried to be John Arlott or Alan McGilvray.

In the real world, my cricket was progressing, too. And fortunately my desire to keep a scrapbook remains as testimony of some of my school-age feats. The first page of one scrapbook I called "Early Days" includes cuttings from papers in January 1965, including a photograph of a young R. Hadlee "cracking the ball to the mid-wicket boundary". The action came from the South Island primary schoolboys' tournament in Ashburton when some of the other lads playing included Warren Lees, Dave Dempsey, Dave Neal (who played first-class cricket for Central Districts and rugby for Marlborough) and Southland's Graeme Thomson, the left-arm medium-fast bowler who played for Otago and toured England with New Zealand in 1978. There's one story headlined: "Chip Off The Old Block". It tells of my performances as a 14-year-old for the High School Old Boys side in the third grade B competition when I evidently took 24 wickets for 51 runs over a period of three Saturdays. And I also hit 125 in 73 minutes! Success doesn't come that easily anymore.

My first year at Christchurch Boys' High School saw me make the school's under-14 top side and, as a fourth former in 1966, I graduated to the third XI, and even experienced the lofty heights of being 12th man for the school's first XI. Despite my upbringing, I still wasn't that well versed in cricket etiquette — I knew I had to wear my whites to perform the 12th man's duties but I mixed that ensemble with black school shoes!

Above: Can I detect the early signs of a young fast bowler's glare in this photo? I'm standing on the far left as a member of the Canterbury primary schools representative team in 1965.

Below: A taste of things to come . . . an early tour as a member of the Lancaster Park club side which toured Asia in 1971.

I copped a hell of a dressing down from the first XI captain, who happened to be Robert Anderson, later to become a New Zealand test player in the mid and late 1970s.

For three years I was in the first XI — 1967, 1968 and 1969 — and cherish as one of my memories the traditional grudge matches against Auckland Grammar School — a team which included Geoff Howarth. By now, I was also well known as Paddles, the nickname which has stuck with me ever since. I owe it to my woodwork teacher, Arch Lamb, at Heaton Street Intermediate School, who was fascinated that I wore size 10 shoes at the age of 12 (I'm now a size 11).

While it's natural to dream of being a New Zealand player, I never seriously considered the prospect until 1969. I'd had some success at different levels of cricket during my school years, without ever believing there was something attainable beyond that, but when Dayle was selected for the New Zealand team to tour England that year, it was all the motivation I needed. One day he brought home jerseys, ties, caps and other gear for the tour, and it became my ambition to have the same. Dayle and I had always been fierce competitors; whatever he achieved, then I wanted to go one better than him, and the fact he was in the New Zealand team to go to England provided me with my goal. I decided then that I wanted to be in the next side to tour the mother country in 1973.

On leaving school I was faced with the task of finding a club to play for; as a Christchurch Boys' High School ex-pupil, that's usually a straightforward exercise. You automatically go to the High School Old Boys club. And, what's more, that's where all Hadlees should go. But I faced a problem. Old Boys already had four good seam bowlers, including Dayle, and there was no way I could break into that senior side. So I bucked family tradition and sought another club. I settled on Lancaster Park simply because I'd be able to use the new ball. I had the fast bowler's hunger then, if in a slightly over-the-top way. As a tearaway, I just wanted to blast people out and to tickle them up with some bouncers. I used to overdo it, I know, but I was impressionable then; there was no real method about the way I bowled — it was just all-out pace and aggression.

It became a little nasty when we played Old Boys, Lancaster Park's traditional arch-enemy. And once again that intense rivalry between Dayle and me came to the surface. When I batted, he bounced me quite a few times, doing all he could to take my head off; I was after him when Old Boys batted, especially when he put me away to the boundary a couple of times. When I got home that night, I was fuming and announced if that was the way Dayle wanted to play cricket, then "I'll bring his head home on a silver platter". Mum and Dad were hardly pleased about the show of animosity and fortunately the bitterness subsided.

In time, I wanted to return to Old Boys to restore my family links, but there was some bad blood between the Park club and me when I left. It's a shame because I remain indebted to people at Lancaster Park. They gave me my start in senior club cricket and I'll always be grateful for that. Quite apart from that, I also had a trip with them to South-East Asia in 1970. But it was only natural that I'd soon gravitate towards my family connections at High School Old Boys.

My first overseas cricket experience came in January 1970, when I toured Australia with the Canterbury Colts side, captained by Rod Fulton (later to play for Northern Districts and then Canterbury at first-class level). Those tours and the early representative outings prepared me for what lay ahead . . . but there was something slightly unreal about it all.

It was surely one of the great sporting ironies — and a disastrous one for Dayle — that his misfortune should open the cricketing kaleidoscope which was to unfold for me.

Few sportsmen have suffered the ill luck which haunted Dayle. When he first made the New Zealand team in 1969 he was a genuine fast bowler of great promise. But then back injuries caught up with him, eventually traced back to the broken leg he suffered playing soccer which had left one leg slightly shorter than the other. He had to readjust, cutting back his pace to medium-fast but was still troubled by his back at various stages until he retired from first-class cricket after the 1983–84 season (with a record of 351 wickets at 25.22 in 111 matches).

In the summer of 1971–72, fate struck Dayle again, only this time it wasn't anything to do with his back. I was quite unprepared for what transpired.

That season I'd been picked for Canterbury B to play against Wellington B at the Basin Reserve, and I prospered taking five for 18 and making an unbeaten 54 not out. We followed that match with one against the New Zealand Brabin Cup (under-20) side in Christchurch during which, late on the first day, I noticed my mother on the boundary looking anything but composed. I found out Dayle had had a dreadful accident, cutting part of his toe off while using a motor mower.

He was obviously out of the Canterbury team to play Auckland in a Plunket Shield match starting the next day . . . and I was his replacement. I'd never wanted the brotherly competition to have this kind of scenario but now I was on the first-class stage. And, terribly nervous, I didn't start at all well, offering Auckland opener Terry Jarvis a juicy morsel with my first delivery in first-class cricket — a waist-high full toss which he sent swiftly to the boundary. The recovery phase was gradual but I had the satisfaction of claiming a test player — Ross Morgan — as my first victim and came out of the innings with three for 57. When I later hit the winning boundary in a fabulous match against Auckland, I was fairly chuffed about life as a first-class cricketer.

We played Northern Districts next and then went on to meet Central Districts in Nelson. The rumour machine suggested I was in line to make the New Zealand B team to play in the Coca-Cola knockout tournament in Australia and, while I was in the field on the third day, I thought I heard my name announced on the radio. Sure enough, the news was confirmed by our 12th man but, while I was elated, I was left wondering: "Why me?" I really couldn't see that I'd done enough to warrant selection in a side which was without the first-choice players who were all bound for the 1972 tour of the West Indies. Certainly in the match against Central Districts I hadn't done anything too astonishing at all, finishing with none for 48 off 12 overs in its first innings and having one for 42 from 10 overs by tea in Central's second innings.

But then came highlight number one in my first-class career. Central was 187 for six with the late Ken Wadsworth in strike. I bowled him an off-cutter on or about middle and leg which he looked to play through the on-side; he failed to make contact, the ball hit his front pad and I won the lbw from Mansfield Rangi. To say Ken was unhappy with the decision was an understatement (he never was one to accept any decision too calmly) and I must admit the ball seemed to be going down leg.

In walked Blair Furlong, who'd toured South Africa with the All Blacks in 1970. My captain Graham Dowling put more pressure on in the

Left: Wellington wicketkeeper Ian Therkleson becomes one of my early first-class victims in the 1972–73 season. About to take the catch is the late Ken Wadsworth.   D.O. Neely Collection

Right: There's that back foot cut — slash — again. And it's produced plenty of runs, as it did on this occasion in my debut test innings against Pakistan in Wellington in 1972–73. I went on to make 46.   D.O. Neely Collection

— 49 —

With Dad at Lord's in 1987 . . . there was so much pressure in the early days being the son of a former New Zealand captain and the chairman of the New Zealand Cricket Council. But Dad's had so much to do with my success — and it can all be traced back to the days when I used to bowl to him in the backyard.

Evening Post, Nottingham

field, I ran in and bowled a fast and straight delivery — which went right through Furlong's defences and into his stumps.

And the score then became 187 for nine when I had the next batsman John Howell — now the New Zealand Cricket Council's national director of coaching — the same way as Furlong. Another fast, straight ball and I'd achieved the unlikely feat of a hat-trick in only my third first-class match. Figures of one for 42 had become four for 42. The start to top level cricket could scarcely have been much better but everything seemed to be happening in too much of a rush for me.

All those kid's games I used to play suddenly had a real-life glow to them.

C·H·A·P·T·E·R T·H·R·E·E

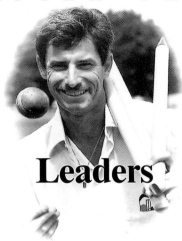

Leaders

Geoff Howarth had come a long way since those eternal grudge matches between Christchurch Boys' High School and Auckland Grammar. It was impossible to forget him. He was yet another of the young superstars Auckland Grammar hailed as future New Zealand material.

The two of us, while schoolboy rivals, were to follow similar paths. We started with something in common when our elder brothers made the New Zealand team for the first time together — the long-winded tour to England, India and Pakistan in 1969. Hedley Howarth, a skilful left-arm spinner, was 25 then and went on to play 30 tests before he was prematurely discarded after the 1976–77 series against Australia. Dayle was only 21; his injury-studded career as a New Zealand seamer foundered on injury early on the 1978 tour of England after he'd played 26 tests.

I loved the matches against Auckland Grammar. They were always competitive and were eagerly greeted by us as the chance to outdo the fancied stars from the north. Geoff and I matched each other for age so there was a fairly even contest between us in the late 1960s. With a reputation which preceded him, he was a prized scalp — and I remember getting him once. Even after years of first-class and test cricket, I still have a vivid recollection of knocking his stumps over back then.

It never proved to be a major setback for Geoff, though. He went on to make his first-class debut as a 17-year-old, playing for the New Zealand Under-23 XI against Auckland in 1968–69, while I had to wait until I was 20 before making the breakthrough for Canterbury in 1971–72. Admittedly Geoff didn't play Plunket Shield cricket until 1972–73 for

Auckland — and didn't make his test debut until 1974–75 — but so much seemed to fall into place for him.

In 1969, he was playing second XI cricket for Surrey and gained a full contract with the county in 1973. He didn't really prosper in two seasons in the Auckland side and, before you knew what had happened, he'd been whipped away by the enterprising folk from Northern Districts. He was only 23, but they wanted him to captain their Plunket Shield side and be their star attraction; their faith in him wasn't misplaced as Geoff celebrated his first season with Northern in 1974–75 by scoring 498 runs at 49.80.

He had it all going for him . . . and always had. As a batsman he had so much time to play his shots; he was a class act. But there was always a slightly casual streak about him and I recall wondering about his dedication. When that was put to the test on the trying tour to Pakistan and India in 1976, he didn't front up so well. In four tests, he did nothing of note but he also fought serious illness. Some doubts were held about him, yet, when the real moment of truth came in 1977–78, he performed. It was the third test against England in Auckland when everyone thought he'd be 12th man. He was retained, scored back-to-back hundreds, and proved once and for all he was a special player.

It was different in 1979–80. With Mark Burgess making himself unavailable after leading New Zealand in nine tests against England and Pakistan, Geoff was now captain, and facing the kind of initiation no one would envy — the West Indians, who had just demolished Australia in the comeback series after the healing of the rift between the establishment and World Series Cricket.

I'd had three New Zealand captains since my test debut against Pakistan in 1972–73. In those early days it was Bevan Congdon, a dour and ruthless leader without much imagination who never impressed me. I played only a handful of tests under him, before he was replaced as captain after the 1974–75 home series against England. I found he was not only a negative thinker but also very demanding. He didn't exactly handle with care the bowlers in the side, including me. When we toured England in 1973, we had a hugely talented side . . . Glenn Turner, Congdon, Mark Burgess, Brian Hastings, Vic Pollard, Ken Wadsworth, Bruce Taylor, Hedley Howarth, Dayle and Richard Collinge. I couldn't believe we lost the series 2–0. We should have won it 2–1 comfortably. But I think Congo's defensive captaincy influenced the outcome significantly because he just wasn't prepared to be assertive and make things happen. The following summer, he led New Zealand to its first test victory over Australia but that was his only win in 17 tests as captain.

Glenn Turner became the next New Zealand skipper for 10 tests against India, Pakistan and Australia from 1975–76 to 1976–77 and, for all his county experience and exposure to different captains, he wasn't much different from Congdon. He was knowledgeable and organised, as you'd expect from a professional but he lacked the gift of getting the players to give him 100 per cent support with his attitude and his reluctance, or inability, to hand out praise. Turns always had this clinical approach about performances; success was no big deal to him and he just *expected* players to perform at the highest level.

The worst side of that philosophy was seen during the demanding times on tour in Pakistan and India in 1976. We were 2-0 down in the series against Pakistan and were in deep, deep trouble in the third test in Karachi, our first innings slumping to 195 for six and we were miles away from making 366 to avoid the follow-on. But Warren Lees batted heroically, making 152 to help us out of trouble to eventually go on and draw the match. When Wally came into the dressing room, the lads were ecstatic but there wasn't even a pat on the back or a 'well done' from Turner. Wally wondered just what he had to do to earn a word of thanks and encouragement from the captain. A captain needs to have respect from his players and, to earn that, he has to try and understand individuals, but Turner never had that quality. Like Congdon, he led New Zealand to just the one victory, in the third test against India in Wellington in 1975–76.

Turner's New Zealand career took a sour twist after the 1976–77 series against Australia, when he began his celebrated self-imposed exile from test cricket. The way was open for a new leader; when Mark Burgess was named as the captain for the series against England in 1977-78, I remember I hadn't been sure what to expect. He was a gifted cricketer and it was logical he should graduate to the New Zealand captaincy. But I wondered about his temperament. He'd always been a volatile bloke, to put it nicely. There was a classic story when once he stormed into the Auckland dressing room after being dismissed, threw his bat and broke the handle. He tossed the bat out the window — and minutes later there was a knock on the dressing room door. A little kid had picked up the bat and asked: "Would you mind signing your bat, Mr Burgess?"

History showed, of course, that Burgess had a magnificent debut as captain, leading New Zealand to its first test win over England at the Basin Reserve. The great start didn't continue though, and Burgess wasn't overly impressive as captain. I doubt whether he actually enjoyed doing the job. To his credit, he was prepared to be aggressive and adventurous on occasions, which was more than could be said for Congdon and Turner.

So, there I was shaping up to life under my fourth New Zealand captain in eight years of test cricket. I wondered whether this would be a new, exciting era. Or would New Zealand cricket muddle along as it always had? In the earlier years, there was an overriding feeling of inferiority. It didn't matter how much talent we had, there was always this attitude that we were just the opposition — an easy target for opposing batsmen to accumulate plenty of runs and for bowlers to collect cheap wickets. We were effectively club cricketers and so it was difficult to motivate the players. Why should it be any different under Geoff Howarth?

I'd been initially surprised about his appointment. He'd proved in the recent series against England and Pakistan that he was our best batsman with four centuries, but your best player isn't necessarily the best captain. He had good credentials, though. He'd been captaining Northern Districts, he'd developed a professional edge through his time with Surrey, and, in the end, I guess he'd been the only serious option for the post.

What I liked about him instantly was his forthright approach. He wasn't frightened or overawed about taking on the West Indies, he wasn't hinting at another imminent disaster for New Zealand cricket. He was altogether more positive than his predecessors. The West Indies, he kept telling us, could be beaten. We could do it if we only had some confidence in ourselves and stopped believing all the advance publicity.

The injection of fresh ideas couldn't have come at a better time for New Zealand cricket but the proof of Howarth's new-style leadership would, of course, be measured by results on the field, not talking and organisation off it. On 6 February, 1980, Howarth made an emphatic and immediate statement about his reign; it may have been a one-day international, and not a test, but our one-wicket win that day at Lancaster Park was the making of the team, the turning point for New Zealand cricket. What mattered more than anything was that we won, not how we won. A week later, we were jubilantly celebrating an even sweeter victory; again it was by only one wicket, and came about amid heart-stopping moments with Gary Troup and Stephen Boock at the crease, but by beating the West Indies in the first test in Dunedin we'd set ourselves up for what became the most glorious phase of New Zealand cricket's international life.

From a schoolboy adversary, Geoff Howarth quickly established himself as my favourite captain. He did so in the brief period which encapsulated an acrimonious series against the West Indies; a contest never forgotten for New Zealand's historic 1–0 series win, but equally remembered for the sour taste left by the West Indians' antics — from Michael Holding kicking over the stumps in Dunedin, to captain Clive Lloyd's surliness, the incompetence of manager Willie Rodriguez, the sit-down strike in Christchurch and Colin Croft's outrageous act of barging into umpire Fred Goodall.

It's an injustice those issues clouded the campaign and partially obscured a summer which should always remain a testimonial to Geoff Howarth, the captain. His impact was both instant and profound; and in following years it was his style of leadership, his demeanour and success as captain which lifted New Zealand cricket into a new realm of acceptance. Through massive television coverage of our WSC campaigns in Australia in 1980–81 and again in 1982–83, Howarth wooed two nations — not just New Zealand, but Australia, too.

He seemed to have an aura about him on the field; where other captains would wave and flap their arms trying to make field changes, Geoff would use just a little motion of the hand, a slight nod of the head. We were conscious of what he wanted and yet he was a bit of a paradox for all his apparent assurance. Off the field he was fairly basic, giving team talks which weren't wonderfully inspiring — they bordered on mundane — because he had some difficulty getting his message across. But put him on the field and he was another person, at once astute, decisive and self-assured . . . a captain very much in charge of his crew, and comfortable in the knowledge that he had their respect as well. He had an air of the cricket aristocrat about him, which was further embellished by his television exposure. He looked the part and coped well as far as the public

Geoff Howarth, seen here with Viv Richards in Trinidad . . . from a schoolday
adversary, he quickly established himself as my favourite captain. I have
tremendous respect for him as a captain, more than any other I played under.

J.G. Blackwell

could see. Back in the dressing room it was a different story. You could see the captaincy drained him totally, both physically and mentally. Before matches he'd be sick with worry and, afterwards, he'd be utterly spent; sometimes, when batting, he was sick at the crease.

That's the price of captaincy. Of all international sports, I can't think of a more demanding and taxing captaincy assignment than leading a side in a cricket test or a one-day international. Geoff Howarth was born to it, though. Accomplished in the role, he also continued to enjoy personal success in the early years, including his test-best 147 against the West Indies in 1979–80 and 137 against India a year later.

New Zealand's ranking as a test power was transformed swiftly as Howarth provided the side with the constant winning experience. After the West Indies, India (1980–81), Sri Lanka (1982–83), England (1983–84) and Pakistan (1984–85) were all beaten by Howarth-led teams in test series in New Zealand. And, in 1983, we had our first test win in England under Howarth, while we also won a series in Sri Lanka. When it was all over for Howarth, he stood alone as by far New Zealand's most successful captain, boasting a record of 30 tests, 11 wins, only seven losses and 12 draws; he'd led New Zealand to more than half of its 21 test victories since the first in 1955–56.

He was equally adept at finding the winning formula in one-day internationals, a form of the game which exploded in popularity during Howarth's reign. It's been a source of growing concern over the last two or three years that New Zealand has fallen well behind as a one-day force, but in Howarth's tenure we won close to 60 per cent of our one-day internationals.

So why did he succeed where so many others had failed? Much of it was to do with his positive outlook but, at the same time, his planning and knowledge was good and he had a flair and feel for captaincy, knowing instinctively when to make decisions. Even though he had a side of good, but not extraordinary, talent, he was able to extract the best from the players. As a decision-maker, he was a bit of a gambler, and one who enjoyed plenty of good fortune; he had an innate ability to make bowling changes at precisely the right time; he had almost a sixth sense when he set fielding traps. Australians, especially, used to marvel at the way he could orchestrate proceedings when he was in the field. It was cricketing poetry in motion. And the best time to witness that was in the one-day arena when the action was at its peak of intensity. There's no question Howarth's leadership won New Zealand many one-day internationals — and tests, too.

The sense of enterprise and innovation was probably best illustrated in his use of Lance Cairns as a batting float in one-dayers. Howarth experimented during the WSC competition in 1980–81 and used him regularly when we were back in Australia for the 1982–83 series. If our run-rate was beginning to lag —whether we were batting first or chasing — then Cairns would go in early, even after the fall of the second or third wicket. It didn't always work but the most celebrated success story came in our clash against England at the Adelaide Oval. Chasing 297 to win — which seemed almost impossible — we were 33 for two, then 96 for three and well behind the asking rate. So Cairns went in at No. 5, blasted an amazing 49 and with Jeff Crowe (50) added 70 runs off only 48 deliveries. That gave our innings impetus and Jeremy Coney and I were then able to attack the winning target and go on to win an astonishing match; but it couldn't have happened without Cairns being used early and doing what he did best. Howarth used him early in all three Rothmans Cup matches against England at home that season and Lancer produced three quick innings of 19, 44 and 21. When the England off-spinners came into the attack, the call went out for Cairns to attack them.

Geoff wasn't afraid to use the same tactic in tests when he felt it was necessary. Such an occasion arose in the second test against Australia in Auckland in 1981–82 when we needed only 104 to win, and had ample time to do so. It was the same target required against the West Indies two years earlier; we'd courted disaster in that chase before winning by one wicket. And when we were 17 for two and then 44 for three there was some cause for alarm. When Howarth himself was out at 44, he sent Cairns in. The result? A bludgeoning 34 and the win became a comfortable operation instead of the nervous one it had threatened to be.

There was also a directness about him which sometimes offended me, but I had to admit he was often right. When I first became a county professional in 1978, I was notorious for eating lots of junk food . . . plenty of fish and chips, chocolate fish and sweets. Geoff gave me a bollocking about it. He told me I'd never become a great fast bowler if I kept eating rubbish. He said I didn't have any stamina, that I was okay with the new ball but couldn't come back late in the day. It was tough to swallow, but it was what I needed. Subsequently, Geoff should have heeded a lot of his own advice.

We did have differences. When I suffered from depression in late 1983 — and seriously considered not playing any cricket at home that season — Howarth rubbed me up the wrong way. He said, in a newspaper article, that I was making so much of my condition just so I could boost sales for my latest book (*Hadlee Hits Out*). That was insulting, hardly the sort of thing for a New Zealand captain to say when we still had to play together. Geoff also made it clear he wasn't too pleased about my decision to reduce my run-up in 1981, and especially in the series against Australia in 1981–82. He wanted me coming in off my long run I was irritated about all the adverse comment about my abbreviated approach and when Geoff was about to put my marker down for Australia's second innings in the Auckland test, I said: "Give me the bloody thing!" I then stepped out my long run, the full 23 paces, and put my marker down.

"What are you doing?" Howarth asked.

"I'm getting back on my long run. I'm pissed off at the moment with what everyone's saying about the short one."

You could see an instant change as a smile came over Howarth's face. As it happened I took five for 63 and we won the test, but it didn't prove anything about what run-up I was best using. I just did it that once out of anger.

Gradually, Geoff lost his touch as captain, although that was linked more to a terrible slump in his own form with the bat. He had great talent as a batsman and in the field. Had he worked harder in the nets and on his fitness, he could have been a better player — and survived longer than he did. It's galling how cruel statistics can be but, after his 137 against India in 1980-81, Geoff never scored another test hundred and even struggled to make fifties. When his eyesight went on him, his timing disappeared and, sadly, he didn't appear to have the dedication and determination to battle through that phase. Glasses or contact lenses were needed — but he never adjusted. It was too late.

Even though he scored 84 in his last test innings in Kingston in 1985, he had to go. Yet, when he was dropped for the 1985-86 tour to Australia, it was tragic to see him insisting he was wrongly done by. If only he'd retired a little earlier, he would have been remembered for so many grand things. The way it was, many cricket people were left with a bad after-taste of a once outstanding player and captain leaving the scene in such a disappointing way. He deserved a better fate.

He undid much of what he'd achieved but that has never stopped me remembering all the good things about Geoff Howarth as a captain. I have a tremendous amount of respect for him, more than any other captain I have played under.

When Howarth was unavailable for the 1984-85 tour to Pakistan, Jeremy Coney had the unenviable task of doing the job effectively on a caretaker basis. Logic suggested John Wright should have been given the post. He'd consistently been Howarth's deputy and I was sure he'd be in charge in Pakistan. For whatever reasons, though, the selectors chose Coney instead and I think this was the only illogical captaincy choice made in my time. Jerry had been an excellent player for New Zealand and, at his peak, was the best No. 6 batsman in the world. It was incredible how many times he produced the fighting middle-order innings which saved or won tests and one-dayers. But Coney as New Zealand captain? I wasn't too convinced. He reluctantly took on the assignment, but, by the end of the tour, indicated he probably wouldn't do it again if it was offered. Coney freely conceded he'd suffered from the pressure, although a tour of Pakistan is never the easiest job for a captain.

His preference was changed by the selectors only months later when they made him captain for the 1985-86 tour to Australia, after sacking Geoff Howarth. It obviously helped, too, that the New Zealand Cricket Council appointed Glenn Turner cricket manager; that was vital to Coney's survival in the job.

New Zealand had a magnificent run of test results while Coney was captain (or should I say, while Turner was guiding the side). There was a 2-1 series win in Australia, giving us our first series win over Australia (plus our first victory in a test on Australian soil) and, in that same season, we beat Australia 1-0 in New Zealand. The tour to England in 1986 produced our first series win in England and, in 1986-87, we came back from defeat in the second test against the West Indies to win the third in Christchurch and square the series. It was Coney's last test and, in the space of about 15 months, he'd led New Zealand in 12 tests for five wins, five draws and only two losses. We won three series and drew one — obviously a marvellous run of results, even more so because two of the series wins were achieved overseas. Even though Coney's New Zealand team lost the 1984–85 series in Pakistan 2–0, with one match drawn, he had an impressive record.

But my lasting impression of Coney as a captain will always be of a leader who operated by remote control. His approach to captaincy was largely through Turner; he appeared to be more influenced by Turner's thoughts rather than having faith in his own judgement. Ultimately, we

Happier times with Jeremy Coney after we'd crushed Australia in Brisbane in the first test of the 1985–86 series.   John Knight

achieved grand results in the test arena but it was a case of Turner virtually directing Coney. There were even times when Jerry left the field to consult Turner about what he should do next. Sometimes he produced a piece of paper from his pocket with instructions or thoughts on it. When it came to tactics and strategy, I always felt it was Glenn who was calling the shots and I don't believe Coney would have been anywhere near as successful as a captain had Turner not been by his side as cricket manager. There was every indication that Turner could, and did, manipulate Coney . . . with healthy results. Left to his own devices out in the middle, Jerry was often indecisive. You could almost see him asking himself: "Where do I go from here? What do I do next?" In the heat of battle Jerry would fidget nervously. He hadn't enjoyed an enormous amount of captaincy experience, so maybe he simply lacked confidence; as a player, though, confidence should never have been a problem for him because he'd proved over the years what a wonderful No. 6 batsman he was.

Jerry's strengths were his ability to communicate his thoughts off the field and his passion for planning and scheming with Turner. He was confident then . . . on the field he seemed lost and isolated, even vulnerable. He was excellent at team meetings where his profession as a teacher was in real evidence. He had a real gift in communicating his thoughts to the players, much better than any other New Zealand captain. And there was generally a freshness about what he had to say. You never felt you were in for one of those tired old approaches so many captains take, simply through laziness or an inability to change the message.

He could reflect on a marvellous return as captain in the first test against Australia in 1985–86. The game plan, hatched so meticulously, worked perfectly on the field but then we lost the second test in Sydney, something which should never have happened. Jerry was guilty in that match of making a number of miscalculated decisions, some of them very late in the match. He used the spinners badly (they didn't bowl as well as they should have either), and he also erred in his use of me on the last day as Australia chased victory. He held me back until the last hour — by which time the Australian batsmen were in full stride — when he ought to have given me a spell just before tea, had me continue for a time after tea and then have a break before bowling eight overs or so of the last 20. It didn't work out that way and I'm still not sure whether Turner had something to do with the strategy.

Generally, the Coney-Turner tandem operated well, but only in tests. All the scheming in the world didn't work anywhere near as well in one-day internationals; in fact, New Zealand's standing as a limited-overs force deteriorated drastically. Where Geoff Howarth had lifted New Zealand to a high plane in the game, we lost our way from the 1985–86 season onwards (and we're still trying to rectify the slide). In Coney's time as captain — including the 1984–85 tour to Pakistan — New Zealand could win, on average, only one in every three one-dayers. There was too much planning, too much theory involved and certainly Jerry himself seemed uncomfortable on the field during one-day internationals. He was a total contrast to the cool and calm aura Howarth exuded.

I will also remember Coney for his decision to announce his retirement from international cricket — before the 1986–87 series against the West Indies. If he was going to quit, surely he could have waited until the end of the series. By making an advance announcement, he opened himself up to criticism; if he failed, people would say he shouldn't have played because his mind wasn't on the job and, if he succeeded, they'd be saying he should play another series. You sensed an easing of the pressure, an increasing sign that he wasn't as dedicated at the crease the further the series went against the West Indies.

To see the way he departed in the third test was a shame, if not a tragedy. We needed only 33 runs to win but lost wickets at such a dizzy rate that Jerry had to go in with the score at 27 for four. And yet he couldn't see it through to the end. In fact, he belittled himself with the way he batted that day, backing off to square leg in the face of the West Indian fast bowlers. It was no surprise when he was out but it was all so undignified for a player who'd done so much for New Zealand cricket. The Christchurch crowd gave him a roaring standing ovation when he walked out to bat, and they repeated it when he departed. As Jerry said later: "It's hard to bat with tears in your eyes." I could sympathise with him. It was an emotional moment and it was sad to see him return to the dressing room, so disappointed. It was even sadder when he threw his bat down, emptied out his coffin and said: "That's it, the end of it. Test cricket's all over for me." And yet he finished with the team's fantastic win over the West Indies.

He changed so much in that last series. Various issues crowded in on him and, because it was his last series, he bowed to some pressure to take over New Zealand's problem No. 3 batting spot. Almost predictably, the move didn't work with Coney out for scores of three and four in the first test in Wellington. He reverted to his customary middle order slot for the next two tests but achieved a measure of success only once, when he made 36 in the first innings at Christchurch. Coney, so well known for his comical side, was no longer the freewheeling funny man during his final series.

Perhaps that also had something to do with the most serious difference of opinion I had with Coney. It happened during the second test against the West Indies in Auckland when we were in poor shape and seemingly headed for defeat. Throughout Turner's reign as cricket manager, we'd become a disciplined and organised outfit, and a team with an outstanding record. But I sensed the regime was losing its edge when, on the third morning of the test, only Turner, Ewen Chatfield, Martin Crowe and I were ready on Eden Park's outer oval for our customary 9 o'clock warm-up. By the time we'd completed one and a half laps of the field, another four players turned up, and eventually some more followed. We looked a bedraggled lot and I told Glenn that the discipline was slack, that something had to be done about it. While he made the point that warm-ups and practices should start on time, he played it a little low-key while I thought a tougher approach might have been in order. We still lost the test although there was a better attitude all round in the latter part of the match. However, I felt compelled to say something about it and, in my column in *Truth*, I said:

One of the most over-worked words in sport is discipline — but we New Zealand cricketers need more of it as we prepare for the third test starting on Thursday.

Frankly, discipline has slipped in this series.

It's simply not good enough, for instance, for players to be late for 9 a.m. practice.

On some occasions only half the team is into its warm-up exercises at 9.10 a.m. To me, that's slack.

No one dislikes warming up more than me. But it has to be done — and on time. It's part of the game and part of the test match routine.

I'd tried to be constructive in my criticism by stirring the lads up, but it had an adverse reaction — and I can see why now. I was speaking out of school and, if I had anything to say, it ought to have been said to the players rather than being aired in public. Fair enough, I guess.

When we assembled in Christchurch for the third test, I sensed something wasn't quite right. I overheard someone say: "Have you read Richard's *Truth* article?" But I didn't give it too much thought — until our team meeting the next night, when the article was produced and read out. I was severely reprimanded which, in retrospect, was more than justified. Glenn said: "All dirty washing should be hung out at team meetings and kept in house. We need to show loyalty to each other and look after everyone." I had to agree, but when I read the evening paper I was more than displeased to see Glenn had made a sarcastic comment about whether I'd be smacked by my parents if I told on my brothers. The comment was also aired on radio and television, indicating there were serious internal problems in the New Zealand team. It seemed to me that Glenn had been two-faced by admonishing me in public when he was the one who insisted such matters should be kept 'in house'.

When the first day of the test was washed out, I asked management for a special meeting to sort out the grievances. With manager Dave Elder there, Glenn could see my point when I suggested he'd been inconsistent, and I told Jerry I felt we weren't getting on; I also wondered why he hadn't spoken to me for two days. He retorted: "I haven't spoken to you for two weeks!"

Coney then accused me of being ". . . disloyal to the team. You've never had the team's interests at heart. You are only one, but there are 10 others in the team. They accept you for what you are because they need you, but don't respect you. I don't respect you as an individual. You always get away with everything." (This was a reference to Lance Cairns being fined for a newspaper article which criticised Geoff Howarth's captaincy, while I had escaped fines.) He went on to say I always received special treatment.

"I don't know who you think you are. The players have remained loyal to you, especially when you've missed the odd practice or team meeting. They've kept quiet about the car controversy. They said nothing when you threatened to pull out of a match against Australia last year. We never know what you are going to say next."

Coney's retort hurt — I was very emotional and upset and felt cornered as things from the past were being re-aired. My commitment and attitude to New Zealand cricket was being questioned yet again. I am proud to be a New Zealander and to represent my country, and my loyalty and commitment are absolute; I have contributed to New Zealand cricket both on and off the field to my best ability. Though there have been problems at times I've always had New Zealand cricket's best interests at heart and I like to think that my efforts and success have helped New Zealand through its remarkable era of the '80s in which it has gained credibility and respect. We have won test matches and series at home and away and I've enjoyed the camaraderie of fellow players. Suddenly Coney's comments were such that not only was he expressing his point of view but also the team's. It appeared the team had turned against me.

Coney's remarks were those of a man under pressure. Perhaps the live interview on television, when he was asked about a rumour that he wouldn't be playing in the third test, was the back-breaker.

After the interview he confronted me: "Did you spread that rumour about not playing in the last test?"

"Don't be so bloody stupid, Jeremy. Why would I do that?"

"Well, the rumour came from this dressing room."

I sensed he didn't believe me, but later it transpired the rumour had come from one of our physios who had heard someone mention the possibility. Eventually, TVNZ found out about it and Peter Williams was asked by his producer to pose the question to Coney. The explanation was made at a team meeting in Christchurch, so exonerating me.

"You owe me an apology," I told Coney.

"What for?"

"You implied I was a liar over the rumour you accused me of spreading," I said.

"I don't owe you any apology. You'll never get one from me."

I was on the defensive throughout the meeting, doing my best to bite my lip. But sooner or later, I had to snap back.

"It's just as well this is your last test, that it's the last time I'll have to play under you," I said. I was emotionally destroyed and felt like walking out. I felt the team, from what Coney said, was against me. It was an utterly unhealthy atmosphere leading into a test.

Fortunately I erred on the side of common sense (with the help and support of Karen and friends), believing I should be able to see out four more days before Coney was finished with test cricket. He was going — but he wasn't taking me with him. I still had to talk to Glenn the morning the match eventually started.

"I have a problem with Jerry. How can he captain me? We're not talking," I told Glenn. "He will have nothing to do with me off the field but he said it's different when we're on it." I found that difficult to understand. How could he turn on and off like that?

Glenn said I'd have to communicate somehow. "If you don't want to address him as Jeremy, then call him 'captain' to get around it."

We won the toss and put the West Indies in. John Wright came to me and said: "The captain has asked me to find out which end you want to bowl from and what field you require?"

In effect, Wrighty captained me throughout the first day.

I started bowling poorly. I was shaken up about everything and was called for a number of no-balls. I took myself off after only four overs, returning just before lunch. Jerry took the first of three good catches off me but we didn't greet each other as warmly as we normally would. There was just a gentle, polite handshake. By the time he'd taken the third catch, we'd warmed to each other. There was more feeling again, but the whole chapter was sad.

How the hell we bowled the West Indies out for 100 in such difficult circumstances was quite amazing. Charlie Chatfield obviously bowled magnificently yet my six wickets were very flattering considering the unsettled air. To win the match was a great victory for New Zealand but my memories were tainted by the unhappy and unsavoury events leading up to the game which nearly brought about my non-participation.

It was an explosion which should never have happened; all it needed was improved communication and understanding. Perhaps, though, we were feeling the weight of different pressures, and incidents like this one triggered greater problems.

In any case, there was a pleasant enough ending as I stood at the urinal answering nature after the match. Who should be alongside but Jerry himself. As he relieved himself, he said: "It's been a pleasure playing with you. All the best for the future." It appeared all had been put behind us. I hope it has —and perhaps we can laugh about it today.

Jerry sent me a Christmas card in late January 1989 (did he forget to put a stamp on the envelope?). And that, I guess, proves real friendships are never broken and forgotten. I will always admire his playing ability, his joviality and his keenness and dedication to his cricket job. He had much to offer New Zealand cricket — and he did so with grit, determination and distinction. I doubt whether New Zealand cricket will ever have another funny man or fighting batsman like Jeremy Coney. More's the pity.

Once Coney had finished, it seemed obvious John Wright would at last become New Zealand captain for the 1986–87 tour to Sri Lanka — but there was an obstacle. Wrighty had his benefit year with Derbyshire and was torn between that and becoming captain. He understandably made himself unavailable so he could work on his benefit, which was the wise thing to do. It was tough on him, though, and there didn't appear to be any obvious replacement, or caretaker for that matter. It was suggested by many people I should take the side to Sri Lanka but I wasn't interested and, eventually, the selectors hit on Jeff Crowe, who'd captained Auckland before and was an established test player even though he had a harrowing time during much of the 1986–87 summer. Chopper proved an excellent leader in Sri Lanka and it was quite predictable that he was retained for the World Cup and the following tour to Australia in 1987–88. Wrighty had to face the prospect that he might never experience the honour of captaining his country.

But the further the summer went, the worse it became for Crowe. After batting well in the World Cup, he totally lost form in Australia, and scored only 78 runs at 13.00 in the test series. It all weighed on him dread-

Geoff Howarth offering Jeff Crowe some advice during the Australian tour in 1987–88? Crowe, while proving a capable captain, was sharing similar batting problems to those Howarth had experienced.

R.J. Hadlee Collection

fully and Wright filled in as captain in a couple of the World Series Cup matches. In all honesty, Jeff was doing nothing to justify his place in the team as a batsman and it became an awful dilemma for him and his fellow tour selectors. He still couldn't bat his way out of the slump in the first two tests at home against England (40 runs in four innings) and so suffered the humiliation of being sacked and dropped totally during a test series. There was nothing else the selectors could really do — and Jeff manfully admitted they were right. There was a lot I liked about his approach as a captain but the facts showed he had a record of five draws and one defeat as a test captain and only four wins and 12 losses when leading New Zealand in one-dayers (including two in Sharjah in 1985–86). What impressed me about Jeff Crowe was his cool, calculating style. He never seemed to be rattled, adopting more of a resigned, philosophical approach. He treated his players with dignity and respect and they, in turn, tried very hard for him — especially in the third test against Australia at the Melbourne Cricket Ground, when we just couldn't take the one wicket needed for victory. He worked so hard on boosting everyone's confidence during the 1987–88 season, while knowing only too well that he was the one who was really struggling. He showed ample courage, but wasn't rewarded.

After the second test against England, John Wright had his chance at last. I first played against him when Christchurch Boys' High met Christ's College in 1969 . . . Wrighty claims he bowled me late in the match! I must say his bowling was never overly impressive and I can understand why he never pursued it. He did, of course, develop into a fine, determined opening batsman and, if anything, improved once he lost his regular opening partner Bruce Edgar after the tour to England in 1986. Without a recognised opener at the other end, Wrighty had to accept further responsibility and he responded wonderfully.

As vice-captain he had been the natural successor to Geoff Howarth. Instead the selectors bypassed him for Jeremy Coney and then Jeff Crowe. I think there was a general feeling that Wrighty was at times too distant from the other players, which might have counted against him in captaincy calculations. He took his game far too seriously, so much so it affected his personality. How then could he automatically change and gain the respect of the players to lead us into battle? The challenge of captaincy and its acceptance is a testing experience in itself. It is a test of character as a person, player and leader. The captain has to be able to cope with the good and the bad without showing too many signs of emotion; sometimes inner feelings and thoughts have to be hidden yet his public and team image has to be relatively stable — not easy to do in adversity.

But my doubts about John Wright's potential as a captain were removed when he captained Canterbury in 1986–87. I was pleasantly surprised about his absolute enthusiasm and his attention to detail. Quite obviously, this was the challenge he needed. Coming late in his career, it was the turning point. One of his great strengths is his devotion to the principle of total team unity, wanting all players to do all things together — and the players have responded and reacted well to his appointment.

His personality's changed quite dramatically since becoming New Zealand captain. Gone are the days when he lived up to his nickname, Shake. He earned that because of his unruly method of dress and for throwing everything into his bag and shaking it up and down so he could close the lid. Now he takes great pride in all he does and is better organised and more relaxed. He retains some of his idiosyncracies. He still enjoys his moments of solitude and another familiar habit has stuck. On arrival at a hotel he always wants to change his room, maybe to get away from the roadside traffic, the sound of the hotel band or the noise of other guests on the same floor. Some things never change.

His record as New Zealand captain may not be overly impressive. After all, there was a draw in the third test against England in 1987–88, a 2–1 series loss in India in late 1988 and then a drawn series against Pakistan last summer. But who could possibly forget that splendid victory in Bombay which allowed us to draw level in the series after being annihilated in Bangalore? His leadership was decisive in the Bombay match. He extracted the best from the tail-end batsmen in both innings after we'd

Can you bowl one more over, Paddles? That's what John Wright might have
been saying in the first test against India in Bangalore in late 1988. Wrighty
waited a long time to become New Zealand captain and our amazing victory in
Bombay was a tribute to his leadership.

All-Sport, Simon Bruty

failed in the top and middle — and it was that which gave our bowlers a chance of grabbing victory. It might have been just one test, but a win in India is an extraordinary achievement, and a tribute to John Wright's talents as a leader.

He also leads the side well enough in one-dayers. Admittedly the series was lost 4–0 in India but in the 1987–88 season he took over from out-of-form Jeff Crowe twice to lead us to important victories against Sri Lanka in the World Series Cup competition, wins we needed to make the finals. And against England, he revived the side after two straight defeats to capture victory in the last two matches to square the Rothmans Cup series; with successive scores of 70, 43, 101 and 47, the campaign proved just how well he could mix the dual responsibilities of opening the batting and leading the side.

His form in the last series against Pakistan may not have been overly impressive — in fact I am sure he was very disappointed — but at no stage did it affect his captaincy. In many ways he's a defensive or safe captain but if he's in a position to take the advantage he'll tighten the screw on the opposition.

Martin Crowe's the natural choice as New Zealand's next long-term captain; I don't see that there's really any other option. He's proved himself to be a capable and positive leader for Central Districts. If he is to do the job, I just hope it doesn't interfere with his production rate as a batsman. He is New Zealand's premier batsman with a magnificent record since his nervous start at test level; one of only four New Zealanders with more than 3000 test runs, he has a great appetite for scoring runs. So much depends on him doing well. Many New Zealand captains have suffered as batsmen when they've been in charge, Howarth being the most obvious example later in his era. But perhaps, like John Wright, Martin Crowe will be ready for a new assignment. Let's hope so.

Just by being a survivor in top-level cricket, I've had the satisfaction (usually) of playing under countless captains, and observing at close range the craft of opposition skippers. At test level alone, the array of captains encountered has been quite staggering.

Among the Australians there have been Ian and Greg Chappell, the excitable Kim Hughes and the long-suffering Allan Border. Ian Chappell was the epitome of a player's captain, the type who would defend his troops to the hilt. As a tough man and a rebel, his style of captaincy was essentially confrontational and ultra-aggressive, sometimes bordering on unacceptable. It was wonderfully successful at the same time, Australia being feared opponents throughout his reign. Greg Chappell was more controlled. Aloof at times, he also demanded and commanded respect but was entirely different from his often outrageous elder brother. He had outstanding results, too, and managed to handle both the captaincy and his responsibilities as Australia's outstanding batsman without undue trouble . . . most of the time. Hughes was a strange captain. He was probably too temperamental and the kind of Australian captain who would cause great concern with his tactical appreciation. He didn't have the total support of his players; more-senior members didn't really respond to someone who rarely led by example. He was somewhat impetuous as a batsman — and that also reflected in his captaincy. And no one will ever forget his tearful end as captain. As for Border, he's had a dreadful load to carry. Despite the pain of leading an Australian side which has won so infrequently at test level, he has lost none of his dignity or class as one of the world's premier batsmen. It's difficult to judge him accurately as a captain because he hasn't regularly had a balanced or competent side to work with, certainly not in the test arena. He's been more successful in one-dayers and there must have been times when he has been frustrated to the point of resigning.

England has become a trend-setter in playing musical chairs with its captains, as proved during the 1988 season when the captaincy went from Mike Gatting, to John Emburey, to Chris Cowdrey and finally Graham Gooch. There were amazing scenes as the England selectors floundered about during the West Indies tour. I've struck a diverse collection of England test skippers including Ray Illingworth, Mike Denness, Geoff Boycott, Mike Brearley, Bob Willis and Gatting.

Brearley, I would say, was the finest captain from my era — he knew cricket, he was intelligent and he studied players. Australian fast bowler Rodney Hogg commented: "Brearley has a degree in people". He could assess situations so quickly, act just as swiftly and usually with staggering results. That was never truer than in the 1981 test against Australia at Edgbaston when Australia, needing only 151 to win, was doing it well enough. Then Brearley brought on Ian Botham, and in an extraordinary spell, he took five wickets for one run to give England victory by 29 runs. Botham abdicated as captain in that series to be rejuvenated as a player when Brearley returned as skipper. Brearley also had a fantastic memory for remembering how any one batsman played, and where he liked to hit the ball. He worked me out thoroughly in the 1978 series in England when he directed his pace bowlers to bowl short at me on leg stump. I didn't handle it well, backing away to square leg invariably, and ending up with only 32 runs at 5.33 in the series — very non-professional.

I didn't play against Botham or David Gower as test captains. Botham plainly didn't have sufficient experience or ability for the task. It was a case of making the best player the captain, and that's so often a recipe for disaster. Gower was clearly too casual and relaxed about it all, although he was the logical man for the job at the time and was resurrected again this year.

As for Bob Willis, he was rather vague as a bloke — but, as a captain, his hard-working style and personal efforts set an example for his colleagues. It was odd to see a side's top strike bowler as captain. The main reason I've never been too keen on captaincy is it's difficult when you're the one who has to try and blast a side out to still think logically for others and plan your strategy. Overall, Willis came through reasonably well although he ought to have blamed the batsmen and his bowlers — and not the pitch — for England's pathetic display when we won the second test in Christchurch, by an innings and 132 runs, in 1983–84.

It was natural that Mike Gatting should be Gower's successor. He'd gathered a lot of experience leading Middlesex; he reorganised England well in the summer of 1986–87 when it won the Ashes series in Australia and also collected two major one-day titles. Gatting didn't really set such a good standard at times — by failing to answer his early morning alarm — but, as a batsman, he responded and performed. For him, there was the embarrassment of becoming the first England captain to lose a test series to New Zealand in England (1986). Generally positive in his approach — he negated that in New Zealand in 1987-88 — he wasn't afraid to sound off about matters which irritated him, like Pakistani umpires. Unwisely, this sometimes led to confrontations which really didn't suit the English way of life or the accepted gentlemanly approach to this grand old game of cricket.

The West Indies moved from one lengthy captaincy reign — that of Clive Lloyd — into another when Viv Richards took over. Lloyd had an easy, almost mechanical assignment. He had four superb fast bowlers and all he really had to do was to rotate them. With excellent batsmen as well, he had magnificent talent to work with. The West Indies couldn't help but be successful during his time. He's admired for making the team a unified force, which isn't so simple in the politically sensitive Caribbean, but his mana as a captain dipped alarmingly amid the antics which poisoned the West Indies tour to New Zealand in 1979-80. At the same time, he remains highly respected as a true professional and gentleman in other countries.

Richards had immediate problems on assuming Lloyd's mantle. Suddenly, there were signs of the political unrest which had been prevalent in West Indian cricket in pre-Lloyd days. In our campaigns against the Windies in 1984-85 and then 1986-87, I wasn't too enamoured with Richards' leadership. There's an arrogance about him, plus an air of excitability — and there was the hint of some racial animosity towards us. He's not the phlegmatic customer Lloyd was. Yet the 4-0 win over England in 1988 marked the start of a phase which suggested Richards was at last at peace as West Indian captain, surrounded by a new band of fast bowlers and a team he could probably call his, at last.

There have been numerous other captains I've played against like Imran Khan, Javed Miandad, Sunil Gavaskar, Dilip Vengsarkar and then skippers in county cricket. One of the best captains I played alongside was Maurice Ryan when he led the Canterbury Shell series side, and I'll always rate Clive Rice extremely highly in my time with Nottinghamshire. They've all had something, some quality or other which gave them the chance to achieve as leaders.

There are so many theories about captaincy. Richie Benaud, one of the best leaders Australia ever had, said: "Captaincy is 90 per cent luck and 10 per cent skill — but, for heaven's sake, don't try it without that little 10 per cent!" Somehow those percentages don't add up, even if Benaud did mean it a little tongue in cheek. I've always believed you have to make your own luck or, as a captain, make things happen on the field. And that's why Geoff Howarth, Mike Brearley and Ian Chappell were such special captains.

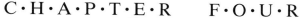

C·H·A·P·T·E·R   F·O·U·R

All Rounders

There's always been a fascination about all rounders, ever since the earliest days when the good doctor, W.G. Grace, dominated cricket. Think all rounders of more modern times and some names come to mind quicker than others . . . like the Australian pair Alan Davidson and Richie Benaud or England's Trevor Bailey.

·And there's the prince of them all, Garfield Sobers. It's a cliche to describe him as the greatest all rounder of them all (and maybe the greatest player, period) because so many people have said that about him through the years. But I can only echo those sentiments about a player who was something else, a true cricketing phenomenon who will probably never be equalled, let alone bettered. He could do it all — bat in the top six and use the new ball (not necessarily a fast bowler but a very good swing one) before reverting to left-arm spin when required. It didn't stop there. He was an outstanding fieldsman almost anywhere, finishing up a brilliant slip, and he also captained without the responsibilities of leadership ever really affecting his game, unlike so many other players.

The beauty about Sobers was not merely what he achieved, though. While he'll be remembered always for his deeds, he's cherished more so for the 'how' factor; to watch him batting, fielding or bowling was to marvel at a pure genius at work because there was so much silky skill, class and panache in all he did. He was an achiever certainly but he was also a pleaser. Just the same, figures are the ultimate tribute to Sobers' all round achievements and his test record constantly amazes any cricket follower: 93 tests, 8032 runs at 57.78 (including 26 centuries), 235 wickets at 34.03 and 109 catches.

I was among a world-wide army of Sobers admirers when I was a youngster but, being more analytical about it now, I think he was a player who excelled when he had good players around him. Strangely enough, when he played for Nottinghamshire, he struggled by his standards because he was among lesser players. He always enjoyed a challenge, matching his boundless talent with fierce determination; the Rest of the World's series against Australia in 1971–72 illustrated that. A young fast bowler named Dennis Lillee had been giving Sobers some problems but he came back to destroy Lillee — and the rest of the Australian attack — with his unbelievable 254 in Melbourne. Another contemporary he had some good battles with was England's Geoff Boycott, although I don't know that Sobers really rated him, certainly not as high as Boycott rated himself. Boycs once said to Sobers: "Are you still playing the game, Gary?" And the reply came back: "If I had to bowl to you every day, I'd play until I was 90!"

To compare today's all rounders with Sir Garfield Sobers is a forlorn exercise; there quite simply isn't room for comparison. While Imran Khan, Ian Botham, Kapil Dev and I all have better bowling records than Sobers we just can't come close in the true all round sense. At the same time, the fascination about all rounders has turned into a fixation today. Cricket has become attuned to the battle of the all rounders in this age, a development which has come about only recently, perhaps since the late 1970s. It may be a by-product of Kerry Packer's World Series days when so much hype was built up in the game. The all rounder has become the player who receives most attention from the media and the public, which is fairly understandable given that these players are constantly involved with either bat or ball, while many of them also become test captains.

During my test career there has been a solid core of all rounders in Imran, Botham, Kapil and myself and, had South Africa not been banished from the international scene, I'm sure my former Nottingham-shire team-mate Clive Rice would have been in the same bracket.

To me, an all rounder is a player who can make a test team as either a specialist batsman or a specialist bowler, and I don't honestly believe I fall into that category. Other people may choose to argue the point but I don't fancy I could play in a test side as a straight batsman; I haven't been consistent enough. On the other hand, Botham, when he was at his best, could make a side on that count and the same applies for Imran and Kapil, plus Rice (who has played rebel tests in South Africa as only a batsman, because of a back injury).

Public opinion — and I guess that of the national selectors as well — places me in the all rounder class but I regard myself as a bowler who bats, rather than a player who can do either task sufficiently well. I think you need a batting average up towards the mid-thirties to be considered a competent batsman and, while I've improved my test batting average from 19.18 in 1978 to about 27.00 today, it's still well short of the standard I'd accept for a specialist batsman. My all-rounder status, at first-class level at least, arrived only in 1981 when I began to make hundreds and more substantial scores on a consistent basis for Notts. My achievements as a test batsman also improved significantly around that time but, with

The battle of the all rounders has been the theme throughout my test career —
and, of them all, Pakistan's Imran Khan has been the best of my time. While
he'd lost some of his pace, he still showed off his classical leap in his delivery
stride during last summer's test series in New Zealand.

J.G. Blackwell

The batsman, later model. Given width to work in, the back foot drive's a real favourite. And the England bowlers gave me ample opportunity to use the shot in the second test in Christchurch in 1983–84.

Patrick Eagar

The bowler, early model. England batsman Dennis Amiss is the nearest spectator in only my second test — the unforgettable match at Trent Bridge in 1973 when we lost by just 38 runs, chasing 479 to win.

Patrick Eagar

It could be wicket No. 96 or 396. It doesn't really make any difference . . . this is what it always feels like — and looks like — taking test wickets. It's pure exhilaration.

just the two hundreds and a 99, I can't compare with my contemporaries — yet, as a bowler, I'm superior on strike rate and wickets taken.

The point is, I never made a conscious decision to become an all rounder in my earlier years. I just slowly developed and, in time, adopted a more responsible approach to my batting, although I've never been able to capture the day-in-day-out discipline required. It's interesting, though, that the introduction of the Deloittes Ratings in 1988, a computerised system of ranking test cricketers on a points basis, worked me out close to the best of the all rounders when combining batting and bowling points.

My battles with Imran, Botham and Kapil have been important throughout my career and I'm sure the media hype about the all rounders has built up the intensity of a Botham v Hadlee showdown or Imran v Botham or whoever. Whenever New Zealand played England, you could bet the old confrontation line about Both and me would be thrown up.

Kapil Dev is a rarity in Indian cricket — a fast bowler. While he's not quite in the genuine speedster class, he still has the ability to bounce batsmen . . . as he did New Zealand's Andrew Jones in Faridabad on our 1988 tour.   J.G. Blackwell

Ian Botham used to be the world's best all rounder but, for all his enormous talent, his general approach to cricket was questioned by many including his team mates. I was delighted to displace him as the world's leading wicket taker in tests. His bowling has deteriorated in recent years and couldn't be compared with Lillee's. He was the master bowler.

Patrick Eagar

But, quite frankly, it's the all rounder who does best in a series who generally affects the outcome; in other words, if I take 18 wickets in a series and my opposite number takes 12, and if I score 230 runs and he makes 180, then I've probably done enough to help my side finish ahead in that series.

One of the vital components in the New Zealand team's test series preparation in more recent times has been that of prearranged private battles, the exercise of pairing off against equivalents in the opposition and looking to outplay them. For the last five or six years, I've picked the all rounder and said: "Right, you're mine." I've concentrated on keeping tabs on him, on trying to outdo him as an extra motivational thing. I look at it as an innings-by-innings operation knowing there'll be a confrontation between the two of us sooner or later . . . at some time he'll be batting and I'll have the ball in hand, or I'll be batting and facing up to my rival. I'll be aware of what he's done in any given match and will dig deep to outpoint him, to return better bowling figures than him or to top his last score. The sight of Imran, Botham or Kapil at the crease gives me just a little more bounce in my step if I'm bowling, a touch more aggression and determination. Don't think it's somehow premeditated that I should have a stronger edge when I'm bowling to them; it's a subconscious reaction.

The way I look at it, the all rounder is the pivotal player in a side. He'll come in at No. 6 or No. 7 in the batting order and, if you can remove him quickly, it turns the whole contest in your favour. If he gets away on you with the bat and makes 80 or 100, you have lost the initiative in the match, which is just what happened when we played England in the third test at Trent Bridge in 1983; England was 169 for five in its first innings but Botham and Derek Randall took England to 355 before the sixth wicket fell. Botham finished with 103 and Randall with 83 as we completely lost all the ground we'd made early on . . . and went on to lose the match by 165 runs.

Obviously, various captains have relied on the all rounders of today's cricket world to single-handedly turn a game around, especially with the ball. As it happens, we've all been strike bowlers during this age and we've usually been called on to try and break a stand, or to come back with the new ball for a fresh burst. It's symptomatic of teams experiencing the greatest problems that they've been without all rounders of genuine ability. England without Botham has been an obvious case in point from time to time, especially in the three-test series against New Zealand in 1986 when Both was serving a suspension for the first two matches in the campaign. England, using Derek Pringle as its all rounder, lost the second test at Trent Bridge by eight wickets; Botham was resurrected for the third test and, with his very first delivery, had Bruce Edgar out, followed soon after by Jeff Crowe and later Jeremy Coney, on a day when he overtook Dennis Lillee as test cricket's leading wicket taker. Then, when England batted, in a test severely affected by the weather, it was Botham who almost overshadowed the England century-makers David Gower and Mike Gatting as he thumped 59 not out off only 36 deliveries. Hurricane Charlie had the final say in that match but the transformation in the England side, with Botham restored, was telling.

Like England, Australia has also been through tough times at test level and, once again, I think that can be traced back to having no true all rounder in the side; it hasn't had one of note for years and that has obviously affected the balance of its side, although Greg Chappell and Steve Waugh may disagree.

The West Indies doesn't really have a true all rounder — but it doesn't need one, not as long as it can rely on four quick bowlers to do the desired job. I suppose that's hard to reconcile remembering what Garfield Sobers did for West Indies cricket; after all, the West Indies side of the modern era is technically unbalanced, usually made up of six specialist batsmen, wicketkeeper Jeff Dujon and any combination of four fast bowlers. But that attack so often reduces opposition batting line-ups to very little and, with batsmen like Gordon Greenidge, Desmond Haynes, Viv Richards and Richie Richardson, not to mention Dujon, the West Indies hasn't needed to deviate. It hasn't been shown up too often.

One-day cricket has helped produce more all rounders, at least of a type. Players like Australia's Steve Waugh who has improved considerably, performing well in both the World Cup in 1987 and in the WSC competition against New Zealand and Sri Lanka in 1987–88. Primarily a batsman, he's a useful change bowler who certainly operates effectively in limited-overs games. He has also bowled very well at the 'death' in one-dayers so has to be regarded as a full-blooded all rounder who still has plenty of potential for further development at test level.

The all rounder's place in cricket's spectrum is further reinforced by gimmicky competitions which are run to try to determine the world's best. A good example is the Silk Cut contest in Hong Kong which I've competed in a couple of times; it's a competition I'd like to win but Clive Rice was on another level. Denied the chance to mix it with players on the international stage, Rice plans meticulously for an event like this and that's why he has done so well. I see it more as a novelty event which, at the end of the day, proves very little . . . but Ricey wants to win it like nothing else, because this is his moment among all rounders like Kapil Dev, Imran Khan, Ian Botham, Malcolm Marshall and others. He sees it as a way of proving himself against the best, in a competition which uses a special points scoring system which punishes dismissals, when you're batting, and rewards wickets taken, when you're bowling. What it does show, though, is that there's unreal interest in the all rounders.

Cricket's critics will write about the world's great batsmen and bowlers but it seems the all rounders command more of the written word for whatever reason. Writers are constantly delving into the psyche of players, trying to work out what it is that makes them what they are and how their personalities are mirrored in their approach to the game.

Somerset captain Peter Roebuck came up with his own analysis on the Hadlee theme when he and Botham put together a book titled *It Sort Of Clicks*. Roebuck wrote: "Richard Hadlee resembles a rickety church steeple, solemn, silent, almost sombre; he is a forbidding man who expects high standards of himself. Alone among the current all rounders, he does not hide his reliance upon statistics, nor his determination to improve them.

"During a day's play — every day's play — he paces himself, not letting his emotions goad him into sudden, draining bursts. His opening spell will be short, and will rely more upon movement and variation than destructive pace. He does not want to wear himself out, for the day, for the season, in hot-headed assault. In mid-morning he'll return for a second brief burst, still rarely reaching full blast. After lunch he will launch a third attack before retiring to slip to be roused only when the tail is exposed. Then, suddenly, he will bowl very fast, determined to add the tail to his haul. Sometimes this tight, disciplined approach infuriates his team-mates who accuse him of lacking the whole-hearted gusto which cricketers expect of each other. Hadlee is sensitive to the charge — which is heard more in New Zealand than in Nottingham.

"The New Zealander is open about his use of figures as a way of disciplining his game. Like Geoff Boycott, he collects statistics rather more obviously than most cricketers but, unlike Boycott, his team rarely suffers from his single-mindedness. Hadlee's character contrasts dramatically with Botham's. Ian tends to regard Hadlee as a bit of a prima donna, perhaps too, as rather a drip. Hadlee, one suspects, finds Botham's vulgarity hard to tolerate."

Some analysis . . . I'll reserve the right to comment!

Newspapers feast on the all rounder line of thinking, most of all in England where the papers — especially the tabloids — seem to run incessant stories on Botham doing this or that.

It was *The Sun* — of London origin, not the ill-fated Auckland version — which set up a so-called battle of the giants during the 1986 England v New Zealand test series. Of course, the confrontation never really happened with Botham being banned for the first two matches in the contest, but Pakistan's Imran Khan was asked to make his assessment on the two of us and "try to settle the argument" about who was the best. Imran judged us this way (giving points out of 10 for each category):

Batting

Botham — He is a far superior batsman to Hadlee. He can deal better with all types of bowling. Although disappointing with the bat during England's tour of the West Indies in the winter (1985–86), he is still better at both defending and attacking the ball at the crease than Hadlee. *Points: 7.*

Hadlee — His batting has improved considerably since the introduction of protective helmets. But because of the pressure on him as New Zealand's only genuine strike bowler, his batting sometimes suffers and in certain situations he is called on to give it a quick slog. *Points: 5.*

Bowling

Botham — There is a vast difference between the quality of Botham's bowling now and in the early part of his career. Once he had the ability to swing the ball away from batsmen consistently. In the last few years, however, he has not been able to swing the ball as much. Because he has also put on a bit of weight, there is less bounce in his action. *Points: 6.*

Hadlee — In the late 1970s, I would have ranked Hadlee and Botham on a par but since then Hadlee has improved as a bowler way beyond anyone else in the game. With his economical run-up, he gets maximum effect with a minimum of effort. He can move the ball both ways off the pitch and that, coupled with his subtle change of pace, makes him a far more dangerous bowler than Botham. *Points: 8.5.*

Fielding

Botham — He is an outstanding specialist slip fielder. Some of his slip catches have marked him out as just about the best in the business. *Points: 7.*

Hadlee — It is difficult to compare the pair in this department because Hadlee operates in the outfield. Because of that he is not in the limelight as often as Botham, but is safe and reliable. *Points: 6.*

Experience

Botham — He has played more tests than Hadlee but, judging by his performance in recent years, it seems as though he has not learned much from his experiences or used them to improve his game. *Points: 7.*

Hadlee — Although he has not played as many tests as Botham, he has been playing international cricket longer. And the more he has gone on, the better he has made himself as a test cricketer. Even at 35, he is still willing to learn and try to improve his game, as is shown by his latest performances against England. *Points: 7.*

Stamina

Botham — Ian has tremendous durability, and seems to bowl forever. Even when he has not looked 100 per cent fit, he has shown remarkable stamina. *Points: 8.*

Hadlee — He is a superb athlete who also has the ability to bowl for long spells. It is impossible to separate the pair in this category. *Points: 8.*

Temperament

Botham — He takes greater risks than Hadlee and is always prepared to experiment — especially with his bowling. He is always prepared to keep going, even when he's being hit. That's why he keeps collecting wickets. He also still manages to produce outstanding innings under pressure. *Points: 7.*

Hadlee — He does not take any risks, relying more on consistency. He has a carefully thought out mode of attack and is always prepared to work hard for his wickets. Maybe he should take more risks, but he has won many matches single-handed for New Zealand. *Points: 8.*

Dedication

Botham — Although the more talented cricketer, apart from bowling, he has not improved at the rate he promised when he first burst on to the scene. And the physical appearance of the two players illustrates their individual dedication. *Points: 6.*

Hadlee — He is totally devoted to cricket and, without that application and dedication, he could never have reached his present heights as one of the game's top stars. *Points: 8.*

Total points — *Botham 48, Hadlee 50.5.*

  Naturally I was flattered to find Imran rating me so highly (except in the batting category!), because there's nothing better than receiving that kind of compliment from one of your peers; especially someone like Imran whom I rate the best all rounder of these times.

  So, taking the idea on board, I decided to come up with my own ratings for my rivals, broadening the scope slightly by introducing a captaincy component, because the players I've analysed all have leadership experience at international level. I've also included one player who hasn't had the fortune to play test cricket — Clive Rice. I think he deserves to be considered even though his rating must suffer through not playing the genuine article, just the watered-down version of rebel tests.

  Ian 'Beefy' Botham seems a good target to start with. His life in

When I'm batting, the sight of one of my all rounder rivals stiffens my approach just that much more. And I made the most of it when Ian Botham bowled in our second innings in the Trent Bridge test in 1983, hitting 92 not out and going on to be named man of the series . . . a personal triumph over the Englishman.

Patrick Eagar

cricket has never been comfortable — and he has only himself to blame for much of the trouble he's been in. Both has always been a larger-than-life character who has been dogged, even hounded, by controversy of some shape or another. Drugs, booze, women, brawls, assaults, bans and fines have almost been par for the course for him. He's been in strife for things he has written, and for comments he has made, and then, in 1988, his whole career was put on hold when he needed major back surgery. He's just so different from me in every respect and at times his general attitude towards cricket has left a lot to be desired; even some of his team-mates have been disappointed with his approach to training and practice. And yet, on the field, there's no greater trier.

Forgetting the personality factor, though, I've always admired his enormous ability as a cricketer, even though he hasn't harnessed that talent as he might have. He was the world's greatest all rounder a few years ago, but then his halo slipped, and I've got to say it gave me immense pleasure to pass him in India in 1988 as test cricket's leading wicket taker. It always rankled me that Botham was the world record-holder because, frankly, I don't rate him as a bowler these days. While he may have taken more wickets than Dennis Lillee, I could never accept his ranking at the top.

Botham's done some good things outside cricket — like his walk for leukaemia — but for the purpose of this exercise I'm judging him on his cricketing performance:

Batting — Obviously a gifted batsman with a track record to back him up, including 13 test centuries. He can utterly destroy the best attacks when he's in the mood. Being in the mood is the critical factor, though, because there have been too many occasions in the latter part of his career when he has batted carelessly and lost his wicket unnecessarily. For all that, a big performer with the bat who has proved he can turn tests as well. *Points: 7.*

Bowling — Nothing like the bowler he was in the late '70s. Then he could swing the ball and bowled with genuine pace at times. As he became more overweight, he lost the bowling art and his achievements in the last few years have been singularly unimpressive. Has a remarkable ability to take wickets with poor deliveries. He could no longer command an England team place as a bowler alone, which wasn't the case early in his career. *Points: 4.*

Fielding — Unquestionably a magnificent fieldsman at slip, but gives the impression he's a little laid back at times. Has excellent reflexes and has grabbed some wonderful catches behind the wicket. *Points: 7.*

Experience — Can't be faulted on the score of test experience. Of the players under review, he and Kapil Dev have played the most test cricket (more than 90 matches each). But, as Imran says of him, he doesn't use his accumulated experience to good effect. *Points: 6.*

Stamina — Whatever deficiencies there may be in his bowling nowadays, Botham has never been short on stamina. His spreading girth would seem to suggest he could bowl only in short spells but nothing could be further from the truth. Given the chance, he will bowl and bowl and bowl. *Points: 8.*

Temperament — Has a sound temperament, generally, for the game. Not one to get too upset or despairing if things are going against him. Has the attitude that, if he keeps going when bowling, he'll eventually succeed. There might be a question mark or two over his batting temperament, though. Guilty of indisciplined batting on numerous occasions. *Points: 7.*

Dedication — Must score low here because, of the all rounders under the microscope, he's definitely the least dedicated. Too casual about fitness work and match preparation; he just doesn't work as hard as he ought to and it's that slackness which largely accounts for his downward slide. *Points: 4.*

Captaincy — Didn't appear to have a great deal of perception of what test captaincy was all about, or have the players' whole-hearted support and the job affected his own performances. He couldn't motivate others by leading from the front with inspired individual performances. To be fair, he had an unenviable task starting his England captaincy reign against the West Indies in 1980 before quitting during the 1981 series against Australia. Had little previous experience but Botham, always one for the ultimate challenge, failed to live up to expectations. *Points: 2.*
Total points: 45.

Kapil Dev has been something of a freak in Indian cricket, providing that country with one of its rare quality new-ball bowlers. Born in 1959, he's easily the youngest of this group of all rounders and yet he's closing in on 100 tests. He's also well into the 300-wicket club and is undoubtedly in the top bracket of all rounders. So, how does he rate?

Batting — An exciting strokemaker, he's prepared to take risks. He looks to dominate an attack as soon as he can, settling in for just a few balls and then unleashing in often devastating fashion. Exciting to watch. While flamboyant, he's still reasonably selective about what ball to hit. *Points: 7.*

Bowling — Kapil's not a genuine pace bowler but certainly a very capable operator with the new ball, easily the best India have had in a long time when you remember they've used players like Madan Lal to open the attack. Leaves a bit to be desired with his technique, especially the way he lets his head fall about, but he's definitely a useful bowler in all sorts of conditions. While he's proved himself all around the world, his strike rate has dropped off over the years. *Points: 6.5.*

Fielding — Such a supple athlete, Kapil's brilliant in the outfield, in the West Indian style. Very loose and almost casual, he can stoop down, pick up the ball and flick it back to the wicketkeeper in one movement. He'd be the most talented fieldsman of all of us. *Points: 8.*

Modern-day test cricket has become a battle of the all rounders, and in two series — in 1980–81 and 1988–89 — I've had the chance to square off against India's Kapil Dev.

S. Utpal

Stamina — Difficult to fault. When you play in the kind of conditions he's used to in India, you need ample stamina just to survive. Has had some injury niggles but keeps coming back so he must be rated for his ability to recover and for his capacity for hard work. *Points: 7.*

Experience — No shortage of test experience since his debut against Pakistan in 1978–79 when he was a teenager. Has crammed a lot of test cricket into a short period but, unlike the other all rounders, has only limited county experience through brief stints with Northamptonshire and Worcestershire. *Points: 8.*

Temperament — Can be a little fiery and hot-headed. Must be vulnerable on this score in view of some of the problems he's had with Indian authorities and his subsequent loss of the captaincy. He can be upset and, if niggled, will react, which is not unusual for Indian and Pakistani players who tend to be somewhat excitable. *Points: 5.*

Dedication — Came into test cricket as a youngster and has fulfilled all his early promise . . . so he must be fairly dedicated. A lot of players can burn themselves out and lose interest when so much is asked of them so soon, but Kapil has survived. That's a tribute to his tireless devotion to his profession. *Points: 8.*

Captaincy — Didn't achieve too much as Indian captain, although there have been so many captains through the years that he was never given the real benefit to develop into the position. I don't think he knew how to win games with his captaincy; and India has had relatively few test wins in the last few years. He may have been tactically deficient or he might have been a victim of the political pressure which abounds in Indian cricket. He did, however, lead India to its World Cup victory in 1983. *Points: 5.*

Total points: 54.5.

Imran Khan's the all rounder I most admire and respect of those I've encountered in my time. I'd unhesitatingly tag him the best of this age; the difference between Imran and Botham is summed up in one word — dependability. Imran has been so much more consistent, able to turn on one good performance after another with either the bat or ball. You just never know with Both. He might be out of this world one moment but then fickle for long periods. I'd line Imran up like this:

Batting — Imran's the most refined batsman among the all rounders of my time. More subdued, he's technically very sound and is prepared to build a long innings where most of the others tend to attack from the start. This is not to say he doesn't look to dominate because he's adept at coming down the pitch to the spinners, but is more circumspect against quick bowlers. *Points: 7.*

Bowling — Initially only a medium pacer before suddenly developing into a genuine fast bowler. Tends to come in wide of the crease and angle the ball in to the batsman; able to get a lot of lift and can be quite lethal even with the old ball. Came back superbly from injury problems and, while he's not as quick as he was, he's still effective and respected. *Points: 8.*

Fielding — Previously rated as useful, until Pakistan's New Zealand tour last summer. He'd slowed down considerably in the field, letting the youngsters do the chasing. On that evidence, he was no better than mediocre. *Points: 5.*

Experience — Has packed in an enormous amount of experience at all levels of cricket. First played test cricket as a teenager against England in 1971. Has used his knowledge to good effect, showing an ability to perform in all manner of conditions. Hasn't been so keen to play in series in Pakistan in recent times. *Points: 8.*

Stamina — Imran has no shortcomings in this area. He has a magnificent physique and comfortably handles long bowling spells while still maintaining his pace. Even when he came back from injury, Imran didn't have problems with stamina at the bowling crease. *Points: 8.*

Temperament — A cool operator, generally unflappable. Has the ability to change mode to suit the circumstances in a match. Can switch his batting approach from tight defence to aggressive hitting if required, and can also tailor his bowling to suit. He's essentially an attacking cricketer but I'd still term him a safe one. However, he has had problems off the field with Pakistani administrators and selectors. At times, he has questioned the timing of internationals in Pakistan (claiming it has been too hot) and he has had so much influence the selectors have changed teams because he has said he wouldn't play otherwise. All in all, I'd say he has had too much power for the good of cricket. *Points: 8.*

Dedication — Imran trains hard and works diligently on his game. Disciplined about his fitness and attitude towards cricket. *Points: 7.*

Captaincy — Another facet of his game which disappointed in New Zealand last season. Tends to be a solid captain but proved to be a bit negative in New Zealand. Didn't always exercise control over his players. Not an astute skipper. Created some strife when he closed Pakistan's innings in the Wellington test when I needed one more wicket to give me my 100th bag of five in an innings. Stopped me inching closer to 400, too. *Points: 5.*

Total points: 56.

I have no trouble in lining Clive Rice up in this exercise as well, even though he fails the test cricket qualification (through no fault of his own). I played with him for 10 years and saw him perform on all the first-class grounds and against top international players in England. He has rated very well and deserves to be considered along with the other all rounders:

Batting — Very watchful and desperately determined. A bit like Boycott in some ways in that he would play a bowler out. Generally a collector of runs but, when he drives, he does so very firmly. Isn't afraid to pull the quicks either when aggression is required. A very good all-round batsman, better than the rest of us. *Points: 8.5.*

Bowling — When I joined Notts in 1978, Rice was as lethal as any other fast bowler around; he got the ball through very quickly and, when he learnt how to swing the ball, it added a new dimension to his game. However, back and leg injuries restricted him and, when he eventually came back to bowling, it was as a medium pacer, although he couldn't be underestimated. Bowled more loose balls than the rest of us but was just as capable of removing a batsman. *Points: 5.*

Fielding — A very good slip, probably averaging about 80 to 85 per cent of chances offered, which isn't too bad. Also sharp at leg slip where he took a lot of good catches for Notts. Only steady in the outfield, lacking pace when turning and chasing. *Points: 6.*

Experience — Misses out here because he hasn't played test cricket but I'm considering him more as a first-class all rounder and giving him a special rating on that basis. Scores well through experience on the county scene. *Points: 5.*

Stamina — A strong, fit man who enjoyed some benefits through living and playing some 5000 feet above sea level in South Africa. Had a great capacity for work and pushed himself physically to keep in shape. Probably did more than anyone else on the county circuit. *Points: 9.*

 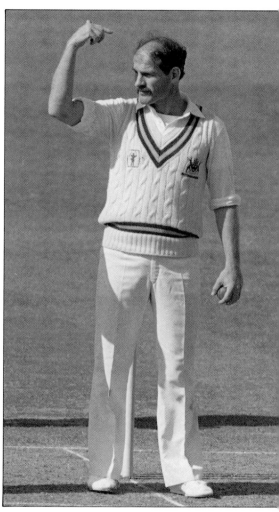

Left: Pakistan's Imran Khan is unquestionably the finest all rounder of my time, but there were two areas of his game which disappointed me when he toured New Zealand last summer — his captaincy and his fielding, both of which have declined considerably.   J.G. Blackwell

Right: He's been denied the experience of playing test cricket but South African Clive Rice still deserves to be considered in any list of today's outstanding all rounders. After 10 years with Nottinghamshire, it was impossible not to be impressed with his ability as a player and captain.   Patrick Eagar

Temperament — Usually unflappable and got on with the game; no histrionics, just played it hard but fair. Didn't quite do himself justice on many big occasions, like one-day finals at Lord's (the 1987 Natwest final being an exception). He rarely managed the magical important innings when run-chasing in the second innings of county matches. He also had a tendency to fail against West Indian bowlers on the county circuit. While it was the ultimate challenge for him to compete against them, the West Indians usually had the better of him. *Points: 6.*

Dedication — Ultra-determined to do well. Because he missed out on test cricket, he was dedicated to proving himself whenever he played in the company of top players. It was his only way of measuring his ability, as he did when he was called into the Bicentennial test match at Lord's in 1987. There was just no way he was going to lose his wicket. *Points: 8.*

Captaincy — A tough and demanding leader, he expected everyone to be at optimum all the time. He commanded and demanded that kind of effort but I thought he was a bit inflexible. Tactically he was sound but not overly innovative. I'd call him a percentages captain. After being sacked as Notts captain, he was reinstated and played a major role in our successes. He had a creditable record as Notts skipper although I thought he was prone to drift at times; perhaps other things were on his mind and distracted him. *Points: 6.*

Total points: 53.5.

I've got no qualms about rating Imran the best — while Botham is well down. Botham was undeniably brilliant in the earlier phase of his career, but I've looked at the players over their entire careers with a special view to analysing their performance in more recent times. And I don't think there would be any argument that Botham's on shaky ground on the basis of displays later in his career.

It's pertinent in that regard to look at some facts and figures from the 1987 calendar year, the last time the four of us (excluding Rice from this, naturally) were all in test circulation. Significantly, Botham scored only 248 runs at 27.55 (highest score 51 not out) in six tests in 1987 while, in the same period, he took just seven wickets at a cost of 70.28 each.

Imran played in 10 tests in the 1987 calendar year, scoring 515 runs at 57.22 and taking 29 wickets at 29.20 while Kapil, in nine matches, totalled 349 runs at 31.72 and captured 23 wickets at 35.47. My return in seven tests that year was 336 runs at 48.00 and 39 wickets at 20.74.

It doesn't really matter who's the best. It's a case of . . . we're only as good as our next performance. That's the way we are judged by cricket writers, commentators and the game's lovers. I'll leave it to you to decide.

C·H·A·P·T·E·R F·I·V·E

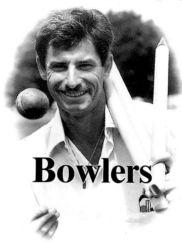

Bowlers

In the early 1970s, he hurtled in towards the crease, intent on projecting the ball as fast as he could. The action was raw, the end result sometimes erratic but he was undeniably fast, very fast. And aggressive, too — as Gary Sobers and the Rest of the World XI discovered in Perth one December day in 1971.

The World XI's first innings total read a paltry 59, Sobers one of four batsmen dismissed for a duck by one D.K. Lillee, who'd taken eight for 29 from just 7.1 overs! It was the day Dennis Lillee really announced his arrival, even though he'd made his test debut earlier in 1971 — and taken five wickets in his first innings.

He'd toured New Zealand with the Australian B side in 1969–70, taking one for 92 off 21 overs in the only 'test' he played. But, by early 1973, Lillee had broken down — stricken by a back injury on Australia's tour of the West Indies. In plaster for six months because of a stress fracture, he was off the international scene for two years undergoing treatment and rebuilding ever so gradually. It had to be wondered whether he'd come back at the highest level and, if he did, just how effective he would be. Lillee, of course, defied logic; he went on to become the master fast bowler. And when age began to catch up, the legs weary and the hair thinning on top, DK cut his pace, his run-up and still lost little. To me, he was the complete fast bowler — a beautifully balanced, rhythmical approach to the wicket, the perfect side-on delivery, a wonderful action and the ability to make the ball talk — at pace. He was the archetypal pace bowler, too . . . the kind who showed his disgust and annoyance when appeals weren't upheld; the kind who chipped batsmen; and the kind who perfected the evil look at the target of his attack.

I marvelled at Dennis Lillee. As a youngster, I was just like any other kid who was fanatical about cricket. I had my favourites but, even though I was into my 20s — and a test player myself — when Lillee was at his best, he was always my idol, my role model. Injury hadn't stopped him. He'd returned an even better bowler as he refined his control while losing none of his firepower. That courage alone was a wonderful example for me — he was saying: "Don't give up." He had a powerful influence on my development as a bowler, both in a technical sense and in the way he presented himself.

While I haven't, fortunately, been through the same injury nightmare as Lillee, there have been similarities in our careers. We were both wild bowlers initially, searching for pace above all else. Gradually, we both honed our bowling approach and evolved into bowling "old age" by modifying our game still further. In many respects, I copied Lillee. I studied him and analysed everything he did, asking myself why he did it and then deciding whether there were aspects of his approach I could build into my own game. I couldn't have had a better example to follow.

But there were other influences, too. Back in the 1960s, I used to watch the New Zealand bowlers Frank Cameron and Dick Motz. Cameron was so steady and reliable, taking 62 wickets in his 19 tests. Motz, the first New Zealander to take 100 test wickets, is the best Kiwi pace bowler I've seen. Strong and with a nice technique, he swung the ball away and used the off-cutter as his main delivery. I recall him giving the Indian batsmen plenty to think about when he took a magnificent six for 63 at Christchurch in 1967–68.

Of course, Dad and my brothers had much to do with my evolution as a fast bowler and yet, there was a time as a teenager when I wondered whether I had the ability to be a quick bowler. At school, I always tried to bowl fast but a competition at Christchurch Boys' High School all but told me I ought to forget it. You had to bowl at one stump and also try to pitch the ball in a marked area on a length — I was eliminated almost immediately, landing halfway down the track, nowhere near on target and using a wind-up action. The only pole I could hit was the one way over on the leg-side holding the net up! I even considered concentrating on spin bowling and batting after that experience but, through more doses of bowling to Dad and Barry in the back yard, I realised perseverance was the better option.

The real spur for me was provided by Dayle. By the time I joined him in the New Zealand team in 1972–73, persistent back trouble had reduced him from a strike bowler to a stock bowler. He refused to succumb to the problems which plagued him, though, and the fact he still enjoyed success was the greatest tribute to his tenacity (and a lesson for me as well). It was one of the special thrills of my career to be able to play alongside Dayle in the test arena. There were a number of times when it seemed the 12th man's job was a choice between the two of us but, from the 1973 tour of England through to his last test in 1977–78, we actually played in the same test side 10 times and enjoyed some memorable moments.

The first came in our fifth test together — New Zealand's historic first win over Australia in Christchurch in 1973–74 when I collected seven wickets in the match and he took five; we were also together in the amazing Trent Bridge match against England in 1973 when we were out for 440 chasing 479 to win; there was the Basin Reserve win over India in 1975–76 when I captured 11 wickets and Dayle three; and then we played together in New Zealand's first test victory over England in Wellington in 1977–78, 10 wickets for me but none for Dayle in his last test as he fought his back injury bowling into the wind. Another "Hadlee Test" I'll always remember was the one against Australia in Sydney in 1973–74 when the rain robbed us, Dayle and I taking seven of the Australian first innings wickets. So there's pleasure in knowing we took 72 wickets between us in those 10 tests, and shared in the winning feeling three times.

Even though I didn't lack for influences — either in my formative years or later in life — there's no doubt in my mind that 10 years in English county cricket was the making of me as a fast bowler. Early on I relied on natural ability and did very little work on fitness. I never made national Brabin Cup or Rothmans teams, nor was I selected for the New Zealand Secondary Schools side. I never deserved to either because I didn't work at my bowling. Perhaps I depended on reputation and the family name too much, and thought things would just happen. It's never quite that simple, but it took me a long time to digest the realities of cricketing life. I found the pace of first-class cricket too much to handle; the idea of playing three days and then having a day or two off before launching into another Plunket Shield match was almost beyond me. I didn't understand — nor was I really told — what training and preparation was all about, how vital it was to the creation of a first-class cricketer. Not until I joined Nottinghamshire in 1978 did I learn more about the need for training and the discipline required to practise constantly; it became an occupational necessity as a professional.

Now I look back on 18 seasons as a first-class cricketer to see I've bowled something like 65,000-plus deliveries (without considering limited-overs games). And, when I stop to reflect on a figure like that, I really wonder how it all happened following those early years of uncertainty, when I lacked confidence and guidance. While I enjoy batting — I like being involved actively in a match at all times — it's the sweat and hard toil of bowling over after over which has meant the most to me. I've conceded more than 25,000 runs but I've taken 1447 wickets at a career average of fractionally under 18.00, and nothing can replace the satisfaction those statistics give me.

What I've achieved with the ball underlines the essence of what the game is all about — it's based on a private duel between batsman and bowler, with the bowler dictating the play. It all hinges on where he pitches the ball; he governs what will happen to a large degree. Will it be a dot ball? Will runs be scored? Will it be a no ball or a wide? Or a wicket delivery?

Success comes about through a whole myriad of factors. You first need the weaponry to make it work — if you're a quicker bowler, the commodity of genuine pace is obviously the first key. Then there's the ability to bowl a consistent line and length and the talent to move the ball both in the air and off the pitch, not to mention having a store of varying types of delivery. Stamina, tenacity, concentration and dedication are priorities, too. But assuming you have all those things, there's still much more to it.

Critical to my career has been my mental method of attack and the way captains have used me. While basic ability must be there in the first place, it's worth very little if a captain doesn't harness the talent correctly, or if he sets wrong fields. Captains like Bevan Congdon and Mark Burgess tended to over-use me, rather than giving me sharp bursts — probably because they felt I was the bowler more capable of striking. They'd keep me on for over after over, turning me effectively into a stock bowler instead of the spearhead I was supposed to be. But then Geoff Howarth came along and he had the ideal recipe . . . a burst of five or six overs, maybe seven, with the new ball, a rest and then back for another foray and so on. I'd have perhaps five or even six spells on a given day's play, meaning I was nearly always sharp and keen each time I was to bowl again.

Equally crucial are the mind games I play as a bowler. I rarely stand at the top of my mark and think: "What will it be this time . . . shall I bowl him the leg-cutter? Maybe the slower ball?" No, I have a definite plan for every batsman who's in the firing line. It's a case of constant analysis, of watching all batsmen to see what sort of pitch conditions they're suited to, or are uncomfortable on. I analyse a batsman's range of shots, checking whether he favours the drive, the cut, the pull or the hook. How does he handle the shorter delivery? What about his judgement of line? Does he let the ball go outside off stump or is he prone to hang the bat out a little?

I store all that information and have a picture in my mind of any batsman as he walks out to face me. There aren't too many batsmen I haven't encountered when I go in to a test match; I might have bowled to them in county cricket or in some other first-class match. The ones I know nothing about, I do research on. So, even before an incoming batsman faces a ball, I'm giving myself a mental print-out on what he's all about. When he takes guard, I have another look. If he leaves a couple of stumps exposed, he wants me to bowl straight at off stump so he can play me through the off. That should give me a good chance of nicking him out, if I can get him to nibble at deliveries a bit wide of the off stump (because he has to reach for the ball). If he takes middle, he's going to hit me fairly straight on both sides of the wicket. If he has a low grip, he favours the cut or the pull. A high grip and he's going to play straight. I look at the pitch conditions, take into account whether I have an attacking field or a defensive one. Is the batsman in form? If so, how do I give him a single so I can get his partner down the other end? It's a thinking game.

But sometimes my mental preparation hasn't been as sharp as it could be, or I haven't had the foresight to alter my strategy when Plan A hasn't worked. It happened in Brisbane in the first test against Australia in 1987–88. When we had played Australia two years earlier, we fancied we could always lure David Boon into chasing wide deliveries and have him caught by the 'keeper or in the slips. And so I went into the match at the 'Gabba with that picture of him in my mind, meaning I bowled from close in to the stumps, bowling wicket to wicket and making the ball move away towards slips. But, much as I tried, Boon just kept leaving me alone — I couldn't believe it. Every time I bowled straighter, he worked me away on the leg side. He'd become so disciplined. I tried to make adjustments but it was too late. He went on to make 143 in Australia's first innings total of 305, the key innings in its decisive victory, a win which ultimately gave Australia the series.

I blame myself for what happened in Brisbane. I should have deduced much earlier in his innings what he was up to instead of adhering to a plan based on the way he'd played me two years earlier. Only later, I read an article about how the Australian batsmen had devised a scheme to deliberately upset me. Letting me go outside off stump was one part of the plan and another was to unsettle my routine. Normally I like to walk back to my mark and come straight in for the next delivery, so the Australian batsmen did some gardening, took a new guard or did anything to hold me up. They also took as many sharp singles as possible, ensuring the batsmen were always rotating the strike. It all served to upset me and put my bowling rhythm out of kilter. They were smart and their plot worked. All credit to them because they won the mental battle. I mucked up in that match and firmly believe my failure to sort Boon out contributed significantly to our defeat.

It was then up to me to introspectively dissect my performance, and to rectify my errors. I was much more flexible in the second test in Adelaide. I knew I had to bowl to Boon from wider on the crease, so I varied it, sometimes going wide, then closer in. I bowled around the wicket at times, varied the pace and I also started bowling into the track. Boon never looked the part at any stage and I had him out for six, dragging a wider delivery on to his stumps. Only three balls later I also had Dean Jones for a duck. I'd made modifications and they paid off. I had a track in Brisbane which should have worked for me but had taken only three for 95 in Australia's first innings. With a changed approach, I collected five wickets in Adelaide and 10 in the third test in Melbourne.

There's a message there about staying cool. As a bowler, it's so easy to become frustrated but, if you are upset with what's going on (or not going on), you can lose sight of the real objective. It's all about controlling yourself, ensuring your temperament is right for the occasion. It's something I worked on because, in my younger days, I was uncontrolled. I'd carry on when catches were dropped or when decisions went against me. It was not until I went to Notts that I appreciated how much energy I was wasting. I don't talk to or sledge batsmen anymore. I use the look or the glare instead. It's far more sensible. I'm not outwardly aggressive in the style of a Lillee or some others but there are still players who believe I intimidate them.

I dismissed Greg Matthews several times in 1985–86 and he said of me: "He doesn't sledge you but he does intimidate you. He's actually one of the most aggressive bowlers I've ever faced. He uses eye contact — he has a presence."

Another key to my development was the support of the New Zealand selectors. Having picked me on raw potential in 1972–73, they decided to invest in me and the policy of selectorial consistency was naturally a huge confidence booster for me. The truth is, my record was anything but flash and, after my first seven tests, I had 20 wickets at 36.75. The selectors persevered until the third test against India in 1975–76 when I must have been so close to not playing. It's history now that I took 11 wickets in the match and made the breakthrough. I stress my case because it's vital the same sort of faith is shown in any other player earmarked as a long-term future prospect. Take Danny Morrison who came into the New Zealand test side against Australia in 1987–88; by the end of the summer, he'd played six tests and taken 16 wickets at 38.93, a record remarkably similar to mine. He was in only his fourth test when he had a five-wicket bag, a feat I didn't achieve until my ninth test.

There has, of course, been quite a fixation about trying to unearth a new long-term strike bowler to take over from me and I've often marvelled at the rapidity with which potential performers have been tried and discarded. Over the last 10 years or so, all manner of quick bowlers have been given a chance —Brendon Bracewell, Gary Troup, Martin Snedden, Gary Robertson, Mark Carrington, Richard Webb, Derek Stirling, Sean Tracy, Stu Gillespie, Willie Watson, Brian Barrett and Morrison providing testimony to the number of bowlers the selectors have dabbled with. The casualty rate has been high with very few really progressing.

I had much to do in the early 1980s with the New Zealand Cricket Council's so-called search for my new-ball successor, seeing much of the talent at the coaching clinics Geoff Howarth and I used to run (subsequently the NZCC employed Dennis Lillee to run the fast bowlers' clinics). I had to analyse the players for their faults, attitude and so on. So many of them have faded away, proving useful enough performers at first-class level but unable to make that jump to the next level.

Stirling was one of the most interesting cases because he was one player the selectors stuck with, taking him on tours to Sri Lanka, Zimbabwe, Pakistan, the West Indies and England. I remember Dad thought he'd play for New Zealand when he saw him as a 16-year-old — and potentially he was a very exciting prospect. He was big and strong, had a high action and was quite quick. He had one or two technical problems with his front arm and back foot but the real worry was his attitude. I wondered whether he was fit enough and whether he was prepared to put the work in. It was a bit of a kick in the backside for him when he returned from the 1984–85 tour of Pakistan to find he wasn't wanted at all for the home series against the Pakistanis. In Pakistan (when I didn't tour), he'd been given the new ball as the main strike bowler; evidently he bowled impressively and caused some of the Pakistani top order batsmen some problems. I don't think he was strong enough mentally to handle the snub for the home series, though. And while he was spasmodically effective in England in 1986, it was clear he hadn't developed as well as he ought to have, proving too erratic in line and length. And so he has a test record of 13 wickets at 46.23 in six tests, which probably won't be added to.

I thought Sean Tracy had loads of potential. While he had technical deficiencies as well, he had plenty of heart and always wanted to bowl as fast as he could. It was a disappointment he didn't make it because Dayle also spent quite a bit of time working with him. Again, attitude problems prevented his progress.

But there are younger quick bowlers who have come through well so far — and the sign of one or two more on the horizon. I like the look of Danny Morrison and believe he'll be around for a long time, provided he's handled with care. He lacks height for a fast bowler — under the general rule — but he compensates with his determination, aggression and enthusiasm. He's quicker than he might appear, he bounces the ball and he adds genuine firepower to the New Zealand attack — and that's something we haven't had for a long time. I'm sure he'll really make it.

Willie Watson's more in the stock bowler mode, I guess, and I must say I initially doubted his future as an international player. But he's improved markedly and, like Morrison, I'm sure he'll be a New Zealand player for some time. He might appear relatively innocuous from the boundary, but he's deceptive. He can move the ball around both in the air and off the track and has the ability to bowl one or two extraordinary balls which make him a dangerous proposition for batsmen.

There's also rich promise in store in Chris Cairns and Shane Thomson from Northern Districts plus Wellington's Stephen Hotter. And perhaps there's still time for Brian Barrett to make it again after touring England with the New Zealand team in 1986. The future looks reasonably healthy.

But New Zealand's pace bowling resources have tended to revolve around a handful of very familiar names. In my early years, Bruce Taylor and Richard Collinge were the established frontline bowlers, Collinge a great trier whose left-arm angle made him a threat (he always seemed to have the wood on Geoff Boycott). Taylor, now a New Zealand selector, was lively and able to produce the golden delivery out of nowhere. Those two joined Motz in the 100-wicket club at test level, Collinge having the New Zealand record at 116 until I overtook him in the first test against the West Indies in 1979–80.

For the greater part of my test career, my partners have been Lance Cairns and Ewen Chatfield, with Martin Snedden moving in and out of the side since his arrival in 1980–81.

Cairns finished up with 130 wickets at 32.91 in his 43 tests but, while he was a grand worker, he had a tendency to be rather erratic and inconsistent, especially at the pace he bowled. Generally used as the first change or into-the-wind bowler, his primary task was to bowl accurately in an effort to contain. But, with his ability to bend the ball in quite outrageously, Cairns often wanted for control and was picked off too easily at times.

Chatfield has been anything but inconsistent; he's the absolute opposite, surely the most consistent line and length bowler in top-level cricket. Most countries in the world wouldn't entertain using a bowler of Charlie's type with the new ball in test matches but, whenever he has shared opening duties with me, he has been the ideal foil. He bowls so

Above left: Danny Morrison on the follow-through . . . he adds genuine firepower to the New Zealand attack and I'm sure he'll be around for years.

Above right: Other countries might shudder at the thought of using a bowler of Ewen Chatfield's type with the new ball in tests — but he's been a great foil for me. He has to be the most consistent line and length bowler in world cricket.

J.G. Blackwell

tightly and gives so little away that I'm free to attack. Yet, given the right conditions, he can be dangerous and effective. I need only cast my mind back to Lancaster Park and the third test against the West Indies in 1986–87 to remind me of that. Chatfield was all but unplayable as we rolled the West Indies for only 100 in its first innings; I didn't bowl outstandingly but still took six wickets while Charlie had four for 30, when he really deserved six. He has also proved — as Cairns did — that age should never be an obstacle. In fact, when the three of us played together in a test for the last time (against Australia in Perth in 1985–86), we were an aged lot . . . Lancer was 36, Charlie was 35 and I was 34. And last summer, Charlie was still there at 38 with me 37! It's pertinent that Chatfield was 32 before he finally established himself as a test player in 1982–83; his earlier experiences in the mid-70s had seen him discarded and, when he returned to the New Zealand team in 1980–81, he was wanted only as a limited-overs bowler. He kept fighting, and made it back into the test side where he has been a fixture ever since, thoroughly deserving his 100th test wicket in Sri Lanka in April 1987.

Martin Snedden may well develop on Chatfield lines. While he first played test cricket in 1980–81, he has been only sparingly used. He's still only 30, though, and gives every indication of gradually sharpening his craft as a medium-fast bowler in much the same way Chatfield has.

Throughout my years as a test player, New Zealand has only very occasionally fielded a new-ball attack of the true kind. We've worked within our own limitations and concentrated on frustrating opposition batsmen, often fiddling sides out rather than blasting them out. It's worked well, too. After all, we didn't need burning pace to skittle the West Indies for 100 in 1986–87, or to dismiss England for only 82 and 93 in Christchurch in 1983–84.

Our attack has been distinctive but undoubtedly effective. At the same time, I've played against some of the world's outstanding fast bowlers — the West Indies were always a daunting lot. The combination of Andy Roberts, Michael Holding, Joel Garner and Colin Croft was awesome in 1979–80 at a time when the West Indies was perfecting its recipe for pace, pace and more pace. By 1984–85 — when we toured the Caribbean — it was Malcolm Marshall, Winston Davis, Holding and Garner and they battered us physically and mentally. It's not a pretty way to play cricket, having fast bowlers belting in and bruising and maiming batsmen. I can't accept the game should be played that way, not when the assault is so merciless, so relentless and so furious, and aimed at physical intimidation. It also takes its toll mentally. But the method remains the same with each passing year, only the names change every now and then. By the time we played the West Indies again in 1986–87, Holding and Garner were on the way out, Marshall was still there and he'd been joined by Courtney Walsh and Tony Gray in the test attack. Now Patrick Patterson and Curtly Ambrose are there, too. Just when will it end?

Holding, all lithe elegance in his approach and action, Roberts and Marshall rank among the most exceptional express bowlers I've struck while Garner, with his steep bounce and seam from such a great height, has been one of the outstanding fast-medium operators.

Lillee I unhesitatingly tag the greatest there's been. He was complete. And Pakistan's Imran Khan is also an excellent pace bowler, able to move the ball — especially so when the ball is old — and to extract awkward bounce from the pitch. For sheer unpredictability, Lillee's Australian team-mate Jeff Thomson was unbeatable. With his slinging action, Thommo would spray the ball anywhere and everywhere. He was frightening to face at his sharpest and I've rarely seen anyone bowl as quickly as he did to New Zealand's John Morrison in Wellington in 1981–82.

Among the band of fast-medium or medium-fast bowlers encountered, Ian Botham is the most bewildering. He was a fine bowler when I first tangled with him in New Zealand in 1977–78. He had an excellent outswinger and cut through plenty of test line-ups but, in time, the good life caught up with him. He didn't appear to work on his game as diligently as he might have, and the supply of wickets dwindled. Although he became test cricket's leading wicket taker for a time, he tended to capture many of his wickets with poorer deliveries in latter years.

A quick bowler I may be, but it's the spinners who fascinate me most and, sadly, New Zealand has been thin on good quality spinners at test level. We've had more than useful left-armers in Hedley Howarth (86 wickets in 30 tests) and Stephen Boock (74 wickets in 30 tests) plus John Bracewell's off-spin which has netted 82 wickets in 35 tests. Another left-armer was David O'Sullivan but, while he took 523 wickets at a cost of about 25.00 each in a long first-class career, he was a disappointment at test level with only 18 wickets at 67.83. He had the distinction of being called for throwing when he bowled in Australia in 1973–74 and also gained some notoriety as one of the slower fieldsmen seen at international level. When we played Australia in the first test in Melbourne on that tour, Daffy waddled off after a straight hit, dived and just pulled the ball up inside the boundary. After the ball had been relayed back through three players, Daffy thought he'd done a great job restricting the batsmen to three runs. In fact, they'd run five when he could have let the ball go and they would only have had four!

As a generalisation, New Zealand spinners haven't been match-winners — and I know Bracewell has proved the exception on two occasions, once against Australia in Auckland in 1985–86 (when he became the first New Zealand spin bowler to take 10 wickets in a match) and then against India in Bombay in 1988–89 when his eight wickets in the match helped us to an incredible victory. Usually, though, they've been selected to fill a stock bowling role, coming in to bowl several overs so the seamers can have a break, or to add a little more variety to the attack. There was a time when Frank Cameron was the convenor of selectors that New Zealand went into tests with four seamers, Cameron always believing they could do the job just as effectively if there wasn't a good enough spinner on hand.

New Zealand spinners haven't been big turners of the ball either, a legacy of the pitches they have to bowl on more often than not. Bracewell can give the ball a useful tweak but he's liable to bowl at least one loose delivery an over, which is a bit of a luxury in test cricket. His aggressive temperament stamps him as the least likely spin bowler in international cricket; spinners are generally cool and calm operators where Braces is outrageously volatile and over-keen at times. There have been occasions when he has lacked patience. Instead of trying to tempt and frustrate batsmen, he'll try and bowl wicket deliveries all the time and that can be expensive. He's also one of the world's champion appealers, using a fast bowler's mentality; this approach would be somewhat frowned upon in English county cricket. But he can be a source of great amusement. He appeals when guys are so clearly out just to hit back at the umpire: "Oh, is that really out? What do I have to do to get him out?" The same bloke is one of the world's greatest triers who cares more about the team's needs than his own achievements.

It's in spin bowling where New Zealand cricket needs to work just as hard as the pace area. We've had fast bowlers' clinics but, until the summer of 1988–89, we lacked the equivalent for spin bowling. Dayle did some work with spinners yet he's hardly the right person to do it with his background as a seamer. The NZCC is now using former Australian test

Opposite: A study of the master. Dennis Lillee's caught in a magnificent shot in the take off position at delivery. His action encapsulates what fast bowling's all about — and why he was the model I used to develop my bowling, both physically and mentally.

D.O. Neely Collection

offie, Ashley Mallett, a move which should be applauded although the likes of Howarth, Boock and Bracewell might have far more to offer in terms of bowling in New Zealand conditions.

The shame about test cricket over the last decade has been the virtual disappearance of spinners, especially leg spinners. The English spinners, brought up on a diet of county play, tend to be very defensive. The Indian trio of Bishen Bedi, Bhagwat Chandrasekhar and Erapally Prasanna were enthralling to watch, each of them contrastingly different — Bedi with his lovely control of flight with those nagging left-armers, Chandra with his brisk version of leg-spin and Prasanna with his rhythmical off-spin. England's Derek 'Deadly' Underwood was the only one of his type, a left-armer who used a fairly long run-up and was well, just deadly, if he had the chance to bowl on a wet pitch.

There aren't all that many memorable spinners left in pace-dominated test cricket today. One exception is India's boyish-looking Narendra Hirwani who routed the West Indies in his test debut in late 1987 and took 20 wickets in three tests against us in late 1988. But how good will he prove to be when he bowls outside his home country? The most exciting to watch is Pakistan's Abdul Qadir. He's all arms and legs and poses all sorts of threats to the batsmen. He's a rarity.

If only test cricket could revert to the balance of former years when spin bowling was equally as important as pace. The preoccupation with the quicker bowlers (the West Indies have a lot to answer for) means test cricket's much poorer for it.

Bowlers come to appreciate something else which is essential to their performance — and I'm not talking about considerate umpires. It's your team-mates and their ability to accept chances in the field, never mind those specially gifted athletes who can turn seemingly impossible chances into wickets.

As a fast bowler, I need support from everyone but particularly from the behind-the-wicket cordon — the wicketkeeper through to the gully. In my earlier years, I bemoaned the number of catches missed in the slips at test level but, in later years, the catching success rate has been much healthier. And the principal reason for that was the return of Jeremy Coney to the New Zealand team in 1978–79. He really was a wonderful second slip who had the oustanding record of 64 catches in his 52 tests and, of that tally, a very high proportion — 27 — were off my bowling. I couldn't have asked for a more competent catcher than Coney; he rated among the very best in the specialist position. It took time to find a first slip I had absolute faith in but that player was found when Jeff Crowe came into the New Zealand side in 1982–83. While Jeff's had problems at times commanding a regular place in the New Zealand side, there's no question he's the most accomplished catcher we've had at first slip. He's an excellent judge in the critical spot and his value there was merely under-lined in India late in 1988 when, without him, we had great difficulty with our catching in the slips area. I've always felt comfortable knowing he has been at first slip; it gives me, and the other bowlers, so much confidence. It was great to see him back in the team for the games against Pakistan last season. He deserved his recall with consistent form — and returned a more relaxed and technically better player. Hopefully, he will continue to play for New Zealand for some years to come.

But the man who sees most of the catching action is the wicketkeeper and, after the late Ken Wadsworth, I've had Warren Lees, Jock Edwards, Bruce Edgar, Ian Smith and Tony Blain as test 'keepers. Mostly it's been Smith, who started his career with Central Districts before shifting to Auckland. And, with more than 40 catches off my bowling, I have a lot to thank him for. While Wadsworth was more than competent, Smithy is the best 'keeper I've bowled to in New Zealand. His glove work is just so good; technically, he's a superb operator behind the stumps. Easily New Zealand's most experienced 'keeper at test level (with 48 appearances), he had a wonderful season internationally in 1988–89 and, if ever there was an illustration of how good he is, it came in the two tests against Pakistan. The tourists batted only twice in the series, making 438 for seven declared in Wellington and 616 for five declared in Auckland. For 732 minutes at the Basin Reserve and then 808 minutes at Eden Park, Smith had to be alert, vigilant — and he didn't let up. He allowed just one bye in Wellington and none in Auckland — in more than 25 hours behind the stumps. He saw only 12 wickets fall while 1054 runs were scored and yet he coughed up just one bye. Amazing. But the best example of a 'keeper being on top of his game came late on the second day in Auckland when Pakistan was 480 for four and Javed Miandad was 271. Smith was alone behind the stumps with not one slip in. Against all expectations, Miandad got an edge to Ewen Chatfield, trying to dab the ball through slips. It went low and wide to Smithy's right but he still had the agility and zip to swoop down and across to glove a wonderful catch. That's what top-class wicketkeeping's all about. He also backed up his 'keeping by batting outstandingly throughout the summer, scoring more than 300 runs at an average of about 46.00 in five tests.

He was outstanding last season but it hasn't always been that way. There have been times — now seemingly gone —when he's had an attitudinal problem. He used to drift and allow his concentration to slip — which we're all guilty of at times — but he's generally done a magnificent job and deserves to be tagged the best wicketkeeper in international cricket today. The 'keeper is the vital link in a team, because he's in the best position to analyse, judge and give advice to bowlers and captains about field placements and batsmen's weaknesses.

I rate England's Alan Knott the best all-round 'keeper I've struck, equally adept standing back to the quicker bowlers or up over the stumps for the spinners; Australia's former 'iron gloves' Rod Marsh became a wonderful exponent of the art when taking the fast bowlers — and he had plenty of practice from Dennis Lillee and Jeff Thomson; Bob Taylor was the most unobtrusive, a thoroughly efficient 'keeper in every sense; and India's Farokh Engineer, who played a lot of cricket for Lancashire, was stunning standing up for the spinners (and again he had ample opportunity courtesy of Bedi, Chandrasekhar and company).

As slip specialists, I've seen no one to rival Ian and Greg Chappell who grabbed a fabulous ratio of catches which came their way while Derek Randall — perpetual motion and perpetual humour at any time —

was one of the great outfielders, a man with such astonishing anticipation and speed to the ball. I could go on — Viv Richards is brilliant just about anywhere, Roger Harper's outstanding for his speed and throwing on the turn while Craig McDermott has one of the best arms I've seen throwing from the deep. David Gower (cover), Clive Lloyd (cover), Gus Logie (bat-pad), Bruce Yardley (gully) and Ashley Mallett (gully) are just some players who've been excellent specialists.

It was a strange thing, but not so many years ago, New Zealand was renowned for its exceptional fielding. Perhaps because it was deficient in the batting and bowling departments, it made up for it with death or glory work in the field. Of course, there's been a transformation over the years with New Zealand proving to have more than average batting and bowling talent — but the improved test performances have come at a cost to the general standard of fielding.

. . . c. Smith b. Hadlee. Dennis Lillee had a great ally in Australian wicketkeeper Rod Marsh. And my most frequent partner in destruction has been Ian Smith, surely the best 'keeper in international cricket today. More than 40 of my test wickets have come through catches gloved by Smithy — I couldn't ask for anything better. And last summer, the little man was at his best. All-Sport, Simon Bruty

J.G. Blackwell

J.G. Blackwell

R.J. Hadlee Collection

My own fielding isn't so wonderful once I'm too far away from the wicket; the aging process has made me too slow and my throwing arm is, dare I say it, of the pop gun variety. But I've always enjoyed fielding in the gully or at first slip to the spinners. I'm proud of at least three catches I've taken in tests — all of them in the gully and all of them at Wellington's Basin Reserve. There were two in the same England innings in 1983–84, one off the right-handed Chris Smith and the other off the left-handed David Gower. And, in 1980–81, I took another sharp one off Kapil Dev in the first test against India.

I guess New Zealand cricket followers will always remember two other "catches" even more vividly, one in 1980–81 and the other in 1987–88.

The first one was Martin Snedden's famous catch which wasn't given in the Benson and Hedges World Series Cup final against Australia at the Melbourne Cricket Ground. A catch, which, if upheld (as it ought to have been) might very likely have prevented one of the worst acts perpetrated in the game of cricket — the under-arm act which happened in the same match. Greg Chappell was 58 when Snedden raced in from the boundary to take the "catch" only to find the umpires ruled it out after consultation (and Chappell went on to make a critical 90 before later pulling the under-arm trick). I'm still astounded whenever I think about that catch.

There's never any shortage of incidents involving New Zealand and Australia cricket encounters, and the other one which ranks right down there with the mullygrubber is the so-called catch Australian wicketkeeper Greg Dyer took to dismiss Andrew Jones in the third test of the 1987–88 series. Yet again it was the MCG which was the stage for controversy in the field; Jones was given out on 40 when he was seemingly taken down leg-side by Dyer off Craig McDermott. It soon transpired —from one angle of the television replays — that Dyer had actually grassed the ball and picked it up off the deck in his other hand. He maintained later he thought he'd taken a fair catch, but it's difficult to believe he couldn't have known he'd dropped it. He received a lot of flak over that non-catch — and perhaps he deserved it.

It was all the more unpalatable for us because of Jeff Crowe's gallant gesture during the second test of the series in Adelaide. When Allan Border was 66, and on his way to 205, Crowe appeared to snatch a great catch at wide mid-on only to come up claiming he'd dropped it. Only he could have known he'd spilled the chance and he called Border back. It was a wonderful move on his part but, just a couple of weeks later, Dyer did his bit. Apparently, Jeff's gesture meant absolutely nothing; it was an instance of gentlemanly conduct which has been missing from the game for years but it must have been lost on Greg Dyer.

C·H·A·P·T·E·R   S·I·X

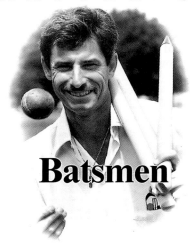

Batsmen

It was the classic confrontation . . . fast bowler to opening batsman.
I bounded in off my long run-up, bounced the batsman and was
despatched for four, just the kind of action which heightens a quick
bowler's fury. Lance Cairns handed the ball back to me as I returned to
my mark. "Give him another one, but a little quicker," he told me. Okay.
Let's see what I can do. Again I thumped the ball into the deck but with
a little more pace on it, again the batsman looked to put me away to the
boundary, only to miscue — and I had him out caught and bowled! I'd
done it! I'd dismissed Geoff Boycott, deceiving him with the Andy
Roberts' theory of bowling lifters of different pace.

Unfortunately, it wasn't a real triumph — by that time Boycott had
made 131 in the second test of the 1978 series at Trent Bridge! For me,
though, the wicket was important. It was the first time I'd taken his wicket
— and I did it again in the third test when I bowled him for only four.
But I dismissed Boycott only twice in 10 test innings I came up against
him.

The names of other batsmen may flow freely as outstanding players
of my time — Greg Chappell, Viv Richards, Glenn Turner, David Gower,
Gordon Greenidge, Allan Border, Javed Miandad, Sunil Gavaskar and
Martin Crowe. That's quite a line-up of batting talent.

But Boycott's the one I rank above them all, at least from a fast
bowler's perspective. He was anything but flamboyant; there wasn't a
batsman who was more dreadfully dour than him. He could never be
regarded in the same breath as Chappell, Richards and others in the classical

batting sense because he eliminated many of the flashy shots from his game. But he was prolific, phenomenally so, and he was a true practitioner of the batting art in its purest technical form. A man despised by so many for his singlemindedness and selfishness, he was the batsman I found the hardest to dismiss. He wasn't the best, aesthetically, but he was certainly the best in terms of preserving his wicket. He was a wonderful judge of line in letting the ball go and had an incredible appetite for making runs. He'd bat all day, gradually wearing down each bowler and, eventually, he'd have a hundred (and with more than 150 first-class hundreds his theory certainly worked).

There was, however, much resentment of Boycott, the way he quite clearly batted for himself and seemed to ignore his team's requirements. It was evident even when he played for the Yorkshire colts that he was never going to be a player who suited his side's needs; the captain once sent a player in to specifically run Boycott out because he was making no effort to score. Many years later, the same thing happened in England's

The joy of dismissing top-flight batsmen . . .
Left: Lord's, 1978, and the bails fly as I castle the hardest of all batsmen to dismiss — England opener Geoff Boycott. Looking on are Boycott's opening partner Graham Cooch and an almost-smiling Dickie Bird, the umpire I most respect.

Patrick Eagar

Right: Gordon Greenidge is undoubtedly one of the best batsmen around today — and forms a superb opening partnership with Desmond Haynes — but I've managed to dismiss him six times in tests, this time caught by Jeff Crowe for two in the third test against the West Indies in Bridgetown, Barbados, in 1985.

Brooks La Touche

second test clash against New Zealand in Christchurch in 1977–78 — Ian Botham was sent out with orders to run the slow-scoring Boycott out, and Boycs was captain of that side. Botham accomplished the mission.

Just about anyone and everyone has some Boycott story or comment. Alex Bannister once wrote: "He occasionally bats with the joviality of an undertaker." Dunedin golf professional John Evans asked Boycott to sign a bat, which I'd also autographed. "I'll sign above him because I'm a better batsman than him," said Boycott. Evans replied: "But he's a better bowler than you." "Yeah — but this is a bat!"

There's little doubt Boycott was self-centred. Rumour has it that one day, while sitting in his car watching cricket, it started to rain. Boycs turned on the windscreen wipers — not so he could see out, but so people could see in! An egotist? For sure. But there's nothing sinful about that because he was proud of his wonderful achievements.

Boycott used to calculate his season so he knew exactly what he needed to do to top the county averages, and I'm sure he planned a few not outs along the way just to compensate for unexpected failures. I can't disagree too much with his approach because, in many ways, I'm the same. I put that down to pride and setting out to do the job you're employed to carry out. At the same time, Yorkshire hardly ever benefited from Boycott's tunnel-vision approach. It won very little and it was significant that when Yorkshire won the Benson and Hedges Trophy in 1987 — and improved its placings in other competitions — it didn't have Boycott.

I never had much to do with him as a player. He used to be very tense and private, and a man with a fierce belief in his own ability. Even when he was 47, he believed he was good enough to play for England . . . and he certainly couldn't have done much worse than many of those who have played for England in recent years. Now he's much more relaxed about life, chatty, friendly and approachable as I discovered when he was in New Zealand for England's tour in 1987–88. Where he was moody and often aloof in the past, he's altogether more pleasant now the shackles of playing the game have been removed.

Boycott was a marvellous technician with superb powers of concentration, but you rate batsmen for different reasons. Greg Chappell was such an elegant, fluent batsman, never the collector of runs Boycott was. He stands out as the kind of batsman I like to watch — but not necessarily to bowl to. While I had Chappell's wicket six times in tests, he was still the sort of batsman who looked to dominate from the start, and very often did. Because he played so many shots, the bowler naturally had more of a chance than he did against, say, Boycott and Chappell's liking for the drive meant he was often nicked out; he had all the shots — he could drive beautifully, was good on the cut and the pull while he was also adept at chipping bowlers away on the leg side.

I'd list Chappell as the best batsman I encountered, in the all-round sense. He was still technically sound and could tear attacks apart, which Boycott couldn't do. I never felt Boycott was in charge when I bowled to him, even though he was very difficult to remove, but Chappell was a constant threat. And those who witnessed his wonderful 176 against New

Zealand in Christchurch in 1981–82 will know what I mean. Chappell reached 76 not out when stumps were drawn early on the first day — and then went berserk the next morning in a batting display which was classic Chappell, brimful of graceful strokes. There was nothing any of the New Zealand bowlers could do as he added exactly 100 runs to his overnight score in just 107 minutes before he was out well before lunch. Gary Troup's 11th over went for 20 runs and his figures read one for 53 off 11 overs. Martin Snedden finished the Australian innings with two for 89 from 18, Lance Cairns none for 74 from 21 and me six for 100 from 28.5 overs. We all suffered from Chappell's murderous artistry.

West Indian Viv Richards fell into the same category as Chappell — another player who has always wanted to be the master of the bowlers. I don't think he's as technically sound as Chappell was, but there's not a bowler in the world who can quell Richards when he's on fire at the crease. He doesn't just try to dominate the bowler in the obvious way of putting the ball away to the boundary; he also intimidates them with the way he carries himself physically, using body language to show who's in charge. He'll eye-ball bowlers arrogantly, often looking disdainfully down his nose at his opponents. He's like a fighter waiting for the next round of a bout. He might pummel the top of his bat handle or adjust his ever-present maroon West Indian cap, all little signs he is toey and itching to demonstrate his talents. A player of enormous confidence, he never wears a helmet; perhaps he wants to accept the challenges of the short-pitched ball from the fast bowler! That's his style.

Even early in his innings, he likes charging fast bowlers, looking to hit them back over their heads for four or six, or he'll innovate by backing away to square leg and positively smashing the ball through the off side. A wonderful player off his legs, he effortlessly puts quick bowlers away to the fence or over it anywhere between backward square and mid wicket, relying greatly on his wonderful eye. His weakness is the ball marginally outside off stump and nipping away; he still looks to hit those deliveries through the on side, wandering across his stumps and maybe nicking to the 'keeper or slips. But it can be so humiliating bowling to him when he's in the mood to rip an attack apart in an hour or even less. He's done it so many times, you lose count. There was his astounding 189 not out in a one-day international against England in 1984, or his 56-ball hundred against England on his home ground in Antigua in 1986, the fastest in test history.

Of course, he was a significant absentee when we beat the West Indies in 1979–80 but he profited against us in the West Indies in 1984–85. He wasn't anywhere near as successful in New Zealand in 1986–87, becoming yet another of the world's great batsmen who have failed on our pitches (Gary Sobers, Zaheer Abbas and Sunil Gavaskar among those who have struggled in New Zealand). In fact, Richards scored only 77 runs at 19.20 in four test innings; after opening the tour with a 28-ball 54 not out in a one-dayer against Auckland he had test scores of 24 (28 balls), 14 (10 balls) and one going into his last knock of the series. Again there was no semblance of patience or any intention to build an innings, even though the team was in dreadful shape. He simply took to me, carving boundaries out at will until I was taken out of the attack — but he eventually self-destructed for 38 off 37 balls (and West Indies was decisively beaten).

That was a cameo Richards display exemplifying his approach when confronted by a bowler who represented a threat. Richards batting against Hadlee . . . those were the sort of confrontations he enjoyed. The same thing happened in a Sunday league match in Bath in 1986. Somerset was coasting along with Richards on about 30 when Clive Rice brought me back on to try and take a wicket, or to slow down the run rate. I achieved neither in the first over as Richards played some big shots to take 12 runs, but I soon bowled him. Somerset lost its last five wickets cheaply and Nottinghamshire won the match. Richards hadn't shown responsibility and it was that kind of performance which highlighted Somerset's decision to sack him and Joel Garner after the 1986 season.

There's no question about his entertainment value, though, or his ability to murder sides on his day. Take the one-day international in Dunedin in 1986–87 when he hit 119 off 113 balls and then did us with the ball as well, taking five wickets. There isn't a more dangerous or destructive batsman in world cricket. David Lloyd, the former England batsman, tells a story about Richards playing against Glamorgan, and having some trouble getting bat on ball to fast bowler Greg Thomas. He kept playing and missing and Thomas said: "Viv, it's red and it's round." That tickled Richards up just a little, so he thumped Thomas's next delivery back over his head and into a pond for six. Richards told Thomas: "You know what it looks like, man, you go fetch it."

What Viv Richards has more than any other of his adversaries is the ability to excite, entertain and still be prolific. I mean, the man has topped 7000 test runs at an impressive average well above 50.00 after more than 100 tests. And he has also scored more than 6000 runs at 50-plus in one-day internationals . . . all of which is simply staggering. People will travel almost anywhere to watch the 'Master Blaster' — just to see him bat, and that alone is value for money.

Gordon Greenidge and Desmond Haynes have given the West Indies one of the most outstanding opening combinations seen in test history — and they're two players I've enjoyed dismissing a number of times in tests: Haynes seven times and Greenidge six. After the 1986–87 series in New Zealand, Martin Crowe suggested Greenidge was perhaps the world's best batsman and it was difficult to disagree with his assessment. After all, Greenidge made 213 against us at Eden Park and scored centuries in two of the three one-dayers. He can be very watchful, all the time just waiting for the loose ball he can hit . . . and then he really hits it, as he did in that double century with seven sixes and 20 fours. His hunger for big scores — he had three double centuries at test level in a three-year spell — classes him as one of the greats of my era. And the way he works in with Haynes as an opening partner has been exceptionally beneficial and critical to the West Indians' success at international level.

The challenge for most bowlers is making the adjustment when you're faced with left handers and, for that reason alone, Australia's Allan Border can be difficult to bowl to. With more than 7000 test runs to his name, Border's one of the best batsmen of this age for his run-gathering and his fighting qualities; he's probably more tenacious than most of his contemporaries, by no means pretty technically but superbly gritty. Like all left handers, he has a natural weakness to the delivery wide of the off stump. Bowl to left handers at off stump, middle or leg, and they're fine; they play you easily, relishing the chance to play off their toes through the on side. They become so accomplished at playing on-side shots because the natural tendency is for right-arm bowlers to stray on to leg stump. I prefer to bowl to right handers and find the adjustment required for lefties difficult to make at times. It's not easy to bowl consistently to the left handers but, provided you can find that line just outside off stump and get the ball to jag away, you have a good chance of dismissing them. Statistics show I've taken Border's wicket six times. I've done even better against his one-time Australian team-mate Greg Matthews, dismissing him a total of eight times in six tests in 1985–86. Like Border, Matthews was more a collector of runs and another fighter. He was a little down about it when I had removed him in five successive innings in Australia and, when he came out to bat in the second innings in Perth, he said: "Just take it easy, Paddles — you've got me out enough times this series." "I'm just getting looser," I said, "I want to make you six out of six." Soon after I did.

Test cricket's leading run-maker is a man I hardly bowled to in the latter part of his test career — Sunil Gavaskar. Known as the little Indian master, he scored more than 10,000 test runs yet the last time we clashed in a test was as long ago as 1980–81. So, it's awkward to make an accurate assessment of his ability. Of course, he has the figures to back him up but I recall he managed just one half-century in New Zealand in 1980–81. As a batsman, he was a split character; he could be terribly introverted and play the real anchor role, or he could explode for no obvious reason. He was technically sound and watchful, but I found I could nick him out on occasions.

One batsman who must always be ranked in the top echelon is Pakistan's Javed Miandad. His performances are underestimated because he's scored so many of his runs at home, and it's interesting that he's hardly ever given out leg-before by Pakistani umpires. Funny that. However, Miandad has a test batting record of exceptional quality . . . anyone who has scored 7422 runs at 57.09 (and scored 21 centuries) deserves the utmost admiration. He was only 19 when I first saw him in Pakistan in 1976; he made 27 and 138 not out for the Chief Minister's XI and then had successive test scores of 163 (in his debut innings), 25 not out, 26, 206 and 85. He averaged 126.00 in that series, then 99.00 in New Zealand in 1978–79 and 84.25 back in Pakistan in 1984–85. He may have

Happiness is . . . outfoxing Australian batsmen.
Above: David Boon drags a delivery on to his stumps to fall for only six, in the second test against Australia in Adelaide in 1987–88. R.J. Hadlee Collection
Below: Robin Bailhache's finger sends Dean Jones on his way — caught by Ian Smith — in the same Adelaide test. Jones had made much of the fact he was ready to confront me in the series but I had him three times (and he lasted only three balls in Adelaide). R.J. Hadlee Collection

failed in New Zealand in the return series but, in last season's reduced programme of just two tests, he had his best moments against us (and he'd had enough magnificent ones before). He opened with 118 in the Basin Reserve test and then produced one of the great innings at Eden Park, making 271. It was an immaculate display, stressing just what a quality player he is. The shame for Miandad was that he came so close to topping his test-best 280 not out; and evidently he also had designs on Gary Sobers' record 365 not out.

So, he emerged from the brief series with 389 runs at 194.50, proof if it was required that this man is an outstanding player against all types of attacks. And the fact that two of his biggest test innings — 260 against England in 1987 and his 271 against us — have been scored overseas also shows he can make test runs anywhere, whatever the cynics might say. I've now clashed with Miandad in 11 tests spread over four series and I've managed to dismiss him only four times (Ewen Chatfield seems to have an easier time removing him than I do). I find him an awkward player to topple. He can be so annoying, too; he likes to chat and egg players on. He's been guilty of over-reacting on occasions and can be a little volatile. But, as a batsman, Javed Miandad has many qualities to recommend him. He's adventurous, prepared to move his feet to the spinners, and to come down the pitch to hit them back over their heads for four or six . . . as Stephen Boock discovered during his mammoth 271 last summer. And he's also murdered some of the finest fast bowling attacks in the world.

There have, of course, been my special favourites. Greg Matthews was one of them because I took his wicket eight times and Australian openers David Boon and Geoff Marsh were other enjoyable opponents, Boon falling to me eight times as well, and Marsh seven. And then there was the Sri Lankan opener Sidath Wettimuny who fell six times in 10 innings against me. Openers have been good to me, accounting for around 25 per cent of my test victims.

But at the top of the pile is my old Nottinghamshire team-mate Derek Randall, who managed to satisfy my wicket-taking desires no fewer than nine times. Because I played with him for so many years on the county circuit — and bowled to him an awful lot in the nets — I had the advantage of knowing the way he played. He was a fidgety player and a chirpy character who gave the impression of being very confident when, in fact, he was quite insecure and hopelessly nervous in the dressing room before going out to bat. For the first few overs, he rarely looked comfortable but, if he could overcome that phase, chances were he'd play a fine innings; and he made two centuries against New Zealand, 164 in Wellington and 104 in Auckland, both in the 1983–84 series.

He was technically vulnerable and I always fancied removing him in tests, as the statistic of nine dismissals in 14 completed innings against me would testify. I was just fortunate I knew his traits and idiosyncracies. He also liked chatting and cracking jokes with close-in fieldsmen, and if players didn't respond, he'd become annoyed and uptight. So our policy was: "Don't talk to Arkle."

It's my New Zealand team-mates I've seen the most of. And, over a period, we've had some thoroughly proficient test batsmen.

The further John Wright's career has gone, the better he's become as an opener, with a slight hiccup against Pakistan last summer. Gradually, he's improved his record to the point where his average is edging the mid-thirties and includes seven centuries and a 99; after 63 tests he holds — and deserves — the New Zealand test runs record at 3635, passing former recordholder Bevan Congdon's 3448 during the series against India in late 1988. It's an excellent effort for a player who's been forced to enjoy test life on New Zealand's more demanding pitches, and also a credit because his statistical record was scratchy for so long.

Wrighty's been just the opening batsman New Zealand's needed, so utterly dedicated to the team cause of seeing the new ball off and, over the last few years, he's had to function without a regular — and successful — partner at the other end. For so many years, New Zealand's batting order was headed by Wright and Bruce Edgar and, while not near the Gordon Greenidge-Desmond Haynes partnership statistically, they were invaluable test openers. Wrighty curbed many of his natural instincts as a test batsman, eliminating the riskier shots, but the same player could be spectacular at any other level — and occasionally in the test arena, as he showed with his glorious 141 against Australia in Christchurch in 1981–82. He has played so many crucial innings for New Zealand and, while we lost the series 2–1 in India last season, it was then that Wrighty's batting was quite exceptional in adversity. With Martin Crowe unavailable for the tour, Wrighty was the only batsman of genuine test experience . . . and he responded marvellously to the responsibility of being captain and our most vital batsman, putting together a string of consistent scores and averaging almost 40.00.

Geoff Howarth, at his peak in the late 1970s and early 1980s, was one of the world's premier batsmen and a lovely strokemaker but, as I discussed in the captaincy chapter, he steadily lost his touch later in his career as the demands of leading New Zealand affected him.

There wasn't a No. 6 batsman to match Jeremy Coney at his best in the mid-1980s, when his batting average approached 40.00. He finished up with 2668 runs at 37.57 in 52 tests. He had such wonderful qualities to battle and then counterattack after middle order collapses, collecting three centuries with his 174 not out saving the first test against England in 1983–84 and his unbeaten 111 helping us to a tense two-wicket victory over Pakistan in 1984–85. But we all admired him most when he refused to succumb to the West Indies' mean machine in the Caribbean in 1984–85 . . . at least not until he was physically maimed when he had his left forearm broken by a rising Joel Garner delivery in the fourth test. To come out of the series with 241 runs at 48.20 was testament to his courage, and ability — although there were some of us who thought he was lucky when he had his arm broken. At least he didn't have to bat again! His farewell series against the West Indies in 1986–87 was a poor one but, even when he was captain, he coped reasonably well with the added pressure, scoring 634 runs at 30.19 in his 15 tests as skipper.

When I consider New Zealand batsmen, I'm drawn principally to Glenn Turner and Martin Crowe, the two Kiwis who have consistently been world-class performers.

Turner made an intriguing study from the awkward youngster who had difficulty hitting the ball off the square to the audacious operator he became in the twilight of his career. As a younger player, he wasn't unlike Boycott in the way he concentrated on technique and occupying the crease. Although he had an unusual grip and stance, county cricket and the advent of the one-day game enabled him to become highly regarded as a batsman on a world scale. His record for Worcestershire was fabulous — 22,298 runs at 52.10 in 284 matches, including a fantastic 72 centuries and 93 fifties. And, when he retired, he'd scored more than 34,000 first-class runs at 49.70 including 103 hundreds.

Turner more than stood up to scrutiny at test level as well with 2991 runs at 44.64 in his 41 matches — but there'll always be regret he didn't play much more test cricket. He returned only briefly against Sri Lanka, and then essentially so he could play in the World Series Cup competition in Australia in 1982–83 and the following World Cup tournament in England. Even today he could still be playing, if he was interested, and the pity is New Zealand never saw the best of him. Worcestershire had that privilege.

As New Zealand's first true pro, Turner was often seen as an antagonistic troublemaker for the New Zealand Cricket Council, having a seemingly endless list of grievances he wanted settled. But, no one player did more to set up the future for professionals who followed him, including Geoff Howarth, John Parker, John Wright, Martin Crowe and me. I enjoyed his company and his advice when he was playing, and also when he became cricket manager. He was an excellent and thorough cricket manager. Well organised and very knowledgeable, he had plenty of theories about the way the game should be played. He didn't fit the norm in many respects. He was prepared to stand up to officialdom but wasn't strong on handing out encouragement in the accepted manner. An apparent lack of understanding and sympathy for his players was emphasised during our 1985–86 test series in Australia. After making a brilliant 188 in the Brisbane test, Martin Crowe had a difficult time in the Sydney match — as most of us did — when he made scores of eight and a duck. We were in Perth preparing for the third test when Hogan told us at a team meeting that he had lacked confidence and hadn't known what shots to play in Sydney. He said he was feeling negative and uptight about it. Glenn told Hogan he was a New Zealand player and that he found it hard to believe he could have such an attitude problem. We were staggered to hear Martin's admission; you don't expect that from your best batsman. Turner's way, though, was to say: "I'm surprised to hear this", rather than helping him by saying: "Okay, but what can we do to help? What's wrong?" It just didn't seem to be his way.

But as a batsman and a player who assisted me, it's difficult to fault Glenn Turner, although his approach against the quick bowlers was often questioned the longer his career went. In one match at Trent Bridge, he made a 50 mainly by backing away to square leg and guiding the ball over slips or popping it over cover, as well as walking outside his off stump and trying to chip over mid wicket. It just wasn't Turner and eventually he missed a slower ball and was bowled around his legs. He retired hurt in the second innings, copping a delivery in the ribs when he backed away to Mike Hendrick. He seemed to become a reluctant batsman against genuinely quick bowling and made a form of protest about short-pitched bowling when Worcestershire played the West Indies in 1980. According to *Wisden*, Turner didn't want to play the match because he had a back strain, but the club forced him to; he batted recklessly in the first innings and then, late on the second day, slogged his way to 45 off only 24 deliveries in Worcester's second innings. Just before stumps, he was out treading on his wicket, apparently quite deliberately.

Turner's display was read as a double protest — one at having to play against a touring side and also because he'd been disturbed about, and had criticised, the West Indians' general conduct and persistent short-pitched bowling against New Zealand earlier in the year. He was interviewed by the club's cricket committee chairman Roy Booth but a statement revealed no more than the fact the club was satisfied Turner had no grievances with Worcestershire as such.

There were regular taunts that Turner wasn't really prepared to face quicker bowling and he certainly didn't play the real pace men in an orthodox manner. But the fact is, he still fronted up to the quickest of the time in county cricket. Whatever theories there were about him, I admired him greatly as a batsman of the greatest quality — I just wish he had played for New Zealand much longer than he did, especially in the test arena.

Martin Crowe has certainly overcome his rough initiation to test cricket when he had to face the menace of Dennis Lillee and Jeff Thomson as a 19-year-old in 1981–82. Just like me, he had to wait some time before the breakthrough with his century against England in 1983–84, but he prospered as selectors retained faith in his obvious talent, in much the same way the selectors had done with me in my formative years as a test player.

He's an excellent technician, ruthless on himself about perfecting his technique, and he has hardened his attitude towards the game. Not unlike Viv Richards, he likes to use his physical presence as an added weapon and I think I've had some influence on his physical and mental approach to the game. He has little charts in his cricket case and uses the motto P-A-D-D-L-E-S as a motivational aid, each letter triggering a key word for him. Hogan's had a swift rise in cricket; even by the time he was 25 he was benefiting from all the by-products of being an international cricketer of some standing. The difficulty for him is handling the successes both on and off the field, knowing he must continue to perform.

Look at Crowe's career record and you find he's already sixth on the list of New Zealand's first-class run-scorers, and with easily the best record. By the end of the 1988–89 season, he'd scored 13,785 runs in 174 matches at a fantastic average of 56.26, including 48 hundreds. But it's in test cricket where he's improved in real leaps; in 44 matches, he now has 3035 runs —only John Wright, Bevan Congdon and John Reid have more for New Zealand — at an average of 45.29 with a record 10 centuries. In his last 21 tests, and including the 1985–86 twin series against Australia, he's been phenomenal, up with the best in the world — scoring 1922 runs at

Left: A player with a full array of shots and the talent to become one of the genuine greats — Martin Crowe. There's poise and elegance about his batting, matched by a hunger to be the perfect batsman.

Right: All sides need opening batsmen with John Wright's qualities of patience, dedication, concentration and determination. There's nothing glamorous about opening in tests but Wrighty, with his peculiar upright stance, has played a priceless role for New Zealand.

J.G. Blackwell

an average of 64.06 and including eight centuries! In the 1987 calendar year alone he amassed 4000 first-class runs, yet there are still nagging little flaws for him. Three times in the 1987–88 series against Australia he made scores he couldn't go on and convert into three figures — 67 in Brisbane and then 82 and 79 in Melbourne. He can't be expected to succeed all the time but it's often the bad ball or a bad shot which brings about his quite unexpected downfall. Momentary lapses are costing him.

I've had some engrossing tussles with Crowe — and still haven't taken his wicket in a first-class match. It's something Hogan always reminds me about and I suppose it's possible I could finish my career without ever having his scalp (not that it really matters). I tried desperately hard to dismiss him in a county championship match against Somerset at Trent Bridge in 1987. Crowe made 93 in Somerset's first innings and, along the way, had his thumb broken by Clive Rice. The lasting memory I have is of bowling to Hogan for about eight or nine overs and dominating him so much the umpire at my end, Barry Leadbeater, said:

"If this was a boxing match, the referee would have stopped the fight." It's interesting that Crowe's life as a county pro is now, in effect, over. The difficulty he had was becoming a full-time county player when he was already an established international, when usually players start off in the county game and then progress to the top.

He has the talent to become one of the great batsmen, and I suspect he'll go on and do that, provided he can overcome the slight attitude problems he has. He's so disappointed when he fails to achieve his goals, like the double hundred he'd set himself for against the Australians at the MCG in 1987–88. He had further setbacks in the first test against England in Christchurch the same summer when he was out for scores of five and six. However, rather than stew on them each time he immediately offered to be my runner when I batted, for I was hampered after straining my calf muscle on the first day of the match. It was a significant change in attitude for Hogan; he was showing signs of being more philosophical about the game.

So, as Martin Crowe evolved from the fragile young genius into the proven world-class player he is, New Zealand cricket's search turned to the pursuit of new long-term batting talent —and, in the last year or so, we've unearthed two quite exceptional prospects. One was 27 before he was selected for New Zealand, while the other player's had a close association with Martin Crowe ever since his schooldays at Auckland Grammar.

Andrew Jones made his first-class debut, for Central Districts, as long ago as 1979–80, before moving to Otago and then Wellington. But not until 1986–87 did he come into the national side, very much a late developer it would seem. For a few years, he'd been a thoroughly efficient first-class player but, given the chance by the national selectors, his development as an international batsman has been stunning.

He was laughed at in Australia in 1987–88 because of his unorthodox technique, jumping around the crease a little like Derek Randall. But Jonesy really did have the last laugh when he hit a magnificent 150 and a second innings 64 in the second test in Adelaide, coming out of the series with 323 runs at 53.83. And now, after such a belated entry into the test arena, Jones has already scored 751 runs at 41.72 in just 10 tests.

While he's proved to be a consistent and reliable performer at No. 3 in test matches, his continued success in the one-day arena — as either an opener or at No. 3 — have been mindboggling. He made the Australian tour a personal triumph by amassing more than 400 runs in the World Series Cup competition, averaging 52.00 and scoring five half-centuries. But that was nothing compared to what he did last summer when he put together a sequence of six consecutive one-day fifties, 57 in the final match in India and then 55 not out, 62 not out, 67, 82 and 63 not out at home against Pakistan. So, in a span of 28 one-day internationals, he has accumulated figures even the great Viv Richards would be proud of . . . 15 fifties and 1226 runs at 51.08. His strokeplay in the air off the back foot is something to see, his cover driving's superb and his wristy on-side shots have proved to be totally effective against many fine attacks.

The player with something of Martin Crowe about him — apart from the fact he bats left handed — is Mark Greatbatch. Now 25, there's little doubt he'll also serve New Zealand well for years to come. In only a limited time at international level, he's quickly established himself as a fine batsman. After making a hundred in his debut test against England in 1987–88, he's managed a 90 not out, a 76 and a 64 as well in only 11 innings to average close to 60.00 from his first six tests. There's much I admire in him — he's technically sound, has good concentration and he's a great competitor. Quite apart from his batting, he's an important team member with his general attitude; a fully committed fieldsman, he hypes the players up with his enthusiasm and constant encouragement. There's no question the side misses his inspiration when he's not on the field.

My own attitude to batting has undergone telling change since my nervous first steps as a test cricketer against Pakistan in 1972–73. While

Andrew Jones sweeping in India last summer and proving there is a place for late starters in international cricket. While he's now 30, Jones has been outstanding in just two years at top level, whether it be in tests or one-dayers. Already he has scored more than 700 test runs while he's topped 1200 runs in one-dayers at an average of more than 50.00   J.G. Blackwell

Talking batting tactics with Martin Crowe — but not as batting partners. In this instance, Crowe was kitted out as my runner during the Eden Park test against Pakistan last summer. J.G. Blackwell

I began with an encouraging 46, my approach to the batting art wasn't as serious as it might have been in those days. I was more inclined to bat adventurously, in the hope I'd have a quick and productive innings. The accent used to be on scoring runs at great haste rather than measuring the performance and picking the right ball to hit. I had spasmodic successes, most notably 87 against Pakistan in Karachi in 1976-77 — which helped us save the match — and then a memorable 81 against Australia at Eden Park the same season, when I had the immense satisfaction of hitting Lillee back over his head. He was devastating that day and our position was so hopeless — we were 31 for five when I went out to bat in the second innings — that I had nothing to lose. And on the day it worked.

I reached my batting nadir on New Zealand's tour of England in 1978 but then county cricket and the arrival of the helmet served to transform me.

I became somewhat apprehensive against the quicks in the 1978 series. The moment the ball was pitched short, I'd back away to square leg, not wanting to get in the line of the ball. It wasn't pretty and it certainly wasn't effective. But the introduction of the helmet — thank you again to Kerry Packer's World Series Cricket days for another innovation — was a saviour and confidence restorer for me. We wear so much protective gear on our bodies when we bat that it makes sense we should protect our heads. The helmet has become more refined from the early years when it resembled a motorcyclist's helmet, or even an astronaut's headgear. Initially, it was a strange experience getting used to it but, apart from the protective element, it has other advantages, as the cynics point out — you don't have to comb your hair when you go out to bat, a helmet is economical because you can also use it if you own a motorbike and, of course, it blocks you off from the verbal abuse handed out by close-in fieldsmen! There are disadvantages, too. You can't always hear your partner's call, you are deprived of a souvenir because players swap caps not helmets and it gets hot and sticky inside a helmet.

Some of the players of yesteryear regard the arrival of helmets as an unnecessary intrusion but I believe they're a fine invention. There aren't too many cricketers around who don't use them at some stage.

It was county cricket which really forced me to become more responsible about batting, and alerted me to the fact I could be something of an all rounder, although not quite in the class of Imran Khan, Ian Botham or Kapil Dev, all of whom I rate as superior batsmen. I'm not technically efficient really. I tend to be too loose and have a habit of sparring at the ball, hanging the bat out without moving my feet (which is often a failing with left handers, I guess). I'm more a basic striker of the ball, with a liking to loft the ball and go for boundaries if it's pitched up in the slot. While that's a strength of mine, it's also a weakness and, over a period of time, I've been worked out by most bowlers. They generally bowl more tightly to me now, keeping the ball just short of length so I can't free my arms and swing the bat. It means I've had to look more for ones and twos in later years, not that I've been averse to the change in emphasis. After all, when my first-class career began I batted at No. 9 or No. 10 and, when you bat there, you tend to go for your shots with much the same applying when I settled into the No. 8 slot. At Notts, though, I began to find myself in at No. 7 and even No. 6 and the upswing in my batting record obviously reflects the greater faith placed in me. By the end of the 1980 English county season, my first-class batting average was only about 23.00 yet, at the end of the 1987 season (my last with Notts), I had a career record of 11,349 runs at 31.79 in 320 matches. My batting return for Notts alone was much more impressive — 5854 runs at 38.76 in 148 matches including 11 centuries. Until I began with Notts in 1978, I hadn't scored a first-class century but I broke that barrier immediately and now have 14 in total (the other three all for New Zealand including two in tests).

There's been a matching improvement as a test batsman. Where my batting average used to hover around 19.00, I've been able to bolster it to 27.00 or so, sometimes nudging 28.00. I still have a tendency to bat irresponsibly at times — as I did twice in our test loss to Australia in Brisbane in 1987–88. Then I was entrusted with coming in at No. 7 but surrendered my wicket with careless shots both times. Even in India last season I got myself out several times trying to slog the spinners when perhaps a more refined approach was required.

Overall, I'm far happier with my batting output, though. And I can also look to an improvement in one-dayers, principally because I've been given greater responsibility there as well, if belatedly. I often thought New Zealand didn't derive full benefit from me as a batsman in limited-overs matches. I was seen as a pinch hitter in the Lance Cairns vein but that wasn't me. I need some time to go out and build an innings; I proved in Australia in 1987–88 that I could pick up ones and twos and keep the innings moving, if I went in with sufficient overs left. I finished up making 206 runs at 34.33 and managed a healthy strike rate.

C·H·A·P·T·E·R   S·E·V·E·N

The Ultimate Experience

Ask me how many tests I've played and I can tell you, I'm up to 80 — or I should be but for the NZCC abandoning the first test against Pakistan in Dunedin earlier this year. I still feel robbed, perhaps even cheated, about that test; it deprived me personally, and us as a team, because it was a match some of us still wanted to play, even though the weather had prevented any action at all on the first three scheduled days. It was a test, after all.

Quiz me on most things about my test or first-class career and chances are I can fire off the answer as quick as you like. Test wickets? Now, that's obviously elementary. That's a figure imprinted on my brain, now up to 396 (how I wish it was 400). What about first-class wickets? I instinctively know I've got 1447. And first-class hundreds? I'm sitting on 14.

But turn my attention towards the one-day game and I'm quite lost. I realise I'm past the 100 mark in internationals, only because someone told me the clash against Sri Lanka in Hobart in 1987-88 was my 100th one-day international. I also know I've taken well over 100 wickets in one-dayers, thanks to a quick check of my trusty *Cricket Almanack of New Zealand*. Really, it just doesn't fuss me that much.

And the one-day game certainly wasn't on my mind as I sat in our dressing room after the third test against Pakistan in Auckland last season. Another achilles complaint flared up on the second day of the match and I knew I wouldn't be able to play again, so missing the Rothmans Cup series against Pakistan. Just for a few moments, I was in a bit of a daze. It was the end of another summer for me — my 18th at first-class level since my debut in 1971–72 — and I knew it was one of the final chapters in my career, maybe not my last playing summer . . . but not very far from it. I have a habit of saying my body can take only so much. On the evening of 28 February, 1989, that never seemed truer. Time was catching up.

In those 18 years as a first-class cricketer, I'd played 333 matches including 79 tests, more than 100 one-day internationals and countless more one-dayers for Nottinghamshire and Canterbury. More than 460 first-class innings, 1447 wickets, more than 65,000 deliveries bowled. Mind-boggling stuff if you want to be blinded by figures.

But what gnawed away at me about the 1988–89 season was that scheduled first test against Pakistan in Dunedin. I'll never accept the match should have been abandoned after three days of rain. The fact was, two days and a possible 180 overs remained; we could have played a lot of cricket in that time and, on what was a decidedly sporting pitch, a result wasn't anything like impossible; the way it played in the substituted one-dayer proved that and so did the following Shell Trophy match between Auckland and Otago, when the home side made just 50 in its second innings on the last day. I wanted the test to go ahead not only would it give me the chance to add to my tally of test wickets (and I never turn down that sort of opportunity) but most of all, because it was a test match. And any test, even boring ones like the clash against Pakistan in Wellington last season, is special, very special. It's the pinnacle. Test cricket's the sole reason why I've played on for so long; without the test article, cricket wouldn't be worth it for me. That's why it irks me that I don't now have a career total of 80 tests — and that I therefore haven't reached the milestone of 400 test wickets.

Nothing beats the atmosphere of a test match. One-day internationals may draw crowds of 40,000-plus and generate an air of intensity and passion among the spectators, but that still doesn't pump the adrenalin for me. I feed off and thrive on tests. In one sense a test match is the most demanding form of the game — as it should be — yet it's also the easiest to play, simply because you have the best conditions to play in (or you should have). You play in expansive stadiums, the pitches are hopefully good and prepared to last five days; there are no distractions like there are at club level where other cricket's going on around you. The test match is the focal point. People are there watching you.

Even after 79 tests, the first is the one I remember vividly, principally because I felt so awkward about being there with all those other experienced internationals like Glenn Turner, Bevan Congdon, Brian Hastings, Mark Burgess, Bruce Taylor, Hedley Howarth and Richard Collinge. I wasn't alone as a debutant; John Parker also played his first test in that clash against Pakistan in Wellington in 1972–73, and Wasim Raja did likewise for the tourists. For Parker, it was an unforgettable debut — he broke a bone in his hand when fielding and was unable to bat.

It's so easy to be over-awed when you're on the test stage for the first time. You look around and see so many people there, many of them concentrating on you because they know you're playing your first test. That was particularly true for me on 2 February, 1973, because I had the

Test cricket's a duel of wits as much as anything, and England's David Gower and I were, well, trigger happy about the first test at Lord's in 1986. Gower's been one of the long line of England captains in my time, a sign of the selectorial inconsistency which has plagued England for so long.   Phil O'Brien

first over with the new ball when Pakistan decided to bat . . . and Sadiq Mohammad sent my very first delivery to the fence.

After your first test, there are so many doubts. Did I do enough to warrant selection for the next test? Or will I just be forgotten about? It takes time to become accustomed to this new territory, to feel part of the team. While I didn't play again in that series — Dayle came back from injury for the second and third tests — I was one of the lucky ones who ultimately survived.

In later years, when I moved into the professional mode, I often said any day's cricket, even in a test, is "just another day in the office". That's no more than a disguise, a bit of psychology designed to try and relax me and ensure I stay low-key about the game. In truth, a day's play never is another day in the office. Especially in a test, it always means much more than that.

On the first morning of a test, there's natural apprehension, essentially because you don't know what the day holds in store. Will the weather allow a start? If so, what about the toss? If we win it, will we bowl or bat? If we're playing a test at home, or if Karen's on tour with me, she knows to leave me alone on the morning of the first day of a test. I'm scratchy, quite moody and likely to behave a little irrationally. For home tests, we usually assemble about two days before, starting off with a light practice. The following day's the big session and on the eve of the match there's the normal routine of a team meeting and sometimes a team dinner. By then, I'm soaking in the atmosphere, reading the papers to see how ticket sales are going, watching the weather and so on. I'm interested in all the preview talk.

We're at the ground early on the first day. It's quiet, not eerie, just quiet. The only people about tend to be the groundsman and his staff when we arrive nearly two hours before play's scheduled to start. Eden Park, Lancaster Park, the Basin Reserve or Carisbrook . . . it's the same at any of New Zealand's test venues early in the day. We warm up, jog around, do a bit of fielding practice, have some throw downs. Still not many people in the ground. Nearby, the opposition are doing the same thing, warming up, getting ready. I always take a sly look at them to size them up. I notice Javed Miandad's hitting the ball sweetly. That could be ominous. Or maybe I notice someone's struggling — so I fancy taking his wicket — or someone else isn't moving too freely. It's all information to lodge in the memory; it could be useful later on.

There's anxiety waiting for the toss. Finally, when the call comes, I know whether I have to move. If we're bowling, it's straight into the changing routine, some stretching and the all-important matter of selecting the ball. I want immediate involvement in any test — or any match — and the act of winning the toss and putting the opposition in is the course I favour.

Always I dream of the perfect test. We win the toss, I've picked a ball which looks and feels rather special and the weather and pitch conditions are made to suit — it happened just that way at the 'Gabba in Brisbane in November 1985. If ever a test was made in heaven, this was it.

I'd done nothing wonderful in the lead-up. Against South Australia my figures were 19-7-38-2 and 12-3-30-1, then 26-7-53-0 and 15-6-15-1 against Queensland at the 'Gabba. I wasn't that pleased with the way I was bowling. So the main practice session before the test became an important one for me; normally, I like to bowl only for about 20 minutes, never pushing myself to the limit. Bowling and bowling in the nets isn't for me, unlike many other players. I've figured out what's best. But before this test I needed more work. For 40 minutes I stuck at it, working with cricket manager Glenn Turner in a session designed to get me bowling from as close to the stumps as I possibly could. Turner formulated the rubbish-bin theory; the rubbish bin was the 'umpire' and we worked out a method of placing the bin/umpire back from the stumps to give me the optimum chance of bowling wicket to wicket. That was the secret. We'd hatched a vital component in the match plan for the Australians.

I'd never known a test when we had prepared so thoroughly and planned so meticulously, and yet there was nothing in the early stages of the tour which suggested this would be an extraordinary match. We'd never won a test in Australia and there wasn't any hint we were about to alter history; certainly we hadn't been overwhelmingly dominant in the state matches against South Australia and Queensland.

But there was a dream-like quality about the first morning of the match. The atmospheric conditions were clammy, humid and there was low cloud and the threat of showers; my fingers were twitching. The toss was another triumph. Jeremy Coney called correctly and in no time it was all happening.

South African-born Kepler Wessels took strike and instantly scored a single . . . which offered me the attractive prospect of bowling to Australia's happy hooker, Andrew Hilditch. Now, Hilditch was as partial to the hook shot as I used to be to chocolate fish, so it was only natural we would exploit his partiality — and weakness — for one of the riskier shots in the game. As it happened, we never really had time to give him the bait and set the trap; he simply obliged without any prompting, whipping a slightly shorter delivery to fine-leg where Charlie Chatfield held the catch above his head. Only five balls into the test and we were away. One wicket, especially an early one, doesn't necessarily determine the course of a match — but in this case we felt it would.

Everything was humming from the outset. The ball was going through well — bouncing, seaming and swinging. I had a perfect ball, a nice dark one which felt good in my hand and, with Chatfield operating from the other end, the Australian batsmen were uncomfortable, not able to cope with the moving ball for a long period. Despite such psychological ascendancy, it took us time to gain more statistical success; not until just before lunch did I lure David Boon to chase a wider delivery and offer Coney's sure hands the kind of morsel they love at second slip.

The real bonus came after lunch. My first ball was a loosener, a delivery which showed all the signs of a player who might have had a little too much to eat at the break. For reasons known only to him, Allan Border was drawn to this wide offering when he might well have let it sail through to the 'keeper. He launched into a cracking cover drive, but hit it aerially and precisely to Bruce Edgar at cover. Soon after, 72 for three became 82 for four when I also had Greg Ritchie's wicket. Then, nicely on cue, the light faded shortly after the tea break, the day ending prematurely with Australia 146 for four. It was a promising position for us, although not commanding, especially with Wessels in on 69 and Wayne Phillips on 25.

However, the abbreviated day benefited us, and certainly me. It meant I returned for the second day as fresh as I'd been at the start of the first. It was like starting a new test match; the ball still had sufficient shine on it and the pitch and weather conditions were again in our favour. What followed in the next hour would have been unbelievable, except that I was there taking part in some of the most sensational scenes I've witnessed in my career. We'd gained confidence from our deeds on the opening day without quite taking a stranglehold on the match. Now we did.

It was incredible to think Australia, within an hour of the second day starting, was all out for 179. It was positively out of this world to find I'd taken nine wickets myself and had a part in all 10 dismissals by taking a catch from Geoff Lawson to give my Canterbury team-mate Vaughan Brown his first test wicket and, as it happens, his only one. There I was so close to all 10, within reach of emulating Jim Laker's 10 for 53 against Australia at Old Trafford in 1956. This was a freak happening. I swear the ball talked throughout that test innings; I've never seen a ball behave and respond the way that one did. It's trite to say it, but that is by far the best bowling performance I've achieved. It would have to be, wouldn't it? You dream of figures like this . . . 23.4 overs, 4 maidens, 52 runs, 9 wickets. But you never expect them to happen, and definitely not in a test.

They were nine wickets to cherish, and all contributing to a bowling display I regularly refer to when I need inspiration. For almost 10 years, the seven for 23 I took against India in Wellington in 1975–76 had been my standard, my best figures in first-class and test cricket, figures I matched against Sussex in my second year with Notts in 1979.

It just happened so quickly. Wessels added two runs before he was beaten by the pace off the pitch and out leg-before; Greg Matthews was ruffled by one where it hurts and then I got the next right through his defences to bowl him; Wayne Phillips is always a candidate to drag an inside edge on to his stumps and he did this time; Craig McDermott became another victim of the moving delivery, edging to Coney at second slip; and Bob Holland was the easiest of all, fending a short-of-a-length delivery off his hip to Brown in the bat-pad position.

The statisticians had a picnic with the nine-wicket haul. It was the fourth best analysis in a test innings; outside Laker's 10 for 53, the figures were the best at test level this century; I became only the 10th player to take nine wickets in a test innings; and the return of nine for 52 was the best in 232 tests played in Australia.

Good as the figures were, they wouldn't have meant half as much if they hadn't catapulted New Zealand to a test win. I revel in personal success but always I want such feats to lead to the grander prize of test victories and series wins. This time, the theme of perfection was maintained throughout. Our specialist batsmen performed magnificently, led by Martin Crowe's splendid 188 and John Reid's 108 as they put on 224 for a New Zealand third-wicket record (bettered in 1986–87 by John Wright and Crowe against the West Indies in Wellington). For the best part of two days we made Australia suffer and, in gathering gloom, I had the added satisfaction of making 54 — the 50 off only 41 balls — as we went on to 553 for seven declared, New Zealand's highest total in a test.

Day four . . . two days left to bowl Australia out, the home side trailing by 374 runs. What a position to be in! With play beginning at 10.30 (to compensate for Brisbane's poor twilight), we immediately had the Australian second innings teetering —and this time Chatfield was the destroyer, not Hadlee. First Wessels was out for three and then Boon for one. Play was halted at 11.00 to mark Remembrance Day by a minute's silence. We stood in a huddle and I have to admit a lack of courtesy by failing to honour the period of silence . . . the ball lay on the ground in the middle, I would be bowling to Hilditch when play resumed and I said: "Think Hilditch, think bouncer, think hook shot, think catch, think out!"

This time we brought our plan into play and, just as unbelievably as the first innings, Hilditch couldn't help himself. I fed him a short delivery, he impulsively hooked and there was Chatfield doing the business again — from the very first ball after the break! It showed gross irresponsibility and indiscipline on Hilditch's part as Australia plunged to 16 for three.

The test was definitely ours. It was only a matter of time.

Australia slipped further to 67 for five before Border found an ally in Matthews. They batted on and on, first Matthews going through to his maiden test hundred — and going way over the top when he celebrated it — and then Border to his 15th. We were getting a bit weary, jaded and had some moments of reservation but, just before stumps, Coney took the new ball for me to have a desperate crack. It worked. Minutes into my spell Matthews was gone, caught by Coney for 115 and we knew the rest would be academic.

From 266 for six, Australia was all out for 333 on the fifth day and again I had five wickets in an innings — six for 71 off 28.5 overs — and match figures of 15 for 123. More statistical delight — my best match figures in first-class cricket and comfortably the best in New Zealand's test history (beating the 11 I'd taken against India in 1975-76 and the West Indies in 1979-80). And the feat of taking nine wickets in an innings and scoring a 50 in the same match was unique in test cricket! That was incidental. At last New Zealand had won a test in Australia, and done it stylishly and emphatically, as the winning margin of an innings and 41 runs would suggest. It's the most perfect match I've played in, quite beyond comparison.

It was yet another step in New Zealand's growth as a test power; when I first entered the test arena, in 1972-73, there was little expectation or anticipation about a test match. New Zealand had won only seven times in 102 tests; it'd been beaten — all too often heavily — on 46 occasions and could cherish just one series win, against Pakistan in 1969. Was it any wonder that New Zealand's attitude to test cricket then was one of hope and little more? A test match was a big sporting occasion but we were hardly on the same plane as the All Blacks.

Then it began to happen . . . New Zealand's first test win over Australia in 1973-74, another win against India in 1975-76 and more history with the Basin Reserve victory over England in 1977-78. I was involved in each of them but it was still difficult to escape the impression New Zealand was no more than a part-time test winner. After all, 10 wins, 64 losses and 62 draws in 136 tests was hardly powerful stuff as New Zealand cricket moved into the 1980s.

It was then that New Zealand's test cricket story began to really unfold through success against the West Indies, India, Australia, Sri Lanka, England and Pakistan plus an away series victory over Sri Lanka. Going into the 1985-86 campaign against Australia, New Zealand had proved itself as an effective force at home without managing quality success — no insult to Sri Lanka intended — abroad. That's why that wonderful five-day experience at the 'Gabba meant so much — and a few weeks later we'd further embellished our standing by winning the third test in Perth by six wickets to clinch our first series in Australia 2-1 (after a disappointing second test defeat in Sydney). The entire series was an expression of New Zealand test cricket's total evolution. It was quite clearly my peak as a test bowler, the series in which I proved to myself that I could perform consistently in any conditions.

I'd had success on other tours before, but this series was a revelation

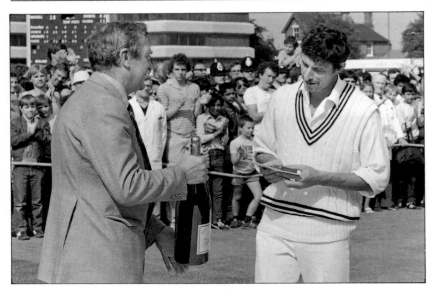

Above: The rewards which go with success, something I have always enjoyed.
After the fourth test against England at Trent Bridge, in 1983, it was the accolade
of man of the series, finishing the series with my 200th test wicket and 92 not out
in Nottingham. Jim Laker made the presentation. Patrick Eagar

Below: Three years later, unbridled jubilation in our Trent Bridge dressing room.
We'd just beaten England by eight wickets in the second test (to set up our first
series win in England) and 10 wickets and 68 had landed me the man of the
match award. John Bracewell, Jeff Crowe, Ian Smith, Evan Gray and
Martin Crowe ensured the champagne didn't go to waste. Robert Rathbone

to me. I felt I'd moved up to another plane. The 'Gabba was made for my bowling; I didn't have to intimidate to profit, just bowl wicket to wicket and let the swing and seam work for me. On to the Sydney Cricket Ground and, on a turning track, I still took seven wickets in a match so dominated by the spinners they took 25 of the 36 wickets which fell. And in Perth, on a pitch which offered variable bounce, I had 11 wickets in a test for the third time. In just three matches, I'd taken 33 wickets at 12.15, including five bags of five wickets in an innings! I was knocked over. I'd started the series with 266 wickets and finished it with 299; I imagined the chance of joining the 300 club was some time off but, suddenly, I was on the brink. In fact, I should have taken my 300th in the Perth encounter when I had a crack at Bob Holland, but I couldn't complete the job, leaving me stranded with one wicket needed.

The series was a total triumph for New Zealand cricket, and for me personally. For the second time in successive test series in Australia, I'd been named the man of the series (the previous instance in 1980–81); it's the kind of acknowledgement which makes it that much more worthwhile. I received a set of gold goblets again — very nice, too — but my target was an even more glittering prize. As in other years since Kerry Packer transformed Australian cricket, there was a car at stake for the player named the International Cricketer of the Year — it was an Alfa Romeo and I had designs on it. Viv Richards (three times), Dennis Lillee, Bruce Yardley and David Gower had all gained the accolade so it was only natural I wanted to try and emulate their achievements. Obviously, I'd made a useful start in the race through taking 33 wickets in the test series but we still had to return for the World Series Cup competition against Australia and India. I had fair success, scoring almost 200 runs and taking 15 wickets and learned some time before the end of the one-dayers that I couldn't be headed for the big prize; I was well clear with Martin Crowe finishing second and India's Kapil Dev third (not an Australian in sight).

As far as I was aware, there was no discussion in a team meeting on tour about what to do with the car if one of us happened to win it. I don't believe we ever talked about the idea of selling the car in such circumstances and pooling the money for distribution among the players. Bruce Edgar maintains the matter was discussed but I don't remember it. Certainly there was a ruling, or agreement, on such matters when cars were at stake at home. However, I'm positive there was no such undertaking for tours. Twice I'd won a "car" as man of the series at home, but we were given the cash equivalent to put in the team fund (cash always goes into team funds); at no stage was I given the keys to the Toyota cars.

So, as far as I was concerned, there were rules at home, but not overseas. To be honest, I don't think it entered anyone else's mind that one of us might win the car, even though I thought otherwise. The aim was to try and perform consistently over a period of three months with the Alfa Romeo the prize at the end. Along the way, win bonuses or cash from player-of-the-match awards went into the team fund — which everyone could share in — but the car remained a separate issue. Players who won gold trays and goblets kept them as a reward; they weren't asked to sell them off. Was the car any different? Once I knew I'd won it, I wanted to keep it. It was as simple as that. Jerry Coney asked me in Launceston (where we played our final WSC match) what I intended doing with the car. "I want to keep it," I said.

As we flew from Launceston to Melbourne — after we'd been knocked out of the competition — a note was passed around informing us there would be a team meeting at the airport in Melbourne to discuss team funds and some other administrative matters. I knew what was going to happen — and sure enough the subject of the car was the hot topic for discussion. The team viewpoint was expressed that the car ought to be singled out as an article for the consolidated fund — I emphasised I wanted the car for myself because I'd won it through my own performances. I maintained everyone had an equal opportunity but that provoked arguments, some players maintaining all rounders like me had an advantage over specialists like a wicketkeeper or a bowler of Ewen Chatfield's type. There was a clash of interests there. And yet, over the years, I had, through various awards and cars, contributed more than $50,000 to team funds; not that it worries me — I'm happy to contribute but that's a huge input and all I actually received for my performances was the same cut as anyone else involved in the carve up. I saw some injustice that there was now feeling against me for wanting to hang on to this car.

There was a vote on the issue which Coney, in his autobiography *The Playing Mantis*, called "a senseless premature vote that merely highlighted the division within the team". It worked out 7–5 against me having the car. John Wright spoke out for me, saying he thought I'd earned the car, had contributed much to team funds previously and had been a great servant to New Zealand cricket. He thought it would be a nice gesture for the team to reward me. I appreciated his stance, significantly coming from a fellow professional.

Some of the newer players in the side — like Ervin McSweeney and Stu Gillespie — I seem to remember abstained. There were 14 of us in the team but only 12 voted. I distinctly recall Coney, Edgar and John Bracewell being strongly against me hanging on to the car. Jeff Crowe voted for me but Martin Crowe was initially in the other camp. One crucial vote might have been Lance Cairns' as he'd been involved in the first phase of the tour, but not the second.

An enormous backlash followed when I spoke out publicly about the controversy; I was upset. And it was interesting that public sympathy was about 99 per cent in my favour. Newspaper editorials came out in support of me, I received so many letters and calls from people expressing their best wishes and saying I was doing the right thing. At the same time, my public outburst wasn't good for New Zealand cricket or for the team. As a unit we suffered because there was this split, not just behind the scenes anymore, but for the whole nation to see.

It was badly handled. A rushed meeting at the Melbourne airport was not the right place to discuss it as there was never a real opportunity to talk about the topic rationally. No one had thought it through carefully and sensibly. Had I been forced to take the cash equivalent for the car — which was valued at $A30,000 — we would have received a cheque for the cost price only, or about $A14,000. There would have been only $1000 per player but, in New Zealand, the vehicle was valued at $NZ52,000. Arrangements were made for it to be shipped and it arrived safely at my home although the overall issue still hadn't been resolved. There was also the matter of taxation. Because I was a professional, I was liable to pay tax on the car (prizes are taxable). I understand if an amateur had won the car, it would have been tax free.

I subsequently talked to various people about my actions, Lance Cairns being one of the first I approached and he backed me to the hilt. Going on the count of the airport vote, that made it 7–6 against me. Then I was interested to discover Martin Crowe had changed his mind. Darryl Sambell, who then managed the business affairs of both Crowes, had told them the players should gift the car to me and, on reflection, Hogan saw much merit in that idea. So, on an unofficial count, the vote was now 7–6 in my favour.

The problem continued to fester, so much so there was more interest in sorting it out than our first practice sessions before the Basin Reserve test against Australia just a few weeks later. The media were there to record the result of a special team meeting — not the practice session or anything else — and this time the discussion was carried out properly, in an in-depth and constructive manner. I eventually agreed I'd breached the players' code of ethics about the car, so I donated it back to the team — and they, in turn, gifted it to me for services rendered. It was then up to me to make some kind of reciprocal gesture of goodwill to the team, to

The infamous Alfa Romeo, or *that* car. This was the vehicle which created all the fuss within the New Zealand camp after I was named the International Cricketer of the Year in Australia 1985–86.

J.G. Blackwell

ensure they benefited in some manner. The primary concern for me was that it was a vital step towards healing the rift which had developed. Sadly, there was still some resentment but we had a test match — and a series — to prepare for against Australia.

Coney later introduced me to some people who had a time-share resort in Taupo. I was happy to lend my name to promoting the place for no personal fee if, in return, the players and their wives, girlfriends and families could all have a free week's holiday. It seemed a good way of settling everything but then it must have fallen through as I never heard anything more about it from Coney. Some players harboured some bitterness about the deal, especially Bruce Edgar, while some didn't seem too fussed at all. The whole business left a sour taste but, thankfully, it was sorted out reasonably amicably in the end.

It was to this backdrop that I was trying to tune in to another big moment in my career — my 300th test wicket and the right to join Dennis Lillee, Ian Botham, Bob Willis, Lance Gibbs and Fred Trueman in that elite group (a club which has since grown through the addition of Kapil Dev, Imran Khan and Malcolm Marshall). There were probably some players who thought I'd deliberately held back in Perth to ensure I'd take my 300th at home — but that's totally untrue. I have a real hunger for test wickets and want them wherever I happen to be; the 300th certainly wasn't a consideration at any stage of the Perth match. But, the way it worked out, the Basin Reserve was set to be the scene for another milestone.

I'd have to say the car business hadn't helped my mental preparation but there was, like the world record attempt in Christchurch two years later, enormous interest. There was a huge first morning crowd at the Basin and Jeremy Coney's move to send Australia in set it up nicely for me. However, the first session passed wicketless — and the second, too. By tea, I was becoming a little anxious. But at 4.08 I managed to hurry a delivery into Allan Border's pads and umpire Fred Goodall thrust his left finger skyward. Jubilation again in a summer which was brimming with so many high points. An added thrill was knowing I'd reached the landmark 300th by capturing the wicket of a high-quality performer like Border.

It's a sadness for me that so many highlights have been hounded by the spectre of controversy. The home campaign against Australia in 1981–82 was soured by the outcry about my transition from the old long run-up to the shortened version, a development which met with limited approval even from my own team-mates. In 1983–84, I battled serious illness to play against England, there was the pesky car business in 1985–86 and the vicious contretemps with Coney during the 1986–87 series against the West Indies. All the trouble served to upset the balance without ultimately destroying the pleasure I've extracted from the big matches and big moments in my cricketing life.

It's a source of immense satisfaction that I've been associated with New Zealand's growth from the shaky beginnings of the early 1970s through to the golden period in the 1980s. Of my 79 tests, 20 have resulted in wins and, during the '80s we became a force only just inferior to the

West Indies at one stage. In the last 10 years, we've shown our teeth by putting together a record of 17 wins, 15 losses and 26 draws in 58 tests. We've won nine series, drawn five and lost six. And, at home, we've been close to unbeatable with 10 wins, only two losses and 16 draws including six series wins and no series losses. The transformation hasn't come about by accident; it can be traced back to sensible selection policy most of the time (especially in Frank Cameron's era) and players who began to believe in themselves.

At the same time, we needed the rich phase through the 1985–86 period and then on to the home campaign against the West Indies to convince the cricket world we had something. Beating Australia twice in back-to-back series in 1985–86 was significant but even more telling was the 1986 series triumph in England and then the third test comeback which enabled us to square the series against the West Indies at home in 1986–87. Three series wins and one squared — with two of the successes overseas — was the equal of anything the West Indies could boast at the time, perhaps even better.

When I reminisce about my test career, there are countless memories from the flood of victories; Lancaster Park 1973–74 because it was my first experience of winning at test level, not to mention New Zealand's first over Australia; Glenn Turner's twin hundreds in the same match, seven wickets for me, success for Dayle and Dad weeping tears of joy in the dressing room afterwards. Picture the Basin Reserve in 1975–76 and I remember I should have been made 12th man. I played but was only fourth off the rank with the ball in both innings and took seven for 23 in the second — 11 wickets in the match — to set me up in test cricket. I'm still at the Basin, it's 1977–78 and we're playing England who need only 137 to win. We bowl them out for just 64 and New Zealand at last has a win over the Mother Country. That was another great — and emotional — moment, marked by considerable personal satisfaction because I'd contributed with 10 wickets. The West Indies at Carisbrook in 1979–80 stands out because it inspired our first series win over the Caribbean kings. It was a sour match — and a bitter series throughout — but there was so much to savour, especially the heart-in-the-mouth sight of tailenders Gary Troup and Stephen Boock scraping together the four runs needed as we escaped with a one-wicket win. Another 11 wickets for me, seven of them leg-befores!

A theme develops when you analyse it. Without being egotistical about it we've won most tests when I've done well. Of the 20 victories I've been part of, I've invariably made a big personal contribution. Although, I took only four wickets against India in Wellington in 1980–81, four against Sri Lanka in Christchurch in 1982–83 and four against Australia in Auckland in 1985–86. The most famous failure of all was at Headingley in 1983 when I had match figures of none for 89 in our first test win in England — but I made 75 in our first innings and was with Jeremy Coney when the winning runs were scored; a temporary role reversal! Overall, though, I've had a fair say; if I've taken 10 wickets in a match, it's helped bring about a test win — at least on eight occasions . . . against India in 1975–76, England in 1977–78, the West Indies in 1979–80, Sri Lanka in

1983–84, Australia twice in 1985–86, England in 1986 and India in 1988–89. The one exception was that Melbourne Cricket Ground test in 1987–88 when 10 wickets weren't enough to bring about victory.

But one of the great ones for me, especially from an all-round standpoint, was the second test against England in Christchurch in 1983–84. The England players were petrified about the Lancaster Park pitch which, to be fair, wasn't wonderful. But they over-reacted and put themselves out of the contest even before a ball had been bowled. Bob Willis misread the pitch totally and, along with his other bowlers, bowled far too short on it. That suited me. I was able to play freely against badly directed bowling, racing to 99, only to fall to a catch behind off Willis. It wasn't a century — and I joined John Beck as the only other New Zealand player to be dismissed for 99 in a test — but it was probably worth 150 in the circumstances. Certainly it's one of my most fondly remembered test innings, ahead even of my hundreds against the West Indies and Sri Lanka. I went on to take eight for 44 as well, as England was dismissed for 82 and 93; to think England couldn't match my own batting total in either innings. Quite remarkable.

After Brisbane, circa 1985–86, my other favourite overseas test is the one against England at Trent Bridge in 1986. There's a singular thrill about playing tests at my two home grounds, Trent Bridge and Lancaster Park. The figures there tend to reflect the inspiration I find at both venues; I've played four tests in Nottingham for 182 runs at 36.40 and 20 wickets at 28.00 while 13 tests in Christchurch have returned 476 runs at 31.73 and 69 wickets at 22.04 (oddly enough I've taken five wickets in an innings six times at Lancaster Park, but never 10 in a match).

Trent Bridge had been the scene for my 200th test wicket in 1983 but, by then, New Zealand was on the end of a 3–1 series defeat. It was different in August 1986; we'd come out of the drawn Lord's test with fair credit, and now set ourselves for a bolder showing. Being Trent Bridge, I had no difficulty in gearing myself despite the counter attractions and commitments of my benefit year programme. With Ewen Chatfield out of action with a broken thumb, our pace attack lacked experience and proven ability. Derek Stirling and Willie Watson had to play but, by the end of the first day, we had England in trouble at 240 for nine. When England was all out early on the second morning for 256, we'd completed an excellent start to the match, and an excellent beginning it was for me when I had six for 80, setting a world record by taking five wickets in a test innings for the 27th time.

Disappointingly, our batting response flirted with danger. While John Wright reached 58, Jeff Crowe, Martin Crowe and Jeremy Coney all scored 20s only to disappear at crucial times until we were teetering at 144 for five. Evan Gray was steady, though, so steady he spent 299 minutes making 50, including just two fours. He was just the ally I needed, though, as I made 68 and we added 95 together — and the value of Gray's exceptional patience (which prompted one wag in the crowd to ask: "Is there anyone in there?") was further emphasised when he and John Bracewell then put on another 79 for the seventh wicket. With Bracewell going on to a magnificent maiden test century — helped by

Stirling and Watson — we made 413 to take a lead of 157.

We could now visualise the result we'd come all this way for, only to have most of the fourth day rained out. Mercifully, the weather was suitable for play on the fifth day. I collected four wickets in the second innings to give me 10 for the match, Braces had three and Stirling two as England succumbed for 230. There was an odd moment in England innings when night watchman Phil Edmonds, one of the more eccentric players on the world circuit, lodged a complaint about my wristbands.

"Umpire! Would you ask the bowler to remove his wristbands — they're upsetting my concentration," he asked umpire Ken Palmer.

I said to Palmer: "He's got to be joking! That's the first time in my 16-year career that I've been asked to do that."

It was, however, a reasonably civil request so I obliged. But, while the next over was in progress, I had time to digest the situation so, just before I started my next over, I said: "Umpire! Would you ask the batsman to remove his helmet — it's upsetting my concentration and I can't see the whites of his eyes."

Palmer was unimpressed. "Stop the nonsense and get on with the game," he told me.

But this all had a sequel as we chased the 74 required for victory. Martin Crowe and Coney were batting and Edmonds was bowling his left-arm spinners, wearing a white Swatch watch on his left wrist. Hogan quite nonchalantly asked the umpire if the bowler would remove his watch, which Edmonds did. A single was taken, Coney was about to take strike but stopped and said: "Umpire, would you mind asking the bowler to put his watch back on again, please?" For the first time in his career, Phil was stumped for words!

The win complete, I again had the satisfaction of another man-of-the-match award, this time at my other home ground and on an occasion when I'd put together one of my best all-round performances in a test, definitely up there with the effort at Lancaster Park in 1983–84.

The test series which thoroughly tested our character and resilience was the one against the West Indies in 1986–87. This could have been another distasteful campaign for the memory of the last visit by the West Indies in 1979–80 still lingered. The New Zealand Cricket Council scarcely helped by undiplomatically naming Fred Goodall as one of the umpires for the second test in Auckland. Such an appointment was bound to antagonise the tourists, and it did. Goodall was put under severe pressure in the field — especially through unreasonable behaviour by captain Viv Richards — and he erred by making some bad decisions. They made only minimal difference to the eventual result because we played so appallingly, losing by 10 wickets.

What with my off-field problems with Coney, the omens weren't bright for the third test. They were even less so when the entire first day's play was lost through rain. With the West Indies 1–0 up in the series, any thought of a result was difficult to imagine in four days, especially against a side with the talent of Gordon Greenidge, Desmond Haynes, Richie Richardson, Viv Richards, Gus Logie and Jeff Dujon . . . not the sort of batting line-up you'd expect to cough up twice in four days.

Mentally, I was totally unprepared for the match after the bitter conflict with Coney. I didn't feel like playing, not when I couldn't communicate with my captain. Play I did, though, and I didn't regret it. By lunch on the opening day, the mighty West Indies had been reduced to an unbelievable 67 for six before being dismissed for just 100. While I had six wickets, it was Charlie Chatfield who deserved six. He bowled impeccably as only Richardson (37) and the last pair, Tony Gray (10 not out) and Courtney Walsh (14), reached double figures.

Through several contributions — most notably a 156-run stand between Martin Crowe (83) and Jeff Crowe (55) — we made 332 for nine declared. In the strange position of trailing by 232 runs, the West Indies proved slightly more awkward to dismiss in its second innings but the batsmen still had a tendency to keep going for their shots, rather than to battle and try and save the match. However, it was Martin Snedden who excelled this time, picking up five wickets for the first time in a test innings to fire the West Indies out for 264. We needed only 33 to win and got there, not without some drama as we lost five wickets. It was a famous win, completely against the odds.

Our greatest foe, even amid the triumphs, has been our inconsistency. We can put together a strong test display one moment, only to crumble in the next match; or we will create a base through dismissing the opposition cheaply, only to fold for even less when we bat. Having dismissed the West Indies for only 100 we may have nurtured thoughts of: "What on earth will their attack do to us if we can get them out for 100?" We overcame that inner fear.

Inconsistency again dogged us in India late last year. The first test in Bangalore was a non-event. No team could have countered their spin attack on such a devil of a pitch (and, of course, we also had to battle an illness epidemic which laid most of us low in one swoop). But we fought back outstandingly in the second test in Bombay. In the first innings we were 158 for eight and recovered to reach 236 and in our second Ian Smith and John Bracewell (again a batting saviour) salvaged a desperate predicament of 181 for eight to see us through to 279. Bracewell spun the Indians out for only 145 and finished with eight wickets for the match. I had 10 and we'd miraculously beaten India by 136 runs — and we did them at their own game. I'll never know how we managed that 27th test win for New Zealand — only the second in India.

But then our old bogey returned. We couldn't follow up with a potent showing in the series-deciding third test in Hyderabad, collapsing for only 124 in our second innings and watching India win by 10 wickets. A test win in India is a fantastic achievement — it can never be overstated — but it's so miserable when we fail to compete the way we did in Hyderabad.

My career's been littered with horror shows mixed in with the increasing number of magical moments. Like the two losses in only three days against Australia in Brisbane and Perth in 1980–81. Those performances gave birth to the slogan: "All I want for Christmas is a five-day test". The Eden Park show against the West Indies in 1986–87 was abysmal as was the first test against Australia in Brisbane in 1987–88. We have a weakness for allowing our concentration and discipline to slip; one moment we can fight so doggedly, even heroically, only to virtually surrender the next.

That's not to say there haven't been sufficient instances of battling out of threatening spots. One of the best Kiwi fightbacks was fired by Coney's 174 not out against England in 1983–84 when we were 244 runs behind on the first innings and drew the match. And we were in real strife when Ewen Chatfield came to the crease to join Coney with 50 runs still needed in the third test against Pakistan in Dunedin in 1984–85. With Lance Cairns injured, we were down to our last pair but Charlie, one of the world's best-qualified No. 11s, fought it out and almost carried New Zealand to victory himself, taking much more of the strike than Coney.

We struck a slightly ticklish position against Sri Lanka in Colombo in 1986–87. We fielded a side without the unavailable Wright and the retired Coney and, when we were 99 for four replying to Sri Lanka's snail-paced 397 for nine declared, the situation was delicately poised. When I came to the wicket to join new captain Jeff Crowe, we were 160 for five and supposedly out of danger on an easy-paced pitch, yet the occasion still called on us to bat and bat . . . and bat. Jeff had elevated me to No. 7 in the order and wanted me to bat as responsibly as the position demanded. Some 406 minutes later I was still at the wicket on 151 not out, my second test hundred and, with Chopper (120 not out), I'd helped add 246 in an unbroken stand. It was never going to bring about a result in what was a timeless test but there's satisfaction just the same from proving to yourself that you can bat for that long — and it was by far the longest time I've been in the middle in my career.

An international match which rates as a genuine highlight is one in which I had very little success — none for 71 off 21 overs and 36 in my only turn at bat. It was the MCC's Bicentennial match against the Rest of the World at Lord's in 1987. It was such a splendid occasion, a real showpiece but ruined by rain on the last day which unfortunately prevented the likelihood of an excellent finish. Mike Gatting made 179 and Graham Gooch 117 for the MCC in our total of 455 but Sunil Gavaskar had the joy of top-scoring for the World XI with 188. There was a big shout for lbw from the first ball he faced and he later said, "At least I can't get a pair in this match." He was out for a duck in the second innings, when the World XI was 13 for one, chasing 353 to win in just over a day. Gate receipts totalled more than £750,000 for the game. It was a thoroughly grand event, one in which I was thrilled and privileged to be involved.

When I switch to my Canterbury career, my memory is not so sharp on the finer points, which is perhaps inevitable as I haven't been able to play for the side too much in recent years. If there haven't been inter-national commitments then injuries have been a factor. One of my best seasons was in 1986–87 when the timing of the West Indies' tour enabled me to appear in all eight Shell Trophy matches and I emerged with 45 wickets at about 12 apiece. However, I've managed only 62 matches for Canterbury since my first against Auckland in 1971–72.

Undoubtedly the best years were those spent under Maurice Ryan's leadership. He was a canny skipper, able to extract maximum effort from his players; they were profitable times, too, times when the three Hadlees — Barry, Dayle and I — turned out for Canterbury. The side was rich in characters of the ilk of 'Mad Pete' Coman and the late Ken Wadsworth. Ken's death through cancer in August 1976 was so tragic. He was only 29, an outstanding wicketkeeper and batsman, an aggressive and competitive player. I recall the pain he was in from cancer towards the end, but he still dragged himself out to play, all the time maintaining there was nothing wrong with him. It was a cruel loss so early in life, a tragedy for New Zealand cricket. His funeral was the first I've ever attended and I'll always remember his wicketkeeping gloves and New Zealand cap on his coffin.

A few years down the track, Ash Hart became Canterbury's wicket-keeper and he — along with new-ball bowler Craig Thiele — provided me with one of my most enjoyable memories of the matches I'd played for Canterbury. It was a Shell Trophy clash against Wellington in Rangiora in 1984–85. We led by only 102 when our ninth second innings wicket fell at 206. This was the signal for Thiele to join Hart at the wicket; Hart went on to make 36 not out and Thiele 49 as they added 87 for the last wicket. When the innings closed at 293, Wellington needed 190 to win but

Some of my best days of first-class cricket were played under Canterbury captain Maurice Ryan in the mid–1970s. He's one of the smartest captains I've encountered.

That winning feeling . . .

Above: That marvellous moment at the Basin Reserve after New Zealand's first test victory against England in 1977–78. Enjoying every second with me are captain Mark Burgess (left), John Wright and Robert Anderson (right).   Peter Bush

Below left: More history in the shape of New Zealand's first test win in Australia — at the Gabba in Brisbane in 1985–86. A great moment for us all especially for Martin Crowe, who made 188, while I took 15 for 123, including my test best nine for 52 in Australia's first innings. That was the perfect test.   John Knight

Below right: A test win against all odds came for New Zealand in Bombay in late 1988. And while I took 10 wickets in the match — for the ninth time in tests — it was John Bracewell who had a profound influence with both bat and ball, twice rescuing us with the bat and taking six for 51 in India's second innings.

All-Sport, Simon Bruty

Trent Bridge . . . an inspirational place to play cricket at. As 'home' for 10 years, it came to rate as one of my favourite grounds. And one of the greatest occasions there was this one: it's action from the second test against England in 1986 — me bowling from the pavilion end — when we beat England by eight wickets (and went on to win our first series in England).

Ken Kelly

An historic photograph . . . three Hadlee brothers all in the same New Zealand team. Dayle (left), Barry and I were selected for the 1975 World Cup in England, and we all played in the cup match against England at Trent Bridge. While that was Barry's only outing for his country, Dayle and I played in 10 tests together, including three which produced New Zealand wins.

Patrick Eagar

slumped to five for five early on and was eventually all out for 107, a win to Canterbury by 82 runs from an improbable position. Later in the season, Hart and Thiele again confounded Wellington at the Basin Reserve, putting on 80 for the last wicket with Hart making a career-best 70 not out and Thiele 28 to lift our first innings total from 193 to 273. It wasn't enough to save us from defeat that time, let alone inspire victory. But the deeds of average first-class cricketers like those two are sometimes easy to forget amid the maze of so much international and other first-class cricket. While it's great to aspire to the heights, it's the bread-and-butter blokes like Hart and Thiele who ultimately make it all possible for those of us at the top.

It's rather obvious by now that I'm not too big on one-day cricket. I'm the first person to recognise its importance because, even though it's an unsatisfactory version of the game, it's a necessary evil — it pays the bills by drawing the paying public in vast numbers. Most players accept limited-overs cricket for what it is. They cope with and adapt to it as a necessary part of the calendar.

But I find it difficult to enjoy because of all the restrictions, which makes it a game of chance as opposed to one of skill that you see in the test arena. It's frustrating for a bowler of my type to operate at the 'death' of a one-dayer with five men on the boundary. Or, what about batting when you need 50 runs off 30 balls to win a match? It just becomes a slog.

The system in England locked you into five or six days of normal cricket on end, when you worked on and observed all the principles of playing the game properly. Come Sunday and everything went haywire as limited-overs madness took over. Batsmen slogged, bowlers were defensive and fieldsmen ran around madly. Greg Chappell once said: "I can hardly remember an innings I've played in one-day cricket, but there are several I can remember in the test arena." I can only concur, certainly from a bowling viewpoint.

The inference must be that I've never derived any enjoyment from the pyjama game. Wrong, even though there are a lot of games I couldn't tell you a thing about. There's satisfaction in knowing I've managed three half-centuries in one-day internationals, 79 against England in Adelaide in 1982–83, 71 against India in the same city in 1985–86 and 52 on a sad day against Sri Lanka in Hobart in 1987–88 when we lost the match and I fell out with the local spectators.

There have been five-wicket bags, too — five of them, the most recent against Pakistan in Dunedin last summer. Five wickets in limited-overs internationals is rare, so to have five is pleasing.

And there are some games which arouse my consciousness, most of all New Zealand's famous win over the West Indies in Christchurch in 1979–80 when we recovered from 80 for six and then 134 for seven to beat the World Cup holders. Coney finished on 53 not out and, with my 41, we put on 60 for the eighth wicket to eventually help New Zealand through to 207 for nine. A seemingly squeaky one-wicket win — and a prelude to our first test winning margin in Dunedin just a week later. It was just one of several times the Coney-Hadlee partnership worked in international cricket.

I suppose the most famous instance was the 1982–83 match in Adelaide when England's 296 for five off 50 overs really did seem unattainable. With the asking rate so close to six an over, Jeff Crowe's 50 and Lance Cairns' swift 49 — after he'd been sent in early — gave us some hope until they were both out at 166. Jerry and I refused to believe the task was beyond us, even in the scorching heat. We just worked away with modest early aims, intent essentially on ensuring the singles came. Small aims became bigger ones and when I was out for 79, we'd put on 121 together; when Jerry swatted the winning runs we were home with seven balls to spare and four wickets in hand. Now, while I may be averse to one-day cricket, I was swept away in the atmosphere of that match.

As I was at the Sydney Cricket Ground on 13 January, 1981 . . . New Zealand playing Australia in the WSC competition. We'd made 220 for eight and Australia, in strife at 123 for five at one point, reached the last over needing eight to win. Martin Snedden was the bowler. A two came off the second ball and singles off the next three. Snedden with the last ball, three runs needed and Doug Walters facing. He drove the ball slightly wide of me, I dived, flicked the ball back to the bowler's end and Shaun Graf was run out trying to complete the second. This was high drama under the SCG lights and, yes, I enjoyed that match, too.

Of course, 1 February, 1981, lights up another day in limited-overs history not to be forgotten . . . for all the wrong reasons. New Zealand playing Australia, six runs needed to tie the match and Greg Chappell perpetrated the dastardly deed which took cricket's code of sportsmanship lower than it had ever gone. The underarm act lives on. It's been so well documented by so many over the years it would be tiresome to go over old ground again now. Suffice to say, it remains one of the two most repugnant acts I've witnessed in cricket, or in any sport — the barging of umpire Fred Goodall by West Indian bowler Colin Croft being the other.

That match had a brighter sequel a year later when Australia toured New Zealand. The opening Rothmans Cup match in Auckland was an occasion quite unique in New Zealand cricketing history. Officials had expected a big crowd, interest being built up to fever pitch as a chance to gain some revenge on Chappell for what he'd done at the Melbourne Cricket Ground a year earlier. But no one was prepared for what actually

One-day cricket's not a special fancy of mine . . . but there have been some special memories just the same . . .
Right: It could be a good spot-the-ball photo. In fact, my throw has just hit the stumps to run out Australia's Simon Davis in the Rothmans Cup match at Eden Park in 1985–86. N.J. Smith
Left: Jeremy Coney and I were invariably tossed together as batting partners at crucial times in one-day internationals, and we had some great successes — like the one-off clash against the West Indies in 1979–80 and the classic chase for 297 to beat England in Adelaide in 1982–83 N.J. Smith
Below: What a lovely sight for New Zealanders, but a sorry one for Australians! The scoreboard shows it clearly — Australia all out for only 70 in a World Series Cup match in Adelaide in 1985–86, after we'd reached 276 for seven. A win by 206 runs! J.G. Blackwell

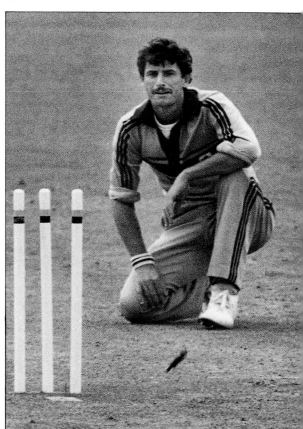

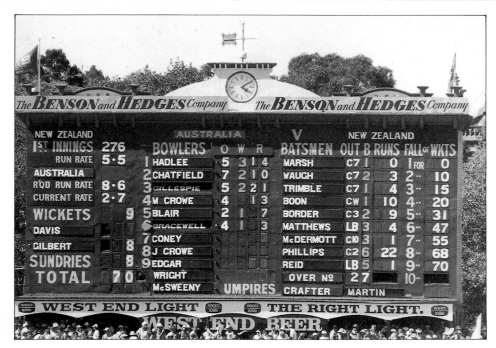

NEW ZEALAND		AUSTRALIA		V		NEW ZEALAND				
1ST INNINGS 276		BOWLERS	O W R		BATSMEN	OUT B	RUNS	FALL of WKTS		
RUN RATE 5·5		1 HADLEE	5 3 14		MARSH	C7 1	0	1 FOR	0	
AUSTRALIA		2 CHATFIELD	7 2 10		WAUGH	C7 2	3	2··	10	
RQD RUN RATE 8·6		3 GILLESPIE	5 2 21		TRIMBLE	C7 1	4	3··	15	
CURRENT RATE 2·7		4 M CROWE	4 1 3		BOON	C W 1	10	4··	20	
WICKETS 9		5 BLAIR	2 1 7		BORDER	C3 2	9	5··	31	
DAVIS		6 BRACEWELL	4 1 3		MATTHEWS	LB 3	4	6··	47	
GILBERT 8		7 CONEY			McDERMOTT	C10 3	1	7··	55	
SUNDRIES 8		8 J CROWE			PHILLIPS	C2 6	22	8··	68	
TOTAL 70		9 EDGAR			REID	LB 5	1	9··	70	
		WRIGHT			OVER No	27		10··		
		McSWEENY		UMPIRES	CRAFTER		MARTIN			

happened when 43,000 people crammed into Eden Park. The ground was full to overflowing, spectators ringing the boundary rope so everyone could fit in. It was the birth of cricket madness in New Zealand, the day Kiwis switched on to this contrived version of cricketing fare.

The day had all its trimmings. Anti-Chappell banners dominated the scene. It was a wonderful atmosphere. Chappell was greeted by the thundering noise of 43,000 people booing him (at least it seemed like everyone in the crowd booed him). And when he came out to bat later in the day, there was more derisive booing and cheering . . . and the appearance of a lawn bowl on the field. Jeremy Coney, never slow to introduce some levity, picked up the bowl and returned it appropriately — underarm. Chappell actually moved from villain to hero that day, making a wonderful century which won the crowd over.

Some of New Zealand's one-day matches have been dreadful. It's the nature of the game that a good match tends to be remarkably good — like the one in Adelaide against England — while the bad ones are indescribably horrible.

What about the clash against the West Indies in Berbice, Guyana, in 1984–85 — the West Indies 259 for five from only 43 overs. New Zealand out for 129 with eight of us bowled. We'd flown to Berbice in a small plane and a helicopter and, because of aviation demands, we had to leave as soon as possible; some of the players soared away in the helicopter while the rest of us were left doing little to hold up the West Indies' progress to what was to become a 5–0 series whitewash.

Another disaster was the 1983 World Cup encounter with Sri Lanka in Derby. It was John Wright's home ground. He'd said to us: "Tell me what sort of pitch and outfield you want, and I'll sort it out. Leave it to me." Well, we were inserted and disappeared for only 181 after being 116 for nine at one stage. We made Sri Lanka fight for success but couldn't prevent them winning by three wickets. It was a shock upset, a catastrophe for our semi-final plans in the competition.

That's the one-day beast showing its true colours. The game's so often a lottery that class doesn't always win. Is it any wonder I seek out the game's genuine article for solace?

C·H·A·P·T·E·R   E·I·G·H·T

The County Decade

"**H**ow would you like to go to England and play professional cricket?" The thought was at once scary, and exciting. But I was much too young to even consider the possibility. After all, I was only 17, and the poser of the query was not some English county club director, but my father.

It was in the late 1960s when Dad first suggested the idea. Of course, it was fantasyland stuff then. How could I, no more than a raw, teenaged cricketer, believe I'd really have the chance to play cricket on a year-round basis, and be paid for doing the job? I was happy enough then to pay to see the best play. Dad thought Colin Cowdrey might be able to help out; nothing ever eventuated, nor did I really expect it would.

For the next few years I was content to play cricket at whatever level I could and combine it with an everyday working life. But when I toured England with New Zealand in 1973, the meaning in life began to change.

Ray Illingworth led England to its 2–0 test series win against New Zealand but, wearing his hat as the Leicestershire captain, asked me about joining the club. Leicester had a problem because the outstanding Australian fast bowler Garth McKenzie was due to retire and Illingworth wanted me to consider being his replacement. It was an enticing prospect but I discounted it as I was still an unrefined, young player, barely on the international scene and a long way from developing my potential. I was wary about trying out the county life at that stage, influenced as I was by some sound advice from cricketing people who'd counselled me against the thought. And even more significantly, I was settled at home, I was enjoying my job and life there; there was something else, too. I had a fiancée waiting in Christchurch and we were about to be married. Why should I allow county cricket to intervene in such a state of bliss? So I happily declined.

Over the next few years, there were more overtures, firstly from the New Zealand captain, Glenn Turner, who suggested I might like to join Worcestershire in 1977. The club's old West Indian warhorse Vanburn Holder was almost finished and Glenn wanted me to come over — but again I politely declined. I wasn't ready or overly interested.

The cycle began to alter somewhat when I received a phone call from Essex's Doug Insole in 1977. He said he'd like me to link up with Essex for the last six to eight weeks of the English season because it had a two-edged problem; West Indian Keith Boyce was injured and the left-arm pace bowler John Lever was on test call for the series against Australia. Essex was doing well in various competitions and was keen to bolster its ranks. When the club offered me £700 a month, return air fares, accommodation and half of Karen's air fares, I could hardly refuse. They were good terms and I agreed; but, literally hours before I was due to fly out, there was another phone call saying I would have to sign a three-year contract. With that news I was instantly negative and turned down the offer.

Perhaps it was going to be only a matter of time before I took up life as a county pro. It was no accident that I eventually moved to England — but the way it happened was almost a total accident, or at least a coincidence. It all came about in April 1978 when I partnered the New Zealand captain, Mark Burgess, in the world indoor double-wicket tournament at Wembley in London. In the lead-up to the event I had a bust-up with my employer, resigning from my job as a sports goods manager; the job allowed me to fulfil my cricketing commitments until this event, when I was refused permission to go. The easiest solution was to terminate my employment.

On arriving in London, the word had spread about the South African all rounder Clive Rice being sacked by Nottinghamshire, because he had signed a three-year contract to play for Kerry Packer's World Series Cricket venture. The club was looking for a replacement quickly and, on advice from England batsman Derek Randall and Mike Harris (who'd played in New Zealand), Nottinghamshire's chief executive Phil Carling contacted me. He wanted to talk about a professional cricketing life and I told him: "I'll talk terms."

Within hours he was in London. Quite by accident, he'd picked the perfect time to approach me. With no job at home, and the lustre of professional cricket now having considerable appeal, I was in a mood to jump at the chance. When I told Karen of the news, she was slightly apprehensive but still supportive and, after sorting out affairs at home, she arrived in England to join me on a new phase in my career, one which would be the making of me as a player.

The focal point of being a Nottinghamshire player was being associated with the Trent Bridge ground. I played there for New Zealand in the marvellous first test of the 1973 series when, needing 479 to win, we reached 440. John Arlott describes Trent Bridge as "mellow, intimate and nostalgic"; qualities I couldn't appreciate when I arrived on a cold April morning in 1978. I was then a Notts player, but it was 10 years later that I fully understood how right Arlott was about the ground.

When my life as a county player ended after the 1987 season, I could digest how much 10 years at Trent Bridge had aided my cricketing education, and how much playing there had meant to me. There'd been legendary players before me including Larwood and Voce plus Sobers and, during my time, there were outstanding performers in Randall, Harris, Rice, Hendrick, Robinson, Broad and Hemmings. The memories will last of the players and the team I was part of — and so will the memories of the ground and its facilities, which underwent some change.

It was sad to see the disappearance of the Old Tavern, a sportsman's haven which made way for a car park for committee members and players. However, the new Larwood and Voce Stand has a tavern underneath it and it's a treasure chest of cricketing memorabilia. The most telling metamorphosis at Trent Bridge was the most important — the work done on the pitch. When I began in 1978, pitches produced were white featherbed tracks but that all changed, thanks to the work of Ron Allsopp and his ground staff. He began leaving more grass on them and suddenly we had result pitches. Opposition batsmen, who'd previously welcomed a visit to Trent Bridge, rather feared the trip there. Runs were much more difficult to come by and the new-ball welcoming party of Rice and Hadlee also ensured they left Nottingham with a few bruises to remember their stay.

My first season with Notts was notable for both its brevity and instant success. I had but a limited time with the side before taking up my commitment with the New Zealand team for the tour of England. I managed only seven matches, the first against Pakistan when I took only one wicket in a rain-affected match. From then on, the wickets came, perhaps because I was new on the county scene and many batsmen were unaware of my capabilities. There were several useful hauls — four bags of five in an innings and one of 10 in a match — as I came out of the shortened programme with 37 wickets at 15.00. I had to be satisfied with my opening gambit in the county game and I was positively elated with my batting. Until 1978, my highest score in some 57 first-class appearances was 87 against Pakistan in Karachi in 1976. But, against Derbyshire, I progressed to the dizzy heights of scoring a first-class hundred, not without significant help from fellow New Zealander John Wright. He spilled a catch from me from the first ball I faced and then misfielded a push to mid-wicket when I was 99 and looking for three figures; thanks to Wrighty I was able take the single. Then, in Derby's first innings, the first ball I bowled to him, he hooked and was caught on the fine-leg boundary! A memorable match for both of us.

The century had a marvellous consequence because I was presented with my county cap, well ahead of the normal schedule, and when I left the team to join the New Zealand side, Notts was near the top of the championship points table after three wins. While it failed to win another match, and finished 13th in the competition, it was still an improvement

from dead last in 1977. The New Zealand tour was also unsuccessful — we dropped all three tests — but, with 41 wickets on tour my first season in England with 78 first-class wickets was a highly satisfactory start.

One of the problems of being an international cricketer is the difficulty of being able to turn out for your club. It is, I guess, a little like the predicament so many top New Zealand rugby players face; take the Auckland players who are All Blacks. It's nothing these days for them to play little, or no, club football because they face so many representative commitments. And initially I struck much the same sort of problem at Notts. In 1978, I toured England with the New Zealand team and so the club saw little of me and, in 1979, the second World Cup tournament meant Notts again suffered.

But perhaps the outstanding feature of the year was a change at the top in the Notts side. Mike Smedley was captain when I arrived, and he was a fair batsman on good batting tracks — but he had a reputation as a defensive, if not boring, captain. Notts wasn't in a winning mode under his leadership. Far too often he took the draw option instead of chasing a possible victory. He was so well known for it that he apparently once told Ron Allsopp: "If you leave grass on the pitch, I'll be sacked." This was a sad commentary on Smedley and explained why Trent Bridge pitches were so flat.

In a year when I was able to play only 12 first-class matches, my best performance of the season coincided with Smedley displaying the worst traits of his captaincy style. By this time, Trent Bridge pitches were becoming a little more lively and, against Glamorgan, I took seven for 28 when we knocked the Welsh county over for only 141 in its second innings. I went even better when we met Sussex, again at Trent Bridge, but only after Smedley had very reluctantly declared, to leave Sussex a target of 219 late on the last day. He just didn't like being adventurous but we had Sussex barely clinging on at 64 for nine at stumps (and I took seven for 23, my best figures for the club and equalling my test best against India in 1975–76). It was no surprise that Smedley lost the captaincy soon after. While it was bound to happen, it was still a sad sight seeing him standing in the showers alone after manager Ken Taylor had given him an ultimatum: Resign as captain, or be sacked. Smed wouldn't go voluntarily so his contract was terminated.

That brought in the Clive Rice captaincy era. Notts had been anti-Kerry Packer during the World Series Cricket days and had sacked Rice, enabling me to join the club; when faced with a legal threat, Notts reinstated Rice. Now he was well and truly back — not just as a player, but as captain. He wasted no time making an impact as a demanding and, at

Above: In the beginning . . . my first year with Nottinghamshire in 1978 and the sponsored car which clocked up a few miles around England that season! While Stephen Boock (right) and I travelled with the New Zealand team, Karen and Boocky's wife, Heather, did a share of sightseeing.

Below: The all-important local . . . no sports team should be without one. The Friday night regular for us was The Griffin in Plumtree Village, Nottingham.

times, ruthless leader. He called a team meeting on the eve of our Gillette Cup match against Warwickshire in Birmingham, and wanted everyone there at 8.00 p.m. That irked Eddie Hemmings because he was staying at home some 80 kilometres away — but Rice told him he had to be at the meeting, which showed all of us Rice meant business. He demanded results, action and a positive attitude. He was hellbent on shaking Notts cricket out of the slumberous state it had been in — and he quickly achieved what he was after.

But the season was one of frustration personally. When we beat Warwickshire by 79 runs in that Gillette match the victory had a painful price for me . . . I tore the hamstring in my left leg and didn't return to full fitness until our match against the touring Indian team in late August. If I'd been frustrated by injury, this game proved a mortifying experience. With Rice and I revelling on the green pitch, we beat India by six wickets, the two of us taking 15 wickets for only 142 between us. However, I experienced my most sickening moment in cricket when I hit Mohinder Amarnath near the temple. He fell badly, hit the wicket and was unconscious. It was discovered he had a hairline fracture of the skull; it could easily have been fatal but I was greatly relieved Jimmy recovered and later excelled again as a test batsman, as well as playing a key role in India's win over the West Indies in the 1983 World Cup final.

The year didn't look too healthy statistically. I took 47 wickets at 16.02 but my batting tailed off alarmingly with only 193 runs and a highest score of 41. I found myself wondering whether I had the make-up to become an effective and efficient county pro. Could I cope with the day-to-day existence? Was I up to it physically? And what about the injuries? I had quite a few niggling and serious injuries in 1979, something which had never happened before. This occupation was proving much more arduous than I'd imagined. I couldn't toss it in yet, though.

Injury is, of course, the greatest fear for any sportsman and, in 1980, the six-letter word utterly depressed me. If I didn't have some injury worry, I had another. A left ankle complaint which affected me during my stint with Tasmania in 1979–80 — and continued to hamper me during New Zealand's test series against the West Indies — became a critical concern. It gave me excruciating pain when I landed my left foot in delivery and, by the end of the season, I'd appeared in just eight first-class matches. One of the precious few matches was an extraordinary game, though.

We met Australia towards the end of the season — it was in England for the Centenary Test at Lord's — and Rice wanted to take the chance of playing the club's three overseas seamers . . . South African Ken Watson, Rice himself, and me. In an incredible display, we beat Australia by an innings and 76 runs after rolling it for 207 in its first innings, Watson taking five for 57 while I collected the wickets of Graham Yallop, Kim Hughes and Rod Marsh for 29 runs.

We faced an Australian pace attack of Dennis Lillee, Jeff Thomson and Len Pascoe and yet we reached 465 with Rice making 90 and me 68. The sweetest sight was the bowling figures with all three of the quicks going for more than a hundred runs — and they were undoubtedly

Early days at Notts training with Derek Randall and Trevor Tunnicliffe. While there was quick success, two injury-studded seasons in 1979 and 1980 convinced me I wasn't made of the right stuff to succeed as a county cricketer. How things changed!

Patrick Eagar

frustrated. Balls squirted through third-man or edged over slips drew a typical reaction from Thommo: "Do you want me to put a rattle on it so you know when it's coming?"

One of our batsmen, Roy Dexter (who had a season of club cricket in Auckland), was quite a big lad and, when Loosehead Len Pascoe hit him in the chest, Ted didn't flinch or rub the affected area. He just stood firm.

"Top guts, mate. Top guts," said Pascoe.

And, as he walked back to his mark, he turned to Ashley Mallett at mid-off and said: "Hey Ash, in my youth he would have gone down — but I'm an old man now. That's why he's still standing."

At the end of the second day, I was named player of the day and presented with a racing bike. After acknowledging the sponsors and thanking them for the award, I told the audience: "I have a problem, though. How can I get this bike home, 20,000 kilometres over water?" Lillee, who was standing next to Rice, said: "With the bloody luck he had today, he could walk on water. I don't know why he can't ride the bloody thing home!"

Australia batted even worse in its second innings, slumping to be all out for 182 as I took three for 39. It was a sensational triumph for Notts, the biggest over Australia since 1888. It partially compensated for the depressing, injury-studded year I had; with 29 wickets at 14.13, I topped the national bowling averages and also scored 231 runs at 28.87, but it just wasn't working out as I'd hoped. I was anything but happy with my development as a county professional. Despite my injury problems, I had survived by bowling from a shortened run-up — that wasn't the way I wanted to play the game, though. So, towards the end of the season, I decided there really was no option. I'd have to quit playing county cricket, and I relayed my decision to Ken Taylor and the club that I wouldn't be returning to Trent Bridge in 1981. I felt embarrassed collecting a weekly pay cheque when I knew I wasn't capable of providing an honest day's work for my employer. It was a degrading and depressing experience to go through but the decision to leave was the only one I could make.

I made my final appearance at Trent Bridge in our last Sunday league match against Lancashire and, from my eight overs, I had a career-best return of six for 12 which preceded an emotional farewell. Standing on the balcony of the players' pavilion, I was in the company of the legendary Nottinghamshire duo Harold Larwood and Bill Voce; Larwood was back in England for the Centenary Test (and it wasn't until the summer of 1987–88 that I met him again at his Sydney home, enjoying a wonderful time chatting with him). The Trent Bridge crowd applauded and cheered, I waved at them and called Ricey over to support me. I was visibly moved by what was happening. Human emotions took over as tears flowed and I savoured the moment. I'd been with Notts only three years but Rice and Hadlee had been a useful combination with the new ball. Now it was all ending. With Mum and Dad also present, I'll remember the event as a sad one, yet still one of the greatest of my career. It was over . . . so I thought.

I'd heard club officials had worked on Dad that day, using him as a lever to make me change my mind and stay with Notts. And later, John Heatley, the club chairman, summoned me to the president's room and said: "We want you back next season, even if you decide to bowl off two paces." Suddenly it dawned on me. Why should I bowl off 25 paces when I'd had success off 15? Until that moment, I had never considered the possibility, always believing a new-ball bowler had to charge in off a long run. Now it all seemed so different.

"I'll think about it and let the club know in a couple of months," I told John. I received a vote of confidence from the club's committee and I knew the players and supporters wanted me to reconsider and return. And Clive Rice was doing all he could to urge me to stay. But the scars of the 1980 season were deep. I had a lot of thinking to do. I'd started out with a three-year contract and that had been completed. Did I really want to quit now? Or should I investigate giving my whole career a new edge?

After some weeks of thought, I decided it was worth it. I could modify my whole approach to bowling by using a shorter run-up, one which would be economical in all respects. The way I saw it, I had to make the change if I wanted to survive as a professional; I couldn't go on the way I had been because I simply couldn't cope physically. John Heatley's idea appealed to me greatly the more I considered it, but making it work was another matter. So when I checked in at Trent Bridge in April 1981, there was a slight fear of the unknown. Would I be able to continue as a genuine strike bowler, or would I become another stock bowler?

There was no need to worry. Notts had a fantastic year and so did the remodelled Richard Hadlee. I moved through the season unhindered by injury, missing only one of the 22 county championship matches and being rested for one Sunday league game. As a bowler, it was my year in every way with 105 wickets at 14.89, topping the national averages for the second year running — and, better still, seeing the success translated into Notts winning the county championship for the first time in 52 years.

Scenes of unbridled joy and emotion were in evidence as we stood on the players' balcony at Trent Bridge, rejoicing in the club's triumph. There was such a sweet irony in it for me. To think I had been standing on the same balcony only a year earlier to bid the fans farewell — and now I was back acknowledging their cheers, still a Notts player after all, and part of a team which had earned a place in history. The twists of fate!

Sir Garfield Sobers greeted the victory as "a great achievement after all those years without success" and 'Basher' Hassan, then 37, relished his first moment of success in 17 years with the club. "I never thought the day would come — certainly not during my career. I'm just grateful I was still around when it happened."

Reg Simpson, the former England player, shed tears on the pavilion, and little wonder. He'd been associated with the club for 40 years without savouring such elation. "No matter what is achieved at Trent Bridge in future years, there will never be another day like it," he said. "In my time we came close, but we never had sufficient quality bowlers to go out and win matches. Today we have."

The elusive title came about through a magnificent sequence of results. Of our 22 games, we won 11 with eight of the victories coming at Trent Bridge. I was delighted with my form because I'd been so consistent all year and felt I'd contributed to the effort — and earned my pay, unlike the previous season. When we rampaged to three successive home wins over Worcestershire (by 10 wickets), Yorkshire (by six wickets) and Lancashire (by eight wickets) I had a hot phase when I collected 21 wickets but, generally, I harvested wickets steadily with only four bags of five wickets in an innings, and none of 10 in a match. In one season, I had completed the transformation from an out-and-out fast bowler to a fast-medium operator, relying much more on economy of effort, tight line and length and a good deal more guile.

And while I was elated to take 105 wickets, I was just as chuffed with my batting when I was able to score 745 runs at 32.39. There was one century — 142 not out against Yorkshire, my best effort in first-class cricket — and three other scores of more than 50. I began to appreciate I had some ability in the all-round sense; until then, I'd never taken my batting too seriously. I believed I was primarily a strike bowler who could bat a little. But, in 1981, I batted at No. 6 at times, which brought about a change in my batting approach because I had to accept more responsibility and be more selective about my shotmaking. Suddenly I had to exercise real discipline as a batsman.

Ken Taylor seemed to extract more out of my all-round efforts (it was interesting that Rice also did exceptionally well with both bat and ball,

1462 runs at 56.23 and 65 wickets).

"You'll have to have a go at the double next year," Taylor told me.

"What double?"

"The double of scoring 1000 runs and taking 100 wickets in a season."

I hadn't been aware of the double and didn't really see how I could be a serious contender. After all, the double hadn't been completed since 1967, when Middlesex's Fred Titmus did it. But he'd had the benefit of playing 28 matches and now the county programme was restricted to 22 games.

For all the success both Notts and I enjoyed, there was ample controversy in 1981 — and it was all to do with the pitches prepared by our groundsman Ron Allsopp. We played 10 matches at Trent Bridge with nine of them producing results; it was a sharp contrast to events in the 1970s when Trent Bridge matches were inevitably draws. But because there were so many results — and because Notts won so regularly and decisively —there was much criticism aimed at Allsopp doctoring pitches to suit the Notts attack. It was all so much tripe. The fact is Ron did no more than abide by a directive from the Test and County Cricket Board which required all groundsmen to produce pitches which encouraged positive cricket, pitches with pace in them and also something for the spinners. And that meant we had a pitch which virtually guaranteed results at Trent Bridge — and we were lucky to win the toss almost every time and put the opposition in. And yet, when Leicestershire won the toss, they opted to bat first and lost by eight wickets!

Ron's a fabulous groundsman ·and, interestingly enough, Geoff Boycott wrote of him in an article: "Ron Allsopp is one of the best groundsmen in the world." Ron begged to differ: "I am the best!" I couldn't agree more because he has the gift of being able to prepare all manner of pitches — a featherbed for a five-day test, one which will seam and bounce or a turner. In my 10 years at Notts, I would say Ron was the subject of reports to Lord's on only three or four occasions for substandard pitches . . . and that's a useful strike rate for a man who produced 100-odd first-class pitches at Trent Bridge in my time.

The cynics of the county circuit labelled him "a greenkeeper for Hadlee and Rice". It's strange the barbs all came in the year we won the title; I'm sure there wouldn't have been any complaints if we'd missed out. And it was also ironical, despite so much adverse comment, Ron Allsopp was still rated second best in the groundsman-of-the-year competition for first-class pitches and top dog for one-day pitches.

Allsopp admitted to much concern when he decided to prepare better pitches at Trent Bridge. He was worried he might have gone too far . . . but the 1981 championship victory was ample comfort for him. Admittedly, I collected the majority of my wickets at Trent Bridge — 60 compared to 45 away from home. But I'd emphasise some of my best performances came on tracks which were low, slow and unresponsive. I had seven for 25 against Lancashire at Liverpool, six for 61 against Essex at Chelmsford and four for 19 against Yorkshire at Bradford. Food for thought?

Obviously the Trent Bridge pitches suited the Hadlee-Rice attack but the best possible ammunition to fire at the detractors was that our off-spinner Eddie Hemmings also profited in home matches. Of the 90 wickets he captured, 60 were taken in Nottingham!

Having done so well in the first-class arena, we needed to find some remedies for our one-day performances, which weren't so flash. So, in 1982, we wanted to retain the county crown and also excel in the various limited-overs competitions; the year of great expectations was the way I looked at it. After all, the county championship pennant flag flapped high above the Trent Bridge pavilion when I returned to Nottingham for the new season, and there was also cause for much expectation with the arrival of the England seamer Mike Hendrick from Derbyshire.

Ultimately we didn't win anything but had our steadiest and most consistent season. We made the final of the Benson and Hedges 55-over competition — the club's first appearance at Lord's — and took fourth

The man who changed the face of Nottinghamshire cricket as much as anyone was head groundsman Ron Allsopp, surrounded by his ground staff after our county championship success in 1981.

J.M. Sumpter

place in the county championship plus fifth in the Sunday league. However, there were so many disappointments for us, nearly all of them related to injuries. I'd been excited about a strike force of Hendrick, Rice and Hadlee yet the three of us bowled together in only one match — against Somerset in the Benson and Hedges final at Lord's. Rice returned from South Africa with a neck injury, which gave him extreme pain whenever he bowled; Hendrick was troubled by hip and groin problems which allowed him to bowl only 244 overs in the county championship; and I had a succession of worries, mainly with further hamstring trouble, which restricted me to 403 overs and saw me playing as a batsman only on a few occasions.

I was downhearted about my troubles. I began the season exceptionally well and, halfway through, had taken 49 wickets; I was right into the groove of being a county pro. My short run was now second nature, even though it had caused enormous debate back home when we met Australia in a three-test series. Where the run-up was an accepted fact in England, I was despised for changing by so many people at home. I'd proved in 1981 that it didn't impair my effectiveness — if anything, it improved me — and now 1982 was going the same way. But then I ran into hamstring trouble again and could manage only 12 wickets over the second half of the programme.

I missed five matches at one point but when I returned against Yorkshire I limped off again — and not because of the hamstring. After a collision with Yorkshire batsman Neil Hartley, our legs got tangled up and I had to put ice on a badly swollen ankle. As we travelled to London after that match for the Benson and Hedges final, I couldn't help thinking I would miss playing at Lord's. We'd reached the final following an astonishing semi-final win over Lancashire. As we chased only 182 to win, we slumped to 116 for six and needed 67 to win off the last nine overs. I hadn't played for some time and was dreadfully out of touch but, after a lucky let-off, I was able to blast 55 in 49 minutes, after taking 30 minutes over my first 10 runs. It was a great way to make it through to the final and, I suppose, just making it that far marked a major triumph for the side.

But, on the trip to London, I wondered if we were ready. It was a big occasion and I could see the nerves were taking over. History shows we bombed out, all out for 130 and then saw Peter Roebuck and Viv Richards both make half-centuries in Somerset's nine-wicket win. It was just another chapter in the learning experience for us all. In five years of county cricket I'd digested so much in my bid to become a more complete bowler, a more complete player, and these kinds of setbacks were part of the process. The one aspect about county cricket is the number of opportunities you have to rectify your mistakes; because you play so much cricket, you never lack for opportunities to regain lost confidence or to play yourself back into form. All I could think after the Lord's disaster was that we'd return and do much better. Prophetic words, indeed.

The hamstring continued to plague me but it didn't interfere when I made the first of two first-class centuries for the season, 131 against Surrey followed by 60 against Lancashire. I was then persuaded to play as a batsman only against Gloucestershire and profited with 64. The next day, I was promoted to No. 3 for our Sunday league match against the same side — and hit a century. This batting wasn't such a bad business with a 91 following against Glamorgan and then my second century — against Worcestershire — and so I finished the season with 807 runs at 31.04 plus 61 wickets at 14.57, top of the national averages for the third successive year. Ken Taylor had believed I could do the double and 1982 told me he was right; what I needed was a full, injury-free season.

There was never a chance of 1983 being a possible double year, not with the third World Cup on followed by New Zealand's tour of England. And with the weather appalling it was difficult to fit in too much early-season play for Notts. I played just five matches and didn't achieve anything too wonderful with 13 wickets and 119 runs, the one bright note being an innings of 103 against Sussex at Hove in the opening championship match, while I also collected seven wickets in the match. The season was even worse for the club. We finished 14th in the county competition, bottom of the Sunday league and we were knocked out in only the second round of the NatWest Trophy competition. While we made the quarter-finals of the Benson and Hedges, we suffered a decisive seven-wicket defeat by Lancashire . . . it was a dreadful season.

A Sunday league clash against Somerset stood out for the private battle between Viv Richards and Ian Botham to score centuries, Viv making 117 not out and Botham 85 in a total of 279 for three from their 40 overs. Richards took a sedate 99 minutes over his innings, Botham just 46. Ricey threw me the ball when they were batting saying: "Good luck, I've wanted to see this battle for some time." Eight overs cost 48 runs but Eddie Hemmings had 88 runs taken off his eight and Mike Hendrick 62!

I made a sentimental return to Trent Bridge during the season, playing for my country in the fourth test against England. It presented a chance for a 'local' duel between Derek Randall and me, Derek out-pointing me in England's first innings when he made 83 — although I eventually had his wicket — while I castled him for 13 in the second innings.

We were well beaten by 165 runs to lose the series 3–1, but the match at Trent Bridge meant so much to me, and not just because I was playing on my other home ground. I also took my 200th test wicket when I bowled Norman Cowans for 0 — and I can thank Bob Willis for giving me a chance to do that. For starters, he didn't enforce the follow-on, even though England had a lead of 213 after dismissing us for 207. And then, instead of declaring England's second innings at some stage, Willis opted to bat right through until England were out for 297, giving us a seemingly impossible winning target of 511. I could easily have been left on 199 but I heard Willis say to Allan Lamb: "We'll give him a chance." As I walked off the field, Bob was at the dressing room door to congratulate me, a nice touch and evidence of the respect you build up for players in the healthy atmosphere which generally pervades the English county scene. I also made 92 not out in our second innings to go with my earlier scores of 84, 11, 75, 6 not out, 0, 30 and 3; my best series as a batsman with 301 runs at 50.16 to top our averages. With 21 wickets as well, I was named man of the series, a nice accolade to receive in front of Notts supporters.

For the club, it was a terrible year and Ken Taylor implored we do infinitely better in 1984. To a point he had his wish granted — Notts finished second in the championship, we were also runners-up in the Sunday league and semi-finalists in the Benson and Hedges competition but what became an enormous season for the club, and for me, had its twists. We lost Hendrick, forced to retire with a hip complaint after two troubled years with the side. When he arrived in 1982 he maintained he felt good for another five years and it was flattering to hear him say his major regret on quitting was: "Unhappily, I never really had a chance to link up with Richard Hadlee and that must rate as the biggest disappointment of my career." In the limited appearances we had together, it was a pleasure to watch Hendo in action; he had such a high, side-on, over-the-top action, allowing him to extract bounce and seam off the pitch and, coupled with his almost flawless line and length, he was one of the best bowlers of his type I saw.

I'd had personal problems in the off-season, plunging into a state of depression in late 1983 before snapping out of it for New Zealand's home test series against England. It was a traumatic time and only through the help of family and friends did I emerge from it to have a magnificent series against England — especially the second test in Christchurch — followed by 23 wickets in three tests in Sri Lanka.

By the time I returned to Trent Bridge for my seventh year with Notts, I was back in my normal mode, brimful of goals I wanted to achieve, not least the apparently elusive county double of 1000 runs and 100 wickets. I admit now I chose a mechanical, even clinical, way to go about it but I didn't see how the double could happen if it wasn't meticulously planned. After all, there were any number of outstanding candidates who hadn't managed it — Mike Procter, Imran Khan, Kapil Dev, Clive Rice, Ian Botham and Malcolm Marshall just some of the players with the potential to be double achievers who had failed. Why, not even the great and incomparable Gary Sobers had done the 1000-100. Since the county programme had been reduced in 1969 only five players had managed to top 1000 runs and 75 wickets in a season . . . Mushtaq Mohammad (1969), Tony Greig (1971), Richard Hutton (1971), Keith Boyce (1972) and Procter (1979).

It wouldn't be a simple exercise of just going out and seeing what happened, hoping injury didn't intervene. No, it had to be a computer-like operation. I knew I had the ability but the unknown factors were critical. How would the weather behave? Would there be injuries? And then match situations might dictate against having sufficient opportunities while mediocre performances would be an ever-present threat.

The calculation was straightforward enough. With the schedule now up to 24 matches, I figured I'd play in 20 of them, so I'd need to average 50 runs and five wickets a match. But I believed I'd need other targets, or motivational crutches, to help me along, and I kept a list of them in my cricket coffin:

1. First bowler to reach 100 wickets.

2. Better career-best first-class figures of 7–23.
3. Take 10 bags of five wickets.
4. Take 60 wickets at Trent Bridge, 40 away.
5. Better career-best batting of 142 not out.
6. Score 600 runs away from home, 400 at Trent Bridge.
7. Three centuries and six fifties.
8. The double.
9. Player of the Year.
10. All Rounder of the Year.
11. Help win 10 matches in the championship with an inspired performance.
12. Take 25 catches.

I didn't achieve every goal. Essex's John Lever beat me to 100 wickets and I failed to improve on my career-best bowling figures of seven for 23, seven for 35 being my best in 1984 (I had to wait until Brisbane 1985–86 — and a test match — to hit new bowling highs). But many of the other targets were at least matched, if not well and truly surpassed. Take the batting; by scoring 210 not out against Middlesex at Lord's I went way beyond expectations and I also managed 711 runs in away games plus 468 at home, again more than planned for. I'd hoped for 10 bags of five wickets or more in an innings but finished instead with six (three fives, two sixes and one seven); what helped dramatically were the 11 instances of four wickets in an innings. My split of wickets away and at home was also bettered — 74 at home and 43 away. So much went right in terms of my targets — but that's because I wanted everything so much. And in the end I had it all, including the prized Player of the Year and All Rounder of the Year awards.

While I had a basic plan, I also had a much more detailed budget. I was adamant achieving the double had to have a mathematical edge to it. I finished up remarkably close to my projections:

I budgeted to play 20 championship matches but played 24.

I budgeted 31 innings and had 33.

The target of 1000 runs became 1179 in reality.

I envisaged a batting average of 34 but it was 51.26.

I estimated I'd bowl 750 overs but I bowled 772.

I anticipated 250 maidens. I bowled 248.

I thought I'd give away 1500 runs but yielded 1645.

I needed 100 wickets and finished with 117.

The budget of a bowling average of 15 turned out to be 14.05.

After each match, I religiously jotted down my performances and calculated whether I was ahead or behind budget. By 24 September I had the vital 100th wicket against Lancashire at Blackpool and, just three days later, the magical glow of the 1000th run came in front of my home crowd

One of the great characters of Nottingham, and English sport, is Nottingham Forest soccer manager Brian Clough. He's a loyal supporter of the Notts cricket club and presented me with a medal after I did the county double in 1984.

R.J. Hadlee Collection

at Trent Bridge against Warwickshire. I went out to bat needing 21 runs and everyone at the ground knew it, including the Warwickshire players. After I'd scored a couple of singles, the Warwickshire wicketkeeper, Geoff Humpage, said: "Two down, 19 to go." When I heaved a boundary wide of mid-on off Chris Old, I'd completed the double in my 21st match of the season.

Despite the euphoria, I felt a tinge of regret about the 1984 season because, despite my double effort, we failed narrowly to win anything tangible. We just missed out on the county championship and also ran close in two of the one-day competitions — and I'd even had budgets that year in the one-dayers. There was an equivalent double in the Sunday league of 400 runs and 20 wickets; I managed the wickets with 23 but, when Ian Botham dismissed me for 14 in the final league match of the season, I was just one short on the run count.

For all the personal effort, and that of my team-mates, we were unable to round the year off with at least one of the major trophies — and Ricey had worked hard to extract the best from all of us. He set targets for every player that season and I noted with some interest that the goals he listed for me were 999 runs and 99 wickets. He was either taking the mickey out of me or using his own psychology to push me further (without ever knowing just how methodically I'd planned my assault on the double).

I was running smoothly for the first half of the season, ahead on the wickets and runs counts but, by the 17-match point, I began to fall behind on the runs side. I still needed 330 runs so a couple of big scores were vital to put me back on target. Our match against Middlesex at Lord's didn't seem the likely opportunity for a decent score when we slumped to 17 for four but Rice said to me: "Go out there and score a double century!" Really! The long and short of it was I did just that. I was driven on by rage to an extent, annoyed so much of our good work was being ruined by this batting collapse. The double hundred became the key to the whole exercise; without it I would have struggled to make the 1000-run factor. By this time I was becoming obsessed with the double. I'd go home and always think about what I had to do tomorrow and in the next few matches. I suspect Karen was becoming sick of the whole deal and was probably more relieved than me when it was all over.

Fred Titmus was one of the first to acknowledge my feat, the first double in 17 years: "Hadlee's a super cricketer and I wholeheartedly congratulate him. He is by far the best bowler of the world's top all rounders. Now he's proved that the batting side of his game is top class as well."

He went on: "To me it (the double) was always important, but then I wouldn't have been much of a cricketer if I hadn't managed 1000 runs and 100 wickets in our seasons. To be honest, I always used to make bloomin' sure I played against Oxford and Cambridge. They were better in those days than they are now, but it was still a good opportunity to get a few statistics under your belt. Credit to Hadlee for missing out those games and still making it."

The failure to win the county championship hurt. I thought of the "ifs". Had I dismissed Terry Alderman in the last over against Kent we would have collected the 16 points which could have ultimately given us the title. And there was the last match of the season against Somerset at Taunton when Ian Botham set us 297 to win off 60 overs; I was out controversially for 28 when Jeremy Lloyds caught me on the boundary and crashed into the advertising boards. Was it, in fact, a six? The umpires said not and we went on to lose a fantastic match by just three runs, allowing Essex to win the championship by 14 points. If — that word again — we had beaten Somerset, the title would have been ours.

I wasn't in marvellous shape for the start of the 1985 season. Who would be after a test series against the West Indies in the Caribbean? A tour involving four tests and five one-day internationals left me drained mentally and physically, the experiences in the last two tests in Bridgetown and Kingston leaving me spent; the cricket was demanding, beyond reasonable expectations, as most of us were battered, bruised and effectively shell-shocked from the persistent short-pitched bowling we had to endure. For all that, I still found appeal in the grind of the county pro's life; it can be so remorseless, moving from one venue to another, involved in a three-day match one day and then into a limited-over encounter the next. You're constantly on the move to set up camp for your next match; there's so little respite. But there's a sense of normality about the county game where it's still competitive yet is played with more respect and skill. It was comforting to be back in an atmosphere where fast bowlers weren't consistently banging the ball in halfway down the track. There's no skill in that but there is when you bowl in English conditions where you have to use swing and seam to take wickets; it's a better test of the batsmen, too. They're not forced into protecting their bodies, continually pinned on the back foot.

But, after the freakish feats in 1984, the 1985 season was a mediocre one for Notts. We slipped to seventh in the county championship, 12th in the Sunday league and didn't qualify for the Benson and Hedges competition. So our efforts were concentrated on the NatWest Trophy more than anything. And I performed only modestly. After nine matches I had only 20-odd wickets and 370 runs and ultimately managed just 592 runs at 32.89 and 59 wickets at 17.38, not marvellous from 19 matches even if weather tended to limit opportunities.

The big development of the year came in the captaincy area. Clive Rice was having his benefit year, which isn't such a wonderful time to also have captaincy responsibilities. It so happened Ricey injured a hand and was out of action for two weeks and, rather than giving the captaincy to a home player, it was given to yet another foreigner — me. I welcomed it. I'd been meandering along a little and the leadership challenge was the ideal tonic. Rice's injury was probably timely because the side wasn't doing so well at the time under his directorship; with his benefit on, he had so many commitments to various functions and it was clear he was distracted more often than not, unable to concentrate totally on the captain's role. The players weren't enjoying their cricket and there was talk behind the scenes that a change was needed to give the side a lift, to bring in fresh ideas and inject new-found enthusiasm. It didn't matter who did the job, we just needed someone else, even on only a short-term basis.

We found ourselves without a captain on the morning of a vital Nat-West Trophy second-round clash against Warwickshire at Trent Bridge. In fact, the toss was only minutes away when Ken Taylor asked me to take over; there wasn't much time, but a team talk seemed to spark instant enthusiasm. I couldn't match the keenness by winning the toss and we were put in on a fresh-looking pitch but, despite a bad start, we were able to score 251 off 55 overs (Tim Robinson making 98 after retiring hurt early in his innings, while I hit a 50). And then, in the field, we did enough to win by 86 runs, creating an air of jubilation in the club after the period of confusion we had been going through.

I led the side in three county matches as well and, while we failed to push home for a win in any of them, we had the edge in all three games. The lads were responding well and we also won two Sunday league matches. The boss (Ken Taylor) must have liked what I was doing because, during our match against Northamptonshire, he said: "Clive will be fit for the NatWest quarter-final against Gloucestershire." I immediately assumed that would mean Ricey would regain the captaincy, which didn't bother me too much. But then Taylor said: "Things are going so well I want you to keep captaining the side, but I don't know how I can tell Clive."

"I don't want to cause any problems. I'm quite happy for Clive to take over," I said, but the head man had spoken. The job was mine, and I assumed he passed on the news to Ricey. There was an odd sequel the next day, though.

"I've had an absolute nightmare about the situation," Taylor told me, "and I've come to the conclusion Clive is the club captain and should captain the team against Gloucester." I accepted his decision but it was a bit of an odd business. We duly beat Gloucester but only after the rain-affected match had spanned three days, and then faced Worcestershire in the semi-finals. After it had scored 232, we were left on 137 for four and faced the assignment of making 96 to win from only 14 overs the following day. With Robinson making 139, we were able to scrape through with four balls to spare — and so make the club's first NatWest Trophy final.

The memories of our last Lord's final in 1982 — the Benson and Hedges decider against Somerset — had some poignancy, mainly as a source of motivation. We had to prove to ourselves that we could perform when the heat was on before a huge crowd. We had to do infinitely better than we had in 1982. With Rice winning the toss, we had to gain some early advantage but that theory was soon destroyed as Brian Hardie made 110 and Graham Gooch 91 to help Essex to 280 for two.

The target seemed to be almost out of reach yet Robinson (80) and Chris Broad (64) gave us a great start only to both be dismissed when one of them really needed to bat through. The loss of Rice didn't help and it eventually fell to Derek Randall and Duncan Martindale to put us back in shape. They reached the last over with 18 runs needed. Derek Pringle obliged as Arkle hit 2, 4, 2, 4, 4 off the first five balls and two runs were required off the last delivery, Sadly, Randall was caught at mid-wicket and we had to stomach defeat by one run.

There was utter despair — and a deathly silence — in our dressing room but we could take solace from the fact we'd regained our confidence after the humiliation of 1982. It was then I said: "I can't leave the club until we win a one-day championship. My job at Trent Bridge won't be complete until it's done."

Whether that could happen in 1986 was difficult to perceive. I'd always thought 1984 was a strenuous year but it was a doddle compared with what I faced in 1986 — there were commitments to Notts as usual, New Zealand was touring England and the club had generously granted me a benefit in only my ninth season, giving me an enormous chance to secure the future financially. It was going to be a demanding year without doubt.

Critical to my benefit operation was John Farrar, who'd been involved — very successfully — in Geoff Boycott's testimonial activities. I engaged him to run my benefit, to organise the myriad of activities and functions which would make it a success. Just as crucial in this whole scenario was the New Zealand Cricket Council which granted me permission to join the New Zealand team for only the three tests and the two one-day internationals, so enabling me to continue playing for Notts and chase the demanding benefit trail. Better still, the NZCC gave approval for the New Zealand players to appear in some of my benefit matches (which they did at Hitchin near London and Cleethorpes).

The first of my benefit functions was a dinner at Hatfield near London in early April, where Jimmy Greaves and Ian St John were guest speakers. By the time it was all over in November, I had attended well in excess of 100 different fund-raising events. There were twilight cricket matches against local club teams, unofficial international one-day games, raffles, ground collections, dinners, darts nights, pub crawls to raffle autographed bats, golf days, square dances, boxing nights, sports quizzes, cabarets and barbecues. You needed willpower to last the distance, and to ensure you weren't swept along in the tide of never-ending drinking and eating!

One of the big successes was a golf day in Nottingham during the second New Zealand-England test, when players from both teams were involved along with Glenn Turner and Richie Benaud. And my test match dinner during the same match was another huge event, when Jeremy Coney and Benaud were guest speakers followed by the multi-talented Peter Brackley, a television commentator-cum-comedian whose show was a sheer delight.

Oh yes, and there was plenty of cricket as well. Notts failed to snare any titles but competed solidly by placing fourth in the county championship, third in the Sunday league, and making the semi-finals of the Benson and Hedges competition and the quarters in the NatWest Trophy. And while I was burdened with New Zealand team and benefit responsibilities, I was content with my returns from 14 matches for Notts — 57 wickets at 14.47 and 720 runs at 55.38, the bowling return including five bags of five wickets in an innings and one of 10 in a match while I hit two hundreds and three fifties. Had I not missed 10 matches for Notts, I'm sure I would have done the double again; there would have been ample time to score the 280 runs and take the 43 wickets needed. As it was, I came out of the English first-class season with 76 wickets — 19 in the three tests against England — plus 813 runs.

One match I salivated about was the clash against Somerset at Trent Bridge where my target would be Peter Roebuck, the Somerset opening batsman. In the New Zealand summer of 1985–86, he'd written some things about me which I didn't overly appreciate, labelling me "austere and morose" as well as saying I lacked a sense of humour and was a bad influence on a team. He had his say during the time of the Alfa Romeo car controversy following New Zealand's tour of Australia.

But on 4 June I had a chance for some form of revenge. I was fired up and could take out all my aggression on Roebuck when he opened the Somerset first innings — and I did. Ricey won the toss, put Somerset in on a fast, green and bouncy pitch and I had my chance. The ball bounced and moved alarmingly, Roebuck taking a physical battering when he was hit in the ribs, on the gloves, on the helmet and the inside thigh. He was a sore lad but, would you believe, he was still there six and a half hours later on 221 not out! He'd had the final say once more!

Two limited-over games stuck in the memory — for opposite reasons. In our Benson and Hedges quarter-final against Essex at Chelmsford, we were chasing only a moderate score of 196 to win but weren't too well placed at 126 for six. Yet, of the next 71 runs scored, I was able to make

61 of them to help us through to the semi-finals, only to lose to Middlesex at Lord's. The other match was our NatWest Trophy quarter-final against Surrey which developed into one of the most frustrating matches I played for Notts. We dismissed Surrey for 204 and I had the satisfaction of a very pleasing bowling performance of 12–4–17–5. But, incredibly, we were bowled out for just 158 and my 54 off 76 deliveries counted for nothing. Receiving the gold award as man of the match was of no comfort; there's nothing that hurts more than seeing individual efforts of such a kind effectively wasted.

There was genuine delight in my match of the year — the second test against England at Trent Bridge — when I was named man of the match after scoring 68 and taking 10 wickets in our eight-wicket win but the season for Notts was another of those annoyingly close-but-not-quite affairs.

I was undecided about returning in 1987 although Ricey had decided he would have one more year. In any case, there was still benefit business to be attended to. It was a massive success on all fronts but I needed so many people to help me . . . John Farrar, Richard Tennent, Sue Fenton, my benefit committee, the New Zealand team, the Notts club and supporters . . . and Karen, of course.

It was a Saturday night in January before I seriously addressed the question of what to do in 1987.

"What are we going to do about England?" I said to Karen. We talked it through and, really, I had to return; it was the right and proper thing to do. I wasn't about to take the benefit money and run so I knew I must do one more season, just to show my appreciation to all the Nottinghamshire cricket people and fans who had helped me so much. After our share of successes and magical moments plus failures and disappointments, it also seemed perfect for Ricey and me to bow out together.

My mission would be to try and help Notts win a one-day crown. I knew we could do it so, after ringing Ken Taylor with the news I would be back, I wrote to him saying I'd like to play all one-day matches but make limited appearances in three-day games. I was picking and choosing yet my terms were happily agreed to. I guess I knew it would be all so different when I arrived; I wouldn't be able to resist playing in every match possible because I'd have another shot at the double, albeit with a more casual approach this time.

I started a little later than usual, initially delayed because of New Zealand's tour to Sri Lanka — which was subsequently abandoned after bombings in Colombo — and then returning to New Zealand. Karen needed an operation and I didn't leave for England until she had recovered sufficiently, taking Nicholas with me while Karen followed later with Matthew and her sister Janice.

The start to my 10th and last season was horrendous. We faced Leicestershire in a Benson and Hedges match, were rolled for 74 and lost by eight wickets. Absolute disaster. There were five ducks in our innings; Rice, Paul Johnson and I drove to Leicester in the same car — and didn't score a run between us. And I'd travelled 20,000 kilometres to suffer the ignominy of a first-ball duck, leg-before to West Indian Winston Benjamin who also took a hat trick. Was this to be the tone of my farewell season?

We had blown out in one of the limited-over competitions and there would be obstacles during the season. We'd face the loss of players to the England test side, the Bicentennial match at Lord's would also cause problems and there was, of course, inevitable concern with injuries. Yet another complication was Ken Taylor's idea to groom Tim Robinson for the captaincy, meaning he would share the job with Ricey. In theory it was a smart move but, in reality, it caused more headaches than anything and the decision was eventually, and wisely, made to persevere with Ricey.

There was nothing outlandishly exceptional about our start to the season, with seven successive draws in county championship matches before we beat Kent at Canterbury. Then the wins began to flow until we were up near the top of the points ladder; crucially, we played Essex and Gloucestershire when four of us — Chris Broad, Bruce French, Rice and I — were committed to the Bicentennial match. Both matches were drawn, meaning we'd need outstanding results in our last four matches of the season. Failing to do so against Leicestershire and Derbyshire, we were under unreal pressure to score big points against Sussex and Glamorgan. The return from the final match was perfect and, after taking our first innings total through to 300 for five, Rice (104 not out) and I (15 not out) walked off Trent Bridge having batted together for the last time, being greeted by a standing ovation which had the lump-in-the-throat feeling running again. It would obviously be one of those emotional seasons. We won easily to take a maximum 24 points . . . and then had to wait anxiously for a few days to see how Lancashire fared in its final outing; but it was unable to do the job required and so Notts had won the county title for the second time in my era.

We were a transformed unit in the Sunday league, becoming a major force, if terribly inconsistent. We seemed to account for the fancied sides only to stumble on the lowly-ranked ones. We should have coasted to the league title, only to have a rough run towards the end, losing to Derbyshire, having the match against Essex washed out before beating Surrey in our last match of the season . . . with two balls to spare! That left us on 44 points and Worcestershire 42 with one match to play — against Northamptonshire — which it won to leave us second. It was ultra disappointing to reflect on so many missed opportunities during the season.

With our run in the championship, the Sunday league and the NatWest Trophy, we were actually in a remarkable position at one stage to perhaps complete a treble of titles never before achieved. Ken Taylor adopted the attitude that one title would be realistic and I agreed. It was optimistic to think we'd win two titles and three would be beyond a dream. The Sunday league result proved the futility of thinking too confidently about three crowns.

But the NatWest represented a real chance of making it two in any case. With a second-round win over the strong Middlesex side we were well set and followed by disposing of Derbyshire in the quarter-finals and then Gloucestershire in the semi-finals. Then we went off to Lord's again to face Northamptonshire, a side of some ability with Allan Lamb, Wayne Larkins, Geoff Cook, Nick Cook and Winston Davis.

The match had to be reduced from 60 overs a side to 50 and Northants, after winning the toss, reached 228 for three through a lovely innings of 87 by Larkins and Lamb's 41. For the third time in a Lord's final, I failed to take a wicket but I was delighted I conceded only 29 runs from my 10 overs.

Right: Team-mates and friends do battle for Nottinghamshire for the last time. In our last innings together at Trent Bridge, Clive hit a century and I was left 15 not out to round off 10 great years with Notts.

Below: The Rices and the Hadlees at Trent Bridge . . . Clive with Mark, Sue with Jackie, Karen with Nicholas and me with Matthew. R.J. Hadlee Collection

Another career highlight . . . the second hat-trick of my first-class career in Nottinghamshire's county championship clash against Kent at Canterbury in 1987.

Above: The hat-trick became a possibility when Derek Aslett's off stump was knocked out of the ground (Neil Taylor being bowled for four from the previous delivery). Peter Wayne

Below: So former England batsman Chris Tavare became the key — and he sent an edge to first slip where Clive Rice juggled the catch before securing it. Peter Wayne

Weather problems throughout the day meant only 21 overs of our innings were completed when stumps were drawn, meaning the match would have to be carried over to a second day — and we were in tatters at 57 for four with Broad, Robinson, Randall and Johnson all out cheaply. The break worked to our advantage because it broke the roll Northants was on. We had time to reflect and reassess our strategy before resuming the mission to score 172 runs from 29 overs. We needed six an over and were running out of frontline batting resources, with Rice (20 not out) and John Birch (9 not out) to be followed by me.

The restart was delayed on the Monday but we struck some trouble when Birch was bowled in the 29th over to leave us 84 for five. Ricey and I looked for ones and twos, adding 62 in 12 overs but then he was caught at mid-on for 63 . . . 146 for six and Bruce French came in to join me. I couldn't feel too confident because he'd hardly scored a run all season. I decided I had to attack boldly when Chippy Williams bowled his last over. There was a six over mid-wicket, a skied drive to mid-off next ball, which Robin Bailey pulled out of because of the sun, so allowing us to score two more runs. And the next delivery Lamb missed a difficult chance which went for four. We finished up taking 15 off the over to give us at least some hope.

Still we needed 57 off five overs but Frenchy proved the killer of Northants' hopes as he raced to 35 off 27 balls, surely his most valuable innings for Notts. The last over arrived . . . eight needed and David Capel bowling.

The match situation reminded me of a vital Sunday league match against Gloucestershire at Morton-in-Marsh earlier in the season. After the game was reduced to 20 overs, we bowled Gloucester out for 111 and coasted for much of the time. But, after the loss of wickets in the middle order, we arrived at the final over needing nine to win; I had a single off the first ball — which was unfortunate — and Andy Pick failed to score a run off the next three. We scrambled a leg-bye off the fifth delivery so I needed to hit a six off the last ball just to tie the match and give us two vital Sunday league points. A slash and I had a four to the wide third-man boundary — but we lost by two runs. It was such a depressing result, one which ultimately cost us the title.

So, the scene was much the same — only on a much bigger stage — when Capel had to bowl the last over of the NatWest Trophy final. Would this be Morton-in-Marsh all over again? This time, I was there again only French was in strike. He drove the first delivery straight towards me, I took off for the single and somehow got the ball tangled up in my feet — who else could do that? — which left Capel the simple task of picking the ball up and breaking the wicket to run French out.

Out strode Eddie Hemmings to join me. I told him: "Everything's under control. We'll do it." Capel roared in, the ball pitched full outside off stump. I laid into it and knew it was six — over long-off — as soon as I hit it. That was the ball game in effect. The rest was a formality. With 75 runs scored off the last eight overs and, with my 70 not out off 61 balls, I had the fairytale end to my Notts career to win the man-of-the-match award at Lord's. What a way to go out.

This had been close to the perfect season. We'd won two titles and I'd come out of it with 97 wickets at 11.97 — top of the national averages again — plus 1075 runs at 53.75 (excluding the Bicentennial match). That I missed the double so narrowly didn't matter. When I'd topped the 1000-100 marks in 1984, we hadn't won the title; this time I'd just failed — but we had the crown. The one individual display I cherished was the one against Somerset at Trent Bridge when I scored a century and had bowling returns of six for 42 and six for 41.

So what did 10 years of county cricket mean? In cold statistics it meant 148 first-class appearances for Notts, 5854 runs at 38.76 (11 centuries and 29 fifties) and 612 wickets at 14.75 (38 bags of five in an innings and five of 10 in a match). It was 10 years which made me as a cricketer, a decade of county life which sharpened and refined my skills. I don't believe you can compare performances with others from another era but committee members, friends and supporters paid me the highest compliment when they claimed I'd contributed more to Notts than the greatest all rounder there has been, Gary Sobers. Ricey also made a magnificent contribution with more than 13,000 runs at an average of about 45.00 in 210 matches plus 350-odd wickets at 25.00.

Our goodbyes were low key. I was relieved to have county cricket out of my system at last. There's no question it had been good to me — and good for me — but it's one of the most onerous assignments to play the

It took three visits but finally we got there in 1987. After failing in two previous one-day finals at Lord's, our big moment arrived at last in the NatWest Trophy final in my last season with Notts. And again there was a special glow about the occasion for me with 70 not out gaining me the man of the match accolade.

Bill Smith

One of test cricket's outstanding fast bowlers was Harold Larwood and, during our 1987–88 tour of Australia, I met him again at his Sydney home (some eight years after standing on the balcony at Trent Bridge with him). As a Nottinghamshire legend, he had plenty to tell me about English cricket — but I wasn't so keen about his offer of having a beer at 8.45 a.m. on the day I visited him!

Mark Baker

game so solidly for so long. I left believing Notts could go on achieving and it was amazing my replacement — West Indian fast bowler Franklyn Stephenson — immediately did the double, achieving it in the last match of the season by scoring back-to-back hundreds to bring up the 1000 runs part of the deal.

Much was said about the state of English cricket during my stay with Notts. There was a complex about it in many ways and, to be honest, England has had disappointing results at international level. The same old excuses are trotted out for England's demise — too much one-day cricket, too many overseas players in England, poor pitches and the need for four-day cricket. They're valid, to a point — but it all really comes back to the attitude of the players. They need the will to prepare properly for inter-national cricket by training and practising diligently; they need the will to adapt to different types of cricket and conditions; and they need that hunger to want desperately to succeed.

I don't see too much wrong with the diet of one-day cricket on the English county scene. The players can cope with it, but the county championship needs to be revamped. Provided pitches are of a satisfactory standard, then four-day games are desirable at first-class level but it should be stressed world-class players cannot be expected to perform in substandard conditions. It's the overseas players who have made the county game the commodity it is today; without those players, I dread to think what the standard would be like. The idea of clubs having two foreign players on their books is a good one; the rules allowed us to do that at Trent Bridge although other clubs had just one . . . and that created an inequality.

For all the problems English cricket has, there's a lot of talent in the county game, and I'm talking about homegrown talent. Admittedly, there are a lot of very average — some well below average — players who masquerade as professionals. But there are many capable performers; what they desperately need, though, is to be given a fair go by the selectors in the test arena so they can develop some confidence. For some crazy reason, the selectors mowed through more than 30 players during the 1988 series against the West Indies — and that's downright ludicrous. If a player's good enough to be picked in one test, then surely he should be given at least two or three tests to try and prove himself. Precious few debutants are successful; it's not unusual to take four or five or even 10 tests before potential is fully reached. There's a bloke by the name of Hadlee who knows something about that. English cricket is certainly not short of problem areas to address, but there are obvious remedies if some common sense is used.

I'll never lose touch with the English county season. After 10 years the county syndrome is ingrained — and I don't regret that. England can take credit for developing countless international players, a lot of them ineligible for England. I'm one of them.

C·H·A·P·T·E·R   N·I·N·E

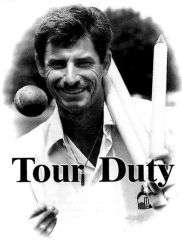

Tour Duty

T our — now there's a word which conjures up all sorts of exotic and romantic images, one which tickles and arouses the senses of adventure and, by implication, tends to be equated with pleasure, enjoyment and excitement.

And haven't I heard those sentiments expressed time and again about the international cricketer's lot. What a life you must lead? Tours to England, the home of cricket and all its traditions, to the heart of calypso in the Caribbean, to sun, sand and surf in Australia and the ultimate cultural experiences provided in India, Pakistan and Sri Lanka.

On the face of it, 18 years in top cricket does read like a travel log — tours to Australia in 1972; England in 1973; Australia in 1974; the first World Cup in England in 1975; Pakistan and India in 1976; England (and Holland) in 1978; the second World Cup in England in 1979; Australia in 1980–81; Australia, again, plus the World Cup and a full tour of England in 1983; Sri Lanka in 1984; Australia in 1985; Australia and the West Indies in 1985; Australia in 1985–86; England in 1986; Sri Lanka in 1987; Australia in 1987–88; Sharjah and India in 1988. On top of all that, I tripped to and from England every year from 1978 through to 1987 during my Nottinghamshire career.

But, for a real slice of touring life, try this sample from my tour diary in the West Indies after the 1984–85 New Zealand season:

Kingston, Jamaica
Friday, 3 May (day 55)

Had a practice at 9.30 a.m. today at the Melbourne Oval, where

Michael Holding plays his cricket. Outfield was poor — bumpy, patchy and stony in some areas. The bowlers couldn't use their full run-ups and we were unable to have fielding practice on the ground.

However, the pitch played well so the batsmen had a reasonable workout. Went to Sabina Park for fielding practice. Watched the West Indians practise next to the test pitch. Obviously gives them a huge advantage because they can work out in conditions resembling those when the test starts tomorrow (the fourth and last test). Strange that we never have the same opportunities — or is it?

Down to 13 players to choose from. Lancer wasn't considered because of the dizzy spells he's been having. Seems it could be a continuation of the problems he had after being whacked in the head by Wasim Akram at Carisbrook a few weeks ago. He's going home tomorrow. Stirls was omitted so we'll have 12 players to pick the final 11 from tomorrow. Braces will have to play, even as a batsman — surely he would do better than Ruds. Ruds will probably come in at No. 6 this time with everyone else moving up, meaning Mantis will be at five. Geoff Howarth and Ruds are both out of form but have to play so Boocky will probably be left out.

The message came out loud and clear at the team meeting tonight. Put all efforts into this test and forget about holidays and the tour coming to an end. We've been done 5–0 in the one-dayers and losing the third test by 10 wickets in Bridgetown has been no help. All out for 94 in our first innings with the quicks Marshall, Garner, Holding and Davis splitting the wickets. We have to put that behind us. We still have five days of tough cricket ahead of us and, if we play well, we could upset. I sense the will has gone from the majority of the players. Dominant thought seems to be to get this test over and done with so we can get out of here.

Saturday, 4 May (day 56)

Lancer left for home today after watching the morning's play. Boocky predictably left out. Surprisingly, Howarth won the toss. First time in the series. He wanted to bat first but consensus was to bowl. Could see Geoff was upset because he differed from the rest of us but I guess we felt if we batted first and were bowled out cheaply, the test and the series was as good as over.

The pitch looked rock hard, white with patches of green. Unlikely to assist seamers. Our medium pacers were reasonably easy to play. Greenidge and Haynes had little difficulty getting the West Indies off to a quick start. Greenidge went first, caught by Jeff Crowe off Hogan for 46. Richardson and Haynes in no trouble until Mantis dismissed them both in similar fashion — chasing wider balls and slashing uppishly to cover-point area where Chopper caught Haynes, and Hogan took Richardson. The home side was 164 for three.

Gomes and Richards looked set for a big score until I had a

new spell. Bowled well before lunch with eight overs for six runs and, at tea, had none for 16 from 12. I set Viv up for the bouncer and pull shot — but then didn't bowl one. Bowled line and length instead, it kept a bit low and hit him on the pads — out lbw although he claimed he'd hit it. I heard two sounds but it must have been pad, then bat, and he was given out, much to the crowd's displeasure and Viv's annoyance — 207 for four.

Logie was out first ball, caught by Hogan at third slip — 207 for five and we were back in the game. As Logie returned to the pavilion, Viv appeared in the players' box, waving his arms to the umpire and pointing to the scoreboard, implying: "Look what you've done. You've allowed them back into the game." Viv's been a little undignified as captain recently.

Gomes and Dujon looked set to bat till stumps but the second new ball arrived with 20 minutes to go. Gomes was beaten outside the off stump frequently so I moved Braces from leg gully to third slip and bowled at Gomes' legs — he spooned up a catch to Wrighty at square leg and was out in the last over of the day — 273 for six. Honours about even.

Had to be reasonably satisfied but could have been a lot better if a couple of bowlers hadn't been off line. Troupy was pulled, cut and driven for 73 off 12 and Charlie Chatfield conceded 57 from 16. Good bowling from Hogan, Mantis and Braces. My three for 32 off 18.1 was good reward yet I deserved better. I thought there was some justice in this game.

On the trip back to the hotel saw the contrast of the slums and dirty areas alongside the plush homes. Also passed the statue of reggae king Bob Marley.

Sunday, 5 May (day 57)

The Windies continued, adding 90 before being dismissed for 363. I finished with four for 53 from 28 overs. Made sure Garner and Marshall received a few bouncers — some good ones, too. Whatever I was able to give them, they've replied with five times as many in the series so far.

We got off to a bad start again. Geoff waved at a short ball and spooned a catch to Gomes at cover-point, Chopper was caught at second-slip trying to cut Marshall, and Hogan tried to pull Walsh and was caught at fine leg. So we were 30 for three. Wrighty was handling the situation well. At tea we were 41 for three with the Mantis being peppered with short-pitched deliveries.

Rain during the interval delayed play for 65 minutes. When it resumed, Mantis was soon in trouble. Garner bowled another short one, Mantis tried to get out of the way but was hit on the left wrist. An X-ray later revealed a break and he returned to the hotel with his arm in plaster, the test and series over for him. In some ways, many of us consider he got out of the series well with only a broken arm because someone could easily have received a really serious injury through the persistent short-pitched bowling. Now we know how the Aussies felt in the

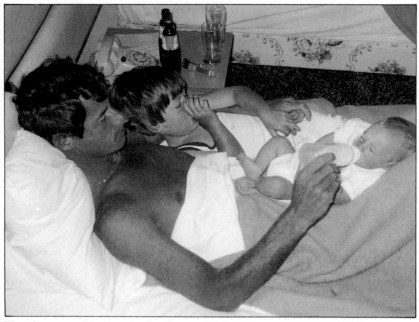

The pleasures of having the family on tour in the West Indies in 1984–85. You become the all-purpose man — cricketer one minute, then baby sitter the next. I feed Matthew while Nicholas sleeps on. R.J. Hadlee Collection

Bodyline series! It's so frightening — and painful — what we've been facing.

Ruds had to bat next, about 30 minutes to go until stumps. He was hit on the helmet first ball. Both he and Wrighty were hit on the shoulder but Ruds soldiered on until 5.30. However, the umpires decided there was time for one more over. Wrighty checked the time with the umpire at the bowler's end and at 5.30 he still wasn't in position. Marshall got another ball to lift, Ruds followed it and was caught by Dujon from the fifth delivery of the over — 65 for four and effectively 65 for five with Coney absent. Ruds was obviously disappointed and upset. It has been a trying series for him and everyone else. A 19-year-old has been put in the firing line against a deadly Windies pace attack and has come out with scores of 0, 0, 4, 0, 2 and 1.

We still need another 98 to avoid the follow-on and, with our top order all but destroyed, I can't see the tail order surviving for long. The players dismissed had all played bad shots, but who can blame them. Life in the middle is hell. There's no enjoyment out there.

The last hour's play wasn't cricket — it was carnage. Marshall and Garner peppered all the batsmen with short-pitched deliveries. Up to three bouncers an over and two or three other deliveries into the ribs. They bowled to hit, and it was overdone.

Action can be taken by the umpires if they feel short-pitched bowling is persistent. Obviously they think it's okay.

There was an incident in the stands today. Two spectators had a fight with machetes and police had to draw their guns to stop it. One offender was apprehended but the other absconded. The incident typified our day — we're also fighting, fighting to save our lives and stay in the game.

Monday, 6 May (day 58)

The newspapers were full of yesterday's battle. "Sunday afternoon is usually a peaceful time, but for the New Zealanders, Sabina Park was nothing short of hell as the ball whistled through the air, then exploded off the pitch like bombs — with the partisan crowd cheering and screaming at their obvious discomfort."

We started badly today. Smithy was out for 0, Troupy for 0 and Charlie for 2. Bowled out for 138, we were asked to bat again after Wrighty had made 53, Braces 25 not out and me 18.

Richards obviously had to put us back in and must have fancied bowling us out again quickly. There were a few wisecracks in our dressing room about our predicament. "I'll be able to catch an early flight to England," I said. Hogan said: "I checked out of the hotel last night." We needed to lighten up a bit but we also needed someone to remind us of our job. Geoff told us: "This is still a test match. We've got something to play for and we must keep going forward." I don't think any of us believed we could avoid defeat, especially once Wrighty was out for 10 and we were 13 for one, with Coney unable to bat.

But for the rest of the afternoon we had the pleasure of watching the captain and Chopper stage a remarkable fightback which has given us hope; they batted together for nearly four hours and took the score to 211 for one at stumps. Chopper completed his second test hundred and still needs another 40 runs to bring up his 1000 in tests. He was in complete control, showing and executing a full range of attacking shots and dogged defence.

There'd been a strong suggestion Braces should open the innings and let Geoff bat down the order, which was what Geoff wanted from the outset only to be shot down by the selectors. I told him he should make the final decision. He simply replied: "The sooner I get in, the sooner it will all be over." That's how resigned he was to another failure. Our manager John Heslop's even tried some hypnosis on Geoff on tour . . . nothing has worked, though. But today something went right. After four hours, he was 78 not out.

He struggled for a while but after tea produced some of the vintage Howarth shots we hadn't seen for years. His timing and confidence started to return and he became dominant against this pace attack. We need only 14 runs to make the West Indies bat again and have eight wickets in hand. It's a pity it's the rest day tomorrow because, if they had to bowl tomorrow on a hot day, they could easily struggle to bowl us out cheaply. We still have to think in terms of getting a good lead. If we can manage another 200 runs or so we would have a game of cricket and an outside chance of winning. Can we do it? We have the ability but somehow lack the confidence. Without Mantis the job is that much harder but Hogan and Ruds are both due for runs, and owe them to the team.

The West Indies board of control's dinner was held at our hotel tonight. Our manager made the usual speech and implied everything had been going smoothly. He was obviously being diplomatic — a shame he couldn't have been a little more honest about some of the problems we'd had.

Tuesday, 7 May (day 59)

Rest day. Visited Morgans Harbour at Port Royal, about 15 miles from town. We boarded a couple of launches for a 20-minute trip to a deserted island, Lime Key, for a day of relaxation — lots of liquid refreshments from sponsors Coruba plus food for a barbecue.

We noticed dark black clouds building up towards Kingston and then saw some thunder and lightning. There must have been a lot of rain but it passed. A good easy-paced day all round.

Wednesday, 8 May (day 60)

We had high hopes today. Geoff and Chopper had to get re-established during the next 17 overs and then see off the new ball to tire out Marshall and Garner so the middle order could take advantage.

The first 55 minutes went well but then Richards brought himself into the attack and had instant success, Chopper caught by Marshall when he tried to hit out when he was 112. Then Walsh replaced Marshall, who'd been bowling off a short run, and immediately had Howarth out for 84. Both our established batsmen were dismissed with the total at 223.

Hogan went quickly, trying to duck a short ball from Walsh which seemed to hit his forearm protector. The ball ballooned to Dujon — another bad decision, making it 12 so far in the series against us.

The new ball arrived and there was little resistance with Marshall doing most of the damage. We were all out for a disappointing 283, losing our last eight wickets for far too few. It was a mere formality for the Windies to score the 59 they needed to win.

We had to be disappointed with our 10-wicket defeats in the last two tests but there is certainly no disgrace in losing to the top team in world cricket. They had too much ability all round for us — and, most of all, they had Malcolm Marshall who took 27 wickets in the series.

We can look at our performances and say not many came away with too much credit. The Mantis proved himself, with consistent, courageous displays but paid a high price — a broken arm. Charlie Chatfield bowled honestly with 13 wickets at 33.92. And Chopper came out quite well with 252 runs at 36.00 but younger brother Martin had six failures around his 188 in the second test. Wrighty averaged 30 but should have done better. The skipper finished with an 84 but it still wasn't enough to save his tour.

The word tour takes on much more sinister implications after an ordeal as mentally and physically gruelling as our trek around the Caribbean. It's an area of the world painted as a tourist's haven, which it might well be. But, when you're there on a cricket tour, facing the fury of West Indian fast bowlers who literally want to see blood on the pitch, even Hobart's Bellerive Oval would shape as paradise to me.

A tour of the West Indies puts a different connotation on the word 'tour'; it becomes more like the experience so many Americans went through in the 1960s when they did their 'Tour of Duty' in Vietnam. It's hell on earth if you're there to play cricket. The unrelenting barrage wears down your emotional and physical resistance until you can stand it no more. When you see your team-mates being maimed by fast bowlers intent on causing injury, you'd need to be a masochist to derive any sort of pleasure from the experience.

Go to India, Pakistan or even Sri Lanka and you don't need to see any fast bowlers to give you a dose of the shits. There wouldn't be many players who've toured that part of the world who haven't suffered from diarrhoea or dysentery.

On New Zealand's 1976 tour to Pakistan and India, Robert Anderson was afflicted by the common complaint and sought advice from David O'Sullivan, who didn't have the same problem.

"How do I cure the shits?" Jumbo asked.

"If nothing else works, try cornflour," replied Daffy.

"Will that cure the problem?"

"No, but it sure will thicken it up."

I was so violently ill on that 1976 tour that I swore I'd never return to either country. I stayed true to my word about the 1984–85 tour to Pakistan and the 1987 World Cup tournament, when New Zealand's group matches were played in India. Ultimately, India became an irresistible attraction last year, not because I wanted to tour the country again (at least initially), but because I had some world record business to take care of. Pakistan's patently a country I'll never visit again; I'm not sorry my last chance has been and gone.

As I travelled to India for the 1988 tour, I naturally had some preconceived notions of what might lie in store. I tried to tell myself the country must have improved since my initiation in 1976. My hopes were immediately rocked when I was greeted by a cockroach scampering across the floor when we arrived in the small hours of the morning.

India, Pakistan and Sri Lanka are such lands of contrast compared to the more comfortable touring options offered in England and Australia. One week you might feel outrageously fit — the next you're stricken by some illness which arrives from nowhere, and all you want to do is crawl away and die. Fred Trueman once said there was a species of snake which, if it bit you, could kill you in nine seconds. After three weeks in India or Pakistan you go out looking for one!

That's the way I felt so often in 1976 but the 1988 experience wasn't nearly so bad. However, you always strike some sight which astounds or shocks you.

For a country of so many millions, I guess death through bizarre incidents becomes rather commonplace in India. We learned of two Indian airlines Boeings which had gone down, killing 130 people. One of the planes, which was supposed to have an engine overhaul after 3150 flying hours, had clocked an estimated 51,000 hours when it went down. With the amount of flying we were to do on tour, we were naturally a little anxious. Suddenly the prospect of train travel looked more appealing — until we inspected sleeping facilities on overnight trains; they were about third class by British Rail standards. We would continue to fly instead.

The special secret on Asian tours is obviously to watch what you drink and eat; in more recent years, New Zealand teams have toured that part of the world armed with all sorts of literature, the most priceless being "Doc's Do's And Don'ts." It came courtesy of Dr Richard Edmond, who became a specialist on Asian tours after accompanying New Zealand teams as the official doctor (somehow, the New Zealand Cricket Council decided it didn't need both a physiotherapist and a doctor for the 1988 tour, so we had only a physio). There was one golden rule: If it is not steaming hot — forget it!

There are basic rules for hotels and restaurants:

1. Eat only food that has obviously just been cooked (still steaming).
2. Choose mainly western-style food until your stomach becomes accustomed to local cooking oils, etc.
3. Never eat salads or uncooked foods.
4. Make sure your eating utensils are clean and dry.
5. Drink only fluid that is known to be safe (tea, coffee, bottled water). Remember fruit drinks may be diluted with unsterilised water.

And so it goes on. There are problems wherever you go. Never drink the water, unless it's been boiled. No ice cream. No ice in your drinks. Wash your teeth in sterilised water. And perhaps the trickiest of all is attending after-match functions.

The Doc said: "This is the most difficult time demanding the utmost diplomacy as your hosts will insist you partake of some local delicacy. Unless it is piping hot, you must refuse politely, exuding your natural charm, adding a touch of humour so your hosts will not be offended. If you make a mistake, tell me! I have tablets you can take to prevent you getting gastro-enteritis or dysentery." On the 1988 tour of India, we were taking all sorts of pills. On a good day we'd have four pills to swallow — on a bad day it was 12 to survive!

The Doc also makes a note about a little alcoholic assistance: "Even though you may not be a whisky drinker it is well worth taking a bottle

Karen and I have hardly had a 'normal' marriage throughout my cricketing years even on tour there's seldom time to catch up and relax . . . as we did at the pleasant Indian holiday resort, Goa, during New Zealand's tour of India in late 1988.

All-Sport, Simon Bruty

Touring can be a laborious business, with the accent on constant travel from venue to venue. But there are benefits, especially when tours take you to exotic spots like Goa in India; for a few days I might have been Richard Hadlee, tourist, rather than touring cricketer.

All-Sport, Simon Bruty

I wonder whether we tried the standard test before this meal in India in 1988 . . .
"If it's not steaming hot — forget it!"   R.J. Hadlee Collection

of Scotch and having a nip if there is any doubt at all about any food you
have eaten."

Armed with so much information about eating and drinking habits,
you might find a way to enjoy parts of a tour of India.

What really strikes home, of course, is the poverty. Just travelling
from hotels to grounds you get some idea of the deprived life so many
people lead. Certainly, there were plush hotels and the evidence of people
who lived very well, but the other side left an indelible impression. The
streets alone told a story — heavily crowded with all sorts of vehicles and
people, animals having the freedom of the streets. Often it was just total
mayhem to me. So much noise, horns hooting, so much traffic. On the
streetwalks, people were trying to make a living while others just lay in
the streets sleeping. Beggars would sometimes wander on to the streets
asking for money, many of them having limbs missing. There were utterly
overcrowded houses, the stench of stagnant water and sewage. What
squalor. But there wasn't anything we could do about it except feel
sadness for the people. Maybe they know no other way of life, but I often
wonder why people are brought into this world to be destined for poverty
and a short life span.

One aspect which did impress me on my second tour to India was the
security. We had police escorts to and from grounds and armed guards
and soldiers patrolling our hotels as well. But security at airports had gone
to the extreme. I can accept standard screening and checking of luggage
for bombs and weapons; there are so many crazed terrorists in the world
today. But Tony Blain, Ken Rutherford and I were astonished when we
were asked to remove the batteries from our radio cassettes at Delhi
airport for a local flight. The batteries were put in a plastic bag, stored
in the hold of the plane and returned to us when we arrived in Bangalore!
Does security really have to go that far for an international cricket team?
Surely commonsense could prevail.

As Doc Edmond stresses, it's difficult, if not impossible, to avoid illness at some time in India but it was strange that in idyllic surroundings in Bangalore, 12 of us were affected by a virus right in the middle of the first test. It was a virus which made you shiver, vomit, dry-retch and brought on the worst diarrhoea imaginable. Not even cornflour would have thickened it! It saps all your strength and, for me, it brought back all the terrible memories of the 1976 tour.

It hit the team with a vengeance, after I'd secured the world record and finished the Indian first innings with five wickets. We faced an enormous task just trying to reach 185 to avoid the follow-on but, with Chris Kuggeleijn and I the worst affected by the virus, the chances were even slimmer. We didn't even go to the ground on the third morning; we were just so ill we had to stay in our beds.

I watched on television as Ian Smith and Ewen Chatfield got us closer and closer to our target and then there was a call from Wrighty: "Can you get down here? There's a good chance of avoiding the follow-on."

I crawled out of bed, dizzily, and was picked up at the hotel. Somehow I got changed and padded up. I was in the toilet when I heard a roar. Smithy was out lbw to Kapil. There was another roar and Kuggs was out. I had no idea he'd gone first ball and that I was facing a hat trick. I knew we were close to avoiding the follow-on but I didn't know how many runs we needed.

I felt weak as I took my guard. I adopted a two-eyed stance to give me a better chance of maybe seeing the ball. Somehow I slashed and connected one from Kapil. It went for four and we were safe. It was only a matter of time before I was bowled but I was completely disorientated. I didn't know what was really going on.

That proved to be one of the most courageous days in New Zealand cricket. With the side wiped out by illness, we could barely find the numbers to put on the field when India batted again. We were down to only three bowlers — Chatfield, Braces and Evan Gray. We had five replacement fieldsmen, one of them Jeremy Coney who was in India doing commentary work for Radio New Zealand. Jerry said later: "I stood in slips and looked at the off-side field — and none of us were selected in the side." Apart from Coney himself, there was Ken Nicholson — in India covering the test for Television New Zealand — plus touring team members Tony Blain, Danny Morrison and Bert Vance. After India had quickly made 141 for one declared, Wrighty and Trevor Franklin batted out the rest of the day, putting on 70-plus in an unfinished opening stand. It was one of the finest days in extreme adversity.

And yet, despite everything that happened in Bangalore, I found the 1988 tour quite comfortable!

There was trouble of a totally different type in Sri Lanka on our 1986–87 tour. Before we left New Zealand, we were well aware of the conflict between the Tamils and Sinhalese and I was worried something extreme might happen. It did when, just after the drawn first test in Colombo, a bomb exploded in the city centre, killing more than 120 people. It happened at a bus station only about 600 metres from our hotel — it was now too close for comfort.

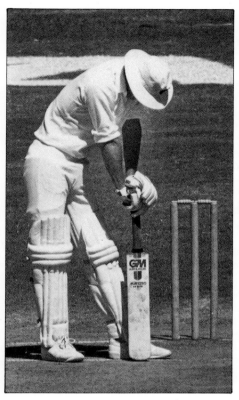

Bangalore, November, 1988 . . . I'd
felt a lot better than the day I went
out to bat to try and help us avoid
the follow-on in the first test against
India.
Above: I felt so weak and didn't
really know what was going on. I'd
been delirious only hours earlier.
Above right: India's Kapil Dev
suggested there is a funny side to
being struck down by the lurgi in
India. Really?
Right: Phew! Time for a rest as
Ewen Chatfield faces Arshad Ayub.
Somehow I'd struck a four by then
to take us past the follow-on.

J.G. Blackwell

There was no doubt these extremist groups had no regard for human life. Despite assurances to the contrary, we had to be at an even greater risk after this episode. Something like 500 people had been killed in the space of about a week. How could we live and continue to play cricket in such an environment? We were in the midst of a civil war.

We had several meetings and the consensus was the tour should be called off. One of the players' wives rang and said she didn't want to become a widow, and some of the Sri Lankan players also told us we should go home.

We had a special meeting with Gamini Dissanayake, a government official who was also president of Sri Lankan cricket's board of control. He made all manner of assurances that we were not in danger.

We realised that if we were to abort the tour, it would be a financial disaster for Sri Lankan cricket, and a sign that we had allowed terrorism to win. A secret ballot came out 10–7 in favour of abandoning the tour and so our manager, Ken Deas, informed the NZCC of our wishes. I didn't see that there was any other option. Player safety had to be paramount — and I didn't feel safe at all in Colombo after that bomb blast. Once again sport had suffered through political troubles.

That experience has, of course, been unique in my career thankfully. But I have encountered cranks and threats on occasions, as I did during the second test in Bombay in 1988. My phone rang in my hotel room at 4.30 a.m. It was the "Inspector of Police" calling. "I ask you get dressed and come to lobby. A car will pick you up and take you to station — there's a fire at your home in Christchurch."

I lay in bed for a few minutes and thought it was strange. If there was a problem at home, family or friends would contact Ken Deas (our manager) and he'd advise me. Half an hour passed and there wasn't a follow-up call. It was obviously a hoax.

I know it sounds melodramatic, but what if I had gone downstairs? Someone dressed up as a policeman may have been waiting for me. I could have been kidnapped or something like that. Crazy? Maybe, but you have to consider such options when you're in foreign countries. You can't be too careful.

I rang home at 8.00 that morning and everything was fine, as I suspected it would be. It so happened I finished with six for 49 in India's first innings that day — so interrupting my sleep had some sort of effect.

One of my most fascinating tours was our trip to Sharjah for the Austral-Asia Cup tournament in 1987–88. I'd missed New Zealand's first venture there in 1985–86 because of my benefit commitments with Notts. But the thought of playing cricket in the desert had some sort of attraction. Sharjah's one of seven city-states in the United Arab Emirates, and it has become quite well known now for this annual cricketing extravaganza. With all its Middle East trappings of desert, sand, Moslems, oil, no drinking and the whiff of the Iran-Iraq conflict out on the gulf, there's definitely a distinctive atmosphere about playing cricket there. We were well beaten in the grand final by India but our runners-up winnings of $US20,000 were not seen by the players. All our expenses and fees came out of the prizemoney, and it was also rumoured the NZCC received

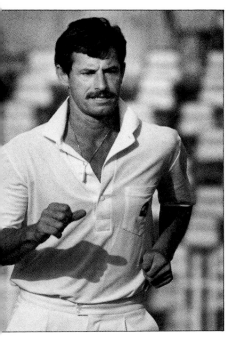

Touring in India . . .
Above: Energetic and keen.
Below: Tiredness is setting in.
Right: The face says it all — total exhaustion!

J.G. Blackwell

On the way to England with the New Zealand team in 1973, flanked by my brother Dayle, captain Bevan Congdon and respected cricket writer Dick Brittenden (left). There's no tour like one to England . . . it's the pure cricketing experience.

further payment as a tour guarantee. That annoyed the players, because we felt we should have been a little better rewarded.

The major bugbear about touring is, of course, the incessant travel and the constant waiting; you require special discipline and tolerance just to cope. In England, the mode of transport's normally a coach. But move to a vast country like Australia and there's nothing worse than the trekking backwards and forwards, especially during the Benson and Hedges World Series Cup competition. If you're not actually playing, you're forever at airports, in planes or waiting to check in or out of hotels. It's three days in one place, then three days in another . . . never time to settle. It asks too much of the players to be performing like robots. And, if you're on a losing run, then it becomes sheer misery.

When it comes to touring, England's the ultimate tour — or it used to be until I began my connection with Notts; then it no longer fell into the realm of being a true tour for me. I was stationed in England in any case, so tours there tended to become a diversion from my county commitments.

But, for sheer charm and the feeling of what cricket's all about, England's a marvellous country to trip around. From the grounds to the crowds it's all so civilised, so traditionally perfect. Because I became so familiar with the venues and cities, it became a little like playing in New Zealand for me, the difference being England oozes cricket in every sense. Everyone's so knowledgeable about the game and so appreciative of good play. There isn't a more satisfying touring experience.

And then there's Australia, a country which exudes sporting confidence, sometimes arrogance but still with an appeal of its own. Again it's all become a little humdrum for me because New Zealand has toured Australia so many times. I mean, I've made eight tours there! Any talk of Australia naturally brings me on to the topic of crowds . . .

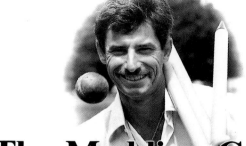

The Madding Crowd

January 12, 1988, dawned as an unexceptional day on cricket's increasingly tedious road show, otherwise known as the Benson and Hedges World Series Cup competition. It was the middle of the pyjama circus season; a few days earlier, we'd been in Adelaide playing Sri Lanka and this time it was still Sri Lanka, but the venue was Hobart.

We'd reached the stage as a team where the constant travel and play was wearing a little thin — and yet we all knew we had to perform. Much as players dislike the abbreviated version of the game, it has become cricket's life support system. The masses love it, that brings in the revenue and keeps us solvent.

If the one-day grind was becoming too much, then we also had other problems. With a string of players injured, we were down to a bare playing 11 for the game in Tasmania's capital and some of the players taking the field were carrying injuries themselves.

Apart from Canterbury and Nottinghamshire, Tasmania had also been a home base for me. I played for the Apple Island state in the Sheffield Shield competition in 1979–80, but returning to the place evoked mixed reactions because there was an element of the Tasmanian cricket public which believed — and still believes — I didn't earn my keep when I played there. That hurts me. It's a slur on my professionalism to suggest I failed to honour my commitment, and I'll always refute any inference that I let Tasmanian cricket down.

The game against Sri Lanka was scheduled for Bellerive Oval, a new venue and a compact, intimate ground. Tasmanian officials were hoping the exercise would strengthen their claims to have a test held at the ground some time soon.

The match itself was important if we were to keep a firm hold on second place behind Australia in the three-team competition. We needed a win but, on an awkward pitch, we were soon in strife at 70 for five, not a healthy time for me to join Tony Blain at the crease. At least there was time for me to settle in for a change, to build an innings rather than go in for a quick slog which is so often the case in these games. And, in time, the runs came — 85 for the sixth wicket — until I was out for 52, only my third half-century in one-dayers (all of them scored in Australia). The runs were vital. They gave us some sort of hope of escaping with a win, but there was something I found disturbing when I was out in the middle.

It didn't take me long to pick up one sign in the crowd, a banner which read: "Holiday Hadlee, back in town like 79–80". It was obviously intended as a poke at me about my efforts that season. There was another banner, too, but I didn't have to read it to learn what it said; the crowd, or at least a fair slice of it, let me know exactly what the message was: "Hadlee is a wanker!"

Perhaps I have thinner skin than some people. What I do know is that I was hurt about this one — the crowd didn't let up with its incessant chant. On reaching my 50, I deliberately gave the barrackers a gesture with my bat. It was probably the wrong thing to do because it only antagonised the crowd and goaded the oafs into more of the same. I could hear the crowd booing, cheering and chanting as I sought the sanctuary of the dressing room after being dismissed . . . but I still had one more obstacle — a spectator who came right up to me and booed me in the face. I shoved him, I'd had enough.

Our innings finished at 199 for seven and so Sri Lanka began its chase with a fair chance of success; again, I was the crowd's target when I bowled, or when I was in the field, especially in the deep. It was "Hadlee is a wanker" all afternoon, and it got me down. As our prospects deteriorated, Jeff Crowe brought me back early to bowl out my overs, in a last-ditch effort to make a breakthrough. As soon as I finished my 10th over, I walked off the field, after asking Chopper whether I could go. I didn't have an injury — I just wanted to get out of the atmosphere. It was a form of protest.

That's the way I remember the events of that depressing day at Bellerive Oval. In the minutes, hours, days and months after the match I tried to fathom why it happened — and I could never come up with any logical answer. I'd done nothing initially to bait the crowd; I'm not a demonstrative person who draws attention to himself on the field. I just try to do my job. But I was hounded that day.

I've always had a thing about crowds and the way they treat players. It's a two-edged sword, I know. As players, we need crowds to watch us; they pay to see us and be entertained. Players, I think, accept that responsibility but, in return, they also expect some respect. The invention of the one-day game, more than any other factor, has attracted a new element of support for the game. It's not always a pleasant experience

A cartoonist's impression of me after we'd beaten Australia in the 1985–86 test series in Australia. But Australian crowds don't see me quite the same way, not on the evidence I've seen.

Moa Collection

playing in front of one-day crowds because they're not as well educated about cricket as those you'd generally find at a test match. However, while such crowds may be short on etiquette they're big on creating atmosphere.

I will always maintain Australian crowds, as a rare sporting (or unsporting) breed, are the most unruly in the world, and events at Bellerive Oval merely reinforced my opinion.

The "wanker" chant and the boos and jeers, the so-called cricket supporter booing me in the face and other events left me totally disillusioned. Later I discovered that even in the members' area people were carrying on like oafs. One of these spectators suggested I was "a weak bastard" when I walked off the field. Even more disturbing was the sight of young kids — probably aged only five or six — who were shouting abuse, no doubt egged on by their parents. It's low when that happens. Is it necessary? There were personal attacks, too, with some people casting aspersions on my parentage. Some Tasmanian officials apologised to me about the crowd behaviour — which was decent of them — but the overriding memory was of Tasmanians letting themselves, and Australians in general, down.

I felt compelled to speak out. To have bitten my tongue and said nothing would have been the soft way out.

The seeds of discontent with certain sections of the Australian cricket public — and it's still a minority, admittedly —were sown during New Zealand's 1980–81 tour. There were two incidents, one in our match against a Victorian XI in Geelong, when I hit their opening batsman Peter Oxlade just above the eye with a rising delivery; and the other in Sydney during a one-day international. The Oxlade event had a sequel at the end of play when a young boy ran up to me and called me "a mongrel". I chased him, grabbing him and asked: "What did you call me?" "Nothing," he said. I repeated the question and this time got an answer: "A mongrel." "Why?" I ventured, and, with all the honesty in the world, he replied: "Because I don't like you." So I told him what the word mongrel meant, impressing on him that he'd probably have his face smashed in if he'd been 18 and used the word abusively to someone else. This lad was only 10!

The whole incident was blown up in newspapers the next day with reporters interviewing the boy. I was, of course, made to look a monster but my reaction was still one of concern that kids could behave like this.

There was another incident in one of our WSC matches against Australia at the Sydney Cricket Ground. Greg Chappell drove over mid-off and the ball was heading towards the boundary with me in pursuit. I was gaining on the ball and would have stopped it about five metres inside the boundary . . . only a youngster did the fielding for me, jumping the boundary fence, picking up the ball and returning it to the bowler's end. I knew the boy's actions would give the umpire no option but to signal a boundary when I had every chance of restricting it to three; you fight to save every single run in one-dayers because they can be absolutely crucial in the final analysis. My next move was, I concede, somewhat foolish, but anger took over. I lined the lad up, ran straight at him, and pushed him back against and then over the fence. A bigger bloke also came on to the field of play and took a swipe at me with a beer bottle.

There was a follow-up in the newspapers that claimed I could be up on an assault charge for my actions. Happily, common sense took over with both parties apologising to each for their actions.

Ever since that tour, I've been on a tightrope with the Australian crowds. It might be deemed a love-hate feeling; former Australian captain Greg Chappell once told me I should view it all as a compliment. The crowds, he said, love to hate me because I'm a threat to Australia's chances. After so many run-ins — including missiles hurled at me — I'd suggest there's no love in the relationship at all.

By berating the Bellerive Oval crowd in Hobart, I invoked an ever-growing monster for the rest of the tour. I talked of the need for stricter crowd control and recommended police or ground authorities should move to eject offensive spectators and to remove distasteful banners. Some Australians, including one or two in the media, misread or deliberately misinterpreted my suggestions. David Hickie, writing in the *Sun-Herald*, branded me "one of the sporting world's great prima donnas" over my criticism of the Tasmanians. He construed my suggestions as advocating silent crowds. He went on in his article: "Anyone seriously suggesting that Aussie crowds ought not be allowed to cheer and boo, chant and jeer and hiss — and as loudly as they like to do it — is in great danger of being branded a thin-skinned wimp. As for suggestions which amount to totalitarian crowd control, this isn't Nazi Germany yet, mate. Is Hadlee seriously suggesting sporting spectators ought no longer be allowed to cheer for their heroes or to boo their villains? This is still a free country, not a police state, isn't it?"

We moved on to Brisbane after the Hobart experience and, naturally enough, the abuse flowed again when we played Australia before a full house of 22,000. The 'Gabba ground is one for which I have a soft spot; remember, it's there I took nine for 52 in Australia's first innings — and 15 wickets in the match — when we won the first test in 1985–86. This match was, almost certainly, my last appearance in Brisbane but I won't remember it as a fond farewell . . . the abuse and the "wanker" call rolled freely. Not just from the outer either, where you'd expect it to come from, but from the main stands and members' areas. I was disappointed that members would stoop so low.

Our captain, Jeff Crowe, had his say about the crowds after the match: "It's sad that everywhere we go, everyone is on the same thing. They love to hate Richard. They know he's a special cricketer, that he's a threat to Australia. But what they say and do is not necessary. No one likes being abused in front of a crowd of 22,000 people. I know it's all part of the razzamatazz in one-day cricket but I don't enjoy it when it happens."

The Hadlee abuse affair even went through official channels with the New Zealand team's manager Alby Duckmanton lodging a complaint with the Australian Cricket Board. Alby was so incensed he felt he had to make a stand: "We're prepared to try and protect our players from organised character assassination," said Duckmanton. "While there's not a lot we can do about it, we can let the ACB know we're not happy. I don't think

Above: There's that word, minus a couple of letters, which caused me so much despair in Australia in 1987–88. It all started in Hobart one January day, a day when a cricket tour turned nasty for me. It never really recovered. R.J. Hadlee Collection

Left: Now, Bob, there's something awfully wrong with the Australian education system when it breeds so many cricket yobbos! That's how I felt after so much antagonism from crowds on the 1987–88 Australian tour. I even challenged Prime Minister Bob Hawke to comment on the issue. R.J. Hadlee Collection

any one player should have to put up with the abuse Hadlee is receiving."

A couple of days later in Sydney, I was on television news programmes challenging Australian Prime Minister Bob Hawke to join the feud, saying: "I just wonder what your Prime Minister thinks about the crowd abuse. I wonder whether he's very proud of the Australian spectators during this (WSC) series. It's a gladiator sport out there. It's like being thrown into the lion's den, and we're on a hiding to nothing. The crowd have got the thumbs down situation — kill, kill, destroy."

That outburst came at a function designed to launch a cricket video I wanted to promote in Australia but the crowd issue, being the business it was at the time, tended to overtake the video promotion. We still had another match — against Australia — to go in the preliminary phase of the WSC competition and my comments, coming on the eve of the Sydney Cricket Ground clash, were scarcely going to enamour me to Australian cricket fans. I still wanted to play in the match but the tour selectors found two reasons to omit me . . . firstly, they wanted to give me a rest before the finals against Australia (this particular match had no bearing on the competition placings) and they seemed keen to avoid another scene which would foster the anti-Hadlee feeling. I suppose my non-selection for the match was something of a tactical withdrawal; as it happened, there was a sell-out crowd for the game and I understand there were plenty of banners which again made it clear what spectators thought of me. I didn't witness them myself. In fact, I didn't go near the ground for the day-night encounter, opting instead to spend much of the day sunning myself on Bondi Beach.

Melbourne was waiting for the first of the WSC finals and I fully expected a reception and a half. The city was full of Hadlee hype, you could say. There were anti-Kiwi jokes on the radio stations and a song was played on one station carrying the title "Don't You Hate That Hadlee" (based on the song put out by the American group The Doors called "Don't You Love Her Madly"). Once again, it was hardly complimentary stuff. As it happened, the Melbourne Cricket Ground wasn't too full at all, certainly not for the first two hours of the match. The crowd reaction was, as a result, slightly muted initially although the Bay 13 people could never be anything less than vocal. We batted first and, when I came out to bat, there was some hooting and carrying on with the Bay 13 lot starting up an English-soccer-style rendition of the well-worn "wanker" line. My public annoyance had perpetuated the whole issue yet I didn't receive the sort of prolonged and frenetic barrage I had anticipated, which was some relief. The signs of ill will were still there in the number of banners around the place — "Hadlee spits the dummy", "Hadlee's worse than a whingeing Pom", "Hadlee's ego — even bigger than Ken Rutherford's nose", and "Even six year olds get on top of Hadlee".

The further the match went — and as we fielded second —the more the vocal aggro grew. I couldn't be thrilled about it but, when Australia was chasing victory, I took the chance to field at third-man in front of the infamous Bay 13 mob. That might have seemed foolish but I wanted to go some way to trying to mend bridges and it was heartening to receive a warm reaction.

The second final, and ultimately deciding match in the series, was even quieter. Again the crowd wasn't overly large —only 29,000 were in the Sydney Cricket Ground for the Sunday match — and it wasn't as overtly abusive as at Hobart and Brisbane. I noted with interest, though, that one offensive sign was removed by ground authorities, one which read: "Paddles the Prick".

Maybe that background goes some way to explaining my mild aversion to Australian crowds. The Aussie fans haven't provided much in the way of humour — I appreciate a little fun from spectators when it's in reasonable taste. I would never deny paying customers their right to enjoy themselves because, as I've said, we are there as entertainers and must be expected to reciprocate in some fashion. The line, however, has to be drawn on the question of decency and that's an area where too many self-claimed cricket followers are ignorant.

I wasn't totally disillusioned with all Australian cricket supporters in the summer of '87–88; it would be very unfair of me to even suggest that. I received some amazing feedback from Australians who were obviously aggrieved that fellow countrymen could behave in such a crude manner. Once I made my stand, letters of support flowed in, restoring my faith that the minority — although a sizable one in Australia — was destroying it for the masses.

The letters said it all for me. One 82-year-old gentleman from New South Wales wrote to our manager:

> "I deplore the unjust and cowardly treatment of Richard Hadlee by some of the Australian spectators. I am ashamed to be an Australian. I cannot understand the reason for the crowds' antipathy towards Richard. Is it jealousy? Is it warped and jaundiced nationalism? Whatever the reason, nothing excuses it and the saddest aspect has been the reported spitefulness of juveniles."

Other letters were more colloquial and to the point:

> "There is only one thing wrong with you — you're not Australian. Wish you were. Stuff the morons. You're a gentleman, just keep bowling them over."

At the time, I also welcomed the fantastic back-up from New Zealanders who posted, faxed or telexed messages of support. It's at times like those that you can never have enough of that sort of encouragement. I gained solace, too, from comments by an Australian psychiatrist who offered his thoughts on why so many Australians had taken a dislike to me.

Dr Bill Wilkie argued it wasn't a straightforward case of bad manners, poor sportsmanship or a strange obsession to be seen and heard on television. No, he put it down to what he called a case of "cultural throwback". He claimed there was "a deep underlying streak of cruelty and intolerance" which had been developing since the first convict ships berthed in Botany Bay! He said Kiwis don't put each other down in the

A lone New Zealand flag in a massive crowd of 71,000 for the World Series Cup final against Australia at the Melbourne Cricket Ground in 1982–83. How I love Australian crowds!

P.G. Bush

way Australians do, that the Australian sense of humour is cruel to those who don't fit in with the group.

That was illustrated during the Benson and Hedges WSC tournament in 1982–83 when the *Melbourne Age* published a list of guidelines for spectators:

1. Never applaud a boundary by an English or New Zealand batsman.

2. Try to be in the toilets or at a snack bar when they score a century.

3. Cheer loudly when an Australian fieldsman cuts off a boundary; hiss when the opposition do likewise.

4. When Australia is in the field, vociferously support all appeals for lbws and catches. Boo the umpire if they are rejected.

5. Reverse procedure of No. 4 when Australia is batting.

6. Jeer all opposing batsmen when they enter the arena, especially the captains, Bob Willis and Geoff Howarth.

7. Constantly refer to England all rounder Ian Botham's physical condition.

8. Destroy all foreign flags (Warning: Don't confuse the Australian flag with the New Zealand one, which is similar. Interfering with the former is an act of vandalism — and the latter is an act of patriotism).

Ted Dexter, the former England captain, once said: "Australians can, and do quite readily and often in my experience, throw off all their 180 years of civilised nationhood; they gaily revive every prejudice they ever knew, whether to do with accent, class consciousness or even the convict complex, and sally forth into battle with dedication which would not disgrace the most committed of the world's political agitators."

One of England's finest fast bowlers, John Snow, observed: "The Melbournians are like piranha fish when it comes to sport. They will devour everything that will satisfy their appetite for competition." Geoff Boycott maintains "they need to have a few of the subtleties of the game spelt out to them". So I'm not alone in having problems and negative thoughts about the "yobbo", the minority Australian spectator.

Sometimes Australian humour does hit the spot, though. After I had questioned the Australian education system, one of the banners during the first WSC final at the MCG read: "Hey, Mr Hadlee! Wots wong wiv our edukation sistom." I enjoy a line like that because it shows some initiative.

There have been any number of other comments I've seen the funny side of over the years, too . . . "Richard Hadlee is called a big 'thinker' only by those that lisp", "Hadlee never gets lost because everyone tells him where to go", and "Hadlee is the only batsman to dent his box from the inside".

When the Central Districts Cricket Association put on a benefit match for me in 1985-86, I had to pick a winner in a banner-of-the-day competition. The match coincided with the controversy over my decision to keep the Alfa Romeo car I'd won as the Benson and Hedges International Cricketer of the Year in Australia — and the banner I selected was a play on the whole affair. The guys who put it together had entered an old model car, which they had drawn lines all over and captioned: "This piece is for Coney", "This piece is for Wright" and so on. I could appreciate that — and there'd be something wrong with me if I couldn't.

I revel in the colour and atmosphere now so evident in cricket crowds, and I'll always cherish the day in February 1977 when the Eden Park terraces invented the "Had-lee! Had-lee!" chant to the deafening accompaniment of clattering beer cans. I'll never know why the revolution happened that day — and that's what it was, a revolution. But, from that day on, there was always a thrill about playing at Eden Park; while it has never been an easy pitch for me to bowl on, the reception from the crowd has always been astounding. I'd come on to bowl and the cans would fire up, the chant would reach sound barrier levels (seemingly). And when I stepped on to the ground to bat, appearing out of the players' tunnel, there was a wave-like roar which bellowed forth from the terraces end, the infamous terraces. As a player, I enjoyed the atmosphere and thrived on it; it hasn't, in later years, been anything like as passionate with the old chant effectively a thing of the past. Of course, the introduction of plastic

Cricket West Indian-style . . .
Above: They breed them big in the Caribbean, from the likes of Garner and Ambrose . . . to their covers. Some 40-odd people were needed to remove the monster covers after a downpour during the fourth test at Kingston's Sabina Park in 1984–85. Soon after, Joel Garner and company made life hell for the New Zealand batsmen in one of the ugliest passages of play I've seen, and Jeremy Coney had his arm broken.

Below: On the field, the 1984–85 West Indian tour was a test of survival for the New Zealand players — but off it, West Indian cricket was, as ever, totally laid back, right down to spectators using nature's grandstands to watch the action.

J.G. Blackwell

Mixing it with Australia . . .
Left: The limited overs batsman; failing to catch up with the legside delivery against Australia in the 1980–81 Benson and Hedges World Series Cup competition. Rod Marsh is the wicketkeeper (and both of us might be accused of having our eyes closed!).

Moa Collection

Below: Australian captain Allan Border tries to look disinterested, I'm indignant about the leg before appeal — and Fred Goodall's raised left finger tells the story of my 300th test wicket, taken at Wellington's Basin Reserve in 1985–86.

P.G. Bush

beer cups hardly helped the cause! However, the afternoon of 26 February, 1977, will always be remembered for the profound effect it had on me, and on New Zealand cricket as a whole.

When Australia's first innings closed at 377, I had the unhealthy figures of two for 147 from 28 overs, but that return told nothing of the drama, passion, excitement and emotion which flowed earlier. Late on the second day, something strange happened. There was an unmistakable buzz in the crowd which just built up and up to an enormous crescendo. The noise mesmerised me and inspired me. Swept along by the emotion-charged atmosphere, I had Rod Marsh out leg-before in the first over of a new spell and somehow failed to remove Gary Gilmour in the same over. Soon after he was dropped. I was functioning at optimum, bowling as fast as I humanly could as I responded — recklessly — to the crowd's urgings and with the adrenalin pouring through my body. Powerless to hold back and conserve energy, I was spent after the most astonishing four-over spell in my career. But that single phase of play meant so much to the game in New Zealand, and to me personally.

The crowd's avid support was a revelation and, while it came at an admittedly sympathetic venue (for New Zealanders), it still sums up some of the differences between New Zealand and Australian crowds. I'm not

Eden Park crowds . . . they've had a big influence on me since inventing the 'Had-lee, Had-lee' chant in the summer of 1976–77. Another fabulous experience in Auckland was the Rothmans Cup match against Australia in 1981–82 when 43,000 spectators crammed the ground for the chance to roast Greg Chappell for his underarm deed of a year earlier.   J.G. Blackwell

about to cast Kiwi spectators as lilywhites; they can be as ill behaved and uncouth as some Australians. How else can you explain the disgusting act when someone hurled a toilet seat on to the field during the first test between New Zealand and Australia in Wellington in 1985–86? There have been instances of loutish behaviour, including the senseless streaker act in the 1976–77 Eden Park clash against Australia — the same day the crowd revolution happened — when Greg Chappell grabbed the offender and thrashed him on the posterior with his bat. Chappell was so worked up he lost his wicket when play resumed after that incident — his concentration had been badly affected.

But while New Zealand crowds aren't blameless, the instances of trouble are more isolated. It's just unfortunate some of the less savoury aspects of Australian behaviour rub off on to Kiwis from time to time.

I've played in front of crowds in all of the world's major cricketing nations and, while Australian spectators are the most agitated and volatile, English crowds are certainly the most appreciative. When you walk on to the field in England, there's a ripple of applause. There are cheers and roars of approval at times to suit, or there are sympathetic groans if you're dismissed or something goes against you. There's still patriotic fervour when England are playing, but the English spectators aren't so narrow minded that they won't, or don't, acknowledge quality play from the opposition.

I've struck very few worries with the yobbo element in English crowds, although the racial issue poses one worrying factor for officials, especially when Pakistan is playing in England.

That happened in 1987 when there were ugly scenes during a one-day international at Edgbaston, scenes usually confined to the hooligan brigade which disrupts so many soccer matches in England. It wasn't pretty when one spectator had his throat cut by a broken bottle. All sorts of missiles were thrown on to the field, several players were very lucky not to be injured and spectators invaded the ground. It was as close to a riot as there's ever been at a cricket match in England; what was most worrying was that the trouble flared through racial tensions in the Birmingham crowd. What emerged from the day of shame was a 12-point plan designed to stem any hint of trouble in the future but, like many other people connected with English cricket, I would suspect this was very much a one-off event. Cricket crowds in England aren't anything like their soccer counterparts, and thank God for that!

Two visits to Sri Lanka soon established crowds on the Sacred Island as similar to those in Pakistan or India — vociferous and unashamedly parochial. On New Zealand's first tour there in 1983–84, spectators became wildly excited when a Sri Lankan bowler took a wicket while fire crackers would greet a local batsman when he scored some runs. The contrast when we did anything was quite the opposite. Bubbling under the surface was an excitability which threatened to get out of hand, and it did after the first test in Kandy. The fans objected to me bowling short-pitched deliveries at the gun-shy Sri Lankan batsmen but, when the captain, Duleep Mendis, failed in both innings and Sri Lanka lost the match by 165 runs, the crowd's resentment changed tack. Riot police armed with tear gas were brought in to quell a post-match uprising when bricks and stones were thrown; both teams needed police escorts and the after-match presentations were, wisely, cancelled. I know some of the Sri Lankan players feared for their safety after losing the test.

The key to much of the unrest is ethnic and religious hostility, which became very obvious when New Zealand toured Sri Lanka again in 1986–87.

In India and Pakistan, cricket supporters are fanatical. They love their cricket and they worship their heroes like Kapil Dev, Imran Khan, Javed Miandad and company; they're just as passionate about overseas stars when they tour. When I first toured that part of the world in 1976, it was everything I expected, and a bit more. The din created by the spectators, especially in India, was so loud it was almost impossible to concentrate.

They have a few props in the sub-continent, articles which come in useful for throwing on to the field, presumably aimed at fieldsmen who might be standing near the boundary. Fire crackers are let off, mirrors are shone in opposition players' eyes, there's non-stop whistling and anything from fruit to a transistor radio are used as projectiles. Transistor radio? Well, one was hurled at me — or in my direction — on the 1976 tour. I couldn't quite figure out whether it was tossed as a sign of annoyance with me or with the radio commentary!

When I was back in India in late 1988 it seemed the Indians had awaited my arrival with anticipation and joy. I had received so many letters of disappointment and regret that I wouldn't play there again and, on arrival and throughout the 1988 tour, I was treated with the utmost respect and courtesy. They enjoyed my skills on the field and were openly appreciative, not to mention flattering, with their praise. Everywhere I went, Indian fans would surround me, or wait for me to leave the dressing room and get on to the bus; they would hang around my hotel room, knock on the door or point and talk and smile. They all seemed to have cameras and used the classic line: "Just one more photo" or "Just one more autograph", with me knowing full well the same lines would be repeated hundreds of times. But there was no mistake they were genuine cricket lovers; they idolised me as much as their own players and some were keen to see me outdo and destroy their own team. It was all quite weird in a way.

West Indian crowds probably fall somewhere between the rest of the world. Caribbean cricket followers certainly know their cricket, which gives them a touch of the English approach. But, while they're learned, they're also enormously exuberant and flamboyant; a cricket match of some importance isn't complete without carnival-like noise and carrying-on. In that respect, they follow the Indian, Pakistani and Sri Lankan penchant for giving a cricketing occasion ample volume. And they also abuse the players, which adds a bit of the Australian and New Zealand supporter to the mix (although they tend to be reasonably witty with it).

It's an engrossing experience playing cricket in front of a West Indian crowd. There's just so much going on. People are perched anywhere and everywhere; I remember seeing photographs of spectators precariously sitting in trees — and I saw that for myself when New Zealand toured the Caribbean in 1984–85. Steel bands play, people dance, people drink — and drink some more — and then there's the cricket. It's like a celebration for them. So many people in that part of the world are struggling to live, either existing in poverty or very close to it. Cricket is a release, and a relief, for them. It's something which makes life worthwhile.

But, like the crowds in the sub-continent, you're never too comfortable. The situation tends to feel like an explosion waiting to happen. One bad umpiring decision (bad, in the sense it goes against the home side) can spark mayhem and there's often trouble among the spectators.

Abusive spectators and violence — so much of it triggered by alcohol — are two areas of concern in crowd behaviour but there's one other, which is peculiar to New Zealand, which also worries me. It's a custom in our country to let the public wander on to the ground before and after play in any match, as well as during the lunch and tea breaks. While it's a nice tradition — nice for the public, that is, who can play their own games of cricket — it's simply not right. It doesn't happen anywhere else in the world; go to Lord's, the Melbourne Cricket Ground, Eden Gardens or wherever and the field of play is forbidden territory for the public. But, come to New Zealand, and chances are the outfield is covered with spectators during breaks in play. Then, at the end of the day, kids pour on to the ground in their hundreds, race across the ground — and across the pitch all too often — to chase autographs. They shouldn't be allowed anywhere near the pitch.

New Zealand has some strange habits, too, about the use of practice pitches. They're prepared especially for the players and yet, in the course of a test match, you find any and everybody batting and bowling on them while the action's going on in the middle.

Cricket needs spectators as does any sport — and the fans want to watch top-level cricket — but it doesn't mean they should run the show. It all comes back to finding the balance between what's fair for the players, and right for the spectators.

C·H·A·P·T·E·R   E·L·E·V·E·N

Turf and Culture

Every sport has its Mecca. In tennis, it's Wimbledon. For soccer, it's Wembley. Golf's is St Andrews or Augusta. And cricket's shrine is unquestionably that venerable ground in London known as Lord's.

I suppose people with a minimal interest in sport might ask why sports grounds or venues take on such divine qualities in some people's eyes. But people who play, or live for, a certain sport will always have a fascination with such places. Anyone who follows Liverpool or Manchester United will have an affinity with Anfield or Old Trafford or, if you're a Nottingham Forest diehard like me, it will be the City Ground.

My sporting interests range far and wide so I derive some indefinable thrill from seeing a rugby union international at Lancaster Park in Christchurch, or Eden Park in Auckland. I'll take in most sports and enjoy the experience of being there and watching it happen in front of me.

An international cricket career stretching back to 1971–72 has made me something of a cricket ground connoisseur. I've seen all sorts; some have pleased, some have excited, some have inspired and some have been downright depressing. And, because I've had the privilege of playing at so many of the world's greatest cricket stadiums, I have developed a feel for some of them. I wouldn't go quite as far as saying grounds have souls, that I experience some kind of spiritual association, but there are venues which do things to me.

Some grounds spark positive vibes. Like Trent Bridge in Nottingham, my other home track, Lancaster Park, the 'Gabba in Brisbane or the WACA Ground in Perth. I look forward to playing at those venues because

I know the pitch ought to assist me at any one of them. That state of mind, the thought of playing there, creates an air of expectancy, which is good for my confidence. Others like the Melbourne Cricket Ground, the Sydney Cricket Ground, Lord's and the Adelaide Oval trigger me because of the venues they are — either steeped in tradition or picturesque, or a combination of both; or I think about the superb facilities they offer the players.

Still others are instant turn-offs. Dunedin's Carisbrook has given me a decent share of test wickets but the place does nothing for me. It's so strange to see an international venue with sawdust underneath the ancient stand and its spartan dressing rooms which, for a time, included a broken mirror in the room the New Zealand team used. We were back at Carisbrook last season for the aborted test against Pakistan — and the sawdust was still there, but almost out of sight. Some carpet appeared in strategic positions for the television presenters. There have been some improvements but it's still an archaic-looking ground, and even more depressing when rain stops play.

Thoughts of my one and only tour to Pakistan rekindle memories — or nightmares — about Peshawar and ants in the dressing room, crawling all over the floor; the room was so tiny we had to stack our coffins on top of each other. There's the old Basin Reserve which was a lack-lustre ground in every sense, except for the pitch which always used to suit the quicks (but no longer does). Then there are other venues — Eden Park, Edgbaston, the new Basin among them — which psyche you out a little because they're so difficult to bowl on — low and slow in pace and bounce. And, yet, there have been a few minor successes.

A ground plays an important part in my mental preparation for a match as I look forward to playing on some while I'm less enthusiastic about others.

I love playing in England and there's no better ground than Lord's. The walk from the dressing room, through the Long Room and on to the ground is an experience in itself. All the old trophies, the photographs, bronze busts and, of course, The Ashes . . . it's just so special to soak up everything Lord's stands for in terms of history and tradition. You're struck by the sight of members wearing the gaudy "bacon and egg" tie. A lot of them sit in their chairs almost half asleep, possibly oblivious to what's happening in the game half the time. It's such a different atmosphere, so olde worlde, but it's always a great occasion to play there in any sort of match, even a county game when the crowds aren't there to add that extra dimension.

Lord's has lost some of its charm, sadly, through the construction of a modern grandstand. It contrasts so starkly with the traditional buildings which give the venue its real character; but Lord's still has its infamous slope. The ground falls away about nine feet from one side to the other, which means the ball will either go up the hill or slope, or down it, depending which end you're bowling from. For the batsmen, picking the line can therefore be rather tricky. I tended to bowl from the Nursery End in my earlier years so my deliveries would go down the hill and away from the right handers. In fact, the ball would do too much and the batsmen could spend all day letting me go, so I switched to the Pavilion End where

Lord's — mecca for any cricket follower with a Royal touch. The New Zealand and England teams are introduced to the Queen during the first test of the 1986 series, captain Jeremy Coney introducing Her Majesty to me. It's yet another of the thrills which goes with playing cricket at Lord's. R.J. Hadlee Collection

the odd delivery might come down the slope — or into the right hander — but the most dangerous ball was the one which held up or possibly moved away up the hill.

I remember how I erred in the third test against England in 1983, when I operated from the Nursery End for the first day and got it totally wrong. I took only one wicket for 70-odd runs off 20 overs. The next day, I changed ends and took four for 19 to finish the England first innings with five for 93!

Lord's has been a profitable ground for me. I've played three tests there for a return of 22 wickets at 18.54, certainly ranking it as one of my most successful venues. In each test I managed a five-wicket bag in the first innings — five for 84 in 1978, five for 93 in 1983 and six for 80 in 1986. I also made my highest first-class score — 210 not out — against Middlesex at Lord's, in 1984. I savoured the marvellous occasion of playing in the Bicentennial test there in 1987 plus three one-day finals for Nottinghamshire (for one win). Lord's, then, has a bit of everything for me — it has history and it's also been kind to me.

Trent Bridge figures prominently simply because it was home for the 10 years I played for Notts. When I first arrived there in 1978, the pitch was a featherbed, white in colour and very difficult to bowl on but, around 1980–81, we began to change the wicket block, producing result pitches. Our groundsman, Ron Allsopp, would leave grass on it and I took a lot of wickets at Trent Bridge; 1984 being a case in point when, in completing the double of 1000 runs and 100 wickets, I captured 74 of my 117 county wickets in 12 matches played at Trent Bridge.

One of the drawbacks in English cricket is the old-school attitude. It's still very much in evidence at Lord's where the "males only" policy stands. This was a major obstacle for Notts because our physiotherapist was a woman, Sheila Ball. An application was made for her to be in our official party for one of our one-day final appearances at Lord's, but the toffs wouldn't have that; only after a great fuss did they reluctantly give permission for Sheila to be part of our squad. The chance was one she made the most of! She changed in our dressing room — stripping down to her bra and panties right beside me — put on her track suit, walked down the stairs, through the Long Room, on to the ground and over to the Nursery End for our warm-ups. You can just imagine the reaction from the old dodderers to such boldness: "What's going on here? No ladies allowed!" Shelia cared not. She went over the top, perhaps in defiance, or ignorance, of the attitude adopted at Lord's about the fairer sex.

When I consider Australian grounds, I feel a bit sad about the Sydney Cricket Ground. Like Lord's, it has lost much of its character through the rush of modern development. The famous hill barely exists now and the new stands don't sit comfortably with me. The only traditional touches left are the old members' stand and the old scoreboard, now an historic building. The SCG has become very much an American arena, dominated by an electronic scoreboard with its instant replays. The pitch has also become a problem, suiting the spinners rather too much. There have been a lot of results in tests there recently but I wouldn't say it's anything like an ideal cricket pitch anymore.

The Melbourne Cricket Ground's a fabulous place to play at, as long as there's a decent crowd in. When there're 70,000 plus, the atmosphere is positively unreal and, of course, there's always the lot in Bay 13 who are an experience on their own.

For obvious reasons, I'm especially fond of the 'Gabba in Brisbane, the scene of my best bowling performance in test cricket in the 1985–86 series. In three tests, I've taken 21 wickets at 16.33. It's a ground with a different appeal, encircled by a dog track, gardens and its own mini hill.

While I've enjoyed significant success in my only two tests in Sydney — 13 wickets at 13.23 — the other productive Australian ground for me has been the WACA Ground in Perth, a venue famous for its bouncy and fast pitch. It wasn't true to its traditional character when we played Australia in the third test there in 1985-86 — it had just been revamped and renovated —but two tests there have reaped 18 wickets (including three bags of five) at 14.55. I can't complain.

The Adelaide Oval's one of the most unforgiving pitches to bowl on but I'd unquestionably rank it among the best in the world for other reasons. There's no more picturesque test venue; it's in a superb setting and it's marvellously appointed. The general facilities are on another plane from most other grounds, too, with the one debit — apart from a pitch which is too good — being the location of the dressing rooms and the players' viewing areas. Instead of looking down the pitch, you're side on which is far from ideal; you seem to spend most of the time craning your neck at right angles to watch the television to obtain a fair indication of what's happening. But the Adelaide Oval remains one of the few grounds in the world which is unspoiled by the advance of time. The old stands and scoreboard have been wonderfully preserved, there's an appealing grass bank area . . . as a venue it's aesthetically appealing. And, while the pitch can be a brute for bowlers, it's by no means impossible to succeed on. The second Australia-New Zealand test in 1987–88 became a real bore — with Andrew Jones making 150 and Martin Crowe 137 while Allan Border made his best test score of 205 — because there was never any likelihood of a result. Yet I had one of my more satisfying bowling returns, taking five for 68 from 42 overs on a pitch which seemingly legislated against quicker bowlers. As a bowler, I prefer my wickets to come a little easier than they do on surfaces like the Adelaide one, but you can't help but enjoy the moment when hard work in unyielding conditions (both the pitch and the searing heat) nets results.

I dislike one-day cricket but, ironically, two of the more memorable limited-overs internationals I've played were at Adelaide. The 1982–83 clash against England will go down as one of the most unforgettable one-dayers, the day we were chasing a winning target of 297 and were looking in bad shape at 166 for five. In a remarkable match we went on to win. Only two days later we had another excellent contest at the Adelaide Oval when, in suffocating heat, Glenn Turner batted himself to exhaustion in making 84 to help us to 200 for nine; then we restricted Australia to 153 to complete a marvellous sweep in that summer's Benson and Hedges

The Melbourne Cricket Ground from the outside, and showing the signs of something else Kerry Packer did for cricket — the introduction of lights and the novelty of day-night matches. It's one of the great grounds to play at, more so when there's a big crowd in to fill out the concrete jungle. J.G. Blackwell

series. I suppose it's pertinent, too, that my next best one-day score was also made in Adelaide, 72 against India in 1985–86, and there have been a few useful bowling returns as well. Most of all, though, the Adelaide Oval sticks in my mind for what it is, not so much for the playing memories. It is the world's most beautiful test cricket ground.

The other test-playing nations, excluding New Zealand, have much in common when it comes to grounds, although I was genuinely surprised about the standard of the venues in Sri Lanka on my first visit there in 1983–84. The test venues were impressive; Colombo has a number of grounds which would be suitable for test cricket and, of the three venues used in the series (two in Colombo and one in Kandy), I found it difficult to be critical. Ground maintenance and scoreboard facilities were excellent and the pitches prepared were outstanding, perhaps a little slow but still offering consistent bounce. I guess I expected to see venues of the type you'd anticipate in third-world countries . . . that is, slightly run down and with tell-tale signs of a lack of finance to upgrade them. That wasn't the case in Sri Lanka.

Go to the West Indies and there's scenic beauty about some of the grounds, like Queen's Park Oval in Port of Spain, Trinidad. There's a back-drop of bush-clad hills and tropical trees surrounding the ground and the wildly exuberant atmosphere at any test match in the Caribbean. But the grounds all too often have a slightly unkempt look about them; certainly they're not in the genre of grounds like Lord's, Trent Bridge, the SCG, the MCG and the Adelaide Oval. The stands tend to be dilapidated and the pitches and outfields don't regularly match the quality you find in Australia or England. That undoubtedly adds to the charm and gives West Indian cricket its distinctive appeal but practice facilities are also often substandard. Countries in the West Indies ooze poverty and it's inevitable cricket venues should also show the signs of that struggle.

When it comes to big venues, India and Pakistan are difficult to top. With such huge populations and such fanatical interest in cricket, the sub-continent countries specialise in monstrous stadiums, generally cavernous concrete constructions which are capable of holding massive crowds. Some grounds have a temporary look about them with stands built from little more than sticks of bamboo and other materials (I guess there's not such a great financial loss when the excitable spectators decide to set fire to a stand, which has happened in that part of the world).

Apart from the heat and humidity factor, grounds in India and Pakistan naturally stand out for the pitches alone. It's rare to find a deck which might give a pace bowler like me some source of encouragement; most of them are no better than baked mud which has been rolled and rolled. The effect, sometimes, is almost blinding. With endless rolling, the pitches take on a glaze which glares back at you. And, the further a game goes, the more the pitches turn into dust bowls . . . which means the spinners usually have a ball.

After first touring India in 1976, I can't say much had changed when I returned for my bid on the world test wicket-taking record in 1988. Two of the test venues were new to me; in 1976, we'd played tests in Bombay, Madras and Kanpur but, on the 1988 visit, only Bombay was retained.

The other tests were played at Bangalore and Hyderabad — and Bangalore was the ground in which I was initially most interested. It was there in the first test that I expected the world record to happen.

I knew something of Bangalore from players in the New Zealand team who'd been involved in the 1987 World Cup; they met India there during the tournament. It's known as the Garden City but the cricket ground, the Chinnaswamy Stadium, didn't quite live up to such a reputation. The stadium itself was captivating with tiered stands all around but the pitch was anything but impressive. While I took five wickets in India's first innings — and captured the world record with my first wicket — there was nothing to recommend the playing surface. It was dreadfully substandard and it was immediately obvious India was going to have all the advantage through its spinners. So it proved. The pitch deteriorated rapidly with the ball turning sharply and bouncing nastily. When I was batting, I pushed forward to a ball which snarled up and hit me on the left shoulder. Predictably enough, the Indian spinners, Narendra Hirwani and Arshad Ayub, had a wicket feast. The memory of Bangalore will live on for my world record moment but the state of the pitch, the defeat and sickness which ravaged the team during the test, made it unforgettable for more uncomfortable reasons.

Bombay's Wankhede Stadium had a much better pitch which, while still low and slow in bounce, at least played well. With so much humidity, the ball swung in the air. As a stadium, it's another concrete maze which erupts into a cacophony of the most deafening noise imaginable when full . . . which I remember all too well on my first visit there in 1976 when the crowd went berserk as Brijesh Patel savaged our attack. Every time he hit the ball, the spectators went absolutely wild and the sound just reverberated all around. The memories in 1988 were much sweeter because we won a dramatic match to record only the second test win by New Zealand in India.

When we travelled to Hyderabad, the test series was beautifully balanced at 1–1 with everything to play for at the Lal Bahadur Stadium. It's a ground rarely used for test cricket. In fact, it was the first time a test had been played at Lal Bahadur Stadium since Graham Dowling's New Zealand team met India in 1969! A long time between drinks. The pitch promised much, having more grass on it than I've seen on a pitch in that part of the world, although the grass was near dead. The ball bounced much more than usual and the pitch also had some pace, yet my return of three for 99 hardly registered as one of my better performances in conditions where I might have done a lot better.

And then we have New Zealand cricket grounds, or should I call them all-purpose sports grounds. The trouble with our venues is an age-old one, that of being too versatile, or being forced to be versatile. Of the four main centres, Auckland's Eden Park, Christchurch's Lancaster Park and Dunedin's Carisbrook are dual-purpose grounds — rugby in the winter and cricket in the summer. Both sports suffer from that predicament; the cricket pitch area becomes boggy in winter and that hardly aids preparation for the following summer. It's cricket which is more disadvantaged because the pitch area takes such a mauling, and it's surely significant that pitches at all three of these grounds have varied in quality. The fact is, the ground staff just don't have a fair chance to work on the wicket block for any cricket season. The Basin Reserve in Wellington is slightly better off as it's not regularly in use during the winter, although some games of soccer and rugby league are played there; and yet the wicket block has still been poor for some years now.

In Auckland and Dunedin the shape of the ground means they're deficient for cricket in the size of the outfield; Carisbrook has short boundaries on the sides. It's too small. Eden Park, with the pitch running on an angle, isn't so bad on the boundaries square of the wicket but the boundary backward of square on the south side of the ground must be the shortest in the world. It's almost impossible to protect when you're in the field.

There's a hassle with the location of the players' viewing areas at New Zealand venues. You're basically sitting among the crowd at large where you can be pestered by kids for autographs throughout a day's play; and that can be distracting and, sometimes, annoying. While a new players' viewing facility has been erected at Carisbrook — providing greater privacy — it is, like the equivalent in Auckland, sited in a side-on position, and the situation's only marginally better in Christchurch. Only at the Basin Reserve is the formula right; there the Wellington Cricket Association has a venue which looks like a cricket ground, unlike the ugly old Basin which had its life span ended after New Zealand's historic win over England in 1977–78. When the new ground, replete with the swept-up R.A. Vance stand, was first used at test level against India in 1980–81, it was something of a trend-setter in New Zealand cricket. The field itself was a genuine test oval, ringed by a white picket fence, although the outfield was atrocious with areas of bare dirt and far too many bumpy patches; even now, the outfield's still not the best. But the players' facilities are very good, resembling those you find in England. At Trent Bridge, for instance, the players have their own room and viewing balcony where they're isolated from the throngs of people. Likewise, at the Basin, there is a special viewing room for the players where they can watch play — and have a view straight down the pitch — either inside behind glass doors or outside on a porch. It's pure luxury compared to what's on offer in Auckland, Christchurch and Dunedin. The only quibble I have is that the concrete walkways from the dressing rooms to the doors leading out on to the ground are dangerous. They should have rubber matting laid down.

The Basin's major drawback these days is, however, the pitch. Where it used to be a haven for quicker bowlers, it's now close to a graveyard. It was in Wellington that I had match figures of 11 for 58 against India in 1975–76 and 10 for 100 against England in 1977–78. Of the nine tests played on the revamped Basin Reserve, we've had just one win of real note, against India in 1980–81 (the other was against Sri Lanka in 1982–83). The last six tests have all been draws and, of the five I've played in — I missed the 1987–88 tests against England through injury — I've captured only 13 wickets at close to 40.00 apiece, which gives some indication of what hard work it now is for pace bowlers at the Basin. And I'm a far better bowler now than I was in the 1970s.

Wellington's Basin Reserve has a balance of good and bad qualities. Since being revamped, it is now, a genuine cricket oval with its picket fence, and it offers good facilities for players. But the pitch is a problem — I find it difficult to take wickets there now — and the outfield still isn't up to standard.   Moa Collection

While I have gripes about Eden Park, Lancaster Park and Carisbrook, there are still things I like about these grounds. After all, there's nothing like playing in front of your own crowd, and we're assured of that wherever we play test matches or one-day internationals in New Zealand.

Logically enough, Lancaster Park, as my true home patch, has provided pitches I've almost always enjoyed bowling on. I've played more tests there than anywhere else — 13 compared with 11 at the Basin and 12 at Eden Park — with my first hometown test being against Australia in 1973–74; I've had great success in Christchurch, apart from the first test against England in 1987–88. In the previous 12 tests, I have taken 69 wickets at Lancaster Park, including six instances of five wickets in an innings, although, oddly enough, not one case of 10 wickets in a match; and that takes me back to an lbw decision Steve Woodward didn't give me in the third test against the West Indies in 1986–87. I hit Courtney Walsh on the back leg and it had to be out, except Woodward didn't think so, and I finished the match with nine wickets instead of 10. While Lancaster Park has been good to bowl on, I've also succeeded with the bat — I made my first test century there, against the West Indies in 1979–80 and 99 in New Zealand's test win over England in 1983–84, when the pitch came in for plenty of criticism from the England camp.

Further south, Carisbrook has been a happy hunting ground with 19 wickets in two tests there against the West Indies in 1979–80 and Pakistan in 1984–85, the wickets coming at a cost of only 11.15 runs each (three bags of five and one of 10 wickets in the match against the West Indies).

Eden Park's one of the toughest places I've bowled at during my test career. It's just so difficult to get it right there because the pitch usually has so little in it for the quicks. Interestingly enough, though, the ground staff produced a seamer for the 1984–85 test against Pakistan, which we won by an innings after knocking the Pakis over cheaply twice. It just shows, it can be done.

Standing out among New Zealand grounds for its beauty is New Plymouth's Pukekura Park, a lovely ground which has never gained real prominence possibly because the boundaries are a little short on the side . . . but it's a venue which rates with the best for its individual appeal.

There's no getting away from the biggest gripe about cricket in New Zealand though — and that's the poor quality of first-class pitches. They have improved on those of a few years ago but there's still ample room for the New Zealand Cricket Council and ground staff around the country to make further improvement. It's a facet of the game which means so much. Pitches which provide inconsistent bounce — and we have too many of them — delude bowlers into believing they're better than they are; wickets come so easily because the pitch too often does the work for them; there's little demand on the bowler to perfect his technique and widen his armoury of deliveries when he knows he merely has to put the ball there, or thereabouts, and watch the track do the rest for him. Just as importantly, the batsmen are unable to advance when they bat on pitches which present such irregular bounce; they can't be in any way confident about shot selection when one delivery might come through at knee height and the next, off the same length, will rear up at chest height. It's so difficult to achieve any consistency as a batsman in such conditions and then, on finding true pitches in Australia or England, it's even harder to discard the old habits and become accustomed to batting on surfaces where you can experience a regular bounce. As for bowlers, they tend to vanish swiftly when they have to bowl on decks which aren't performing the tricks they're used to. The pitch problem in New Zealand is one which can't be overstated.

It was a big issue throughout last season's series against Pakistan, ultimately because the only two tests played were affected by pitches which were just too good.

The Carisbrook pitch for the first test looked a definite result pitch, but we never had the chance to test the theory when the first three scheduled days were washed out — and then the NZCC, in its wisdom, abandoned the match. We did, however, play a one-dayer there to try and recoup lost finances for New Zealand cricket, and the pitch proved to be venomous, immediately suggesting the test couldn't possibly have gone the distance had it proceeded. The bounce was erratic and the ball jagged about alarmingly. Pakistan could make only 170 for nine off 48 overs and I had five wickets in the innings.

The loss of the test was costly for us because it was there we fancied we would win; it was also expensive for me. If I was to reach 400 wickets, then I really needed to have the benefit of bowling in Dunedin.

From there on the series became a dull event by and large, and essentially because of pitch conditions. The Basin Reserve surface was prepared to last and last, never likely to allow a result; the match became unforgettable for its tedium, especially in Pakistan's first innings, when

Shoaib Mohammad batted an agonising 720 minutes for his 163, a knock which spanned three different days and provided the measly return of only 60-odd runs on one day! All of a sudden, on the last day of the match, I picked up two quick wickets to give me four for the innings — my best effort in Wellington for years — only to see Imran Khan declare at the oddest time. I can only surmise he wanted to deny me the chance to move closer to the target of 400.

But, having drawn that match, the pitch which commanded all attention was the one at Eden Park for the series-deciding third test — and the omens didn't look good. The track provoked endless discussion and comment; it was bare of grass, little better than rolled mud. Just about every theory suggested this would be a result match, only in Pakistan's favour. While the Eden Park ground staff had difficulties preparing the surface, we should never have a pitch like that in New Zealand again. The whole home team advantage was destroyed — it was Pakistan who were more at home. Perhaps the ultimate insult came with the naming of the final 12 for the match. Auckland won the Shell Trophy through the best seam attack in the country and yet Martin Snedden, Danny Morrison and Willie Watson were all omitted for the test on their home ground!

While the pitch had pace, and surprising bounce, on the first morning, there was no sideways movement at all which killed Ewen Chatfield and me; as Pakistan compiled a massive 616 for five declared — a record test score against New Zealand — Charlie bowled a mammoth 65 overs for figures of one for 158. I didn't make it through the innings, being struck down by yet another achilles tendon complaint and coming out of the innings with one for 68 from 28 overs; I was stranded on 396 wickets and wondering just what lay ahead. But, if Chatfield and I had problems, then so did our spinners, Stephen Boock, rewriting the record books with one for 229 from 70 overs, and John Bracewell collecting one for 138 from 37. Interestingly enough, the New Zealand attack of Hadlee, Chatfield, Boock and Bracewell had an accumulated age of 142 years — we had to be the oldest attack in test cricket for many years. The way I felt, maybe we should all have been unavailable and let the youngsters bowl on *that* pitch.

The outstanding feature of the game was Javed Miandad's innings of 271 and later he said: "It's like batting at Karachi." And so it must have been, which is just inexcusable. Why should we make overseas sides feel so much at home?

When Pakistan was 289 for two after the first day, Boocky said at breakfast the next morning: "We need three quick wickets and to see a pig fly if we are to get back into this game." To which I replied: "I'd like to see a pig fly first, then we have a better chance of getting three quick wickets."

Boocky suffered the indignity of setting a new standard for the most runs conceded by a New Zealand bowler in a test innings, taking the dubious honour from Fen Cresswell who had held the record with his six for 168 since 1949. When Boocky's 200 was brought up, the crowd cheered and Imran Khan smiled but Boocky, ever the humorist, still saw the funny side. He proceeded to kiss the pitch to mark the occasion! Just

A typical test match day at Auckland's Eden Park. This aerial shot accentuates one of Eden Park's major failings — a ridiculously short boundary behind square on the main grandstand side of the ground (on the right). R.J. Hadlee Collection

before Chatfield bowled the next over, Boocky yelled out to him from point: "Hey, Charlie, I've left some moisture on the pitch — see if you can hit it and use it to your advantage." And Pakistan was only 550 or so for five at the time!

Some questions must be asked about future test cricket at Eden Park. Other venues have lost tests because of poor pitches (the one against Pakistan was poor in the sense it worked against New Zealand) but revenue in Auckland will almost guarantee cricket's always played there.

I'm not saying New Zealand has pitch trouble all on its own. There's always a test pitch somewhere which isn't up to standard — look at the worries there have been at Headingley in Leeds as an example — but our pitches tend to create concern more often, partly because so many grounds are dual-purpose ones and also because we lack the total expertise in pitch preparation. The poser is trying to find the perfect balance, trying to manufacture pitches which offer the bowlers something throughout but never allow them to absolutely dominate the batsmen. I suppose the best example I can think of during my test career was the pitch used for the second test between Australia and New Zealand in Christchurch in 1973–74; it had something for everyone. Australia made totals of 223 and 259, Ian Redpath having scores of 71 and 58 while Ian Davis and Doug Walters also scored half-centuries in Australia's second innings; we scored 255 in our first innings and reached 230 for five in our second to record New Zealand's first test victory over Australia in a match also remembered for Glenn Turner's back-to-back centuries (101 and 110 not out). I also liked pitches prepared in Auckland for tests against Pakistan in 1978–79, the West Indies in 1979–80 and Australia in 1981–82; what I define as a good cricket pitch is not, as some people may surmise, one which necessarily aids quicks. I'm not quite that narrow minded.

My point simply is that we must always strive for much better pitches than we have at the moment. The use of the Department of Scientific and

Industrial Research is a smart move in analysing what we're doing right or wrong while the New Zealand Turf Culture Institute always has plenty to offer. In short, there's no limit to the amount of research which can be carried out.

I like the scheme employed in England where an inspector of pitches is detailed to check out bad reports about pitches; the man filling the post at the moment is Bernard Flack. And because our groundsman at Nottinghamshire, Ron Allsopp, was dedicated to producing result pitches — leaving sufficient grass on them — he was the target of some complaints for doctoring pitches to suit the Notts attack. You could say poor Ron copped a little Flack from time to time. The idea of an inspector of pitches is an excellent one, though, and perhaps in New Zealand we could be stricter about taking action when bad reports are filed about pitches used for first-class matches, perhaps by banning games on that ground for a year or two until the pitch is improved. If that was the case, the Basin would have been out of commission for years!

Groundsmen are obviously the crucial playmakers in this little puzzle. To be fair, many New Zealand curators, as Australians like to call them, don't have a real show of doing their job properly. Some, I suspect, haven't really had the experience or total knowledge to do the task adequately while most have suffered from the dilemma I mentioned earlier, trying to work rugby and cricket together on the same ground.

Russell Wylie has done his best to try and transform Lancaster Park into an English-style ground by providing a lush outfield which, for test matches at least, he mows in the Lord's tradition. But in the old days, Cyril Barnes — and Russ himself when he took over — used to just throw the gang mowers over the outfield. Russ has new ideas and he listens. He's keen to please, keen to learn, which can only help overcome some of the problems there have been at Lancaster Park. The pitch for the 1987–88 test against England was, as an example, not really up to the desired standard, although it nearly produced a result. There have been some much better ones in Christchurch generally, though, especially during the 1988–89 season.

Eden Park was for years under the care of Eddie Thorne, who's recently retired. But what disappointed me was that more use wasn't made of Peter Webb, the former New Zealand and Auckland batsman, who has obvious advantages as a top-level player and knows what the players want. Webby eventually left the Eden Park staff. At the same time, Eden Park has peculiar problems which, I'm sure, are more to do with the soil used in the pitch than anything else. The strip used for the test there against England in 1987–88 was a shocker and there was talk afterwards of the block being dug up and relaid . . . England captain Mike Gatting was so delighted to hear the suggestion he offered to help! There may be mitigating factors which contributed in the preparation but cricket can do without pitches like the one used in that test. Five days produced very little attractive cricket with New Zealand making 301 and 350 for seven declared while England totalled 323 in its only innings . . . 970 runs at a rate of barely more than two runs an over. The Lancaster Park test in the series was equally dreary with only 760 runs scored in a match affected by the weather, the runs per over again just creeping a decimal point above two.

That kind of cricket doesn't satisfy the players or the paying public and that's why ground staff need greater assistance and education in the pursuit of excellence.

It so happened pitches during the 1988–89 season generally appeared to be quite outstanding, judging by the amount of runs scored. A record number of first-class hundreds were made, there were double centuries and declarations, all of which indicated the playing surfaces were excellent. For once bowlers had to work hard on pitches which forced them to rely on skill, rather than variations in bounce and movement to take wickets, and, consequently, many average bowlers were sorted out. The overall improvement is vital for the development of our game and our players, although I must say conditions at some grounds seemed to be rather too one-sided . . . perhaps too much in favour of the batsmen.

Practice pitches are just as crucial and the players are unanimous that more emphasis must be placed on practice facilities at test venues. There's nothing more frustrating than working out on pitches which in no way resemble the surface prepared for the match itself. There have been numerous occasions when practice pitches offered to us have been so poor we've cancelled training sessions and gone somewhere else the following day.

Before the scheduled first test against Pakistan last summer, the practice pitches were diabolical at Carisbrook and yet, on another day, we found quite satisfactory conditions at Tonga Park. Groundsmen should take just as much pride in producing good practice strips as they do with the pitches out in the middle. Of equal concern is the matter of not covering practice pitches; there have been times in Auckland when we've arrived at the ground in the morning to find the practice surfaces unplayable because of overnight rain or dew — and that's simply not good enough.

While it might only be a strip of grass to the uninitiated, the cricket pitch should be a work of art. The ideal one — and it's too rarely seen in New Zealand — should have at least a light covering of grass to assist the new-ball bowlers on the first morning, so the opening batsmen have to battle and graft to survive and establish the innings. Midway through the first day, the pitch ought to flatten out somewhat allowing the batsmen to assume greater control, and forcing the bowlers to rely more on skill and variation to take wickets.

On the second and third days, the playing surface should be at its best for batting. All the quick bowlers can do is toil away as the spinners begin to come into play. Assistance should become more pronounced for the spinners on the fourth and fifth days, reversing the roles where the batsmen are the ones who now need a lot more skill to combat the turning delivery. Perhaps most importantly, the ideal pitch should be firm and the pace and bounce should be consistent, not consistently inconsistent which is so often the case in New Zealand. But is that the impossible dream?

C·H·A·P·T·E·R T·W·E·L·V·E

Decision Makers

Selection in any New Zealand team is supposed to be one of those special thrills in life . . . and it was for me when I was named in the New Zealand B side which played in Australia's limited-overs competition in the 1971–72 season.

I'd been a first-class cricketer for practically five minutes. I was only 20, I'd played just three matches and taken 10 wickets for Canterbury at an average of 19.40, including a hat-trick in my third appearance, against Central Districts. And yet, on that limited background, I was whisked into the New Zealand B team to play alongside such players as Ross Morgan, Mike Shrimpton, Bryan Andrews, Graham Newdick, Brian Dunning and my brother Barry.

I was back in Australia with the full New Zealand side for the Coca Cola tournament the following summer before making an even bigger leap into the test side to play Pakistan in Wellington in February 1973. It was an occasion never to be forgotten; on the first morning I took my first test catch (Zaheer Abbas off Bruce Taylor) and later that day I had my first test wicket (Asif Iqbal) followed by Sadiq Mohammad's scalp on the second day. My bowling may have been erratic — my very first delivery in test cricket was a leg-stump full-toss which Sadiq put away to the boundary — but I was encouraged that I'd come out of my first test innings with two for 84 from 18 overs. By the end of the third day, my debut test was even more memorable after I'd made 46 with the bat in my initial innings.

But whatever joy I experienced in my first steps as an international cricketer was tempered slightly by the unique position I found myself in. I wasn't just another New Zealand cricketer who had broken into top-level cricket; I had a tag beside my name . . . I was the chairman's son. So, while there was understandable elation about vaulting to such lofty heights as a player, there was a self-consciousness that I wasn't so much Richard Hadlee, New Zealand cricketer, but more the son of Walter Hadlee. Dad had captained New Zealand in eight tests from 1945–46 to 1950–51 and just happened to be chairman of the New Zealand Cricket Council's board of control when I became a New Zealand player. Obviously that development could have been viewed cynically by the more sceptical of cricketing people, and I'm sure there was some resentment about my swift arrival. In an ironical twist, much the same thing happened 15 years later in the 1987–88 test series between New Zealand and England. After being close to selection previously, the experienced Wellington captain, Robert Vance — son of NZCC chairman Bob Vance — made his test debut as a 32-year-old in the third test in Wellington, so sparking fresh innuendo about being "the chairman's son".

I could imagine exactly how Bert felt. Along with my brother, Dayle, I'd been through the same scene years earlier . . . and it's a slightly uncomfortable feeling being in the New Zealand side when your father is the gaffer. That's not to say there was a torrent of nasty, behind-the-hand talk all the time. Interwoven in the web of suspicion and criticism was the sharp wit of one clever Aucklander who had the ability to bring out the funny side. Ian Donnelly, a portly off spinner who played for the Suburbs-New Lynn club in Auckland, used to spark plenty of derisive banter on the Eden Park terraces whenever Dayle or I — not to mention both of us — played in Auckland. We could always rely on Donners to stir us, ever so playfully. It was good stuff, nothing offensive, with quite the best touch being his venture into Broadway musicals when he borrowed the universally known song "If I were a Rich Man" from *Fiddler on the Roof* to create his own ditty titled "If I was a Hadlee". Dayle and I invariably bowled indifferently on Eden Park's unhelpful pitch; often our bowling figures would take on an unhealthy look and it certainly took time before I came to terms with the bowling requirements there.

Ian Donnelly didn't miss the chance to prick our consciences when he would lead 'Cans Corner' on the terraces with his rendition which went like this:

> If I was a Hadlee . . .
> Deedle, deedle, deedle, deedle, deedle, deedle, dum,
> I would be in the Kiwi cricket team
> 'Cause I am the chairman's son.
>
> Wouldn't have to bowl straight . . .
> Deedle, deedle, deedle, deedle, deedle, deedle, dum,
> Long hops, full toss, anything will do,
> 'Cause I am the chairman's son.

Donnelly's witticisms had a sequel some years later when, at the tender age of 35, he was picked in Auckland's Shell series squad for the 1981–82 season. What's more, he was selected in the playing side for

Auckland's Shell Cup one-dayer against Canterbury in Christchurch. Who would have thought it possible years earlier that Ian Donnelly, the cheerleader of Cans Corner, would actually face me in a top-level cricket match? But it happened on 9 January, 1982. Now, Donners had no great pretensions as a batsman, and not unnaturally batted at No. 11 (even that was too high for him). So when Auckland's ninth wicket fell, I waved him to the wicket much to the delight of the crowd who were well aware of the significance of the event. I'd been operating off a shortened run-up but, to put fear into Donners' heart, I proceeded to mark out my long run . . . and the not-so-intrepid incoming batsman turned and walked back to the pavilion. Eventually he took guard — from behind the stumps — and finally I charged in off my short run, if with a good deal more zest than usual. The first delivery was full in length and Donners somehow managed to get bat on ball and take a desperate single; a chubby fellow, Donners is not the quickest man between wickets, but he was that day. "Damn it," I thought to myself, "five balls left in the innings and I have let him off the hook." Fortunately, Warren Stott took a single off the next ball and so I had another crack at the Cans Corner man. I considered a bouncer but decided it wasn't worth it; bowling him out would give me more satisfaction. The third ball of the over was a little wide and Donners played and missed. I indicated he should move his front foot across to the line of the delivery instead of backing away to square leg. He pointed to the stumps and said: "All you have to do is bowl straight." The fifth ball was straight and very full and the middle and leg stumps were knocked back. Donners later told his team-mates: "He is quick, isn't he? In Cans Corner I can play him easily from 80 metres, but 20 metres is just a little too close."

While Ian Donnelly found humour in "the chairman's son" business, it was generally a good deal more ticklish than that and I'm sure my father found it awkward to handle at times. With him as chairman, and me as a New Zealand player, we clearly had a clash of interests and, obviously, he had to act in the best interests of the NZCC in the final analysis. Eventually he opted out of discussions or voting on matters concerning me, just as Barry does today as a member of the board of control.

Dad had a special way of dealing with the father-son problem. He'd give me fatherly advice which sometimes might have been contrary to what the NZCC wanted — but that was done strictly on a father-to-son basis. He'd tell me what he thought was right and wrong yet would necessarily have to adopt a different stance in his role as chairman on some issues. One matter which comes to mind concerned my bid to be involved in the World Series tour of New Zealand in the early part of the 1978–79 season. I wanted to play but the board was initially against it and yet Dad told me: "If I was you I'd play World Series Cricket."

Generally, Dad would give me a double-edged view of matters. Without being too positive about some idea, he'd present the facts about a case and suggest what might be more acceptable to the board. If I'd been left to my own devices, I would probably have been belligerent in my approach and told the board: "I want this and I want that and, if you don't meet my requests, something's going to happen." Through talking

When it came to cricket decisions, Dad could give me the low-down from both sides of the fence — as chairman of the NZCC's board of control, and as a father giving his son advice. That enabled me to think more rationally.

to Dad, firstly as a father, and then through the chairman's eyes, I became much more reasoned in my attitude because I had a more balanced view about issues (although that might not always have seemed so, given some of the problems I've had with the NZCC).

Dad's advice had a marked bearing on the way I handled the World Series Cricket venture in 1978–79 and, eventually, the board allowed me to play for Tony Greig's World XI against an Australian side captained by Ian Chappell. Dad, though, had stayed out of deliberations on my application to appear as a guest in the WSC tour in New Zealand; instead his deputy, Bob Vance, chaired the meeting . . . and Dad was out of the room during the voting.

Another issue on which Dad had a major influence was the vexed one about playing in South Africa. It's well known that he sees much merit in South Africa being re-admitted to the International Cricket Conference; in fact, the ICC asked him to be part of a special task force which did a detailed survey on South African cricket. I know he put a lot of time and effort into the project and was disappointed nothing eventuated from it through the ICC.

Having playing connections with South Africa is always in the wind — it blew up again during New Zealand's test series against England in

1987–88. Johnny Fisher, who was in New Zealand with a supporters' tour party, was said to be arranging the latest rebel venture to the republic and, wouldn't you believe it, I was among those who had supposedly been targeted and approached. It was all rather preposterous really but you come to expect that when the topic of South Africa comes up. There's always some rumour about.

While Dad would like to see South Africa back in the official fold, he's realistic enough to know it's just not on. He would tell me it would decimate New Zealand cricket should any Kiwis play in South Africa; the board would find it totally unacceptable if any player hightailed it in search of the almighty kruger-rand. Yet, when the issue has come up on a father-to-son level at intervals, his inclination has been to tell me I probably should go. I don't know whether that's a sign of him hitting back at the ICC for not re-admitting South Africa. Like him, however, I know South Africa's return would mean a white v black cricket world. Cricket has lived without South Africa since 1970, and doesn't seem to be any worse for it, but to turn it around would be tantamount to disaster. With Sri Lanka's admission as a full ICC member, the so-called black countries are in ascendancy — West Indies, Pakistan, India and Sri Lanka against England, Australia and New Zealand. I've always been basically pro-establishment throughout my career, which can be measured by my attitude on a number of matters, including the South African one. I'm not averse to the administrative stand on South Africa and, if it was reversed, I'd still support the establishment. While I've had my share of incidents with the NZCC, I'm by no means a rebel and all problems have been sorted out.

I haven't always sounded my father out about moves I might make and the most significant was my decision to turn professional in 1978. I struck out on my own to forge a full-time career with Nottinghamshire. It happened quickly. Suddenly, I had graduated from the amateur to pro ranks alongside Glenn Turner, Geoff Howarth and John Wright. The metamorphosis from amateur to professional probably tested the father-son association more than anything, although Dad retired as chairman about the time I began with Notts. I sensed instantly that I was treated differently by the board and I found myself looking for extra benefits and concessions in much the same way Martin Crowe has in more recent times. There's an enormous difference between the amateurs and the pros . . . and the amateur brigade are well aware of it. Cricket is a pro's job where the amateur's cricket earnings subsidise income from a more regular form of employment. I'd be the first to say, however, that the pros have been looked after well by the NZCC; you negotiate a deal you believe is reasonable for your talents and acceptable to the NZCC; there are numerous other revenue-winning areas which also require negotiation. A pro cricketer's career can be quite a lucrative business. But bridging the gap from amateur to professional, and avoiding animosity and jealousy, is no simple process. It was Bob Vance who introduced a three-tiered player remuneration system which enabled long-serving players to be paid at a higher rate; the middle tier was for those who had given several years of service and the beginners started at the bottom — and had plenty to aspire to. It was a much fairer system than putting everyone on the same level; it was unfair to see someone like Brian Barrett, who was only 19 and who played sparingly in England in 1986, being paid the same on his first tour as old troopers like Ewen Chatfield and Ian Smith. There had to be a method which rewarded those who had been in the New Zealand team for some time.

But it's perplexing that New Zealand cricket's recent history has been notable for sour relations between the country's two most experienced players and the chairmen of the time. In the 1970s, it was Glenn Turner v Walter Hadlee and, in the 1980s, it became Richard Hadlee v Bob Vance. While my worries with Vance haven't been quite so evident, Glenn's differences with Dad are well-known and well-documented.

Turner's disputes with officialdom didn't begin and end with my father, but the clashes between the two were certainly the most publicised. During the 1987 English season, I learned Glenn had, in his newly-published book, criticised the NZCC and, in particular, my father. As a player, New Zealand captain, member and chairman of the NZCC's board, Dad devoted more than 30 years of life to improving New Zealand's status in the cricket world. Having read Turner's comments, I asked Dad for his comments and he told me:

> "It seems a pity that one who is deservedly among the most highly-rated batsman, should indulge in an unwarranted attack on members of the NZCC's board of control.
>
> "No cricketer in my long association with the game felt so aggrieved as did Turner. Money, tour contracts, air fares, and availability to play for New Zealand all seemed to be problems. Glenn took the view that the chairman could decide all matters and would not accept that decisions were made by all the board members. The NZCC recognised his professional status and treated him as favourably as finances of the time would permit.
>
> "I don't wish to catalogue the many problems but one particular matter raised in his book needs rebuttal. After the 1975–76 season in New Zealand, Turner went to South Africa for a cricketing engagement, leaving his wife in New Zealand. He knew, under the terms of his April 1975 contract, that the NZCC had paid for an air fare which returned him to England for the 1976 summer. Despite this, he asked his wife to approach the council's secretary, Bob Knowles, for an air fare to the United Kingdom. Turner subsequently claimed (in his book) that Sukhi 'felt angry and humiliated' by having to sign an affidavit for an air fare he claimed the NZCC owed him.
>
> "That wasn't true, which Turner admitted later; there was no air fare owing to him. He had already been paid the fare in question, and Mrs Turner did not sign an affidavit. In fact, she requested a loan, in a letter to the council."

The Secretary
New Zealand Cricket Council,
P.O. Box 958,
Christchurch

Dear Sir,
Re: Airfares to United Kingdom

In order to enable me to proceed from New Zealand to the United Kingdom, I would be grateful if you would advance me by way of loan the amount involved in a single economy fare. If approved I will arrange through Air New Zealand the purchase of my ticket and ask them to render the account to the New Zealand Cricket Council for payment.

The amount involved is to be repaid by deduction from any amounts which my husband Glenn Turner may be entitled to collect under the terms of the contract between the New Zealand Cricket Council and himself and dated in 1975, or such other monies as may be due to him by the New Zealand Cricket Council.

Yours faithfully
Sukhi Turner

"As it was clear Sukhi Turner did not have funds to purchase an air fare, we arranged this on her behalf. Perhaps the act could have earned commendation, not condemnation.

"Turner also wrote in his book: 'Every team is a hot-bed of personality conflict where envy, jealousy and ambition work against unity.'

"I enjoyed my cricket; it was an exhilarating and shared experience, and I feel sorry for Glenn Turner if he felt so differently about his career. Hopefully, in time, bitterness will be replaced by tolerance, especially of those people who give freely of their time to develop cricket at all levels."

After reading Dad's response about Turner's criticism — and remembering my own troubles with Bob Vance it might be asked: Why should there be such strife between players like us and the chairmen of our times but by becoming professionals we request special treatment because our needs had become rather different. With cricket, and all its related trimmings, providing our living, we have to fight for a good deal. For me, the pro's life has always meant much more than just playing and training. There have been so many other associated commitments; advertisements, endorsements, speaking engagements or public appearances, all vital if you're to make your profession work for you.

Sometimes one of the appointments might eat into a team meeting or perhaps you have something to attend the night before a match starts, at lunchtime or after practice. It can disrupt the team pattern — which certainly isn't good — and can also generate some resentment among fellow players. But, while I have other responsibilities outside cricket itself, it has to be remembered that I put in the work and effort, I train hard and I'm geared up to play and perform on the field. All these peripheral things have hardly ever affected my level of performance.

But administrators and players alike tend to be very negative about the level of involvement I have in and around cricket. Players like Glenn Turner and myself are sometimes seen as isolated individuals and I'm sure that has been behind some of the problems we've had with top administration. I know administrators in general believe the pros are aloof from the so-called amateurs in New Zealand.

If taking care of yourself to be in the best possible playing shape means becoming aloof, then so be it. I know, as do John Wright and probably Martin Crowe, that you have to be careful to give yourself a chance of performing to optimum level. Whether you do actually achieve such ideals is another matter but at least you give yourself every chance. It hurts me to hear some administrators consider we remove ourselves from the team by sticking to our routines.

Maybe it's the impression I'm seen as a special case which created the personality clash between Bob Vance and myself, a contretemps which peaked in 1987 when I had a bust-up with the NZCC over my non-availability for the World Cup in India. Our relationship reached its nadir when I found Vance almost impossible to deal with.

The World Cup ruckus would have seemed highly improbable after my first dealings with Vance as an administrator on New Zealand's 1973–74 tour to Australia. He was a good team manager, being very much a player's man who was prepared to listen. He'll still listen to some degree but, when he inherited the NZCC's chairmanship from my father in 1978, his personality changed. I don't suppose health and business problems helped. I've always found he engenders a fairly inflammatory atmosphere in any discussion situation and that he's more often than not extremely intolerant and stubborn. It seemed at times that Vance would make decisions on behalf of the board . . . on matters the board knew nothing about. The chairman is not the ultimate decision maker; he must allow his board to make the final move on any matter.

Breaking point in my dealings with Vance may well have come over the World Cup negotiations in August 1987, but an incident a few years earlier did the real damage.

Each year Keith Hancox, the New Zealand Sports Foundation's executive director, holds a special dinner at his place, generally coinciding with the New Zealand cricket team being in Wellington. Along with Karen, I've been invited regularly and always make it a priority to take up the invitation, indebted as I am to the Sports Foundation's assistance.

At one of these dinners a few years ago, Bob Vance belittled himself and offended Karen and me — in such distinguished company — by referring to me in very unsavoury terms. He was blunt and loud. What he said was tactless and in poor taste, especially from the NZCC chairman. Vance probably thought it was amusing and there was no apology about his display to either Karen or me. I couldn't understand why he was so sarcastic and offensive that night.

The incident was probably insignificant, but it was something I didn't

New Zealand Cricket Council Board of Control, 1982
Back row: A.G. Duckmanton, V.J. Chettleburgh, N.G. Ockwell, K.R. Deas,
R.C. MacInnes, G.T. Dowling, I.N. Taylor.
Front row: The late M.E. Chapple, B.J. Paterson, W.A. Hadlee, R.A. Vance,
J.C. Saunders, Sir Allan Wright. *Absent:* J.H. Heslop

forget, especially in dealings with him later. I guess it was the forerunner
to the problems which, unbeknown to me, lay ahead. I'm sure Vance was
a very competent and capable chairman, a good cricket administrator. His
love of the game is unquestioned, but his attitude towards me left a lot
to be desired on several occasions. He proved to be the most difficult
administrator with whom I have had dealings.

My flare-up over the World Cup affair in 1987 was an awkward
moment. A meeting between Vance, the NZCC's executive director
Graham Dowling and myself in London — just before the Bicentennial
match at Lord's between the MCC and the Rest of the World — was an
absolute disaster, finishing with me walking out.

The affair had its origins in a letter I wrote to Graham Dowling on
13 July, 1987, at a time when there was considerable doubt whether I
would, in fact, be available for the World Cup tournament in India. I was
obligated to New Zealand cricket to play anywhere, even in the sub-
continent, an area I was not at all keen about returning to after some
horrific experiences there on my first visit in 1976. But, despite an obligation to make tours even to India or Pakistan, I believed I would be able
to put up a case not to tour when the time arose.

By July 1987 I had to make a move about the World Cup and wrote
this letter to Dowling:

Dear Graham,
No doubt you have been hounded by the media and others about
my availability for the World Cup.

After due consideration I regretfully advise that for personal
reasons I am unavailable for the tour of India/Pakistan in

September/October/November. I would therefore ask you to announce it officially before I make a statement.

The 1976 tour still haunts me and I have no desire to relive the past there again. Some players on that ill-fated tour still have after-effects. If I was unlucky enough to pick up another bug it would greatly reduce my effectiveness for the Aussie tour, which is a little more important than the World Cup.

Like the Sri Lankan tour (in 1987), I'm not happy with the political situation and unrest which appears to be common at the moment. Only yesterday a bomb killed 72 in Karachi and 250 were injured while recently, in India, people were machine-gunned down. While we are not deliberate targets there is still a risk that I'm not prepared to take.

Again, with the demands on players, I'm finding it all too difficult to play and compete at the level I'd like to. There is a lot of cricket still to play in the next eight weeks here in England, then hopefully a month or so off before playing club cricket for several weeks and then to Australia and back home for England.

I'm sure you can appreciate the need to freshen up a little instead of going through the motions and putting in mediocre performances.

I trust the board will treat my decision favourably and understand my situation.

Regards
Richard Hadlee.

I had been ticked off a few times before about going public prematurely on varying matters, so I played this strictly by the book by writing to Dowling first. I'd followed procedure carefully and was hopeful of a satisfactory reaction from the board as I was genuinely worried about going back to India.

But Dowling's reply, dated 27 July, was scarcely one which thrilled me. He told me the board believed I should go to the World Cup and that I had been aware the tournament was on when I completed my newest business arrangement with the NZCC. He also said the "tired" factor was "clearly self-induced by you returning to the UK to play one further season with Nottinghamshire. Tiredness was inevitable". There was a further comment that the board would be fully justified in terminating its arrangement with me. However, the bit which really hurt — not unnaturally — was the disclosure that the board would reduce the financial terms by a substantial amount, for missing the World Cup.

I was furious, to say the least. I saw the NZCC's so-called reduction as outright blackmail — tour India or be penalised was what they were saying. I read it as a fine, not a reduction. And to fine me substantially for missing the World Cup was right out of proportion. I couldn't accept the board's suggestions and a meeting with Vance and Dowling in a London hotel seemed to bring everything to an end, essentially because Vance was so difficult. I've always tried to adopt a reasonable approach to matters like this — I'm open to negotiation and, if there needed to be a compromise in this instance, then I was ready to do business. I agreed there should be some sort of reduction because I wasn't fulfilling my arrangement completely, and I also stood to lose out financially in other ways by not going to the World Cup. But the NZCC decided a hefty penalty would make me change my mind. I indicated a lesser figure was acceptable; Vance, though, wouldn't budge on his best offer so I said: "If that's the way you want to do business, okay!" and walked out.

The board's attitude was one of justifying the amount of the reduction as being in proportion to the period I wouldn't be playing for New Zealand, but I had to see it differently. Maybe the board wanted to force me to go to India and hoped that the figure they came up with would literally scare the pants off me. Perhaps they should have seduced me instead!

I'm sure businessmen would have negotiated a figure in such circumstances so everyone left happy and we could get on with the job. Not Vance. I heard from reliable sources that Vance later told various members of the Australian Cricket Board that I had refused to negotiate — that hurt me and proved he behaved totally unprofessionally, showing disloyalty to me and to the NZCC. Ultimately, the NZCC accepted my original offer of a reduction just a day later. Graham Dowling knew I was in a negotiating mood and that I was keen to sort out everything amicably; but I found it strange they changed their tune so quickly.

There were rumours a prominent New Zealand businessman, known for his generosity to and love of cricket, might have influenced the NZCC's stance. Vance was evidently told: "Sort out the Hadlee business or else . . ." For a day or so, though, I had contemplated life without New Zealand cricket. While that never happened and the affair was sorted out, Vance's negotiating skills had emphasised the rift between us.

The episode had a sequel when Bob Vance decided he didn't want to be involved in negotiations with me in future. That probably suited the board because subsequent matters were handled quite satisfactorily with at least two other board members involved.

My brother Barry, who is my accountant, has been handling my financial affairs since, along with the former Canterbury captain Cran Bull — my solicitor — and Dowling. Because of the obvious conflict in interests, Barry has sometimes been asked to leave the room or pressed not to vote on any issues concerning me, but it has worked out well having him as my negotiator. There could be a clash of interests with the triangle involving my brother and accountant, my solicitor and the NZCC's executive director who was my first Canterbury captain.

Despite various differences, I must say the NZCC's board has made several decisions which have assisted me. One involved the media contracts John Wright and I had during the tour to India in late 1988. We had signed an arrangement with Kapil Dev seven months earlier and were obligated because part of the fee had been paid in advance. However, the Indian Board of Control for Cricket stipulated none of the Indian players were allowed to write newspaper columns; those who contravened the ruling would be severely fined, or banned, as Dilip Vengsarkar was for six months. The Indian board also requested that the NZCC prohibit our players from doing columns, and the tour contract drawn up stipulated this. I was somewhat reluctant to sign the contract in this form but, technically, if I didn't I wouldn't have been on the tour.

However, none of the players were asked to sign until we arrived in Bombay. I said to Dowling: "Our board has no need to be influenced by the Indians. What right do they have to interfere with our existing media arrangements which invariably involve half the team whether at home or on tours? What they decide to do in India with their players is their concern, not ours." There was also the question of loss of earnings if we couldn't write columns.

Dowling obviously saw our point and the problems which could be created. A call to New Zealand and some discussion — no doubt with our new chairman, Barry Paterson — clarified the issue, the board deciding we should honour our existing contracts. Wrighty and I were grateful for that and, perhaps negotiations with a new chairman will bring me back closer to the game's administrators. I'd like to think so; I'd certainly prefer to end my playing days with a much happier relationship with my employers.

Because my career has spanned the era of three NZCC chairmen now, I'm able to sit back and reflect on various differences. I remember the way Dad came into the dressing room after New Zealand's first test victory over Australia in Christchurch in 1973–74. Glenn Turner objected to his presence in the room, believing it should have been an occasion for the players but I believe that's precisely the sort of player-administrator contact we need at times. I think it's a courtesy for the NZCC chairman to go into the changing room and wish the team well on the first morning of a test match or before any day's play, just as it is to offer congratulations or commiserations after a match. I know Dad did that and Bob Vance and Sir Allan Wright have also visited us in recent years, giving us some positive feedback from up above.

What I couldn't agree with were the methods Vance adopted when we played Australia in the first test in Wellington in 1981–82. We'd lost the Rothmans Cup one-day series 2–1, being bowled out for only 74 in the series decider at the Basin Reserve. It was a poor display on a sub-standard pitch. However, before the first test began, Vance visited our dressing room to give us a pep talk. He gave us a real grilling, telling us we had to perform much better in the test series; that job belongs to the captain or cricket manager, *not* the chairman of the board. Telling players how to play is outside the chairman's jurisdiction. Vance erred that day. He should have simply wished us the best and said something like: "We're behind you."

Fortunately we now have a cricket manager to handle the ripping-the-players-apart duties where, in 1981–82, we didn't have such a luxury. That in itself is a sign of the advances New Zealand cricket has made administratively. Positive moves have been made over the years with cricket managers, physiotherapists and doctors being attached to New Zealand teams; it's frightening now to imagine a New Zealand team without such back-up staff.

I've always found it odd that I've run into so many worries with officialdom at home; after all, in 10 years with Nottinghamshire, I never had any upsets. In England, you're able to get on with your job with the minimum of fuss. In New Zealand, there are almost inevitable personality clashes which prevent a cricketer's programme being incident free. I'm sure NZCC board members honestly believe they're doing what's best for the game, but it's unfortunate there are so many problems. Perhaps New Zealand cricket needs to be run by a board of directors like a major company. The best possible expertise needs to be used so rational decisions can be made, allowing the business (sport in this instance) to succeed. If necessary, sports administrators/board members should be financially rewarded, as long as the sport can carry the cost (and I suppose cricket possibly can't).

The NZCC's board of control comprises representatives from the various associations but that means certain areas — like Auckland, for instance — are restricted in the number of administrators on the board. If Auckland can provide two or three astute administrators, why shouldn't they all be on the board? We need the best people in the top jobs. Another fault in the system is the lack of continuity. Some people serve on the board for only a short period before they're pushed out with good minds being lost too soon. There is also a need for more younger, talented people to be involved, men who have recently played cricket and are closer to the modern-day requirements of the game. Cran Bull is a good example. He was voted on to the board as a member of the executive but could quite conceivably be voted off next year in favour of another nomination, a victim of the political power struggle which goes on.

I'm in favour of a fast-track system allowing younger men to get on to the board of control quickly instead of stagnating too long at provincial level. Changes are too slow and we need younger, sharper minds having more say at the top.

The NZCC has been looking at its constitution and changes are imminent to keep pace with today's demands. Significantly, a firm has been investigating the financial structure of major and minor associations, and this might bring forward some important recommendations.

Admittedly, progress has been made through the NZCC's acceptance of players' delegations and from meetings with Shell series captains, or representatives, to discuss matters of mutual concern. However, I'd still like to see more; players and board members should become more involved so they can talk casually or formally about player needs and the general state of the game. We saw the signs of it on the day before the washed-out first test against Pakistan was due to start in Dunedin last season. Both teams and NZCC members were present at a cocktail function, an event welcomed by the players as a chance to mix with the decision makers. Many questions were asked from both viewpoints about cricket — and this communication can only enhance relationships between the players and the men at the top.

There have been times when I've felt some administrators have dominated the sport to achieve their own ends. This undoubtedly happens in all sports, but officials should remember their responsibility is to run the sport as a business for the sport's sake, not for their own. Gone are the days of serving on boards and executives as purely a status symbol;

decisions, positive results — and especially balance sheet profits — are required. In cricket, profits can then be redirected into needy areas to secure the game's future . . . coaching, young players' tours, seminars for umpires and groundsmen, and so on. It's interesting how English soccer clubs like Nottingham Forest have directors who pay for the privilege of running the club. I also understand they're liable, personally, for deficits; you can just imagine the decision-making in a set-up like that! I'm not suggesting cricket needs a similar system — I don't think it would work anyway.

In my time as a New Zealand player there's ample evidence the NZCC has grown up. Bob Knowles used to be the council's secretary, and he was required to do everything, but, after his death, Graham Dowling became the full-time executive director and he now has a secretary under him plus additional staff — and enlarged council offices in Christchurch — to cope with the increased workload. However, I find it puzzling that Dowling, as the executive director, doesn't have a vote at board meetings. He's the link between players, administrators, sponsors and other countries; he's familiar with every aspect of New Zealand cricket. It's possibly fair to say he controls the game — and yet he doesn't have a vote! Perhaps as an employed servant, he's not entitled to vote.

It also became clear the NZCC needed a full-time marketing arm as the game blossomed into a multi-million-dollar business, which has to be run efficiently, preferably by professionals. Television's cricket presence is so enormous now that the council must be prepared to catch, and cash in on, every marketing and promotional chance available.

Some areas of the game are being well catered for. The Dennis Lillee fast bowling clinics have been beneficial (and that's an area I'm keen to be involved in again when time permits) while the introduction of Ashley Mallett to look at the spin bowling talent is similarly useful. I guess people might find it strange that Australians are doing the teaching, but I'm not unduly concerned, provided there is some Kiwi input. We also have schemes and scholarships which allow young players to go to England, the New Zealand under-20 side receives valuable exposure against Australia and twice in the 1980s a New Zealand Young Internationals team has been sent to Zimbabwe. This year a New Zealand Youth team went to England, so our young players are given enormous opportunities. This is important for our future survival at international level.

Despite such advances, I was frustrated by the council in August 1988 when I wanted to run a series of coaching clinics around New Zealand. The cricket coaching proposal was to incorporate six three-day clinics, if it received the go-ahead from the council. I spent hours planning the operation while my business manager from the International Management Group — now the NZCC's marketing company — worked hard to find a sponsor, Dominion Breweries, who had virtually accepted the deal.

But, despite DB's association with the New Zealand team, the NZCC was reluctant to allow them to back the clinics because of the tie-up of alcohol with an under-age scheme. The council wanted DB to go into the arrangement under the Pepsi banner (or low-alcohol beer), but DB didn't agree. The sponsorship was worth between $30,000 and $40,000 to the

If there's something New Zealand cricket has lacked, it has been more regular communication, on a semi-casual basis, between players and top-level administrators. It happened this time when I could chat with Ian Taylor (centre) and Alby Duckmanton, but we need more if the players and officials are to establish closer links.

R.J. Hadlee Collection

NZCC, funding which could be used in other areas of youth development. It all sounded great . . . except for the youth-liquor hassle.

So, IMG was asked to find another sponsor. An interested party was unearthed but the sponsorship offered would barely cover the costs. We would have been forced to cut corners and a proposed internal tour of two or three matches for a team selected from the clinics would have been one of the casualties, and this wasn't acceptable to the NZCC. IMG approached DB again but they weren't keen after the earlier refusal. So everything was cancelled only two weeks before the first clinic was due to be held — six months of negotiation and planning, during which the board had been indecisive, had been destroyed.

Sponsorship is vital to the success of any sport. Running costs for tours overseas — and around New Zealand — are very expensive and, at times, there's a fine line between making a small profit or suffering a huge loss. Large companies want to become involved in cricket because they recognise the opportunities to promote their products through the sport — TV, team associations and ground and media advertising.

New Zealand cricket has been blessed with support — Shell at domestic level, Rothmans internationally, and Dominion Breweries with a vested interest in the New Zealand team. While they are all happy to be involved with cricket, and may feel they've helped our survival and progress, they're naturally looking for some return on their investments. We, as players and administrators, can't expect handouts and give nothing back — exposure is important if these sponsorships are to be retained and renewed.

A major worry these days are the pressure groups like the anti-smoking and liquor brigades who are putting pressure on those sponsors and the NZCC. Restrictions on advertising have been introduced; these minority groups see cigarette advertising as encouraging youngsters to smoke, and that it's detrimental to one's health. Beer advertising and sponsorship is seen in a similar light but I don't believe these two companies — Rothmans and DB — are trying to lure young people to smoking or beer. Everyone has an individual right to choose whether they want to drink or smoke. It's a catch-22 situation because sport needs these sponsors. If they're banned from this sort of involvement, what then happens to one of New Zealand's greatest loves — sport? We can't have it both ways.

The NZCC must remember to cater fairly to the players. That hasn't necessarily been the case in the past. If players are considered and rewarded fairly, they'll tend to stay in the game longer. In earlier times, too many players retired too soon for family, business or financial reasons. We must ensure they remain on the playing fields for as long as possible. There's a cycle which must not be broken if New Zealand cricket is to continue to prosper. It begins with fostering and nurturing targeted players so they'll stay in the side for a long term, so enabling the New Zealand side to perform well. Success on the field is all important to cricket's welfare and, if the cycle is not maintained through early retirements or player resentment, then poor results will become the rule rather than the exception, crowd interest will wane, sponsors will be turned off and cricket will be staring at a crisis. The need for the administrators to consider the players cannot be overstated.

To be fair, the system now is almost acceptable. However, it may be advisable to introduce a scheme where a nucleus or squad of players are contracted to be available to play for New Zealand when required.

This seems to work in Australia, but of course the game is bigger there, and their administrators can afford this type of arrangement.

New Zealand cricket is now entering a new era, certainly from a playing point of view — the glorious '80s have gone, but our image and credibility must be maintained. With changes likely to be made at administrative level the '90s pose a testing time for everyone.

Provided we all unite to serve cricket's best interests we should continue to be successful both on and off the field.

Standing in Judgment

Umpires, as a general breed, are all too often the curse of cricket; it's a human failing to dispute or disagree with decisions made by umpires (or by those in control in any other sport for that matter). I'm not about to take the hero's way out, though. While playing cricket will soon be consigned to history for me, don't imagine I'll do the honourable thing by progressing to umpiring. My mind's set on continuing my involvement in cricket beyond the game, but umpiring's not for me — I haven't got the powers of concentration required.

I have the greatest respect for the job umpires do yet I know I haven't been happy about some umpiring displays I've witnessed. I strongly advocate that New Zealand cricket should bring on more umpires with an extensive playing background in the game. Just leave me out!

It's a sad fact in today's cricket world that apart from England, scarcely a test series goes by without some haranguing about umpires. In England the white-coated ones are consistently a level removed from their colleagues around the world.

The bitterness about umpires reached an all-time low with events in England's series against Pakistan in Pakistan in late 1987. I don't support Mike Gatting's confrontational attitude used against the Pakistani umpire Shakoor Rana; players should never stoop to such levels of blatant umpire abuse, let alone resorting to physically handling an umpire, or prodding him. At the same time, the cricketer in me sympathises with the anger Gatting felt at the time. It was his way of expressing the players' annoyance at the depths to which umpiring standards slipped during that series.

Player after player was 'sawn off' and, when Gatting blew up at Shakoor, he was doing what countless other touring teams have felt like doing for years.

Cricket turned ugly in that series — and there was still more nastiness much closer to home last season. And again the Pakistanis were the central figures. Ultimately, the abbreviated test series of two matches provided little in the way of memorable cricket, but the tourists' antics about the standard of New Zealand umpiring ensured the series was unforgettable for quite the wrong reasons.

It was clear from the outset that Pakistan arrived in New Zealand determined to set upon our umpires, as part of some premeditated plan to show the world something had to be done in the cause for neutral umpires. The players abused and swore at Steve Woodward and Brian Aldridge during the third test in Auckland, Imran Khan berated the quality of decision making and Pakistan's manager Intikhab Alam claimed Woodward and Aldridge were "biased in favour of the New Zealand batsmen". The Pakistanis simply never let up with their neutral umpires call throughout the tour.

All the time, the New Zealand Cricket Council kept its silence, diplomatically — until the very last day of the tour. Then, after we'd secured a seven-wicket win in the final Rothmans Cup match in Hamilton (to clinch the series), NZCC chairman Barry Paterson had his say: "The NZCC rejects any allegations of bias against its umpires . . . it is concerned at the manner in which Pakistani players have put extreme pressure on the umpires — visible signs of dissent and foul language have no place in any grade of cricket." That was just part of an official statement issued by Paterson.

There's no doubt at all the Pakistanis subjected our umpires to undue pressure, or that they abused them, sometimes racially. Imran denied the claims, saying: "None of our players directed abuse at them." That may be so, technically speaking, but words were said. Sometimes players don't line up an umpire and verbally attack him . . . they often turn away and direct their frustrations to the open field, but with the intention that the umpire hears them.

It seems, according to Imran, that a newspaper column I wrote before the tour annoyed the Pakistanis. I said: "New Zealanders shouldn't be so worried by the Pakistani players, but they will pressurise our umpires. Our umpires shouldn't become intimidated by their presence when it comes to making decisions . . ."

If Imran and his players were worried about that statement, then they certainly lived up to expectations by showing dissent and proving I was right. The umpires involved in the series withstood the psychological pressure well, although it's fair to say decisions went against Pakistan — as they did against us. The difference was we got on with playing the game where the Pakistanis let the umpires get to them; they didn't endear themselves to the New Zealand public by making excuses and by perpetuating their crusade for neutral umpires. After all, just who were the Pakistanis to complain about umpiring standards when the most acute problems have historically occurred in Pakistan? Were they trying to cover up for their

Steve Woodward gives Pakistani captain Imran Khan and his players the 'cool it' message after more umpire abuse during the third test in Auckland last summer. There was no justification for the way the Pakistanis treated the New Zealand umpires during the series.   J.G. Blackwell

own inadequacies in Pakistan by calling for neutral officials? Enough is enough. There are difficulties all around the world with umpires but, whatever the strife, the game still has to be played; perhaps teams should first look at their own shortcomings before chastising the umpires.

Any dissatisfaction shouldn't be aired through the media either, especially not during a series, as Pakistan did in this instance; it's common courtesy to wait until the end of a series before revealing grievances. The tour could have been so much happier — and memorable for the right reasons — had the Pakistanis left their comments until later. Then some rational appraisal may have followed instead of the emotive bleatings which rang out throughout the visit.

Incidents on England's tour of Pakistan in late 1987, then Pakistan's trip to New Zealand last summer, may yet turn out to be the awakening the game needed — if the International Cricket Conference wanted evidence that international umpiring must be seriously addressed.

Events in those campaigns once again resurrected arguments about introducing a panel of international umpires, or neutral umpires as some people like to call them. I'm on record as a supporter of the panel concept and it's an ideal I still stand by. The trouble with world cricket is that whenever there are furores like these, authorities just let it ride in the belief the passing of time will somehow eradicate the problems. The next series in Pakistan will probably recycle the same old worries, which is just what happened with Mahboob Shah when Australia played there in late 1988; seven of his decisions were questioned in the first test.

In arguing the issue, some people have harped on the need for neutral umpires to stand in tests because the umpiring controversies and incidents have got out of hand. They see a place for impartial and neutral officials in the same way rugby union, rugby league, soccer and other sports have strictly neutral referees for tests. The question of umpires for test cricket is not one of neutrality as far as I am concerned, though; it's one of competence and having the best umpires to do the job, irrespective of which country they come from. Ideally, I see the need for a panel of maybe 10 to 12 umpires who are paid a basic — and healthy — retainer plus fees and expenses for standing in international matches as they'd have to be on call or be appointed in advance for tests around the world. Obviously that could create complications for an umpire who had a steady job and that's why financial compensation would be so vital.

There will always be obstacles in considering some new scheme like this but international cricket must make a move. I've seen cricket brought into disrepute over the last year or two. It's suffering from a poor image, perhaps not of the same magnitude as that facing soccer, but nonetheless still significant enough to create an air of anxiety. While cricket has been beset by umpiring controversy before, the whole issue has been highlighted lately, and the game and the players deserve much better. If the umpires on test duty are the most capable available, regardless of colour, creed or nationality, then I'm sure players would more readily accept decisions in the dubious category, because the system would eliminate any thought of bias. I suspect an international panel, if selected today, would be dominated by Englishmen but I wouldn't care if there were six Indians and six Pakistanis on a 12-man panel, provided they were the best. There'd have to be constant updating and assessment of these umpires with those not rating with captains or assessors being replaced. It couldn't be a cosy little panel for the chosen 10 or 12; like players, they'd still have to perform.

I know Martin Snedden has slightly different views. Rather than an international panel, he favours the neutral concept and believes there should be a panel of 14 umpires — two from each of the seven test-playing nations. He suggests an ICC fund — with equal contributions from all seven countries — be set up to cover umpires' fees, transport and accommodation costs.

In reality, I wonder just how any panel would or could work because so many questions have to be answered, not the least being the financial one. At a guess, umpires on a panel would probably have to be guaranteed a basic income of about $50,000 a year plus expenses. And, when you look at it like that, and begin to count the cost, cricket might be better off making do with the present system. It's not great — but what else can we do? Maybe some form of sponsorship's the answer.

The very thought of changing international cricket's umpiring structure tells something of the modern age's fixation with what's good and bad about sporting officials. Much is made of the fact umpires are now under intensive scrutiny from television cameras with the repeated replays of decisions given (or not given). While that can be very unfair on umpires it's also a fact of sporting life that their moves will be analysed. Players are under just as much pressure to perform and behave on the field. If we make idiots of ourselves then that's highlighted and umpires, despite their complaints, just have to accept the same consequences if they make mistakes. Television can illustrate some very good decisions, and some very bad ones. How often have we seen replays of a run out showing a batsman literally two or three inches out of his ground and given not out by the umpire? Technically the batsman was out but really an umpire can't rule that way on such a tight call. If he gives him out and replays subsequently show he was right, it could only be regarded as a fluke decision. It's the more blatant incidents which deservedly irk players — and embarrass umpires — which television can highlight well. In truth, replays of such glaring errors are the equivalent of multiple replays of a batsman being dismissed playing indiscreetly. You made an error in judgment, television showed it to thousands of viewers many times over and you have to lump it.

Poor decisions in tests are utterly critical. One bad one, or a collection of them, can not only alter the outcome of a match, they can also ruin or very severely affect a player's livelihood. Even good players have bad patches of form, putting together a run of low scores through a mixture of bad luck and indifferent technique. Should such a player also be the victim of a couple of bad decisions they could very easily contribute to his axing from a test side. A tour place might also hang on them and suddenly the player is in the wilderness. With the combined loss of revenue, a player's international career could be in tatters. That emphasises the importance of the umpire's role and the enormous responsibility he has to make accurate decisions.

Respect between players and umpires is a two-way business which is ultimately so dependent on an umpire's personal qualities and ability. He must know the book obviously but that's nowhere near enough in itself. An umpire needs to have a feel for cricket and, if he has played the game at a reasonable level — and particularly up to first-class standard — it makes a big difference. Then he can understand player frustrations, match tensions and general pressures on the field, as well as being able to sniff out and quell potentially explosive situations. An umpire without the players' respect will invariably find himself immersed in ugly confrontations.

The respect factor is more evident in English county cricket than anywhere else in the world. Players generally have respect for each other . . . and for the umpires. If a player cheats the system and becomes known for nicking the ball and not walking, it soon gets around the counties and he will find marginal decisions going against him. If you're known for fair play, then you're helping each other. My part in the first test against England in Christchurch in 1987–88 was all too brief (and frustrating) but, before straining my right calf, I was a little staggered to witness umpire Brian Aldridge's reaction to the on-field atmosphere between the two sides. He really couldn't credit the banter between myself and some of the English players in the test arena. What he didn't realise was such carrying on is commonplace on the county scene, because of the mutual respect;

you don't survive in that environment if you have a bad reputation. And yet the game still remains competitive.

It all comes back to familiarity, and the difference between umpires who insist on being little Hitlers and those who find the balance between being the ultimate decision maker and doing the job in such a way that they have the players at ease. Trevor Bailey, the former England all rounder, probably hit the spot nicely when he discussed the merits of batsmen who walk. In a newspaper article, Bailey wrote: "I was raised on the principle of walking, which worked well within the narrow confines of the county circuit, where all the players and umpires knew each other well and could afford to tolerate the few who ignored the unofficial code. I first began to have doubts about these ethical conventions on my first tour of Australia. It did not take long to realise their bowlers, with considerable vocal support from the rest of the team, appealed for anything remotely resembling a catch or an lbw, while their batsmen retaliated by invariably staying put. To some extent, their approach stemmed from the umpires not being personal friends, so they were treated as referees and left to make decisions without assistance."

That encapsulates the gulf between umpires in England and, generally speaking, the rest of the world. The difference is more pronounced in New Zealand where most umpires have had little, if any, playing experience. While they have the theoretical knowledge they lack experience in most other areas and tend to become isolated in the top-level cricket environment. It's hard for them to become part of the set-up and so they're aloof, where their English counterparts aren't. Umpires in England are altogether more relaxed and often enjoy a beer with the players at the end of the day.

The nature of the cricketing environments in England and New Zealand, as an example, also accentuates another problem. English umpires are able to subsist on a regular diet of first-class cricket and so they have ample opportunity to hone their performances. Yet in New Zealand, umpires have to fossick for more than a few first-class matches each season. It's not the preparation they need for test cricket. Fred Goodall, New Zealand's best-known umpire, would move from school teaching five days a week to stand in a club match. Later in the season he'd progress to Shell Cup and Shell Trophy matches, maybe doing three first-class matches before going into a test series against a side like the West Indies who would have four fast bowlers operating at ferocious pace.

The jump from club to first-class and then to test cricket is too sudden and a lack of preparation tends to show up in New Zealand umpires.

I've seen it happen regularly in New Zealand cricket where umpires take anywhere up to 20 seconds before giving a player out. To me, there must be doubt when an umpire takes so long over putting his finger up. He has to make decisions on what he sees, what he hears and on the actions or reactions of the players involved. They're the three basic elements I believe an umpire should use and, because all three go together, a decision should be spontaneous. Even if it's wrong, it's done swiftly.

In England the pattern is different. If there's a caught-behind appeal, the umpire will deliberately wait to give the batsman the chance to walk; if the batsman doesn't go then the umpire will give him out. Once again, it's the respect syndrome which exists on the county circuit.

I rate cricket umpiring the most demanding refereeing assignment of any sport but umpires can help themselves by being a little more laid back and relaxed about it. I like umpires who find the time to have a brief chat with a player standing nearby, the batsman at the non-striker's end, or the bowler. Perhaps the umpire might tell the bowler he's close to no-balling or maybe he's in danger of being called for running on the pitch. I believe an umpire needs to chat with players just to break the intense periods of concentration and, at the same time, win the players over a bit with his demeanour.

If umpires refuse to open communication lines, you'll find the players putting pressure on them. I know I've been guilty of standing my ground and forcing the umpire to make the decision instead of leaving when I have known I was out. There was such a case in the third test against Australia in Auckland in 1985–86; I nicked a delivery from Bruce Reid which was caught by the 'keeper Tim Zoehrer and, instead of going, I stood and left the decision to the umpire. I hit the ball all right but was given not out. I know it's not right; it was a case of double standards on my part. However, I took that approach because there were so many batsmen I felt I had genuinely dismissed who weren't given out, or hadn't walked. So why should I? It's one of the unpalatable by-products of poor umpiring or the lack of rapport between player and umpire.

It's common practice today for touring teams to criticise the umpires but I have the impression New Zealand umpires, unwittingly or otherwise, tend to look after the touring sides better than the locals. I'd suggest New Zealand teams have had more rough calls than the tourists in series in New Zealand in my time, and that might be construed as the umpires' way of removing accusations of bias. But, in doing so, they go too far the other way (with the exception of the ill-tempered series against the West Indies in 1979–80 when there was no doubt New Zealand benefited more from marginal decisions). Efforts to do the so-called right thing create so much tension, especially on the question of lbw appeals.

Some New Zealand umpires are very tough on leg-before decisions, especially in the test arena; they seem to adopt a policy of not giving any, or very few. In contrast, English umpires will give batsmen out on the front foot or when sweeping across the line.

The first test against England in Christchurch in 1987–88 was notable for the paucity of leg-before appeals won throughout most of the match. There were none in England's first innings and only one (Martin Snedden) in New Zealand's first innings; England's second innings provided just one lbw before something went horribly wrong in our second innings. Of the four batsmen dismissed — as New Zealand went on to safely draw the test — three were out leg-before. The pressure was on from the bowlers and the England players on the last day and the umpires were giving lbws. I'm not disagreeing with their judgments in those instances because I thought the calls were fair. But they weren't giving any on the first few days of the match and, if the ones on the last day were sound decisions, then some of the appeals earlier in the match were equally clear cut . . . but given not out. It's as if our umpires subconsciously feel guilty they haven't given any lbws and need to get a couple in the bank; they feel too many lbws given will somehow tarnish their reputations.

Fred Goodall gained a place in the record books when he gave me all those lbws in the 1979–80 test against the West Indies in Dunedin (seven of the 11 wickets I took in the match). And Tony Crafter gave me six in the third test against Australia at the Melbourne Cricket Ground in 1987–88. There's nothing wrong with that, though. It doesn't mean someone's not a good umpire because he gives a lot of lbw decisions; if he's giving them, he's a brave umpire and can still be a very competent one. But it's the inconsistent displays, like those in the test against England in Christchurch, which naturally antagonise and annoy players.

New Zealand's 1984–85 tour to Pakistan threw up some horrendous umpiring problems, from what I've heard from the players who made that tour under Jeremy Coney's captaincy. Jerry was sufficiently angered to speak out publicly about the Pakistani umpires at one stage, so giving some credence to what happened when Mike Gatting blew up there in late 1987. I missed that tour and cannot therefore give a first-hand view of the errors made. But New Zealand's 1987–88 tour to Australia was notable for umpiring hassles, too. We lost a lot of confidence in Australian umpires generally, more so than on our previous visits. Some wouldn't make any decisions and some would make them all the time; there was absolutely no consistency. Players don't want umpires who become actively involved in the game when it suits them. Their involvement mustn't waver.

Perhaps the most concerning issue on the tour, though, was the move to give two umpires their first-class debuts in our matches against state sides Western Australia and South Australia. They were, in fact, international matches and surely that's no way to introduce new umpires; they should start their first-class careers in Sheffield Shield matches and work up from there.

In our four-day match against South Australia in Adelaide, we had Tony Crafter at one end and a novice, Daryl Harper, at the other. Harper really struggled. Feelings became a little frayed between Harper and off spinner John Bracewell, so much so, it probably seemed I moved in to stifle a verbal confrontation at one stage when Braces had another appeal turned down. In fact, when I put up my hands in an apparent keep-it-cool gesture, I actually said: "That's 10 (bad decisions), and that one was a shocker!" Some of the Australian umpires scored very low points with us including Mel Johnson, Robin Bailhache, Dick French and Steve Randell. Crafter was one umpire I found good value. He was approachable and made some brave decisions, especially in the amazing third test in Melbourne.

Dickie Bird won't be seen without his constant companion and trademark, his white cap. He's a "human" umpire, one who's prepared to acknowledge players while standing out as an excellent operator, certainly the best I've come across. New Zealand umpires could learn so much from him.   Ken Kelly

But when I think of umpires I've been involved with, England's Dickie Bird is unquestionably the first who comes to mind. He's one of umpiring's great characters, as much a personality as any player. But he's not merely an infectious character; he's undoubtedly the best umpire in world cricket today, and enjoys enormous respect from most players. Dickie's nervous and fidgety and is instantly recognisable by the little idiosyncracies and gestures which are part of his make-up. He's totally aware of these outward signs of nervousness and has said of them: "I am highly strung. All my mannerisms which I have, come out of me when I am on the field, and this helps me to unwind when I am in the middle." As an umpire, he's an outstanding operator, though. To me he's somebody special, one of those umpires who stands no nonsense and gets on with the game . . . but in a friendly manner. He would ask me how my father was or what had happened to John Reid, Bert Sutcliffe and other players of that era. He's not afraid to have a private conversation during play — even if it's something completely divorced from the action — just to give him a break. Otherwise he'll tell you whether you're bowling well, or he might offer the theory you'll get a certain batsman out soon. "Keep bowling there, he might nick one," he'd say to me. Dickie would smile as I beat the batsman again, as if he got a real thrill out of it. Get the batsman out, and his look would say: "I told you so!" In a way he motivated you. It's pertinent, too, that he's an umpire who's played first-class cricket (for Yorkshire and Leicestershire).

Quite apart from his peculiar mannerisms, Dickie is known for one special trademark — the white cap he always wears when umpiring. He lost one of the caps when a supporter came on to the field and took it at the end of the 1975 World Cup final between the West Indies and Australia at Lord's. "But there was an amusing sequel," said Dickie. "A few days later I was travelling on a bus in London, and the West Indian bus conductor was wearing a white cap which looked like one of mine. I said to him: 'Where did you get that cap from?' 'It was from Dickie Bird, the test umpire. He's my friend, he gave it to me,' he said proudly. He then said to me: 'You must have heard of him MAN.' He didn't recognise me and I decided against trying to reclaim the cap."

Another former Leicestershire player turned umpire is Ray Julian, who gave me quite a few lbw decisions, simply because I bowl wicket to wicket and create more chances than most bowlers. He's also known for giving batsmen out quickly and even keeps a count of his decisions. Before a county championship match against Leicestershire at Trent Bridge, I was going through the process of choosing which ball I wanted when Ray asked me: "What end are you bowling from today?" "I'll wait until I get outside and see what direction your hanky is blowing," I told him. "I think you should bowl from the Radcliffe Road end," said Ray. "I'll check it in the middle." As I walked out the door from the umpires' room, I heard him say to his partner, John Hampshire: "Jack, do you mind if I stand at the Radcliffe Road end? I think I'll get a few more today." For the record, I don't recall Ray giving me one lbw that day, although he had said: "I need 45 more lbws to get my hundred for the season."

That genial approach reflects favourably on English umpires in general whereas New Zealand umpires are all too often too rigid. They're not all robots though and there are definite signs they're relaxing and beginning to open up.

My test career began in the days of umpires like Dick Shortt, Bob Monteith, Fred Goodall (naturally), John Hastie and the like, along with a very interesting character in Ralph Gardiner. I first encountered Gardiner in the third test against Australia in 1973–74; he was unforgettable for one reason — his stance. He used to crouch down, with his eyes just above bail height. When the new wave of umpires came along, Goodall remained a constant factor. We had Dave Kinsella at one stage in the 1980s; he was a rarity in New Zealand cricket — a first-class cricketer turned umpire — but there were doubts about his overall umpiring ability. Another who appeared briefly was the late Bruce Bricknell. He umpired one test only (against Australia in Auckland in 1981–82) and was involved in a number of controversial incidents in that match.

One of the survivors has been Wellington's Steve Woodward, who first began umpiring at first-class level in the mid-1970s. As New Zealand's second most-experienced test umpire — behind Goodall — he's improved considerably and has tried to be more relaxed out in the middle, but I've found it very difficult to get decisions out of him. The singular lack has been umpires who are characters. One of the few was former test player Keith Thomson, who came through the fast-track system; he used to hand out advice by saying: "All you have to do is hit that bloke on the pad and there's a good chance he'll be out." He was probably over-involved in the action and now he's off the scene.

Along with Woodward, the cluster of international umpires now includes Brian Aldridge, Rodger McHarg, George Morris and Steve Dunne, who made his test debut against Pakistan last season. They provide the nucleus of the top operators. In general, our umpires have been a rather dour and colourless lot, undoubtedly affected by the dominant figure of this era, Fred Goodall. For too long he mirrored a stiff-upper-lip approach. I think he stayed perhaps one or two years longer than he should have at international level, before retiring in 1988. His undoing was the second New Zealand-West Indies test in Auckland in 1986–87 when he was put under severe pressure. West Indian captain Viv Richards made racist remarks at Goodall — and was seriously wrong to do so — but his abuse upset Goodall's decision-making and concentration. When I was batting, Fred was saying to himself: "Concentrate, concentrate." He was hyping himself up and I just couldn't believe it was happening. You hear players doing that sort of thing, but not umpires. It was very unusual, and a sign to me that, sadly, Goodall was at the end of his international umpiring days.

I always found him difficult to deal with on a player-umpire basis because he wouldn't chat. He'd simply stand there and make decisions. Maybe it was just his schoolmasterly manner, but he'd go by the rule book totally and wasn't at all flexible. He tried to stamp his authority on a match rather than being there to oversee the action, and that inevitably led to confrontation situations.

The very mention of Fred Goodall's name invariably revives talk of the ugly Colin Croft shoulder charge during the ill-tempered series against the West Indies in 1979–80. The incident that seemed to fire the outrageous Croft assault in Christchurch came when I stood my ground after an appeal for a catch off Croft's bowling. I stayed because the series had turned nasty by then anyway, and Fred gave me not out. Croft's act prompted some calls for umpires to have greater disciplinary powers. After all, in a sport like rugby, league or soccer, Croft would have been ordered off and very likely banned for life for hitting an official. But despite what happened at Lancaster Park that day, cricket remains essentially a gentlemanly game and the need for a sin bin or any other form of on-field punishment is totally unnecessary. I could never agree with what Croft did — and no one in his right mind would — yet happenings in that series do highlight one of the crucial umpiring tasks I have mentioned . . . the ability to sense volatile situations developing and the skill to nip the trouble before it really blows. There was a chain of events after Goodall turned down the appeal against me, finishing up with him confronting West Indian captain Clive Lloyd. Lloyd didn't want to know Goodall, though, because he didn't respect him or rate his decision-making. It's that word respect again. The secret is to move swiftly, and not to allow ill feeling to fester and then explode.

As a bowler, I build up a collection of mental pictures of batsmen so I'll know how to attack them when they face me. In exactly the same way, umpires need that kind of knowledge. They need to study teams and players for all sorts of reasons — to establish who the likely troublemakers are in a side or to suss out co-operative players whose common sense they may need in ticklish times. On the score of decision-making alone, an umpire should collect information about the way batsmen and bowlers operate . . . which shots various batsmen favour and the variations a bowler might use. He needs to look for the batsman who plays off the back foot a lot; he must be vulnerable to a leg-before decision if he's struck on the pads. The batsmen who push forward predominantly or perhaps bat a little out of their crease; the lbw odds must be longer for them. Likewise the bowlers have to be studied carefully. If a bowler comes in wide on the crease he can't hope to snare too many lbw victims while someone like me, who bowls very close in to the stumps, should receive a much higher percentage of leg-befores.

One modern-day development which leaves me completely cold is the idea of having women umpires. For the first time, we had a woman standing in top-level cricket in 1986–87 — Pat Carrick — who made her first-class debut in a Shell Trophy match I also happened to be playing in at Lancaster Park.

I find the concept of women umpires quite strange. Should a woman be placed in a man's environment and be subjected to abuse, criticism and frustration from players? That was my argument about Carrick being promoted to first-class level . . . if she wants to be part of the scene she has to accept all the trappings which are inevitable in this level of competition. I couldn't question her ability; I thought she did the job satisfactorily. But, while she may stay on the first-class panel, will she ever control a test match and, if not, is she depriving our top operators from gaining much-

New Zealand's two most experienced test umpires — Fred Goodall and Steve Woodward (holding the helmet). Goodall has now retired from the international scene after a controversial but distinguished career at international level. And now Woodward is poised to overtake Goodall's record of 24 tests.   J.G. Blackwell needed experience and practice for international matches?

While I can't see Pat making it to test level, it's still perfectly conceivable she could. She proved her ability to gain first-class status and could logically be scored well by captains in their reports, even better than some of those umpires already on the international panel. That would suggest she's capable of standing in test matches — but should she? Technically there may be no reason why she shouldn't. We may soon see women rugby referees in a similar situation. But can you see a woman ever officiating in a test between the All Blacks and the Australians! The International Rugby Board would never let it happen.

Of course, women have a point when they state men officiate in women's matches so why not the reverse? But it's not for me.

Another new move in cricket surrounds the use of electronic aids for umpires, or even a third 'eye' sitting somewhere in one of the stands watching television replays of tight decisions before confirming which way the appeal should go. None of these inventions are acceptable to me.

There's talk of umpires having little television screens to watch slow-motion replays as well as the third umpire scheme. But I believe the umpires in the middle are the judges and it's very much part of the game for them to make decisions the way they see them. The umpire at the non-striker's end does have assistance from the square-leg umpire, in much the same way the referee in rugby, league and soccer matches has touch judges or linesmen to call on. Of course, even the square-leg umpires do get things wrong, as Australia's Dick French did with the infamous Greg Dyer 'catch' when we played Australia in the third test of the 1987–88 series in Melbourne. Tony Crafter looked towards French to seek confirmation whether the catch from Andrew Jones had been taken fairly. We all know Dyer didn't glove the catch but French couldn't see what happened properly and the appeal was upheld, when the doubt should surely have been in the batsman's favour.

An area which is always a tough one for umpires to police is that of short-pitched bowling. And, yet again, it's a facet of the game which is hampered by umpiring inconsistency. The short-pitched delivery is part of the bowler's weaponry which, on it's own, may not produce a wicket but it will often unsettle a player and perhaps indirectly bring about his dismissal soon after. As long as bowlers don't overdo it, the shorter delivery is fine. When a bowler uses it three times in an over for two or three overs on end, then it's intimidatory, dangerous and unnecessary. The umpire has a duty in such a situation to warn the bowler.

While I sympathise with Ewen Chatfield, who knows the dangers of short-pitched bowling only too graphically, I could never go along with the idea of so-called non-recognised batsmen being protected from the short delivery. Test cricket is very much a war, country against country, and players who perform at this level have to accept everything that comes to them. Certainly lower order batsmen, without any great batting claims, should be shielded to a degree if they're subjected to persistent short-pitched bowling. But if one of those players hangs around for quite a while — as Charlie Chatfield did against Pakistan in Dunedin in 1984–85 — then he's frustrating the fielding side and must expect a couple of short balls. Charlie himself knows the score, even though he was hit by England's Peter Lever in 1974–75.

I like to use the short-pitched ball sparingly, as a surprise weapon . . . which is the way it should be used. But I can't understand players who deliberately try to hit and maim batsmen; Australia's Jeff Thomson is on record as saying he liked seeing blood. I find that very callous; I've never intentionally set out to hit anyone. It happens sometimes through bad pitches and indifferent technique.

Certainly there have been occasions when I have gone out of my way to bounce players. I gave England's Neil Foster a volley of short-pitched balls in Wellington in 1983–84 as my form of revenge. He'd bounced me when I batted and I figure, if a guy is prepared to give them out, then he has to take them. It helped me get him out, too. In the West Indies in 1984–85, we copped plenty of short stuff, about two days solid of it from the four-pronged fast attack in one of the tests. So I reacted by trying to bowl four or five short-pitched deliveries at Joel Garner and, being the man he is, I could only get the ball up to chest height at best on Big Bird. And yet Wes Hall, the West Indian manager, said the umpires should have taken some control because it was bad cricket. Just who are the West Indies to complain? They serve it out non-stop and here I was bowling a spate of shortish balls in just one over! I was the only bowler in the team who could dish it out and the lads demanded I seek some retribution after what we'd been subjected to. In fairness to Wes Hall, the intent was there in my case so, perhaps, the umpires should have done something to quell what was going on, and prevent it developing further.

While I have some strong views on umpiring standards, I can't say I've had too many on-field problems with umpires, although there was one in the third test against Sri Lanka in Colombo in 1983–84 and another in the third test against India in Madras in 1976.

Indian (and Pakistani) umpires have been called many things and, in the Madras test, I found out why. I bowled a bouncer to Anshuman Gaekwad. The ball didn't bounce much at all, it went through to the 'keeper, Warren Lees, and Gaekwad lost his balance. We noticed a bail had fallen off and we all appealed for the batsman to be out, hit wicket, captain Glenn Turner being adamant Gaekwad had flicked the bail off as he reeled. Both umpires conferred — and gave Gaekwad not out! When we asked why, they said: "The wind blew the bail off." We were incredulous; it was a windless day and, at the end of the over, I snatched my hat out of the umpire's hand and mumbled a few choice words. The umpire approached Turner and asked him to control his player to which Turns replied: "Once he starts whacking you over the head with the hat is when you have to worry." Eventually I knocked Gaekwad's off stump out of the ground, breaking it in two pieces, which prompted one of the players to say: "Bloody strong wind!"

Funnily enough, my little contretemps with an umpire in Colombo in 1983–84 also involved my hat, and again it was all so petty. At the start of one over, I left my hat on the stumps for the umpire (P. W. Vithanagamage) to pick up so I could get back to my mark quickly and get on with the game; he wasn't happy with that so, the next over, I left the hat on the ground and walked back to my mark. Still not happy, he called out to me: "You have to give me your hat. I will not start the over until you give it to me." I was trying to be helpful but he took it the other way.

Proof once again that cricket's umpiring world is bursting with officials who become just a little too power-crazy once they put on a white coat.

Interestingly enough, New Zealand's next test in Sri Lanka in 1986–87 — the only one of the aborted series — threw Vidi and me together again. That time there were no problems, and we had a very happy player-umpire relationship. I'm pleased to say there are people who can forget and get on with the game instead of holding grudges.

C·H·A·P·T·E·R F·O·U·R·T·E·E·N

Hares and Hounds

I t's part of the international cricketer's ritual. You stagger out of bed and stoop to pick up the morning paper outside your hotel room door. Bleary-eyed, still wiping sleep out of your eyes, you immediately flick over to the sports page, searching for what the newspaper has to say about the match you're playing in.

Sometimes you're shocked, other times plain flabbergasted, or sent into a fuming rage; on another morning there might be nodding agreement with the way some cricket writer has encapsulated events, perhaps the odd flutter inside on seeing your own achievements in print.

But one newspaper's never enough. In Australia and England there're a swag of morning papers on offer at the newsagent; and I like to digest what everyone has been writing whenever possible. I'm on the look-out, sometimes as ready to pounce on a journalist as I might be on an opposition batsman when I'm bowling.

Later in the day, the emphasis switches from the written word to the spoken. It's time to listen to the men behind the microphones on radio and television. Their job's often more straightforward; they have to describe events as they see them, or as they happen. But they, too, with their interpretations and comments on the game can infuriate, embarrass, belittle, applaud and inspire.

In cricket, in sport, the media has power, more than many people ever appreciate. Most sportsmen never master the ability to handle or manage the media; a few are champions at it, but not very many.

The fact is, journalists and commentators are seemingly always under suspicion, players wary of what might be said or written about them

— 243 —

tomorrow, next week or next month. There's so little respite. It could be sweetness and light today, but tomorrow doom and despair.

Media exposure's necessary, vital for the well-being of any sport but, too often for sportsmen, it's a necessary evil. Most sporting people are sensitive and critical about the way the media cover their sport. I've certainly been one of that large group. Success in sport brings rewards either through winning matches, or series, or being honoured with man-of-the-match awards. Success also brings increased coverage in the papers, on the radio and on television; it burgeons, snowballs the more you succeed. And then, when you fail, it's still there because, while people like winners, they also revel in those winners tasting failure. It's part of the fascination about sport, perhaps more so about cricket which is so much a numbers game.

I've attracted my share of abuse or negative reaction in the media; I'll certainly concede I've also received untold praise, sometimes bordering on adulation it seems. It cuts both ways. And that's fine, as long as there is a balance.

I wonder if it has all weighed up though. As I'm so sensitive to criticism, I've felt and reacted to the media's rougher side more readily than most of my contemporaries. I've probably had more reason because I've been subjected to a heavier dose of media attack. I know people say you shouldn't read the papers, and there are players who claim they follow that rule, but I don't really believe that. It's natural to want to know what various writers say about a match you're playing in, and what comments they might make about your own performance, or about incidents. Reaction is all a matter of degree. I don't mind the facts. If I've bowled indifferently or hit myself out by batting irresponsibly, then I accept there'll be some adverse comment. So there should be. Over the years, I've become increasingly self-critical of my own efforts. If I've thought I've performed poorly, I've said so in my newspaper columns or on radio; and I've been just as forthright in times of success. You can't pretend to recognise only the good times and ignore the bad.

When it comes to newspapers, I'm well read. I read just about every publication available. I'll digest what has been written and think about it. I try to understand why writers say certain things about me, or about the team I'm in and the way we're performing. If I think someone has got it wrong, then I'll seek the journalist out and try to discuss it with him. The intention's never to have a raging argument, just to establish an understanding. I've never seen any value in sweating and stewing on what a journalist has written. If you're not happy, it's far better to come out in the open and say so.

When I first stepped on to the international stage, the media issue wasn't one for me to worry about. There were plenty of other players who commanded interest then, like Bruce Taylor, Glenn Turner and Mark Burgess. But I soon realised the men in the media underestimate the influence they have. They can destroy a player's confidence and mental approach with just a few words; I know — because I've seen it happen. If a journalist calls for a player to be axed, he may only be expressing an opinion but the comment can have a telling effect, even on the selectors.

I'm not about to indulge in a mindless game of rating members of the media I've encountered in New Zealand, Australia, England, the West Indies, Pakistan, India, Sri Lanka or even Sharjah. There's little to be gained out of classifying the good, the bad and the ugly. My concern is more with the interpretation and reaction to incidents and issues which have affected me during my career. I believe the standard of New Zealand cricket journalism is generally very high. That may reflect on the lack of true competition; with a limited number of papers, there's not so much of the cut and thrust between journalists, which undoubtedly softens the sensational edge which is so prevalent in Australia and England. In those countries it's the startling angle which often becomes more important than the game itself, or at least that's the way it seems to me. You find controversy or incidents on and off the field suffocate the actual play. It's all out of kilter. I can understand why journalists strive to outdo each other . . . but I don't necessarily condone it. It's their way of doing their job, and often they're under pressure from their superiors. It's difficult to argue with that.

What has surprised me, though, is the difference between the media in New Zealand and England; throughout my county career with Nottinghamshire — admittedly away from the glare of the international scene — I never had any problems with the Press. But at home or when I've toured Australia there has often been trouble with the media. In the northern hemisphere I was treated as a professional doing my job but, down under, it's different.

In 1978, I began a long association with *Truth*, providing a regular column until 1987 when I switched to the new Auckland daily, *The Sun*, which sadly lasted less than a year. After its demise, I linked up with the *Auckland Star*. I've also written columns and articles for overseas magazines and papers, and have a weekly report on Christchurch radio 3ZB. I've dabbled in television commentary work, having a taste when I was injured during the 1987-88 series against England, and again last summer during the Rothmans Cup one-dayers against Pakistan. So, while I've been hunted by the media, I've also been very much involved in it.

The media avenue has been a necessary one for me as it has provided an income. I also think the average bloke wants to hear or read views from players who have some experience in the game. A column by a player carries some credibility; it provides some inside comment and opinion from the people who are in the know.

Newspaper columns became more common as New Zealand cricket prospered. While Glenn Turner and I were among the earliest newspaper columnists, other New Zealand players have tried their hand at the exercise — John Wright, Geoff Howarth, Jeremy Coney, Lance Cairns, Gary Troup, Martin Snedden, Jeff and Martin Crowe, Stephen Boock, Bruce Edgar, John Bracewell and Ian Smith among them. As the Danny Morrisons and Willie Watsons settle into international life, they'll no doubt do the same.

Writing — and the word should be used advisedly — columns does set you up a little, though. My columns have generally been ghosted; a professional journalist puts together my thoughts. But you're as suscept-

The Press corps in India in 1988 — the New Zealand Press Association's David Leggat (left), son of former New Zealand test player Gordon Leggat; the *New Zealand Herald's* Don Cameron; photographer Ross Setford; and the *Auckland Star's* Eric Young.   J.G. Blackwell

ible to criticism as the journalists. Your opinion is never going to please everyone and can provoke discussion and argument. It's difficult to be too critical on tour, or during a home series, because the NZCC closely governs the writing of columns; you can't, for instance, comment in a negative way about umpires, team-mates or pitches, and discussion about injuries is prohibited. They're the rules, but sometimes, with a careful choice of words, the ghost writer can still make your point. But go too far and you pay the penalty, usually with a reprimand from the NZCC or sometimes a fine.

I've sailed close on a number of occasions, incurring the NZCC's wrath without, so far, receiving a fine. There have been some reprimands, but as a professional I feel I need to express views which might bring about better results or improved conditions. If we're playing on a poor pitch, why shouldn't I be allowed to say so? After all, it affects the performance of the team; it's a way of putting things in perspective.

I enjoy providing my thoughts for papers and radio, and it's not something I take lightly. There is, however, jealousy from some people in the media about cricketers earning money from columns they don't physically write. I picked up *The Australian* one morning on our 1987–88 tour to see a story from Terry Brindle which started this way:

"One of the unmistakable signs of superstardom is being paid handsomely for doing something reluctantly and not very well.

"As a communicator, Richard Hadlee is a very fine fast bowler."

And it continued further on:

". . . Hadlee has signed a newspaper contract which will turn his innermost thoughts on the coming series against Australia into cash at an hourly rate which is usually the preserve of millionaires and stock market speculators.

"By the good offices of a journalist earning a comparative pittance, he will achieve a level of articulation that will quite probably surprise even himself."

But Brindle's most cutting lines came later in the article when he wrote: "It is fashionable to say that he is unpopular with his team-mates and there is little doubt that if the price of acceptance was loss of his independence, he would not pay it."

I spoke to Brindle about that story and said I thought the story was unreasonable.

Putting a column together is not the simple exercise, for me, which Brindle and others might believe it is. On our tour of Australia in 1987–88, I had daily commitments to *The Sun* throughout a test match. Picture the match at Adelaide, where we spent two full days in the field with temperatures up to 40 degrees and more; there were only a few moments to unwind after the day, before I had to compose my thoughts and discuss my column. It's anything but easy, with the time difference and the pressure of deadlines, to tune in to those kinds of demands after a day in the field.

My 3ZB radio spot has been running for several years, and it's more laid back, more conversational. In England, I'd place a call on Friday nights to do a live interview for 3ZB listeners to hear around 9.30 on Saturday morning. Wherever I was, in a hotel, on the motorway or at a dinner, I'd find a telephone to make my call. Over the years, it's become much more spontaneous and much credit must go to 3ZB announcer Mike Richardson, a Canadian who professed to know absolutely nothing about cricket when we first started doing the weekly slots.

I recall one session when Mike said: "Well, where are you today, Richard?" "I'm actually calling on a car phone and we're lost somewhere in Wiltshire, trying to find the main road so we can get back to Nottingham." Another time was much less exotic. "I'm in a phone box," I told Mike, "and the rain's pouring in. I'm getting wet and feeling miserable." Another phone box call had to be made through the stench of urine. "There's a bit of a smell in here, Mike. I don't think I want to stay in here too long!"

I usually call Mike and, off air, discuss questions and topic areas he could ask me about. But on the 1984–85 tour to the West Indies I struck a hitch one Saturday when I called up and spoke to another announcer who was filling in for Mike. I said: "Well, we'll talk about this and you can ask me about that and that. Do you understand? Everything under control?"

To my embarrassment he came back and said: "Well, Richard we're live at the moment." I cringed. But that bloke didn't do the interview again. As with newspaper columns, I prepare for the Saturday call-up. I'll sit down and reflect on happenings in cricket for the week and make sure it's topical. Of course, we don't stick to cricket alone. If there's a big sporting event — like a rugby match — coming up that weekend, there will always be some comment about it. I love radio, and I'd like to be more involved in it, when I eventually finish playing, with a preference for commentary work.

Cricket commentaries have always been special to me. Like so many cricket lovers, I relished listening to a crackling, old, valve wireless when overseas tests were broadcast. Radio commentary is the one area of the game where there's tremendous scope to enlighten and enliven proceedings for the listener, creating a picture with your words. It is, of course, the one medium which is infamous for its gaffes as well. Because radio commentators do so much talking, I suppose it's predictable they'll slip up more than a few times. Some, like the BBC's Brian Johnston, are famous for the bloopers they make; it's as if they can't help themselves. Johnston owns up to gaffes which have really become part of cricket folk-lore and, even if they're well worn, many still stand up well. It was Johnston who once told listeners: "You join us at an interesting time. Ray Illingworth has just relieved himself at the Pavilion End." There was also the time when a mouse ran across the pitch during a test at Edgbaston; play was held up while the players tried to catch the mouse, the action being caught by television cameras with Johnston behind the microphone. "They are bound to catch it soon — it's got no hole to go down," he said, before adding: "Lucky it's not a ladies' match." Another famous one was: "D'Oliveira is getting badly punished by the Hampshire batsmen. A moment or two before you joined us Barry Richards hit one of Dolly's balls clean out of the park."

Commentators leave themselves wide open. How about these:

"I don't think he expected it, and that's what caught him unawares" — Trevor Bailey.
"Then there was that dark horse with the golden arm, Mudassar Nazar" — Bailey again.
"The Queen's Park Oval — as its name suggests, perfectly round" — Tony Cozier.
"Well, everyone's enjoying this except Vic Marks, and I think he's enjoying himself" — Don Mosey.
"And Marshall throws his head to his hands" — Christopher Martin-Jenkins.
"People started calling me 'fiery' because 'fiery' rhymes with Fred, as 'typhoon' rhymes with Tyson" — Fred Trueman.
"His throw went absolutely nowhere near where it was going" — Richie Benaud.

There are so many more, gems most of them, from out of radio commentators' mouths, although there are precious few credited to New Zealand commentators (they're either too clever or no one has started a list). But one of the better lines, oft repeated but unsourced, is told against a New Zealand player, former test player Bob Cunis: "Cunis. A funny sort of name. Neither one thing nor the other."

When I think radio commentators, I can't help but mention the quite incomparable John Arlott and Brian Johnston, each successful in the medium of contrasting ways, Arlott had a quite unique power with his descriptive ability . . .

> "A constable is using his helmet to cover the streaker's confusion."

> "As the train withdraws from the Warwick Road end, so does Boycott, caught Marsh, bowled Lillee, no score."

> "If you can see the Pennines it is about to rain — if you can't see them, it is raining."

There was no fanfare from him when he retired from broadcasting, no special farewells. In fact, his last words were: "After Trevor Bailey, it will be Christopher Martin-Jenkins." Such a magnificent commentator.

Johnston was so utterly different from Arlott yet complemented his style beautifully. Johnners was a great one for adding '-ers' to anything, so he called me Hadders and, of course, there's Bloers (Henry Blofeld). He had a list of 10 golden rules for radio commentary, the last of which is: "Don't miss a ball. If you do, someone's bound to take a wicket."

The television commentator's task is another matter. The picture's there for him so no scene-setting is required in the radio sense. The biggest problem I found during my brief stints on television was how little time there was to make a point. There were just so many distractions, like the director calling down the headphones: "Commercial break in 10 seconds", or "Camera six, move in on Mike Gatting. Commentator — talk about Gatting for a few seconds." It's difficult to concentrate at times. On radio, it's nowhere near as unnerving, and so there's a better chance for commentators and comments people to develop a rapport.

Richie Benaud divorces himself well from what's going on behind him and through his 'cans'. He's undoubtedly one of the most respected television commentators in the business — experienced, analytical and fair.

The secret with radio and television commentators is the need for thoroughly professional people and, in that sense, I believe it's important to employ former players. Look at Channel Nine's operation in Australia and the commentary team has been studded with former internationals — Benaud, Ian Chappell, Tony Greig, Keith Stackpole, Bill Lawry, Max Walker, Doug Walters, Rod Marsh and Dennis Lillee among them. It's much the same with the BBC's coverage and Television New Zealand has followed the trend through using Glenn Turner, John Morrison, Warren Stott and Geoff Howarth. And Radio New Zealand looks to use ex-players for expert comment as well, like Jeremy Coney and John Parker. It's imperative.

There aren't, as it happens, so many instances of first-class players working as cricket correspondents for newspapers. Because of the nature of the job they either pursue sporting interests in the competitive sense, or they stick with journalism. It's almost impossible to do both. And I don't consider it a fault among cricket journalists that so few have a reasonable playing background in the game. They watch so much cricket, they talk to so many people involved in the game and, in time, they're able to develop the right perspective to be able to write about the sport for the masses. I know a lot of players who say: "He shouldn't be writing about cricket. He's never played the game at a decent level — what would he know about it?" But it doesn't work like that. Some of the better cricket writers haven't had a broad playing background, yet that doesn't negate their ability to pass fair comment.

Just the same, it's the Press which has caused me the greatest anxiety with what I call personal attacks. On numerous occasions, I've felt maligned, chagrined and bitter. Through writing columns and talking on air, many things I've said have backfired on me, or been twisted to work against me.

I'd have to say the phase when I made the transition from my long run-up to the shortened version was the most harrowing. I made the decision to change after the 1980–81 season in the interests of my future in the game but the move wasn't well accepted at all, least of all from the New Zealand media. It was Don Cameron, writing in the *New Zealand Herald*, who angered me most when he suggested I was operating off "a pop gun run-up". It implied I was firing blanks or corks; no longer was I the archetypal strike bowler haring in off a long run. It didn't sit easily with Cameron, or a lot of other people, that I'd made the change. Some time later he modified his stance and conceded the value of what I'd done, which was a credit to him, but that comment was so galling for me. I felt my ability as a professional cricketer was being undermined. Surely I knew what I was capable of and what was best for me if I was to perform in New Zealand cricket?

Through the years the run-ins continued, the next coming in 1982–83 when I had my hamstring injury which prevented me from playing in the Benson and Hedges World Series Cup finals against Australia. I erred badly, I concede, by announcing on radio that I was out of contention . . . before I'd officially told team management. That wasn't on and I really created the fuss in the first place. But that scarcely excused the verbal assaults which followed with even our captain Geoff Howarth obliquely questioning the authenticity of my injury. There were behind-the-hand whispers that I was faking it . . . "Hadlee's just a hypo-chondriac" and that sort of thing. But what irked me more than anything was Armin Lindenberg's suggestion in the *Auckland Star* that I should have painkilling injections so I could play in the WSC finals. That was unbelievable because, had I played with painkillers and further damaged the hamstring, I would very likely have missed the home test series against

It couldn't be said the media always have the best conditions to work in . . .
Above: The Press literally had boxes to watch play from for New Zealand's tour match in Faridabad, India, in late 1988.
Below: And Radio New Zealand commentator Bryan Waddle (second from right) and his comments man John Wiltshire (right) hardly had salubrious surroundings when they called Pakistan's match against the Shell XI at Napier's McLean Park last season.

J.G. Blackwell

Sri Lanka — and I've always rated tests as more important than one-dayers. To have had a jab could have had dire consequences for my whole career. Not everyone was against me, though. Amid the controversy it was stressed by another writer that I'd more than paid my dues to New Zealand cricket. Why all the fuss about missing a few one-day internationals when I could boast a record showing 31 consecutive test appearances since 1975-76, plus an unbroken run of 37 one-day internationals? The argument was proffered that I hadn't let New Zealand down before, so why question it now?

There haven't been many seasons since when there hasn't been some crisis with the Press. In the 1983-84 season I was very upset when a journalist contacted me in Rarotonga . . . where I'd gone to recover from a bout of physical and mental depression. I resented the invasion of my privacy — and gave the reporter a succinct interview, which must have sounded awfully like a telephone being hung up in his ear.

The summer of 1985-86 was a 'biggie' for media strife when I became embroiled in the ticklish negotiations about keeping the Alfa Romeo I won as the international cricketer of the year in Australia. It wasn't so much the stance the media took on my I-want-to-keep-the-car campaign; I'm not sure how cricket journalists viewed my intentions. It was the aftermath which became the worry.

The car furore was still fizzing as we went into the first test against Australia in Wellington, an occasion which had an added edge for me because I was chasing my 300th test wicket. When I had Allan Border leg-before on the first day, I had my thrill. It was a fantastic moment but I confounded the media at the end of the day by refusing to talk about the achievement. The truth was I was tired and not overly happy with my bowling performance on the day as a whole; I just didn't want to talk to journalists about my 300th wicket. I know the newspaper men had dead-lines to meet and wanted their story but, on that day, I wanted to be left alone. I again declined to be interviewed before the second test of the series in Christchurch when I hadn't been feeling well. What followed was a series of articles which attacked me personally. I was anything but delighted and, before the third test in Auckland, I broke away from training at Cornwall Park and called journalists together; I wanted to know what was bugging them and the session became an involved and wide-ranging one. The Alfa Romeo was obviously the hottest topic of discussion but I made it amply clear I was disturbed with some stories which had been written about me, particularly in Australia.

This illustrated perfectly the situation I find myself in so often. Some-thing I'd said in jest on radio about trying to break lanky Bruce Reid's toes had been banner headlined in the *Sydney Sun* as some sort of shock disclosure. My attempt at humour had clearly failed and what had been intended as lighthearted retaliation had been turned back on me. It stemmed from Reid bouncing me out in the Christchurch test and I had said on radio: "There's no way I'll get the ball over his head, so I'll try and break his toes with yorkers."

The press conference also gained extensive coverage in *The New Zealand Cricket Player*. The entire interview was reproduced while Don

Cameron's editorial attempted to dissect my motives for calling the conference. Cameron said the *Sydney Sun* had been quite justified in taking my toe-breaking comments about Bruce Reid as fair material for a story. And he wrote: "But the point is here was Hadlee blasting away at 'the media' for enlarging on his radio comments, when he himself had made his comments in another section of 'the media', a radio station. It looks suspiciously as if Hadlee, having begun some action in 'the media' wanted to act as judge and jury when some other section of 'the media' reacted."

Given all these hassles, it may appear I'm unduly sensitive about it all and feel the heat of the media's words more than some of my contemporaries. That's wide of the mark, though. The fact is Glenn Turner, Geoff Howarth, Jeremy Coney, Martin Crowe and so many others have all been piqued on various occasions about something someone's written about them, or said about them. It seems to happen to me more often.

Probably the most celebrated media problem surfaced early on our tour of Australia in 1987–88. We travelled up country from Adelaide for a one-dayer in Renmark, a match I wasn't originally due to play in. In fact, I was left out of the travelling party . . . but I went because I wanted to visit the area and I also wanted to play the game. The match was fine — we won by 85 runs and it gave me another workout leading up to the test series. There was a dinner function during the brief visit and I was asked to make a speech, just an impromptu thing, and then signed some autographs and drew the raffles. It was a nice day, a pleasant trip all round. But the pleasure was erased the next day when I learned Don Cameron had filed a story for the *New Zealand Herald* which frankly horrified me. He asserted I'd made comments which were critical of Glenn Turner's performance as New Zealand's cricket manager at the World Cup tournament in India.

That staggered me because I didn't even mention Turner's name at all. When I rang Cameron in our hotel to ask what he'd written, he told me he couldn't remember. He also refused to let me see a copy of his story. In time, I had the story faxed to me from New Zealand and my worst fears were realised. Under a headline "Hadlee Cut At Turner In World Cup", the story, published on 26 November, 1987, began:

"A sour note has jarred the harmony so far evident on the New Zealand cricket tour of Australia with public sniping at Glenn Turner, the cricket manager with the team at the World Cup tournament.

"And, to make matters worse, some of the sniping came from none other than Richard Hadlee, very much the senior team member.

"The criticism of Turner occurred at a dinner on Tuesday night in the pleasant South Australian country town of Renmark, where the New Zealanders yesterday won their one-day match against a South Australian Country XI.

"It has now become a New Zealand ritual to attack and blame Turner for New Zealand's dismal showing in the World Cup.

"The New Zealand 'knocking machine' aimed at cutting down men who have contributed much to New Zealand sport in the past is rolling on again over another of yesterday's heroes.

"The first cut might be excused; Mike Coward, a senior Australian cricket writer and a flourishing after dinner speaker, rolled out another Ian Chappell-Turner line, and that squabble is old enough to be worn smooth and without rancour.

"But it did the digestion no good at all to hear Richard Hadlee take a swing, however indirect and over the audience's head, at Turner's alleged weakness in the World Cup in India.

"Turner in India may have been below his past top form. The selectors may not have helped with the team personnel and the players in turn might not have helped themselves.

"But Hadlee had absolutely no safe ground for taking at cut at Turner.

"At least Turner went to India."

Just how Cameron ever construed I'd taken a swipe at Turner from what I'd said, I'll never know. In a speech of little import, I noted that: "In Gren Alabaster we have an astute cricket manager, and we have a good captain in Jeff Crowe." Cameron interpreted that to mean Turner wasn't astute. Alabaster's certainly very astute. He played first-class cricket for more than 20 years, was a national selector and then cricket manager; he had great credentials.

I quickly alerted Gren to what had happened and verified with fellow players and other journalists travelling with us that I had definitely not mentioned Turner's name. To a man, they all agreed there wasn't even the slightest hint of implied criticism of Turner.

To say I was angry was an understatement. I contacted my solicitor Cran Bull about the possibility of legal action. I created something of a scene in our hotel bar in Adelaide one night by thrusting a copy of the offending article in front of Cameron. In time, an approach was made to the *Herald* to establish what had happened with the article, why it appeared in such form and what action the paper was prepared to take. I learnt on tour that Cameron's original copy had been changed but that wasn't my concern; a story still appeared which was damaging and inaccurate, grossly so.

When it became clear the *Herald* wouldn't take any action, we sued the paper and Cameron for defamation. I was prepared to take it to court if necessary. I'd been wronged and wanted justice. The matter dragged on and on until, just before New Zealand's tour to India in October 1988 the *Herald* settled out of court. An apology was published prominently on the paper's leading sports page and there was a financial settlement as well. It wasn't the money that mattered, it was the principle.

Later on that tour Don Cameron had another crack at me after a column I wrote during the second test. When I took five for 68 in Australia's only innings of the match, it was the 30th time I'd taken five in a test innings. In the same match, Allan Border scored 205 — his best in tests — to take his runs aggregate beyond the great Sir Donald Bradman's tally of 6996 and then past Greg Chappell's Australian record

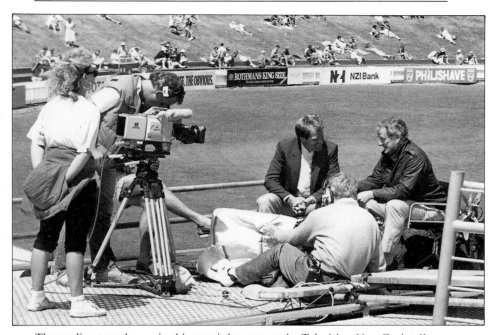

The media at work . . . in this case it happens to be Television New Zealand's Peter Williams interviewing a member of the Press — the *New Zealand Herald*'s Don Cameron. And, from the "pop gun run-up" to Renmark, Cameron and I have had some clashes. On this occasion, he was covering his 100th test, at Wellington between Pakistan and New Zealand last season.   J.G. Blackwell

of 7110. I said in my columns — in both Australia and in *The Sun* at home — that I felt I, too, had topped Bradman. I equate the bowler's five wickets in an innings being the equivalent of the batsman's century; I'd say that's a fair comparison. And the five wickets I took in Adelaide gave me my 30th instance of five which, in my book, put me one ahead of Bradman who scored 29 test centuries. I didn't see too much wrong with that — but Cameron did. He wrote in the *Herald* that I'd come up with "the remarkable piece of rationalisation" that I, like Border, had moved past the great man. He finished up saying: "Still, anyone who bowls reasonably fast and can coax five wickets from a test innings at Adelaide might be entitled to pat himself on the back, even at the risk of dislocating his reasoning process."

Newspapermen are, of course, quick to pick up on stories and some of them don't mess around trying to extract the information they want.

Nottinghamshire was playing Yorkshire in Middlesbrough when Chris Broad was hit on the thumb, casting some doubt as to whether he'd be able to play for England in a coming test. A call went out for a doctor to come to the Notts dressing room and there was a knock on the door. A well-dressed man came in and asked Chris:

"What's happened?"

"I think I've broken my thumb," said Chris.

"How long will you be out for?"

"I was hoping you could tell me that."

"Why?"

"You're the doctor, aren't you?"

"No, I'm a reporter for the *Daily Mail*," said the supposed 'doctor'.

He got his story . . . and later on the real doctor, casually dressed, arrived. Sometimes we all get confused!

C·H·A·P·T·E·R F·I·F·T·E·E·N

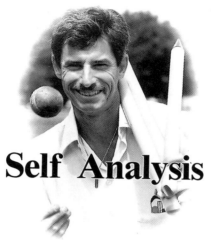

Self Analysis

A professional sportsman in today's pressure-filled world needs the thickest skin possible and there are times I wished I had an armour-plated covering to deflect the snipes and wisecracks fired at me. I've been called many things during my cricket career.

It might surprise those cynics who insist I'm an automaton to hear I have normal feelings, and I'm as sensitive as the next person.

As a professional cricketer I have handled my workload but I haven't coped so well when I've been subjected to pressures directed at Richard Hadlee the person, as distinct from Richard Hadlee the cricketer. I'd like to have been unaffected by some of the comments from fellow players, former players, administrators, the media, spectators and the general public, but I'm vulnerable.

When I started my New Zealand test career in 1972–73, I never envisaged my privacy would be threatened. It was so different then. New Zealand cricket was struggling, and didn't have the profile it was to assume in the 1980s. There was an olde worlde charm about the game. There wasn't the suffocating attention which developed a few years later with the onset of massive television exposure.

Cricket, though, has burgeoned with television generating unprecedented awareness. Sadly, the price we have to pay for being associated with top-level international sport is an intrusion on our privacy. New Zealand cricket graduated in the 1980s and the more successful the national team was, the harder it was on a personal level. While I must expect publicity as part of my involvement in a high-profile sport, it's still something I've never really got used to.

Grahame Felton, a Christchurch motivator, has helped me through the emotional highs and lows. He came along when I required someone to establish some emotional balance in my life.

Everything was catching up with me towards the end of 1983 as I tried to meet too many demands; I simply could not cope with one promotion after another, and an endless round of after-dinner speaking engagements. Something had to give. It was me.

I experienced physical and mental depression, blurred vision, excruciating headaches, chest pains and had a preoccupation with death. I had grave doubts whether I'd ever play cricket again.

By nature I'm positive but I was controlled then by negative thoughts. A visit to a doctor gave me one of the most obvious answers — I had to start saying 'no' to requests for my time. But everything was crowding in on me and playing the home series against England was the furthest thing from my mind.

Then Grahame Felton, who works at the Institute of Management in Christchurch, asked permission of the Canterbury Cricket Association to run a course to prepare the Canterbury team mentally for the 1983–84 Shell series campaign.

He struck a chord with me instantly. If I was to overcome my psychological shortcomings, Grahame was the man who would help. His impact on me was profound. He spent only three hours with the Canterbury team but it was the beginning of the end of my lowest times.

The simple message involved setting goals in life, and adhering to them. My way of adopting the Felton gospel was to list key words and phrases on a card which I've carried in my cricket bag ever since.

I pop up the lid of the bag and there are all the ingredients which help put my life in order — fear is negative, desire is positive, simulation, making it happen, visualising what I want to happen, belief, rewards, control, wanting to achieve, enjoyment and being happy with my performance. It all seems so straightforward but the success of the scheme is putting it into effect — making it happen.

Grahame remembers the initial meetings well. "I thought at the time I could do something to help Richard. He responded very well, sat there writing notes furiously, and absorbed things like a sponge," says Grahame. "He quickly understood the motivational and attitudinal ideas I was trying to get across and put them into practice. The characteristics of human nature need reinforcing, things like discipline, control, self-esteem, self-motivation."

His influence has been an on-going thing. When I'm overseas he may drop me a letter or note with some key words, just to refresh my mind — or he will phone me. I owe it to him that I was able to regain my poise in life and climb back on to the cricket treadmill. Having a motivator or psychologist might not work for everyone but I know it has for me, helping to rebuild my confidence and make me a stronger person.

People develop a morbid fascination about why sporting performers function and behave the way they do; what is in their character which makes them special competitors; how they control their emotions and how they make them work to advantage; how they handle depression one moment, elation the next.

The breakdown was dramatic and frightening but it showed I was susceptible, like everyone else, to everyday pressures. Irritatingly, this phase in my life and other controversies I've been involved in brought critical assessment of my personality and character. I was described, among other things, as being "austere" and "morose". On consulting my dictionary I discovered austere meant "harsh, stern" and morose meant "gloomy, sullen". I've been called moody, brooding, cold blooded, clinical, mechanical, robot-like, big headed and selfish, plus countless other unmentionables.

Dr Max Abbott, director of the Mental Health Foundation, has his own prognosis. He sees me as something of a paradox — detached and somewhat distant, but not aloof.

I'm understandably touchy about such assaults; I view them as character assassination, with the inner me — and not Richard Hadlee the cricketer — being unfairly targeted. As a professional cricketer I may become public property but the real me is a private person.

There is a popular perception of me being the cold, tough, unemotional professional. I can be rather unsmiling and cool on the field, because I try to keep a lid on my emotions. I have to . . . there's obvious danger in becoming too downcast, excited or elated over on-field happenings. I need to keep some sort of control. But there's still a very normal, emotional being inside. I am single-minded, but I have to be to succeed. I strive for excellence, aspiring to perfection; I know it can never be achieved but I try!

Being brought up with a family background like mine ensured I'd have a disciplined approach to life and towards my chosen sport. With my father captaining New Zealand and brothers all playing cricket, there had to be some rub-off. Just being a Hadlee was pressure enough to make the most of my ability in cricket, and yet none of us — and least of all my mother — ever thought any of us would one day make a living out of the game.

Dad's methodical approach as an accountant was reflected in his attitude to sport and life. He was so ordered and there's no question I've been strongly influenced by his values, especially on discipline. Dad, too, has always revelled in facts and figures — through both necessity and fascination — and I've been much the same. Averages, budgets and statistical performances have been, to me, a passion bordering on obsession.

My hunger for cricket figures started at primary school and ultimately this stats mania became important to me in terms of my overall record, my contribution to my team's performance and as a source of motivation. What used to be a hobby evolved to become an integral part of my cricketing career.

It became a cliche to talk about Hadlee's targets. Each time I started a new season or campaign, I seemed to have a fresh target in mind. Depending on whom I was playing against and in which country, I'd set myself a budget of wickets to be taken, the number of runs I wanted to score, and so on. Perhaps this approach fostered an image of me being somehow ruthless and unfeeling in my approach to cricket.

Budget-setting for a test series evolved from my first major success in the international arena, the third test against India in Wellington in 1975–76, when I took 11 wickets in the match. Until then, I'd been inconsistent at test level with wickets coming occasionally and at a fair cost. With 11 wickets in that match — and 12 in the series — I aimed then to take 12 to 15 wickets in a three-match test series. I also tried for man-of-the-match and man-of-the-series awards, using them as extra spurs to retain interest and a purpose.

It's easy for your mind to drift in test cricket, especially when you're in the field. You come out of the bowling attack after your first spell and can sometimes switch off a little, losing your level of concentration. Thinking about targets has helped me. Whenever I bowl, there are four key words as well which aid my purpose — rhythm, off stump, hate and Lillee.

If I finish a spell with one or two wickets, I say to myself: "That's not good enough. I have to do better when I come on for my next spell." In time those mini targets would become bigger ones. I set myself for five-wicket bags, turning that into a world record; I wanted 10 wickets in a match and then the world record for that, too. And finally the world record for test wickets. I have never chased these goals at the expense of my team but the pursuit of a target drives me on to a better performance which, in turn, has to benefit the team.

There have been other targets, too. Instinctively I strive to win any award on offer . . . medals, trophies, cars, man-of-the-match and man-of-the-series awards. One of the most cherished is the Winsor Cup, awarded annually by the NZCC to the New Zealand bowler whose performances in first-class cricket have been the most meritorious. I won the cup 11 years straight from 1976–77 to 1986–87 and, after my 10th success, the NZCC presented me with a replica of the original as a keepsake. I appreciated that because it meant a lot to me.

But in 1987–88, I lost the cup to Ewen Chatfield, the ceaseless work-horse who has done so much at the other end when I've been bowling in test matches. I'm the first to praise Charlie for the job he's done and he had a great home series against England when I was injured, taking 13 wickets at 15.23 in the three tests. He didn't bowl so well in the series in Australia — he was omitted for the second test in Adelaide — but, together with first-class performances in Australia and at home, he finished the season with 24 wickets at an average of 28.00. I was injured in the first test against England, but collected 18 wickets against Australia, finishing the season with 29 first-class wickets at 21.17. Maybe the criteria had changed? Perhaps one-day international performances came into consideration?

There was great satisfaction in regaining the Winsor Cup in 1988–89. Goal-setting implies I must spend hours flicking through cricket data to see which mark I can go for next, but statisticians, writers and fans have provided me with ammunition, too.

Sometimes a milestone just happens as when New Zealand played Sri

Lanka in Colombo in the 1986–87 season. I was batting with my captain, Jeff Crowe — in a long partnership — when we heard the next century by a New Zealand batsman would be the country's 100th at test level. I was on 82 at the time and Jeff was on 95 but my immediate reaction was to go to him and say: "I've got to do that!" He said: "Go for it." In the very next over I collected 13 runs to pull up level with Chopper but, as it happened, there had been a scoreboard error and I was actually 96. I was dropped as I chased the four I needed for the century — my second in test cricket.

After battling for so many years, often in foreign and trying conditions, the world record for test wickets was very important to me. It's also great for New Zealand cricket. The game's history has a preponderance of English and Australian players in the record books. So isn't it something that the two most significant test records — most wickets and most runs — should be held by an Indian (Sunil Gavaskar) and a New Zealander? I wanted the record. I was determined to do it — there were so many people I wanted it for, but perhaps most of all to give New Zealand the record.

I worked just as hard for the English county double in 1984. No one had done the 1000 runs-100 wickets feat in England since Fred Titmus in 1967 and I meticulously planned it. I couldn't have done it otherwise. This is where the single-mindedness comes in; when there's something I want, like the double, then I'm dedicated. When you've played the game for so many years — 13 years at first-class level in my double year — then you need some variation to break the monotony; boredom; provides the motivation. Operation Double enabled me to retain my sanity in 1984, especially after the breakdown problems only months earlier.

I realise I had ample opportunity to reach the world test marks for instances of five wickets in an innings and 10 wickets in a match, plus most wickets overall. After all, I've been able to start with the new ball, have a go at the middle order and come back for the tail, while many of my team-mates have done the hard work at the other end, containing the batsmen. Unlike the Marshalls, Holdings, Garners and company, I've had more chances to take three, four, five or more wickets in an innings. If New Zealand had had another strike bowler operating with me my chances of wicket-taking may have been considerably reduced. At the same time, I've had to perform consistently and stay in shape.

As a youngster there was no real method about my cricketing approach, not even when I moved into first-class cricket. I relied on my natural ability, more or less going through the motions as a bowler and expecting success to come rather than working for it. I didn't appreciate the finer points which went into making a top-level cricketer. As a green 21-year-old my first tour was to England in 1973 and I remember I felt I wasn't given sufficient opportunities to show my ability. Right up until my early international days I played my cricket with no real plan or method of attack.

Only when I began my career with Notts in 1978 was the finesse factor introduced; it provided me with my breakthrough as a cricketer. I became more level headed with the emphasis on achieving day-in-day-out consistency, and my on-field personality mellowed. I had been overly aggressive and flighty as a player with histrionics playing a big part in my game. I disagreed with umpires and chipped players but at Notts, I learnt to accept umpiring decisions which went against me.

Ability alone is not enough, you must also put some order into your life. You don't have to become celibate, a non-drinker or a fussy eater but do things in moderation to ensure you're in the best possible shape to play every day.

If statistics, discipline and county cricket were all key ingredients in shaping me as a cricketer and a person, then so, too, was my role model. There was an extraordinary cricketer who helped me — my idol, Dennis Lillee. I aped him just a little too much at times but his effect on my development was profound.

I'd like to have been judged totally as a player during my career but subjectivity has clouded some thinking. Always, too, the spectre of jealousy — even from peers — has haunted me. I guess that's inevitable when you're regarded as morose and austere.

C·H·A·P·T·E·R S·I·X·T·E·E·N

The Better Half

When you look at the international cricketer's lot today, you wonder how any of them get married, let alone stay married. The attrition rate's high, often a legacy of the strains the pro cricketer's life puts on a marriage. But, when I met a Christchurch girl by the name of Karen Marsh more than 17 years ago, neither of us had any perception of what lay ahead.

Sure it helped that Karen was a cricketer herself, in fact a New Zealand player. But, when she took the plunge with me, we unwittingly started a marriage which has been anything but 'normal'. We've survived as a couple, just as I've survived as a player. Karen has been physically and emotionally strong and her support has been undying and, quite frankly, without it I would not have played the game for as long as I have.

This is her story, her view of life inside a cricketing marriage:

Strange as it may seem, our first meeting in 1972 had nothing to do with cricket; in fact, we met at a soccer party (soccer being Richard's other sport in those days). Eventually, we were invited to a mutual friend's 21st party and, later on, I used a bit of womanly conniving to take Richard to a movie. And, as the old love stories go, we've never looked back, well not very often.

Back then, I was working in a law office and RJ was a section manager in Woolworths across the road. The cheapest item in his section was teaspoons and, consequently, my firm, Bowie, Stringer and McBeath, ended up with an over-supply of them. The sweets section next to his counter was another reason to see him — and I put on half a stone as well!

We were married soon after New Zealand's tour to England in 1973, which meant the wedding arrangements fell on you know who. Richard must have intrigued his team-mates when he managed to buy my wedding dress while on tour (what do they say about the groom seeing the bride's dress before the event?) We actually contemplated getting married before the tour and, to this day, neither of us knows why we didn't — the single allowance in those days was $40 a week while $70 was the married rate, and we could have done with the money.

The first two and a half years of the marriage were notable for the amount of time we weren't together, what with both of us playing cricket and Richard by then on the road selling for a sports firm. We still did very normal things for newly-weds, like buying our first home; times were tough then, and they didn't improve when I lost my engagement ring while playing in the Hallyburton Johnstone national tournament one year. We duly filed an insurance claim and were paid the appropriate amount but, while I was deciding what ring I'd buy to replace my old one, Richard already had the money earmarked for something else — a Para pool!

When he wasn't playing cricket he spent the whole summer trying to dig a hole where he'd decided to place the pool; when it was dry, the hole would cave in and when it rained it would fill in. When he at last won the battle, Richard decided to change the water one night so pumped the water out with the intention of refilling the pool the following day. But it rained overnight and when we woke up the next morning the pool had collapsed.

Bad became even worse when the Burnside Park groundsman miraculously found my missing engagement ring. Richard being Richard said we had to repay the insurance money. Honourable of him, but we had a pool which was now useless and we had to pay back money we'd already spent! And to think Richard's not really a swimmer anyway.

Normality disappeared for the Hadlee household when Richard received his offer to play for Nottinghamshire in 1978; we thought we'd give it a go for three years and then review the situation. With RJ already in England, it was left to muggins to make arrangements in Christchurch before joining him in England. Much of that first season was devoted to following New Zealand's tour of England, Stephen Boock's wife, Heather, and I clocking up more than 7000 miles in Richard's sponsored car as we followed the team around the country. Our budget was well out of the Hilton or Sheraton range and we decided we couldn't entertain the idea of staying in the Savoy in London. No, we were working on a costing which allowed us to spend £2 a night on accommodation (remembering that wives weren't allowed to stay within 200 yards of the team's hotel in those days). So, when we arrived in Nottingham, we looked for a bed-and-breakfast place and found a very reasonable one not far from Trent Bridge, and priced at £2 a night. It was a little dirty and a bit busy — but it wasn't until the next morning we were told it was thought to be a house of ill repute! Our budget wasn't that tight!

Around that time, the treatment of wives really was a bit amazing, although I stuck rigidly to the ruling that players weren't allowed to have their spouses with them. But one morning I had to make a visit to the team's hotel because Richard wanted a pair of boots. I was in the lift on my way back to my hotel and, when the doors opened at the ground level, there waiting to get in were Bob Vance, Wal Hadlee (then the chairman of the NZCC's board) and Graham Dowling. I got such a shock, I pushed the 'door close' button as they were about to get into the lift, hightailed it up to the first floor, got out and raced down the stairs and out the side exit.

Really it was a ridiculous situation in those times when wives couldn't stay with their husbands, and weren't even supposed to be near them. With so much cricket being played now, it would be impossible to impose such a rule. I believe — and I think most wives do — that the first two weeks of a tour are important for the players to be together. But it was crazy how Heather Boock and I literally sneaked around to spend some time with our husbands.

It's also astonishing how many people are under the impression the NZCC pays for the wives to travel; it's a nice thought but the fact is that's a personal expense — and touring becomes an expensive business, especially when I get my hands on the Visa card! Even though we travelled cheaply around England in 1978, the cost soon mounts up.

As if to emphasise the background role wives are forced to take, I had an amazing experience during New Zealand's third test against Pakistan in Auckland last season. In some 17 years as the wife of a New Zealand cricketer I had never been invited to the famous board lunches the NZCC always has at test matches. Lo and behold, I had my first board lunch at Eden Park. History in itself. And wouldn't you believe I had a girlfriend with me and she was also invited — on the first time she'd ever been to watch test cricket!

But back to those early times in England. After the tour in 1978, the 1979 season was also an interrupted one, Richard having commitments to the New Zealand team for the Prudential World Cup in England. We became a little more settled, though, by renting a house not far from Trent Bridge — which soon became known as 'Hadlee Hotel' because of the number of visitors we had from New Zealand; we enjoyed that because we could at least pretend for a while that we were in New Zealand.

One night Lance Cairns called in (he was playing league cricket in Durham) on his way to Heathrow to pick up Sue and the children, and I generously offered my services as navigator. Stupidly, I hadn't taken a look at the car Lance had bought for the season. When I did the next day, I tried desperately to convince Lance he could find his own way out of Nottingham to Heathrow! His powers of persuasion were stronger than my resistance and so I had a job. It took 10 minutes to get the car started and another 10 minutes to free the safety belt which was rusted to the side of the car; I refused to leave without being belted in, primarily because the passenger's seat was in such bad condition it offered no support when I leaned back. Four hours later we found a distraught Sue and the kids at Heathrow. We'd been held up by peak-hour traffic, and the humour scarcely improved when it took us another couple of hours to find the car in the multi-storey parking building. To be honest, I rather fancied leaving the car where it was and putting my trust in British Rail to take us to Nottingham. The chances of survival were infinitely better.

Eventually we were on our way, only to stop on the M1 when Christopher noticed a car behind us flashing its lights. I suspected it was a policeman about to give us the third degree about the state of the car. Instead it was a motorist who told Lance: "Your back door's open." Sue assured the motorist everything was under control; Lance had tied the door up with string, Christopher was holding the door and Sue was hanging on to Christopher. Not exactly out of the defensive driving manual! Eventually the 'machine' got the better of the Cairns family. Sue and the kids were to drive up to Durham to meet Lance after staying with us. But, with all the luggage on board, it collapsed and there it remained outside our place for six weeks.

Because life for us became a diet of travelling to and from England every year — mixed in with stays in other countries when Richard was touring with New Zealand — people assumed it must be a wonderful life. Interesting, maybe, but not always wonderful. It was never easy leaving family and friends for six months every year; it's so nice now to be settled back in Christchurch on a year-round basis. The problems of living overseas were highlighted during the 1979–80 season when Richard was playing Sheffield Shield cricket for Tasmania. We were based in Launceston when I received a phone call one day to say my mother had had a heart attack. Fortunately, we weren't too far from home and I was able to rush back to New Zealand the next day but, when you're on the professional round-about, that kind of thing is a constant worry.

Richard's absences from home — for numerous overseas tours and even home series for that matter — have created their own set of problems. In effect, cricketers' wives have to learn to cope as solo parents and it can be difficult fitting a husband back into a relationship after those longer tours. You become accustomed to managing affairs; you have to. Any emergency or problem is overcome and, in some ways, after managing to keep the telephone connected and the power on while he's away, it's almost an intrusion when your partner returns. I object to passing the reins back over to Richard.

The neighbours can usually tell when Richard's about to come home. When they see me spending a whole day in the garden they know something's up. I always set myself to put the house and garden in some semblance of order about two days before RJ's due home; he's such a stickler for tidiness it's a never-ending challenge to try and meet his standards. Invariably friends will arrive for a quiet drink — which becomes an early morning event — and the garden and house look worse than ever. Richard's only once given me 11 out of 10 for my efforts; I can't live up to his expectations, and gave up trying years ago. Richard at last seems to realise everyone's different (even though it frustrates him).

Once Nicholas came along in 1981, the Hadlee lifestyle became that much more hectic, especially when we were faced with packing up house and moving every six months. Luckily, Nicholas has always been a good traveller and Richard was there to help on the plane . . . for the first five minutes at least, until he plugged in his headphones and slept for the rest of the trip. He has this remarkable ability — remarkably annoying, too — to sleep on command. Although, to be fair, when Matthew arrived the

Look no further if you want to find out who taught Richard how to appeal. I wasn't just being polite asking for this leg before appeal playing for Canterbury in the Hallyburton-Johnstone Shield tournament in 1981–82.

D.O. Neely Collection

duties were shared and we both managed to arrive at our destination in one piece mentally and physically.

Matthew was just one month old when I travelled to the West Indies — en route to Notts — to follow New Zealand's tour at the end of the 1984–85 season. The trip was horrendous from the moment we discovered we had no onward travel bookings out of Los Angeles. With the team already in the Caribbean, I once again had my old travelling mate Heather Boock. After staying in LA an extra night, we eventually got on a flight to Miami, all five of us (I had Nicholas and Matthew while Heather had the Boocks' daughter Lucy). When we arrived in Miami we were once again cheered by the news that our flight had been overbooked by 30 per cent. After hassling for an hour, the airline unearthed four spare seats and decided to allocate them alphabetically. So Janet and John Blackwell — publishers of this book — plus Heather and Lucy Boock had seats. It meant I was left with the prospect of another overnight stay — and knowing Matthew's nappies, milk powder and our clothes were all in the plane's hold and unlikely to be delivered until the following morning in Port of Spain, Trinidad.

Graciously the Blackwells made a deal with the airline. They'd give up their seats provided they were allocated to the Hadlees. Marvellous. A lovely gesture. It wasn't quite that straightforward. With everyone strapped in and ready for take-off, the pilot announced he couldn't leave with all the passengers, fuel and luggage on board. He wanted some passengers to disembark (with the lure of free accommodation); no one wanted to and only after two hours did he succumb, agreeing to unload some fuel. It was a hell of a trip and we weren't too popular with two long-suffering husbands when we finally arrived. Our shares weren't looking any better when Matthew woke up the whole floor on our arrival in the early hours of the morning, demanding milk . . . and the first test was just around the corner.

The next day, Heather, Ian Smith's wife Louise and I went for a stroll in a park near the hotel. There I was pushing a pram with a tiny baby in it and three other kids under five years old walking by our sides, when a tall West Indian came up to me and said: "I'll kill you, whitie." My reply was to burn some rubber off the soles of my shoes and the wheels of the pram as we retreated to the hotel. I very rarely ventured outside the hotels in the West Indies after that, and certainly didn't take the boys out.

Some of Richard's years in the game have been more demanding than others — 1984 was a case in point. I travelled to Johannesburg to stay with Sue and Clive Rice on the way to Notts. Richard met us there after New Zealand's tour of Sri Lanka and, as we flew to England, he went over a whole heap of papers. I asked him what on earth he was doing. Planning his assault on the county double, came the reply. "What's that," I asked, and he explained it was the feat of scoring 1000 runs and taking 100 wickets in a season. My reaction was to say it was impossible — but I should have known this man always achieves something when he sets his mind to do it.

My worry surrounded Richard's readiness for what would be a strenuous assignment. My mind drifted back a few months to late 1983 and the early part of the New Year when Richard was so ill I doubted whether he'd ever play cricket again. For some reason, the pressures got on top of him. He was struggling to cope with the demands on his time; he just couldn't say 'no' and was racing up and down New Zealand giving speeches or making personal appearances. It was a roundabout he couldn't get off. It was a dreadful time at home. No matter what I said or did, it wasn't right and he lost most of his confidence. He wouldn't go outside the gate for fear of being recognised. Once, when I insisted we go for a drive in the car, we had travelled only two or three kilometres when he said: "Take me home".

I did — but I also put in a call to Air New Zealand to arrange a break for all of us in Rarotonga. Off we went, Richard doing his best to travel incognito, wearing dark sunglasses. And while he relaxed in Rarotonga, he had some deep thinking to do to sort out the priorities in his life.

He really was only barely over that phase and yet there he was on the flight back to England planning the double. It was staggering and, in time, I read it as proof he was 100 per cent again. Not until a few months later did I realise the significance of what Richard was striving for. And when he went out to bat against Warwickshire needing 21 runs for the 1000 (having already taken 100 wickets), it was an amazing feeling. When Richard smashed a Chris Old delivery for four, he'd achieved his ambition. I was certainly proud, perhaps a little in awe of a chap who could be so single-minded in his pursuit of a goal which had eluded so many people before him.

From then on, it was like Christmas as Richard was presented with mementoes almost non-stop. The disappointment for him, as he's said, was that Notts never won a trophy that year to climax such a successful season. They came desperately close in 1985 when they made the NatWest Trophy final against Essex at Lord's. I couldn't watch when Derek Randall needed two runs off the last ball to win the game for Notts. He didn't get the runs. Notts had come so close and I was close to inconsolable. Richard was quite philosophical about it, maintaining there'd be another chance.

In 1987 there was, when they won the NatWest final as well as the county championship to complete a fabulous year. Sadly, my health didn't allow me to be at Lord's that day. It was one of the great disappointments to be confined to watching Richard and Bruce French take Notts to victory via television.

My health at the time highlighted one of the problem areas in a cricketing marriage. Because Richard was so locked into his playing career, he tended to overlook my problems. When New Zealand's tour of Sri Lanka was called off soon after the first test in April that year, Richard rang to say he'd be heading for London with Martin Crowe.

I don't think he could believe it when I said: "Afraid not. I'm off to hospital tomorrow and could really do with you here." The fact I hadn't told him I was ill was irrelevant. I just expected Richard to understand. Richard's point was I should have let him know what was going on earlier, while my attitude was one of not wanting to worry him while he was on tour. The trials of being married to a cricketer! Ultimately, Richard did

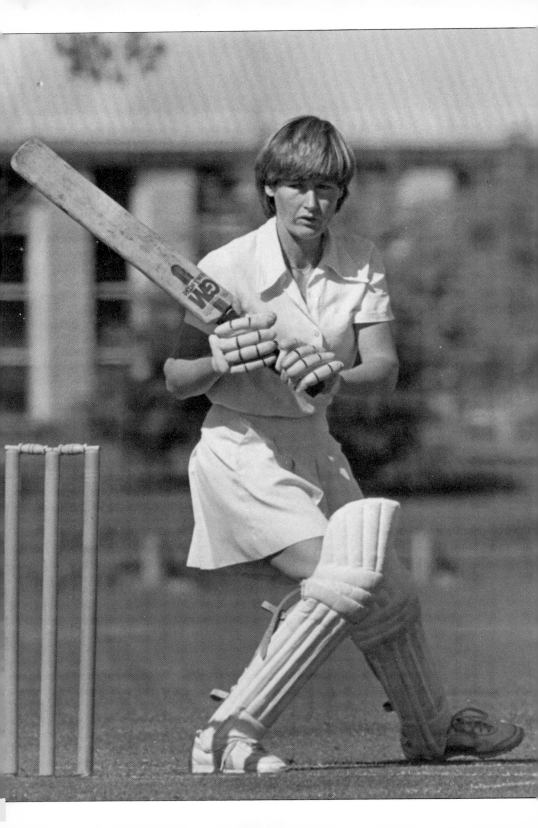

come home and was able to be with me and look after the boys while I was in hospital — and, eventually, I returned to England for the final fling.

The time in Nottingham was marvellous with Richard's benefit year in 1986 one of the real highlights but, in truth, the business of returning to England each year became difficult once Nicholas started school. It wasn't fair on him taking him out of school here and planting him into another in England; I wasn't prepared to subject Nicholas to that kind of programme for more than a year.

It was also hard getting a feel for our real home. We've lived in so many different places in Christchurch. We sold our three-bedroom bungalow in Shirley and moved via Hoon Hay and Avonhead to a five-acre farmlet in Harewood in 1983. The lifestyle attracted us to the land . . . but I do remember a word of warning from Richard's brother, Barry. He told Richard it was all very well waking up to the sound of sheep bleating, horses neighing, dogs barking and so on, but who was going to do jobs like dagging the sheep and generally looking after the animals. A very wise man is our BG. Very fortunately, we had a good friend, Mel Hegan, who was well versed in farming matters and he helped out with the tasks of the type BG queried.

We stayed on our little farm for three years but the final straw came one day when Richard was on tour. For the second successive morning, I was up at six chasing sheep up the middle of the road in my dressing gown. Even though we'd had fences repaired, the sheep or cows still managed to get out.

We put the property on the market the day we left for England in 1986 and two days later we had an offer and accepted it. Now without a home, we left it to family and friends to search for a new home. Wal rang up to say he'd found a place and tried to describe it over the phone. Better still, I said, how about sending us a video. So BG played cameraman and, at the end of the video, Richard's mother, Barry, Dayle and Wal all gave their assessments of the house. And so we told WA to go ahead and buy it on our behalf.

We've needed support like that and it's always been there for us. You really learn to appreciate the value of friends and family after living such a nomadic life. When Richard's been away I've welcomed having my sister Susan stay, especially after a couple of nasty phone calls when we lived on the farm. One call came asking to talk to Richard. "Sorry, he's out," I said. To which the voice on the other end said: "Give him this message (replete with heavy breathing) . . . tell him I'm going to knife him all the way up." I wasn't as concerned about that as his next sentence: "And I'll get your boy as well."

On another occasion there was a call with a similar message and, to my horror, Nicholas had disappeared from his cot one night. RJ was away. I searched the farm and when I found the sliding doors from our

Notice the bat's make . . . we have to keep the sponsors happy in this family.
It's helped being a cricketer myself; I've been better placed to try and understand what Richard goes through.

bedroom were open, I feared the worst. I was about to call the police when I heard a snigger coming from the wardrobe — the little cherub was hiding in the corner behind a big coat.

These are the problems you have to put up with as the wife of a public figure but the recognition's something I find difficult to deal with. In fact, we go out very rarely unless we are with a group of close friends; people are less inclined to barge in if you're part of a group.

Even walking down the street with Richard makes me feel uncomfortable. Only last Christmas, while we were holidaying in the Marlborough Sounds, Matthew and I were delayed in the laundry in Picton and ended up following Richard and Nicholas, plus Candy Brown and her son Jeremy, a little later. As we caught up with them, I wondered what on earth was going on in the street. People were coming out of shops, popping their heads out of cars, turning and staring back down the road. Then I realised they'd seen Richard and all Matthew and I could hear was: "It's him, it's him. My god, he's much smaller than I thought." All good-natured stuff but again it reduces your private life.

And privacy's a commodity Richard cherishes — he likes to get away and relax, away from the pressures which are always there. But there's never a chance to totally escape. When we were in the Sounds last Christmas, the phone rang . . . it was an Indian gentleman saying he'd come all the way from Bombay to meet Richard, just for five minutes.

"I'm on holiday, you'll struggle to find me and you'll probably be wasting your time," Richard told him. The caller was persistent and said he'd come in by helicopter because he was desperate to see Richard.

"If you can find me, we'll have a chat."

I thought it all seemed strange, so unusual I believed it was a friend of ours (Graham Allport) taking the mickey. A call to Graham's place in Christchurch found him out of town, staying in Blenheim, only about 30 kilometres from us. It had to be him.

The next morning the phone went again. It was a cruise boat company informing us a visitor would be arriving in about 20 minutes. "What does he look like?" I asked. "I think he's Indian or Pakistani." "You're pulling my leg," I said, automatically assuming it was one big set-up. Allport had obviously primed up the cruise people and was about to make a surprise visit.

We prepared for his arrival, making a sign to put on the end of the jetty: "Afternoon tea is off. Return to Allports Island (in the Queen Charlotte Sound). Signed Saresh (the name of the supposed Indian gentleman)."

When the boat arrived, I bent down and had a look inside the boat, saying: "Come on out you beggar. We've been waiting for you." And, would you believe, out came a distinguished looking Indian man dressed in suit and tie, carrying a briefcase and camera bag! My heart sank. The joke was on me.

Richard talked to him for about 30 minutes. It all seemed genuine enough and the visitor's dream was fulfilled: "I don't want to keep you any longer. I'll just have a look around and wait for the boat to return to pick me up." That wouldn't be for three hours and some of us became suspicious. We even wondered whether he might have a bomb in one of his bags but our fears were soon allayed when a check found nothing. (We couldn't be too careful after the phone calls and threats Richard received in India in 1988.)

Not until later, when Richard rang his father, did we learn Wal had given the Indian gent our phone number. He was rather amused about the whole affair but had been careful to check him out in the first place . . . if only he'd let us know.

There are so many stories of that type, like the time we arrived in Auckland to attend a sporting function one evening. We travelled from the airport to our hotel by taxi and I could tell the driver — an Indian — looked in his rear vision mirror at regular intervals. Just before we stopped he said: "Oh, my god! Good gracious me! You have the facial features of Richard Hadlee." Richard said: "Do you take an interest in cricket?" He obviously did but, to this day, I'm sure he wasn't convinced it was actually Richard he had in his car. Not that we confirmed it to him, either.

It's the recognition which comes with the profile which has added to the pressures we've felt as a couple. Our marriage has held together while some other couples have found it very difficult — even impossible — to keep things going. I can understand why. The strain is enormous on both husband and wife. The husband has to hold his place in the team and that brings with it publicity — both good and bad — which is sometimes hard to keep in perspective. Richard's moody, testy and restless before a test match. I've been through it so many times I know what to expect. I can feel for him and so you learn to understand and tolerate what's going on, even though it doesn't make it any easier. The wife is the one who has to keep body and soul together — as well as the family — and still remember and consider the assistance the husband needs before a test. Basically, she mustn't let anything annoy or irritate him. Because of the world these cricketers live in, it's also easy for them to bring their public image into their private life. That's where I draw the line and can be heard saying to RJ: "Just who the hell do you think you are?" At times I sense the media haven't helped; they've picked on him personally when surely he should be judged on the cricket field alone.

I've always been there to support him, to help him through rough times — and that's only right. There was the test against England in February 1988, when Richard was hoping to take his world record 374th wicket, but damaged his calf muscle instead. I was delayed having a drink in one of the sponsors' tents at Lancaster Park that evening and arrived home a bit later than planned. I showered and was about to get into bed when I remembered that someone at the function had talked about giving Richard the RICE treatment — rest, ice, compression and elevation. Being the good wife, I floundered about in the dark, pulled back the duvet, elevated his leg on to a pillow (with a slight groan from my patient), replaced the duvet and slept soundly. The next morning I asked whether elevating the leg had helped. "It might have — if you'd elevated the correct leg!"

I'm a great watcher of cricket. I need to be. And one of the highlights was seeing Richard make his world record bid — again — in Bangalore in November 1988. I'd been to India before and knew what to expect yet it's always a culture shock to see the poverty there. One day I was in a taxi with Sue Wright and Viv Vance when a beggar carrying a tiny baby on her hip said: "Please missy, please missy, money for food for the baby." We had no money but offered her a large bag of fruit we had with us . . . "Bah!" she said and almost threw it back at us. We decided she couldn't have been so hungry after all.

On what became world record day, we arrived at the ground about 15 minutes before play started, only to find we were in a tiny stand surrounded by barbed wire. Fortune smiled again because Janet Blackwell was with us and had a press pass. She went off to find someone else who could give us better seats and, within a matter of minutes, the president of the local association came down and guided us to the best seats in the place. Must get myself one of those press passes!

It was an amazing feeling when Richard took Arun Lal's wicket to make it 374. It even brought a tear to my eye — most unlike me — but I knew the work he'd put in over the winter to be in shape for this. I said to him that morning: "Are you nervous?" "Do I look it?" "No," I said, to which he replied: "Good, because I'm not." I must say he gave a huge sigh of relief as he walked back to his bowling mark. So did I!

On the rest day, the few of the team who weren't ill decided to go shopping but Richard said he didn't feel that well; he sat down in a shop and the colour of his face changed quite dramatically. "I've got to go back

Travelling to cricket with Viv Vance in India in a motorised rickshaw.

to the hotel," he said. I continued shopping and returned to the hotel about an hour later, only to find six people in our room attending to Richard. He was violently ill. He'd been vomiting, dry retching and in constant need of finding the loo; he was shaking, cold, goose-pimply, drawn and pathetic. He'd obviously picked up a virus but I'd never seen him looking so bad. That night he was totally delirious, saying stupid things I couldn't understand. He hardly slept, couldn't eat and didn't want to drink, although he was forced to have liquids to prevent dehydration.

How he went out to bat the next day — to help avoid the follow-on — I'll never know. While he's been criticised by some people for supposedly not being a team man, he proved beyond all doubt that day that he was. New Zealand cricket and its world rating are so important to him; he has strived for near perfection and has seen New Zealand cricket change completely, especially in the 1980s. And he's so proud of that.

Another highlight for me through the years was dinner on board the Royal yacht, *Britannia*. When the invitation came for us to attend, Richard checked the dates and said: "Oh, too bad. It's the night of the second day of the test against Australia."

"No, it's too bad for you — because we're going!" I told him.

"Aah," said he, "I guess we are then."

Accepting the invitation was the easy part, but finding an appropriate dress was another matter. I spent days and weeks going from dress shop to dress shop trying to find the right outfit. Finally, I had the ensemble I deemed suitable and was ready to tackle what I thought would be a wonderful, if awe-inspiring, night.

I spent a few minutes at home practising my curtsy, which was a major mistake. I got the heel of my shoe caught in the hem of my skirt and had to do some very quick running repairs.

The night itself turned out to be a marvellous occasion and I really made only one blunder — the Queen walked past me on her way to dinner and gave me a huge smile. I did likewise but it wasn't until she passed the next woman that I realised my mistake . . . I'd forgotten to curtsy!

It was quite off-putting to sit down to dinner with such a dizzy array of glasses, knives and forks but, fortunately, the Queen's then equerry, Major Hugh Lindsay, helped me with the protocol. I was saddened to hear he was the friend of Prince Charles who was killed in a skiing accident in Switzerland in 1988.

Later I met the Queen and it was just as well she was wearing gloves as I was so nervous and worried about doing my curtsy that my palms were wringing with sweat. I really shouldn't have worried because the Queen and the Duke of Edinburgh are experts at relaxing people. I think I even managed to say a few things to them which made sense.

In the real world, time's catching up with Richard. He's now so close to 400 test wickets — and he deserves to reach that mark because he's such a thorough professional. For me, though, life goes on. Other things are just as important to us as a unit. Matthew learning to ride his two-wheeler bike at three years old was probably just as significant but publicly didn't matter a hoot. What matters to us is that Richard and I were both in India

We've never lacked for family support through the cricketing years, especially from RJ's Mum and Dad. We needed them to help us find a new home one year.   R.J. Hadlee Collection

at the time and missed the event. If it's not the world record or striving for 400 test wickets, there'll be something else. It just goes on and on — and somewhere it has to stop. I think his time's not too far away.

For the first time in 17 years, Richard was able to have a holiday at Christmas last year, when we all spent 17 days together with our good friends Candy and Grant Brown in the Marlborough Sounds. And I think those 17 days made RJ realise there's much more to life than the eternal treadmill of international cricket. We had so many laughs we're keen for Christmas 1989 when both families can head to the Sounds again — assuming Richard's not playing cricket, of course. And that's a big if.

C·H·A·P·T·E·R S·E·V·E·N·T·E·E·N

What Now? What Next?

Karen's right. My time can't be too far away and, as I look towards the 1989–90 season as a 38-year-old, that's perfectly understandable. I'm not saying age should be a guide to retirement; that has very little to do with it.

But when you've been a first-class cricketer since 1971–72, it's inevitable there's one question I ask more often of myself, and one I'm persistently asked by others: "When will I give it all away?" I can't accurately answer that because it's foolish to put a fixed time on retirement; rather, as I regularly say now, I monitor my enthusiasm, mental alertness and physical alacrity on an annual basis. There's now a short-term look about my career planning which is the only way to operate at this stage of life.

My last two seasons have been both frustrating and concerning as that enemy of all sportsmen — injury — has visited too often for comfort. Unlike Dennis Lillee, Ian Botham and Imran Khan, the spectre of a serious breakdown hasn't hung over my career at any stage. Lillee needed back surgery in the 1970s — very early in his career — and Botham's back required surgical attention last year while Imran was threatened for a time by a serious shin complaint (and even played tests as a batsman only for a time). I've been blessed in comparison, and that's unusual for a pace bowler. However, the increasing instance of niggling worries has caused me some anxiety, perhaps psychologically more than anything else.

The calf muscle breakdown against England in 1987–88 hurt my right leg, my world record plans, my professional pride and my bank balance;

it abruptly ended the first test of the series for me (as a bowler in any case) and put me out of the other two tests and three one-day internationals. In India last season, my right achilles tendon became a painful worry and forced me home early after the tests; there were no one-dayers for me and I couldn't play in one Shell Cup or Shell Trophy match for Canterbury at home as I set about restoring myself to full fitness for the campaign against Pakistan. And then, in the third test in Auckland, I was hit by achilles trouble again, this time in my left leg. A calf muscle strain and two achilles setbacks in the space of a year? It suggests my body's telling me something.

The breakdown in Auckland reduced the New Zealand attack to just three bowlers as Pakistan went on to 616 for five declared in its first innings, a record test total against New Zealand. I finished with one for 68 from 28 overs while the others had to battle on, Stephen Boock conceding 229 runs! I'm sad to say there were mutterings from one player in the side who suggested I had conveniently become injured, because I'd looked at the pitch and didn't want to bowl on it! It's just staggering when one of your own team-mates thinks that way. I started the series against Pakistan needing nine wickets to reach 400; I desperately wanted that record. The cancellation of the first test in Dunedin was a major blow — it was the sort of pitch where wickets would surely have come easily. I bowled 54 overs in Pakistan's only innings in Wellington — and on a pitch which offered precious little to the bowlers. I was just as keen to fight the odds at Eden Park.

It's in times of injury crisis like this that life without cricket — as a player — comes into sharper focus. And having witnessed cricket evolve through two decades, thoughts of the future provoke some lateral thinking about all sorts of cricket issues.

There was a time after doing the county double in England in 1984 that I could see some attraction in rounding off my playing days with a stint in South Africa for one last pay day. Now my attitude's changed, not because I'm making some personal political statement about South Africa's apartheid policies. I abhor the system and am on record as saying so any number of times. I've always been an establishment player through all the drama of the Kerry Packer upheaval and the vexed and sensitive issue of playing contacts with South Africa. When the New Zealand Cricket Council made its play-in-South-Africa-and-be-banned stand in the early 1980s, that was enough for me. I wasn't about to risk my test career for a rebel tour, despite constant urgings from my Nottinghamshire team-mate and friend, Clive Rice. There was far too much to lose in other ways. If I finished my test career tomorrow, there wouldn't be the same dangers supposedly — but there still would be for my conscience.

There's big money to be made in South Africa. When former Australian captain Kim Hughes was offered $400,000 for a three-year rebel

My body was telling me something during the third test against Pakistan last summer. An achilles tendon injury forced me out of the bowling attack . . . and then cramped my style when I batted. But still not quite enough to prevent a straight drive for six off Imran Khan. J.G. Blackwell

— 278 —

contract, he said: "You have to think of the big amounts of money. You could retire for the rest of your life on that figure." I'd like some of that action but, of course, the South African issue is a little more complicated than that and, put simply, I'm just not prepared to jeopardise my future now by going there (and I'm talking about my life beyond playing cricket in New Zealand). There's too much I still want to do in the game.

At the same time, the South African conundrum angers me for the hypocrisy which abounds. I could argue forever about the rights and wrongs about playing sport in South Africa; there's no sporting matter which polarises opinion more than this one. I don't want to become embroiled just now in those kinds of pros and cons, but I do want to pose some questions about how South Africa's treated in different parts of the world, or at least how sportsmen who have visited the republic are treated.

The hoary old topic surfaced again in late 1988 when England was to tour India, only to have the visit aborted after the Indian government denied entry visas for eight England players who'd been to South Africa; and yet some of those players — like Graham Gooch, Allan Lamb, Tim Robinson and John Emburey — were allowed to play in India in the 1987 World Cup! Consistent, isn't it?

In a bid to rescue the tour-less England side, the NZCC came up with an alternative — a second successive New Zealand tour including two tests and a triangular one-day series involving England plus New Zealand and Pakistan, who were confirmed tourists in any case. There was distinct appeal about the 1988–89 international programme, even though it was, through necessity, arranged rather late in the piece. The season promised a total of eight tests against India, Pakistan and England and, for New Zealand players and fans, the lure of the first one-day tournament at home, a mini World Series Cup equivalent.

But, in this age of political sensitivity and ultra awareness, the Pakistan board opposed the venture and withdrew from the planned series. It wasn't prepared to be involved in a tournament against England because of the South African factor — and yet Pakistan had happily accepted playing against some of these rebels in the 1987 World Cup there and in the test series which followed. What's more, the Pakistani players also lined up against Australian rebel Terry Alderman in last summer's World Series Cup competition. Once again, the officials were calling the tune while the players were pushed around like pawns in this sad game of political-sporting warfare.

The NZCC was in a fix. The first duty was to protect the Pakistan tour which had been set in place for some time, but there was also an obligation to help England out of a spot. The NZCC was riding the horns of a dilemma, and what a dilemma. It was obvious the one-day series was no longer an item and, without it, the NZCC argued a separate tour by England wasn't a viable concern. However, to save the NZCC acute embarrassment, England withdrew gracefully from the tour, giving the Pakistan-India faction some sort of victory. It was all such an unfortunate business and yet another case of the damage politics can do to sport.

Out of this development — and England's aborted tour to India — evolved the International Cricket Conference's look at the entire question of players going to South Africa. The West Indies pushed for a blanket ban on players who'd had contact with South Africa; the Australians favoured all players starting with a clean slate after the January ICC meeting but, from then on, any players going to South Africa should be banned. Ultimately, there has been a tightening up in international circles and players continuing to go to South Africa will suffer. The real sufferers are the English county pros who rely on coaching and playing stints in South Africa for their off-season bread and butter. Now they've been warned — continue to go there and they can forget about their test career for the immediate future. The players are being dictated to again and I always find that repugnant.

An amicable solution to the South African puzzle seems a long way off. I'm a great believer in sport being a unifying force but the elements of pleasure, competition, exercise, enjoyment — and income for professionals — are being undermined by the political threat. It's naive in this age to believe sports and politics don't or shouldn't mix because the two are inextricably interwoven in so many ways; it's a shame but it's an inescapable fact.

Those people in organisations like HART don't unduly perturb me. Anyone in a democratic society like ours has the right to express personal views on any matter in an orderly, peaceful manner — and I respect the rights and views such people may have; I don't have to agree with them, though. What dismayed me when the England tour was such a hot topic last season, was HART's plans to disrupt games by assisting the England team with extra bowlers and fieldsmen. That's just so immature. If protest is the aim then they can march and stand around waving placards and shouting slogans, but going as far as disrupting a sporting contest, by getting on the field of play, is an invasion of civil rights . . . for the players and for the spectators who have paid money to see sport played at top level.

The South African topic — and that of political intervention and interference — will remain an unpalatable fact of sporting life but there are many other areas in cricket which need attention. And there are cures available, some of them rather obvious, others perhaps impractical.

In doing some crystal-ball gazing, I've talked to a number of modern-day test players, just to gauge the depth of feeling in some topic areas. And, in the playing arena itself, there's one issue which has gathered momentum.

Every four years we have a World Cup tournament, an event involving the seven test-playing nations plus one other in either 60-over or 50-over one-day games. And it's a fillip for New Zealand cricket that the next World Cup — the fifth since the concept was introduced in England in 1975 — will be staged by New Zealand and Australia in 1991. The World Cup's important, a prestigious title to win. But the way to find true champions on the cricket stage would be to extend the concept to test cricket; limited-overs cricket may be a crowd puller but the game's a lottery in so many ways. Far better, for cricketers and purists, to have some form of rating of countries at test level — and it could be done.

Martin Crowe wrote in his column in the *Dominion Sunday Times* that a World Cup concept for test cricket "would do a lot to stop falling attendances at test matches. Test matches could be run within existing series with qualifying points for the cup being awarded for one of those tests within a series."

Perhaps points for wins and first innings leads could be awarded — for the first or whichever test in a series — over a period of four years or so with the two top teams playing off in a final, like the rugby league system. Obviously international programmes would have to be rearranged so countries had the chance to play each other at home and away to ensure no one had an unfair advantage; perhaps even one-off tests with World Cup points at stake could be played to avert an overkill of test matches. I believe that's on, especially if administrators are serious about trying to rejuvenate interest in test cricket.

I think it's certainly time the New Zealand players were treated far more seriously, too; in that sense, I'm talking about giving the New Zealand side five-test series. Surely we should be fairly rewarded after the fabulous 1980s when we managed to beat every test nation in at least one test series; when New Zealand toured England in 1983 and the West Indies in 1984–85 we played four tests, but we've never played five in my time. The last time it happened for this country was in the West Indies in 1971–72. We deserve to be accorded the same sort of status as Australia, England or the West Indies both in series in New Zealand and overseas. One of the attractions of the planned 1988–89 season was the prospect of five home tests, admittedly not all against one opponent, but five matches nonetheless. It would have enabled the NZCC to measure interest and I believe the news would have been all good. We may never know now.

I have no doubt a triangular one-day series would boom in New Zealand, too . . . what a shame the theory wasn't tested last summer. It would require some co-operation, but wouldn't it be feasible to lock in with one of the sides involved in Australia's annual World Series Cup competition? India tour New Zealand this coming season, so why not bring in Australia, Sri Lanka or some country from across the Tasman to set up a three-way competition.

And, if New Zealand is stuck with the normal one-day diet of a series against just one touring side, then we should be upgrading such a series to five matches, not four. The crowd at Auckland's Eden Park for one-dayers usually determines the financial success of tours and yet the system allows Auckland to stage just one limited-overs international. Why not start a five-match programme in Auckland, go to three other venues for the ensuing matches and then return to Eden Park for what could be the decider? Apparently it's difficult to persuade touring countries to play an extra game in New Zealand but we've been forced to accept itineraries in India and the West Indies involving five one-dayers. So, where's the consistency? That's precisely where world cricket needs a greater sense of unity and understanding.

That issue falls to the International Cricket Conference to work on and remedy. Cricket's world body meets infrequently — usually once a year — to discuss the game's problems and try and come up with solutions. On a numbers basis, the so-called black countries have it over the rest of

I may be past my 38th birthday but age should never be a factor in retirement.

Sun

the world numerically — the West Indies, India, Pakistan and Sri Lanka can always muster more voting power than England, Australia and New Zealand on matters which might be delicate for whatever reason.

Each country is represented by its chairman or president plus its secretary or executive director (or another board member) . . . two representatives per country. The NZCC's executive director, Graham Dowling, is a former New Zealand captain. Sadly, many of the delegates to the ICC are professional men who have never played the game at all, or at least not to a very high level. And yet these people are entrusted with making decisions about the game. I'm sure these men all have a great love of and for cricket but I see an urgent need for countries to have a third delegate — specifically a former player or perhaps even the captains of the day. The game's for the players and decisions reached by the ICC affect their attitude to and interest in cricket.

The theme of unity is seen to be lacking on a world scale; it also emerges as a problem all too often on individual tours. There are disputes about required over rates and playing conditions, not to mention the international unease about umpires.

The abandonment of last summer's scheduled first test against Pakistan in Dunedin was not, as I've said, a decision I supported. But, having scrapped that test, there was surely some responsibility to come up with a replacement; it could have been managed by giving Napier a test instead of the meaningless Shell XI match it staged (that fixture became a disaster with so many of the originally selected players withdrawing from the Shell XI). I know our captain John Wright believed it was too much to play three tests within three weeks but most of the New Zealand players were keen to have a replacement; Pakistan, on the other hand, had the attitude which most touring teams have, viewing the abandoned match as a draw. And so a test match totally lost ensured the NZCC was on a rocky road financially for the rest of the tour.

Revenue has always been important for any sport to survive. Sports bodies have to explore — and perhaps even exploit — all sorts of income-winning avenues. Cricket, like most sports today, is now commercialised but not yet as overtly as it could be, certainly not compared with some other sports.

American football probably goes over the top with some of its sponsorship gimmicks but, when a sport needs finance to subsist, should there be any rules? Almost anything should be possible and there's one aspect the NZCC could move on very swiftly — and that's the matter of painting sponsors' logos on the outfield at either end of test and one-day venues. And I'm certainly in favour of some bending of the rules about players wearing sponsors' logos on playing gear.

More importantly, the NZCC still has to grapple with a perennial problem — what to do with the Shell Trophy competition. We need to move away from three-day cricket and it's only a matter of time before we will; the Sheffield Shield involves four-day cricket and there's some four-day play now in the English county championship. The gap between three-day first-class matches and five-day tests is too great for players to adjust to. With the four-day game there's more time for proper cricket to be played — batsmen can construct long innings, spinners can bowl long spells and the need to give away quick runs to bring about false declarations would also be less prevalent. With each passing season, the players talk longer and louder about the need for more expansive first-class matches, and that was especially true last summer when so many matches had a contrived look about them; it needed enterprising captains to bring about results — and all credit for the way they did that — but it proved the futility of three-day games. They just aren't long enough.

Martin Snedden's been playing first-class cricket now since 1977–78 and, as one of the real thinkers in the game, he has plenty of theories about the way the NZCC could revitalise the Shell Trophy competition. He feels the council should start with one complete round of four-day games and another of three-day ones, so allowing the council to assess the feasibility of four-day cricket. But the NZCC rejected the idea this year opting instead for two full rounds of three-day games in the 1989–90 season. The question about four-day matches is whether our pitches are good enough. Last summer they generally were, although there must be some doubt whether some of the smaller centres would come up to standard. Costs for running the competition would obviously increase, so who would pay? Would the public be interested? And what about some of the players — would there be problems in being available for the extra cricket involved? Lots of answers are needed but at least the NZCC should give it a trial.

The points system may also need to be addressed. Scrapping first innings points and giving rewards only for outright victories will ensure results are pursued, so generating public interest. At the same time, the points value for outright wins might be reduced from 12, to say eight.

Four-day cricket would see the best emerging more often than not because the game would be played authentically rather than artificially, as it is now.

If the Shell Trophy format is a frequent discussion topic, then so, too, is the matter of a seventh side for the competition. In the last 10 years, Auckland has grown considerably — especially on the North Shore — and there's a strong case now for a North Harbour cricket side. Rugby, softball, bowls and other sports have North Harbour or North Shore bases, so why not cricket. It's a sign of the viability of the scheme that the Auckland Cricket Association, which would be the big loser on the surface, is keen to see such a possibility investigated. As it stands now, too many players are prevented from coming through to first-class level in Auckland because there simply aren't enough team places to go around; where some other associations battle to find enough players of sufficient quality, Auckland seems to have talent to spare. And it's that abundance of players which may well have been a contributing factor to Auckland's indifferent record in the Shell Trophy competition; when it won the title last summer, Auckland ended an eight-year drought since its previous success in 1980–81, the only other time the country's biggest association has won the trophy since the last season of Plunket Shield cricket in 1975–76.

And, talking about the Plunket Shield, that's something which needs to be brought out from its hiding place and dusted off. There's too much history tied up in the old shield not to have it at stake in top-level cricket for some sort of reason. Maybe it could be put up for a special North Island v South Island one-dayer, or even a three-day match. Better still, why not give it Ranfurly Shield-style status. As Shell Trophy champions, Auckland could start off with it this coming season and be forced to defend it in all home games; any Shell Trophy match at home would auto-matically become a shield match as well. But, to wrest it from the holder, a challenger would have to win outright . . . just another idea to inject more edge and interest into the competition.

There's some room for improvements and adjustments at inter-national level, too. Not so much in the playing of the game but in one or two administrative areas. I'm strongly in favour of a new approach in the selection of test teams; rather than picking the traditional 12 players, there's a great opportunity for the selectors to choose, say, 14 players so fringe players and youngsters who are likely test contenders in the near future can experience the test-match atmosphere (without necessarily playing in the game itself).

Money issues are inevitably involved in any cricket discussion among players, and one area for the NZCC to look at is setting up a super-annuation scheme similar to the Australian one. While playing fees have increased considerably, which might be a debit against a super scheme, those who have been in the game a long time — say, 10 to 15 years — would appreciate receiving a lump sum at the end of their careers.

If not a super scheme, then what about player contracts like those in Australia where 10 to 15 players could be contracted to be available to play over a period of time, and be guaranteed an additional income source

The sign of things to come when I finally stop playing. More relaxation will certainly be on at our holiday home in the Marlborough Sounds. And coaching the players of the future could be another pursuit.

R.J. Hadlee Collection

during any given season. It's one way to keep the top-drawer players in the game longer, and it's also a useful way of partially appeasing long-suffering wives who have to put up with so many absences.

I've always enjoyed watching rugby or rugby league internationals and seeing the way the players exchange their jerseys at the end of a series. It's a marvellous expression of goodwill . . . but it's not the kind of thing New Zealand cricketers can do. The NZCC's supplies to players don't extend to providing extra sweaters or caps so we can swap them with opponents; in fact, I was billed $69 by the NZCC to replace a sweater and cap I swapped with Kapil Dev in India last season. Surely some deal could be made with the suppliers to allow test players a small perk. And couldn't New Zealand's sweaters also carry a national logo?

As New Zealand cricket moves into the 1990s, and many of the links with the past two decades are gradually lost, the development and arrival of fresh talent is vital — and I'm encouraged with what's coming through. It's a signal our coaching schemes, youth tours and tournaments are providing valuable opportunities for our players of the future. Young New Zealand and under-20 tours are vital to aid the developmental process because the players experience playing on foreign soil, being exposed to match play nearly every day and being together with players for three or four weeks. If overseas tours are not possible, then at least internal ones should be pursued, ensuring these youngsters have cricket managers of first-class or test experience with them, players like Geoff Howarth or Andy Roberts.

Coaching basically incorporates the principles of playing cricket but can never substitute for actually playing the game; and I'm sure there's a greater need for emphasising the match-playing aspect of cricket among our youngsters. Further ahead they'll find the demands of first-class cricket are enormous but, while they have ability at a young age, they have little idea of how to prepare themselves and exploit their talents. Short cuts should never be taken in learning the game but I've gained the impression some up-and-comers think everything is just going to happen. It takes years of being the apprentice, with problems and failures, to understand that you have to work hard, listen and learn to become a successful cricketer.

While I'm all in favour of tours for our younger players if we're to develop as a playing nation, I can't accept players in these teams should be rewarded with a New Zealand cap and jersey. The cap with the silver fern on it and the sweater with three black bands (if missing the national logo) should be something special for those who make the full New Zealand side. I know it was for me when I first made the national side, and it's still something I cherish. But when I see youngsters in the gear, its meaning is somehow devalued. Give them caps and jerseys of some type, but reserve the privilege of wearing the real thing for the top team.

All this discussion about coaching and youngsters embodies an area of the game I want to be involved in in the not-so-distant future. But I'm a little sceptical about New Zealand's coaching structure which allows for basic coaches at the level-one standard, more advanced ones at level two and the elite at level three, of whom there are about six or seven in New

Zealand. What irks me about the elite grade, though, is that you have to be invited to be part of the exclusive group! The system gives the impression that a talented and competent coach, who's not liked by the people who matter, might never become a level-three coach. Geoff Howarth and I might want to advance to that level and yet we could be prevented from reaching the top, all on a subjective technicality. Ability should be rewarded.

I suppose I have some affinity with women's cricket — after all Karen played the game and reached national honours. Like some other sports in New Zealand they find it difficult to survive.

Some women's and men's sporting bodies have amalgamated — helping each other in the best interests of the sport. Maybe the NZCC could invite the Women's Council to be part of the overall cricket administration in New Zealand. I'm not necessarily suggesting that women should make decisions on the male game but I do see some advantages — assistance in marketing and promotion, finding sponsors, coaching, grounds/pitches, umpiring and so on. Perhaps representatives of the Women's Council could join a subcommittee specifically designated by the NZCC to assist women's cricket in whatever way they feel. Closer ties between the two would be an important breakthrough.

Here I am, 18 years down the track as an international cricketer, trying to solve the game's ills but it's a sign to me there's still excitement ahead when my playing days are over.

I think it makes good sense for me to be involved in both the technical and mental development of fast bowlers in the way of coaching; it's something I tasted in the 1980s when Geoff Howarth and I ran coaching clinics up and down the country. And, after so much first-class and test cricket, I ought to have some knowledge to pass on to young players; it's appealing to me to analyse up-and-comers, to watch their actions and their attitudes. How hard do they train? How diligently do they work on their game? Do they understand what they're trying to do? My wealth of knowledge should be explored and exploited through coaching and I'd like to think I can play a significant role in producing test bowlers of the future. It's also common for former internationals to gravitate towards a selection role; for me, perhaps one day. And there's something attractive about some day managing a touring team and again visiting countries — and meeting players — I've played in. Invariably, New Zealand touring teams are managed by NZCC board members as some sort of reward for their services to the game, but that doesn't necessarily mean they're best suited for the task or equipped to handle it. It's interesting that, for home series, there's been a trend to use non-board members as managers, and that's worked extremely well. Dave Elder had a fair stint at it and he was a wonderful manager; the same applies to Leif Dearsley who managed the team last season.

An involvement in administration or selection would cut across one

Something symbolic? Going out to help avoid the follow-on with Ewen Chatfield against India in Bangalore last season. There can't be too many more test innings left for the two old troopers.   J.G. Blackwell

of my other interests in the game. I want to write and comment on cricket. I've been writing newspaper columns for more than 10 years now and, once I've finished playing the game, I'll be able to comment more pointedly and objectively on the game without being shackled by the restrictions put on players. I've also had a share of television and radio commentary work and this has whetted my appetite for more in years ahead. I'm keen, too, on working in the marketing and sports promotion field and, as my manager's also the NZCC's marketing manager, that could be an avenue for me.

All of that's still in the future, if much more immediate than I might care to admit. In the meantime, I've still got some unfinished business to do as a cricket player. Two achilles injuries didn't take the gloss off my 17th season of international cricket — how could it when the world record came in India and five tests played, most of them on demanding pitches for fast bowlers, provided me with 23 wickets in only six innings? But I didn't achieve the goal of being the first man to 400 test wickets.

The 1989–90 season looms and, with it, the prospect of a series against India. Hopefully there'll also be plenty of other cricket to play, including a series of benefit matches — and even then I may not be finished. Already people are saying to me: "You should do the 1990 tour to England." Who knows? . . . I certainly don't at this stage. But when I do finish, I'll know it's the right time and there'll be no turning back — then it'll be time to face life without playing the game, and what a strange experience that will be.

By the end of last season, interest was growing in Ian Botham's come-back as a player after his surgery last year — and I must say any talk about Both always makes me perk up. It's that old challenge of the all rounders thing again. It always gives me some added motivation.

Some people may believe I hope Botham doesn't make it because I might lose my No. 1 ranking. But at the end of the day, does it really matter that I'm on top? No. I'm contented with my career, I've gone on longer and reached heights that I never imagined I would.

The world record was what I wanted most of all, to be No. 1. I made it, I'm ahead and that's nice, but someone will overtake me one day. It could be Botham, it could be somebody else and whether it takes six months, six years, or 60 years there's someone who'll do it. But, if someone's to pass my final total, I believe they'll have to play test cricket for at least 15 years and average about six wickets a match and, of the current crop of international bowlers, I don't know who could do that. Kapil Dev's not as productive as he once was, Botham's an unknown factor now, Imran Khan's almost finished and I'm not so sure Malcolm Marshall will go on and on.

Good luck to whoever the future No. 1 might be; he'll deserve it. It takes nothing away from my life in cricket — I'm very happy with what I've achieved. And I still haven't quite finished!

Statistics

to end of 1988–89 season

Compiled by Peter Marriott

TEST MATCH CAREER RECORDS

Batting & Fielding / Bowling

		M	I	NO	Runs	Ave	HS	100	50	Ct	O	M	R	W	Ave	BB	5w	10w
1972–73	v Pakistan	1	1	0	46	46.00	46	–	–	2	25†	0	112	2	56.00	2-84	–	–
1973	in England	1	2	1	4	4.00	4*	–	–	–	45	8	143	1	143.00	1-79	–	–
1973–74	in Australia	3	6	0	68	11.33	20	–	–	2	66.7†	9	255	7	36.42	4-33	–	–
1973–74	v Australia	2	3	0	37	12.33	23	–	–	1	50.4†	7	225	10	22.50	4-71	–	–
1975–76	v India	2	2	0	45	22.50	33	–	–	–	48.3†	4	197	12	16.41	7-23	1	1
1976–77	in Pakistan	3	6	2	214	53.50	87	–	1	2	75.2†	2	447	10	44.70	5-121	1	–
1976–77	in India	3	6	0	60	10.00	21	–	–	1	127	18	437	13	33.61	4-95	–	–
1976–77	v Australia	2	4	0	143	35.75	81	–	1	2	72†	7	354	6	59.00	3-155	–	–
1977–78	v England	3	6	1	80	16.00	39	–	–	–	121.3†	26	371	15	24.73	6-26	1	1
1978	in England	3	6	0	32	5.33	11	–	–	3	121.1	31	270	13	20.76	5-84	1	–
1978–79	v Pakistan	3	5	1	115	28.75	53*	–	1	1	117.6†	13	414	18	23.00	5-62	2	–
1979–80	v West Indies	3	4	0	178	44.50	103	1	1	1	161.3	50	361	19	19.00	6-68	2	1
1980–81	in Australia	3	6	2	98	24.50	51*	–	1	1	147.3	35	364	19	19.15	6-57	2	–
1980–81	v India	3	4	0	29	7.25	20	–	–	2	119.3	37	288	10	28.80	5-47	1	–
1981–82	v Australia	3	5	1	92	23.00	40	–	–	2	91.5	25	226	14	16.14	6-100	2	–
1982–83	v Sri Lanka	2	3	1	59	29.50	30	–	–	1	77.3	27	141	10	14.10	4-33	–	–
1983	in England	4	8	2	301	50.16	92*	–	3	1	232	65	559	21	26.61	6-53	2	–
1983–84	v England	3	4	0	144	36.00	99	–	1	3	109.5	33	232	12	19.33	5-28	1	–
1983–84	in Sri Lanka	3	4	0	75	18.75	29	–	–	3	117.5	48	230	23	10.00	5-29	2	1
1984–85	v Pakistan	3	4	0	131	32.75	89	–	1	–	118.5	29	306	16	19.12	6-51	1	–
1984–85	in West Indies	4	7	1	137	22.83	39*	–	–	1	143	33	409	15	27.26	4-53	–	–
1985–86	in Australia	3	4	0	111	27.75	54	–	1	2	169.3	42	401	33	12.15	9-52	5	2
1985–86	v Australia	3	3	1	105	52.50	72*	–	1	2	157.5	36	387	16	24.18	7-116	1	–
1986	in England	3	3	0	93	31.00	68	–	1	–	153.5	42	390	19	20.52	6-80	2	1
1986–87	v West Indies	3	4	2	74	37.00	35*	–	–	2	113.1	20	354	17	20.82	6-50	2	–
1986–87	in Sri Lanka	1	1	1	151	–	151*	1	–	1	38.5	10	102	4	25.50	4-102	–	–
1987–88	in Australia	3	6	1	111	22.20	36	–	–	–	156	44	353	18	19.61	5-67	3	1
1987–88	v England	1	1	0	37	37.00	37	–	–	–	18	3	50	0	–	–	–	–
1988–89	in India	3	6	1	61	12.20	31	–	–	1	100.5	25	252	18	14.00	6-49	2	1
1988–89	v Pakistan	2	3	1	53	26.50	32	–	–	–	82	21	169	5	33.80	4-101	–	–
Total		**79**	**127**	**19**	**2884**	**26.70**	**151***	**2**	**13**	**37**	**20232**	**750**	**8799**	**396**	**22.21**	**9-52**	**34**	**9**

‡577.1 8-ball [†] plus 2602.3 6-ball overs / balls‡

Against Each Country

	M	I	NO	Runs	Ave	HS	100	50	Ct	Balls	R	W	Ave	BB	5w	10w
England	18	30	4	691	26.57	99	–	5	7	5050	2015	81	24.87	6-26	7	2
Australia	22	37	5	765	23.90	81	–	4	12	5851	2565	123	20.85	9-52	13	3
West Indies	10	15	3	389	32.41	103	1	1	4	2506	1124	51	22.03	6-50	4	1
India	11	18	1	195	11.47	33	–	–	4	2471	1174	53	22.15	7-23	4	2
Pakistan	12	19	4	559	37.26	89	–	3	5	2949	1448	51	28.39	6-51	4	–
Sri Lanka	6	8	2	285	47.50	151*	1	–	5	1405	473	37	12.78	5-29	2	1
Total	**79**	**127**	**19**	**2884**	**26.70**	**151***	**2**	**13**	**37**	**20232**	**8799**	**396**	**22.21**	**9-52**	**34**	**9**

In Each Country

	M	I	NO	Runs	Ave	HS	100	50	Ct	Balls	R	W	Ave	BB	5w	10w
New Zealand	39	56	8	1368	28.50	103	1	6	19	9780	4187	182	23.00	7-23	14	3
England	11	19	3	430	26.87	92*	–	4	4	3312	1362	54	25.22	6-53	5	1
Australia	12	22	3	388	20.42	54	–	2	5	3373	1373	77	17.83	9-52	10	3
West Indies	4	7	1	137	22.83	39*	–	–	1	858	409	15	27.26	4-53	–	–
India	6	12	1	121	11.00	31	–	–	2	1367	689	31	22.22	6-49	2	1
Pakistan	3	6	2	214	53.50	87	–	1	2	602	447	10	44.70	5-121	1	–
Sri Lanka	4	5	1	226	56.50	151*	1	–	4	940	332	27	12.29	5-29	2	1
Total	**79**	**127**	**19**	**2884**	**26.70**	**151***	**2**	**13**	**37**	**20232**	**8799**	**396**	**22.21**	**9-52**	**34**	**9**

Home and Away

	M	I	NO	Runs	Ave	HS	100	50	Ct	Balls	R	W	Ave	BB	5w	10w
Home	39	56	8	1368	28.50	103	1	6	19	9780	4187	182	23.00	7-23	14	3
Away	40	71	11	1516	25.26	151*	1	7	18	10452	4612	214	21.55	9-52	20	6
Total	**79**	**127**	**19**	**2884**	**26.70**	**151***	**2**	**13**	**37**	**20232**	**8799**	**396**	**22.21**	**9-52**	**34**	**9**

Collaborators in the Field

41	I.D.S. Smith
27	J.V. Coney
24	W.K. Lees
19	M.D. Crowe
11	J.G. Bracewell, M.G. Burgess
10	B.L. Cairns, J.J. Crowe, G.P. Howarth
8	J.G. Wright
7	K.J. Wadsworth
5	B.A. Edgar, J.M. Parker, substitutes
4	S.L. Boock, B.E. Congdon

3	E.J. Chatfield, J.F. Reid, G.M. Turner
2	M.J. Greatbatch, J.F.M. Morrison, D.R. O'Sullivan, N.M. Parker, K.R. Rutherford
1	B. Andrews, V.R. Brown, G.N. Edwards, T.J. Franklin, E.J. Gray, H.J. Howarth, A.H. Jones, C.M. Kuggeleijn, P.E. McEwan, P.J. Petherick, A.D.G. Roberts, D.A. Stirling, G.B. Troup

Summary of Test Wickets Taken

Batsman No.	Wkts	Batsman No.	Wkts	Batsman No.	Wkts
1	50	5	35	9	34
2	54	6	35	10	26
3	42	7	35	11	17
4	28	8	40		

Batsmen 1 and 2 (104) represent 26.26% of total
Batsmen 1 to 7 (279) represent 70.45% of total
Batsmen 8 to 11 (117) represent 29.55% of total

Summary of How Test Wickets Taken

	Wkts	%
Bowled	83	20.96
Leg before wicket	71	17.93
Caught	233	58.84
Caught and bowled	9	2.27

Test Victims
Number of times dismissed

England (28)

9   D.W. Randall
6   P.H. Edmonds, R.W. Taylor
5   R.G.D. Willis
4   G.A. Gooch, D.I. Gower, M.D. Moxon, C.T. Radley
3   I.T. Botham, N.G. Cowans, N.A. Foster, M.W. Gatting, C.M. Old, G.R.J. Roope, C.J. Tavaré
2   C.W.J. Athey, G. Boycott, J.E. Emburey, G. Fowler, C.L. Smith
1   J.M. Brearley, G.R. Dilley, M. Hendrick, V.J. Marks, G. Miller, G.C. Small, J.A. Snow, J.G. Thomas

Australia (43)

8   D.C. Boon, G.R.J. Matthews
7   G.R. Marsh
6   A.R. Border, G.S. Chappell, G.M. Wood
5   I.C. Davis, K.J. Hughes, R.W. Marsh
4   D.R. Gilbert, C.J. McDermott, G.M. Ritchie
3   R.G. Holland, D.M. Jones, G.F. Lawson, K.J. O'Keeffe, W.B. Phillips, K.R. Stackpole, J.R. Thomson, B. Yardley
2   I.M. Chappell, G.C. Dyer, A.M.J. Hilditch, R.B. Kerr, D.K. Lillee, A.A. Mallett, P.R. Sleep, K.D. Walters
1   R.J. Bright, G.J. Cosier, S.P. Davis, A.I.C. Dodemaide, G.J. Gilmour, J.D. Higgs, R.M. Hogg, B.M. Laird, I.R. Redpath, B.A. Reid, M.R.J. Veletta, M.H.N. Walker, S.R. Waugh, K.C. Wessels, T.J. Zoehrer

West Indies (20)

7   D.L. Haynes
6   C.G. Greenidge
5   A.L. Logie
4   J. Garner, M.A. Holding
3   H.A. Gomes, I.V.A. Richards, R.B. Richardson
2   P.J.L. Dujon, C.H. Lloyd, D.L. Murray, L.G. Rowe
1   C.G. Butts, C.E.H. Croft, A.H. Gray, A.I. Kallicharran, C.L. King, M.D. Marshall, D.R. Parry, C.A. Walsh

India (29)

4   Arun Lal, S.M. Gavaskar, D.B. Vengsarkar, G.R. Viswanath
3   M.B. Amarnath, K. Srikkanth
2   S. Amarnath, Arshad Ayub, B.G. Bedi, C.P.S. Chauhan, A.D. Gaekwad, Kapil Dev, S.M.H. Kirmani, R. Patel
1   K.V.B.J. Azad, M. Azharuddin, B.S. Chandrasekhar, K.D. Ghavri, U.S. Madan Lal, A.V. Mankad, K.S. More, B.P. Patel, S.M. Patil, E.A.S. Prasanna, W.V. Raman, R.J. Shastri, S. Venkataraghavan, Yashpal Sharma, Yograj Singh

Pakistan (25)

6   Mushtaq Mohammad
5   Talat Ali
4   Imran Khan, Javed Miandad
3   Asif Iqbal, Mohsin Khan, Mudassar Nazar, Sadiq Mohammad
2   Salim Malik, Sarfraz Nawaz, Zaheer Abbas
1   Abdul Qadir, Anil Dalpat, Azeem Hafeez, Haroon Rashid, Intikhab Alam, Majid Khan, Rashid Khan, Rizwan-Uz-Zaman, Saleem Yousuf, Shoaib Mohammad, Sikander Bakht, Tahir Naqqash, Wasim Akram, Wasim Raja

Sri Lanka (14)

6 S. Wettimuny
4 L.R.D. Mendis, J.R. Ratnayeke
3 R.G. de Alwis, D.S. de Silva, E.R.N.S. Fernando, S.M.S. Kaluperuma,
  R.S. Madugalle, R.J. Ratnayake
1 A.M.J.G. Amerasinghe, R.L. Dias, A.P. Gurusinghe, V.B. John, S.A.R. Silva

Complete Test Bowling Figures by Ground

			First Innings				Second Innings			
			O	*M*	*R*	*W*	*O*	*M*	*R*	*W*
1972–73	v Pakistan	Basin Reserve	18	0	84	2	7	0	28	0
1973	in England	Trent Bridge	26	5	64	0	19	3	79	1
1973–74	in Australia	MCG	25	4	104	0				
		SCG	9.4	2	33	4	4.3	0	16	2
		Adelaide Oval	28	3	102	1				
1973–74	v Australia	Lancaster Park	14	2	59	3	18.4	3	71	4
		Eden Park	9	1	45	1	9	1	50	2
1975–76	v India	Lancaster Park	12	1	75	0	14	2	64	1
		Basin Reserve	14	1	35	4	8.3	0	23	7
1976–77	in Pakistan	Gaddafi Stadium	19	0	121	5	5	0	36	0
		Niaz Stadium	19	1	77	1				
		National Stadium	20.2	1	138	4	12	0	75	0
1976–77	in India	Wankhede Stadium	29	5	95	4	16	0	76	1
		Green Park	29	2	121	1	15	1	56	2
		Chepauk	21	7	37	3	17	3	52	2
1976–77	v Australia	Lancaster Park	29	1	155	3	13	4	41	1
		Eden Park	28	2	147	2	2	0	11	0
1977–78	v England	Basin Reserve	28	5	74	4	13.3	4	26	6
		Lancaster Park	43	10	147	4	6	1	17	0
		Eden Park	31	6	107	1				
1978	in England	Kennington Oval	21.5	6	43	2	11.3	3	18	0
		Trent Bridge	42	11	94	4				
		Lord's	32	9	84	5	13.5	2	31	2
1978–79	v Pakistan	Lancaster Park	25	2	62	5	26	4	83	3
		McLean Park	25	3	101	4	14	1	56	1
		Eden Park	27	3	104	5	0.6	0	8	0
1979–80	v West Indies	Carisbrook	20	9	34	5	36	13	68	6
		Lancaster Park	23.3	5	58	3	22	7	64	0
		Eden Park	31	8	75	4	29	8	62	1
1980–81	in Australia	Woolloongabba	37	8	83	3	6	0	28	0
		WACA Ground	27	8	87	5	11.1	4	20	2
		MCG	39	8	89	3	27.2	7	57	6
1980–81	v India	Basin Reserve	16	4	62	0	22.3	7	65	4
		Lancaster Park	33	12	47	5				
		Eden Park	27	11	49	1	21	3	65	0
1981–82	v Australia	Basin Reserve	7	2	15	0				
		Eden Park	20	7	38	2	28	9	63	5
		Lancaster Park	28.5	5	100	6	8	2	10	1
1982–83	v Sri Lanka	Lancaster Park	13.3	1	33	4	22	12	27	0
		Basin Reserve	25	9	47	2	17	5	34	4
1983	in England	Kennington Oval	23.4	6	53	6	37.2	7	99	2
		Headingley	21	9	44	0	26	9	45	0
		Lord's	40	15	93	5	26	7	42	3
		Trent Bridge	30	7	98	1	28	5	85	4
1983–84	v England	Basin Reserve	31.5	6	97	2				
		Lancaster Park	17	9	16	3	18	6	28	5
		Eden Park	43	12	91	2				

			First Innings				Second Innings			
			O	M	R	W	O	M	R	W
1983–84	in Sri Lanka	Asgiriya Stadium	20.5	7	35	4	7	4	8	4
		Sinhalese SCG	22	12	27	2	30	14	58	3
		Colombo CCG	22	4	73	5	16	7	29	5
1984–85	v Pakistan	Basin Reserve	32	11	70	2				
		Eden Park	19.5	3	60	4	17	1	66	2
		Carisbrook	24	5	51	6	26	9	59	2
1984–85	in West Indies	Queens Park Oval	24.3	6	82	4	17	2	58	0
		Bourda Oval	25.5	5	83	2	16	3	32	2
		Kensington Oval	26	5	86	3				
		Sabina Park	28.4	11	53	4	5	1	15	0
1985–86	in Australia	Woolloongabba	23.4	4	52	9	28.5	9	71	6
		SCG	24	2	65	5	27.1	10	58	2
		WACA Ground	26.5	6	65	5	39	11	90	6
1985–86	v Australia	Basin Reserve	37.1	5	116	3				
		Lancaster Park	44.4	8	116	7	25	4	47	2
		Eden Park	31	12	60	3	20	7	48	1
1986	in England	Lord's	37.5	11	80	6	27	3	78	1
		Trent Bridge	32	7	80	6	33.1	15	60	4
		Kennington Oval	23.5	6	92	2				
1986–87	v West Indies	Basin Reserve	31	9	77	2	4	0	12	0
		Eden Park	41.4	7	105	6	1	0	9	0
		Lancaster Park	12.3	2	50	6	23	2	101	3
1986–87	in Sri Lanka	Colombo CCG	38.5	10	102	4				
1987–88	in Australia	Woolloongabba	31	5	95	3	8	3	14	0
		Adelaide Oval	42	16	68	5				
		MCG	44	11	109	5	31	9	67	5
1987–88	v England	Lancaster Park	18	3	50	0				
1988–89	in India	Chinnaswamy Stadium	30	10	65	5				
		Wankhede Stadium	20.5	5	49	6	16	3	39	4
		Lal Bahadur Stadium	34	7	99	3				
1988–89	v Pakistan	Basin Reserve	54	14	101	4				
		Eden Park	28	7	68	1				

How Wickets Taken by Grounds

In New Zealand (5)

	M	Balls	R	W	Ave	BB	5w	10w	B	LBW	C	C&B
Basin Reserve	11	2375	966	46	21.00	7-23	2	2	9	4	31	2
Carisbrook	2	636	212	19	11.15	6-51	3	1	1	8	9	1
Eden Park	12	2999	1331	43	30.95	6-105	3	–	6	12	25	–
Lancaster Park	13	3458	1521	69	22.04	7-116	6	–	16	8	44	1
McLean Park	1	312	157	5	31.40	4-101	–	–	2	1	2	–
Total	**39**	**9780**	**4187**	**182**	**23.00**	**7-23**	**14**	**3**	**34**	**33**	**111**	**4**

In England (4)

	M	Balls	R	W	Ave	BB	5w	10w	B	LBW	C	C&B
Headingley	1	282	89	0	–	–	–	–	–	–	–	–
Kennington Oval	3	709	305	12	25.41	6-53	1	–	3	4	5	–
Lord's	3	1060	408	22	18.54	6-80	3	–	4	4	14	–
Trent Bridge	4	1261	560	20	28.00	6-80	1	1	9	4	6	1
Total	**11**	**3312**	**1362**	**54**	**25.22**	**6-53**	**5**	**1**	**16**	**12**	**25**	**1**

In Australia (5)

	M	Balls	R	W	Ave	BB	5w	10w	B	LBW	C	C&B
Adelaide Oval	2	476	170	6	28.33	5-68	1	–	1	2	3	–
MCG	3	1048	426	19	22.42	6-57	3	1	4	6	9	–
SCG	2	418	172	13	13.23	5-65	1	–	–	6	7	–
WACA Ground	2	624	262	18	14.55	6-90	3	1	5	1	11	1
Woolloongabba	3	807	343	21	16.33	9-52	2	1	6	2	12	1
Total	**12**	**3373**	**1373**	**77**	**17.83**	**9-52**	**10**	**3**	**16**	**17**	**42**	**2**

In West Indies (4)

	M	Balls	R	W	Ave	BB	5w	10w	B	LBW	C	C&B
Bourda Oval	1	251	115	4	28.75	2-32	–	–	1	–	3	–
Kensington Oval	1	156	86	3	28.66	3-86	–	–	1	–	2	–
Queens Park Oval	1	249	140	4	35.00	4-82	–	–	1	1	2	–
Sabina Park	1	202	68	4	17.00	4-53	–	–	–	1	3	–
Total	**4**	**858**	**409**	**15**	**27.26**	**4-53**	**–**	**–**	**3**	**2**	**10**	**–**

In India (5)

	M	Balls	R	W	Ave	BB	5w	10w	B	LBW	C	C&B
Chepauk	1	228	89	5	17.80	3-37	–	–	1	–	4	–
Chinnaswamy Stadium	1	180	65	5	13.00	5-65	1	–	3	–	2	–
Green Park	1	264	177	3	59.00	2-56	–	–	1	–	2	–
Lal Bahadur Stadium	1	204	99	3	33.00	3-99	–	–	–	–	3	–
Wankhede Stadium	2	491	259	15	17.26	6-49	1	1	2	2	10	1
Total	**6**	**1367**	**689**	**31**	**22.22**	**6-49**	**2**	**1**	**7**	**2**	**21**	**1**

In Pakistan (3)

	M	Balls	R	W	Ave	BB	5w	10w	B	LBW	C	C&B
Gaddafi Stadium	1	192	157	5	31.40	5-121	1	–	2	–	3	–
National Stadium	1	258	213	4	53.25	4-138	–	–	–	–	4	–
Niaz Stadium	1	152	77	1	77.00	1-77	–	–	–	1	–	–
Total	**3**	**602**	**447**	**10**	**44.70**	**5-121**	**1**	**–**	**2**	**1**	**7**	**–**

In Sri Lanka (3)

	M	Balls	R	W	Ave	BB	5w	10w	B	LBW	C	C&B
Asgiriya Stadium	1	167	43	8	5.37	4-8	–	–	1	1	6	–
Colombo CCG	2	461	204	14	14.57	5-29	2	1	3	2	9	–
Sinhalese SCG	1	312	85	5	17.00	3-58	–	–	1	1	2	1
Total	**4**	**940**	**332**	**27**	**12.29**	**5-29**	**2**	**1**	**5**	**4**	**17**	**1**

FIRST-CLASS CAREER RECORDS

		Batting & Fielding									Bowling							
		M	I	NO	Runs	Ave	HS	100	50	Ct	O	M	R	W	Ave	BB	5w	10w
1971–72	Canterbury	3	3	1	16	8.00	11	–	–	2	55 †	9	194	10	19.40	4-42	–	–
1972–73	Canterbury	5	7	1	80	13.33	50	–	1	5	119 †	18	438	28	15.64	4-25	–	–
	NZ in Australia	1	1	0	9	9.00	9	–	–	–	26 †	3	80	1	80.00	1-32	–	–
	NZ in NZ	1	1	0	46	46.00	46	–	–	2	25 †	0	112	2	56.00	2-84	–	–
1973	NZ in England	12	7	2	74	14.80	30	–	–	–	355	72	1058	38	27.84	5-56	1	–
1973–74	NZ in Australia	7	11	0	197	17.90	49	–	–	3	175.7†	18	728	16	45.50	4-33	–	–
	Canterbury	1	2	1	34	34.00	25	–	–	–	29 †	4	115	6	19.16	4-64	–	–
	NZ in NZ	2	3	0	37	12.33	23	–	–	1	50.4†	7	225	10	22.50	4-71	–	–
1974–75	Canterbury	1	2	1	47	47.00	33	–	–	1	27 †	6	82	3	27.33	2-32	–	–
1975–76	Canterbury	7	10	3	155	22.14	53*	–	1	3	174.4†	27	554	28	19.78	5-53	1	–
	NZ in NZ	2	2	0	45	22.50	33	–	–	–	48.3†	4	197	12	16.41	7-23	1	1
1976–77	NZ in Pakistan	5	8	2	224	37.33	87	–	1	2	109.5†	3	610	18	33.88	5-47	2	–
	NZ in India	3	6	0	60	10.00	21	–	–	1	127	18	437	13	33.61	4-95	–	–
	Canterbury	5	7	1	185	30.83	53	–	1	2	109.5†	13	366	12	30.50	3-21	–	–
	NZ in NZ	2	4	0	143	35.75	81	–	1	2	72 †	7	354	6	59.00	3-155	–	–
1977–78	Canterbury	7	14	3	266	24.18	77	–	2	2	144.6†	30	489	27	18.11	5-28	2	–
	NZ in NZ	3	6	1	80	16.00	39	–	–	–	121.3†	26	371	15	24.73	6-26	1	1
1978	Nottinghamshire	7	8	4	193	48.25	101*	1	–	1	216.3	48	555	37	15.00	6-39	4	1
	NZ in England	10	13	0	149	11.46	40	–	–	9	280.4	72	714	41	17.41	7-77	2	1
1978–79	Canterbury	7	11	3	214	26.75	79*	–	2	2	181.3†	43	495	32	15.46	6-28	2	–
	NZ in NZ	3	5	1	115	28.75	53*	–	1	1	117.6†	13	414	18	23.00	5-62	2	1
1979	Nottinghamshire	12	16	4	193	16.08	41	–	–	5	317	103	753	47	16.02	7-23	2	–
1979–80	Tasmania	6	10	3	160	22.85	33*	–	–	1	173.2	36	477	13	36.69	5-55	1	–
	NZ in NZ	3	4	0	178	44.50	103	1	1	1	161.3	50	361	19	19.00	6-68	2	1
1980	Nottinghamshire	8	9	1	231	28.87	68	–	1	4	222.1	82	410	29	14.13	5-32	1	–
1980–81	NZ in Australia	5	8	2	249	41.50	103	1	1	2	229.3	52	567	27	21.00	6-57	3	–
	NZ in NZ	3	4	0	29	7.25	20	–	–	2	119.3	37	288	10	28.80	5-47	1	–
1981	Nottinghamshire	21	26	3	745	32.39	142*	1	3	14	708.4	231	1564	105	14.89	7-25	4	–
1981–82	Canterbury	7	13	2	408	37.09	83*	–	3	3	332.3	106	642	45	14.26	6-26	5	–
	NZ in NZ	3	5	1	92	23.00	40	–	–	2	91.5	25	226	14	16.14	6-100	2	–
1982	Nottinghamshire	18	28	2	807	31.03	131	2	4	16	403.5	122	889	61	14.57	7-25	4	–
1982–83	Canterbury	2	4	0	112	28.00	46	–	–	4	75.2	25	136	13	10.46	6-43	1	1
	NZ in NZ	2	3	0	59	29.50	30	–	–	1	77.3	27	141	10	14.10	4-33	–	–
1983	Nottinghamshire	5	4	0	119	29.75	103	1	–	3	86.2	28	210	13	16.15	5-72	1	–
	NZ in England	8	11	2	477	53.00	92*	–	5	3	345.1	95	855	36	23.75	6-53	2	–
1983–84	Canterbury	3	5	1	161	40.25	93	–	1	4	72	29	97	12	8.08	4-14	–	–
	NZ in NZ	3	4	0	144	36.00	99	–	1	3	109.5	33	232	12	19.33	5-28	1	–
	NZ in Sri Lanka	4	4	0	75	18.75	29	–	–	3	128.5	50	258	24	10.75	5-29	2	1
1984	Nottinghamshire	24	31	8	1179	51.26	210*	2	7	23	772.2	245	1645	117	14.05	7-35	6	1
1984–85	Canterbury	5	8	2	90	15.00	30*	–	–	–	168.4	57	346	22	15.72	5-46	2	–
	NZ in NZ	3	4	0	131	32.75	89	–	1	–	118.5	29	306	16	19.12	6-51	1	–
	NZ in West Indies	4	7	1	137	22.83	39*	–	–	1	143	33	409	15	27.26	4-53	–	–
1985	Nottinghamshire	19	29	11	592	32.88	73*	–	5	17	473.5	136	1026	59	17.38	8-41	2	–
1985–86	NZ in Australia	5	6	0	151	25.16	54	–	1	3	241.3	65	537	37	14.51	9-52	5	2
	NZ in NZ	3	3	1	105	52.50	72*	–	1	2	157.5	36	387	16	24.18	7-116	1	–
1986	Nottinghamshire	14	18	5	720	55.38	129*	2	3	6	393.4	108	825	57	14.47	6-31	5	1
	NZ in England	3	3	0	93	31.00	68	–	1	4	153.5	42	390	19	20.52	6-80	2	1
1986–87	Canterbury	8	13	3	207	20.70	50*	–	1	7	294.1	86	581	45	12.91	7-49	6	1
	NZ in NZ	3	4	2	74	37.00	35*	–	–	2	113.1	20	354	17	20.82	6-50	2	–
	NZ in Sri Lanka	1	1	1	151	–	151*	1	–	1	38.5	10	102	4	25.50	4-102	–	–
1987	Nottinghamshire	20	27	7	1075	53.75	133*	2	6	16	568	186	1154	97	11.89	6-20	9	2
	MCC	1	1	0	36	36.00	36	–	–	–	23	7	73	0	–	–	–	–
1987–88	NZ in Australia	5	8	3	151	30.20	36	–	–	1	237.4	63	564	29	19.44	5-30	5	2
	NZ in NZ	1	1	0	37	37.00	37	–	–	–	18	3	50	0	–	–	–	–
1988–89	NZ in India	4	7	2	88	17.60	31	–	–	2	124.5	30	307	27	11.37	9-55	3	1
	Canterbury	1	1	0	37	37.00	37	–	–	–	31	11	65	2	32.50	1-25	–	–
	NZ in NZ	2	3	1	53	26.50	32	–	–	–	82	21	169	5	33.80	4-101	–	–
Total		**333**	**464**	**93**	**11715**	**31.57**	**210***	**14**	**56**	**194**	**65423 balls‡**	**2756**	**25984**	**1447**	**17.95**	**9-52**	**99**	**18**

‡1586.6 8-ball [†] plus 8788.1 6-ball overs

Summary

	M	I	NO	Runs	Ave	HS	100	50	Ct	Balls	M	R	W	Ave	BB	5w	10w
Canterbury	62	100	22	2012	25.79	93	–	12	35	12564	464	4600	285	16.14	7-49	19	2
NZ Overseas†	77	101	15	2285	26.56	151*	2	9	31	16927	626	7616	345	22.07	9-52	27	8
NZ in New Zealand†	39	56	8	1368	28.50	103	1	6	19	9780	338	4187	182	23.00	7-23	14	3
Nottinghamshire	148	196	45	5854	38.76	210*	11	29	105	24974	1289	9031	622	14.51	8-41	38	5
Tasmania	6	10	3	160	22.85	33*	–	–	4	1040	36	477	13	36.69	5-55	1	–
MCC	1	1	0	36	36.00	36	–	–	–	138	3	73	0	–	–	–	–
Total	**333**	**464**	**93**	**11715**	**31.57**	**210***	**14**	**56**	**194**	**65423**	**2756**	**25984**	**1447**	**17.95**	**9-52**	**99**	**18**

†includes test matches

By Country

	M	I	NO	Runs	Ave	HS	100	50	Ct	Balls	M	R	W	Ave	BB	5w	10w
In New Zealand	101	156	30	3380	26.82	103	1	18	54	22344	802	8787	467	18.81	7-23	33	5
In England	182	231	49	6683	36.71	210*	11	35	117	31920	1573	12121	756	16.03	8-41	45	7
In Australia	29	44	8	917	25.47	103	1	2	13	6907	237	2953	123	24.00	9-52	14	4
In West Indies	4	7	1	137	22.83	39*	–	–	1	858'	33	409	15	27.26	4-53	–	–
In India	7	13	2	148	13.45	31	–	–	3	1511	48	744	40	18.60	9-55	3	1
In Pakistan	5	8	2	224	37.33	87	–	1	2	877	3	610	18	33.88	5-47	2	–
In Sri Lanka	5	5	1	226	56.50	151*	1	–	4	1006	60	360	28	12.85	5-29	2	1
Total	**333**	**464**	**93**	**11715**	**31.57**	**210***	**14**	**56**	**194**	**65423**	**2756**	**25984**	**1447**	**17.95**	**9-52**	**99**	**18**

Summary of How First-class Wickets Taken

	Wkts	%
Bowled	337	23.29
Leg before wicket	293	20.25
Caught	785	54.25
Caught and bowled	26	1.80
Hit wicket	6	0.41

Ten Wickets in a Match
(18)

11-58	**New Zealand v India**	**Wellington**	1975–76
10-100	**New Zealand v England**	**Wellington**	1977–78
11-141	Nottinghamshire v Yorkshire	Worksop	1978
11-116	New Zealanders v Warwickshire	Birmingham	1978
11-102	**New Zealand v West Indies**	**Dunedin**	1979–80
10-83	Canterbury v Central Districts	Christchurch	1982–83
10-102	**New Zealand v Sri Lanka**	**Colombo**	1983–84
11-76	Nottinghamshire v Gloucestershire	Nottingham	1984
15-123	**New Zealand v Australia**	**Brisbane**	1985–86
11-155	**New Zealand v Australia**	**Perth**	1985–86
10-72	Nottinghamshire v Surrey	Nottingham	1986
10-140	**New Zealand v England**	**Nottingham**	1986
12-81	Canterbury v Northern Districts	Christchurch	1986–87
12-83	Nottinghamshire v Somerset	Nottingham	1987
10-46	Nottinghamshire v Sussex	Nottingham	1987
10-67	New Zealanders v Western Australia	Perth	1987–88
10-176	**New Zealand v Australia**	**Melbourne**	1987–88
10-88	**New Zealand v India**	**Bombay**	1988–89

Five Wickets in an Innings
(99)

5-56	New Zealanders v Lancashire	Manchester	1973
7-23	**New Zealand v India**	**Wellington**	**1975–76**
5-53	Canterbury v Wellington	Christchurch	
5-47	New Zealanders v Prime Minister's XI	Rawalpindi	1976–77
5-121	**New Zealand v Pakistan**	**Lahore**	
5-28	Canterbury v Auckland	Christchurch	1977–78
5-50	Canterbury v England XI	Christchurch	
6-26	**New Zealand v England**	**Wellington**	
5-25	Nottinghamshire v Derbyshire	Nottingham	1978
6-39	Nottinghamshire v Yorkshire	Worksop	
5-102	Nottinghamshire v Yorkshire	Worksop	
5-29	Nottinghamshire v Warwickshire	Nottingham	
7-77	New Zealanders v Warwickshire	Birmingham	
5-84	**New Zealand v England**	**Lord's**	
6-28	Canterbury v Central Districts	Christchurch	1978–79
5-50	Canterbury v Auckland	Christchurch	
5-62	**New Zealand v Pakistan**	**Christchurch**	
5-104	**New Zealand v Pakistan**	**Auckland**	
7-28	Nottinghamshire v Glamorgan	Nottingham	1979
7-23	Nottinghamshire v Sussex	Nottingham	
5-55	Tasmania v Queensland	Hobart	1979–80
5-34	**New Zealand v West Indies**	**Dunedin**	
6-68	**New Zealand v West Indies**	**Dunedin**	
5-32	Nottinghamshire v Hampshire	Nottingham	1980
5-61	New Zealanders v Queensland	Brisbane	1980–81
5-87	**New Zealand v Australia**	**Perth**	
6-57	**New Zealand v Australia**	**Melbourne**	
5-47	**New Zealand v India**	**Christchurch**	
7-25	Nottinghamshire v Lancashire	Liverpool	1981
6-60	Nottinghamshire v Essex	Chelmsford	
5-47	Nottinghamshire v Lancashire	Nottingham	
5-34	Nottinghamshire v Northamptonshire	Cleethorpes	
5-81	Canterbury v Wellington	Wellington	1981–82
5-49	Canterbury v Northern Districts	Christchurch	
6-26	Canterbury v Auckland	Christchurch	
6-40	Canterbury v Central Districts	Palmerston North	
5-35	Canterbury v Wellington	Christchurch	
5-63	**New Zealand v Australia**	**Auckland**	
6-100	**New Zealand v Australia**	**Christchurch**	
6-65	Nottinghamshire v Lancashire	Manchester	1982
7-25	Nottinghamshire v Hampshire	Nottingham	
5-64	Nottinghamshire v Derbyshire	Chesterfield	
5-21	Nottinghamshire v Sussex	Hove	
6-43	Canterbury v Central Districts	Christchurch	1982–83
6-53	**New Zealand v England**	**The Oval**	1983
5-93	**New Zealand v England**	**Lord's**	
5-72	Nottinghamshire v Middlesex	Nottingham	
5-28	**New Zealand v England**	**Christchurch**	1983–84
5-73	**New Zealand v Sri Lanka**	**Colombo**	
5-29	**New Zealand v Sri Lanka**	**Colombo**	
6-52	Nottinghamshire v Essex	Chelmsford	1984
5-35	Nottinghamshire v Hampshire	Bournemouth	
7-35	Nottinghamshire v Gloucestershire	Nottingham	
5-61	Nottinghamshire v Worcestershire	Nottingham	
5-40	Nottinghamshire v Lancashire	Blackpool	
6-55	Nottinghamshire v Warwickshire	Nottingham	

5-46	Canterbury v Wellington	Rangiora	1984–85
5-74	Canterbury v Auckland	Auckland	
6-51	**New Zealand v Pakistan**	**Dunedin**	
7-34	Nottinghamshire v Middlesex	Lord's	1985
8-41	Nottinghamshire v Lancashire	Nottingham	
9-52	**New Zealand v Australia**	**Brisbane**	1985–86
6-71	**New Zealand v Australia**	**Brisbane**	
5-65	**New Zealand v Australia**	**Sydney**	
5-65	**New Zealand v Australia**	**Perth**	
6-90	**New Zealand v Australia**	**Perth**	
7-116	**New Zealand v Australia**	**Christchurch**	
5-41	Nottinghamshire v Leicestershire	Nottingham	1986
6-31	Nottinghamshire v Derbyshire	Derby	
6-33	Nottinghamshire v Surrey	Nottingham	
6-42	Nottinghamshire v Warwickshire	Nottingham	
6-80	**New Zealand v England**	**Lord's**	
6-80	**New Zealand v England**	**Nottingham**	
6-51	Nottinghamshire v Essex	Nottingham	
5-39	Canterbury v Auckland	Auckland	1986–87
5-44	Canterbury v Northern Districts	Gisborne	
5-28	Canterbury v Otago	Alexandra	
7-49	Canterbury v Northern Districts	Christchurch	
5-32	Canterbury v Northern Districts	Christchurch	
5-32	Canterbury v Auckland	Rangiora	
6-105	**New Zealand v West Indies**	**Auckland**	
6-50	**New Zealand v West Indies**	**Christchurch**	
6-44	Nottinghamshire v Kent	Canterbury	1987
5-29	Nottinghamshire v Leicestershire	Nottingham	
6-53	Nottinghamshire v Sussex	Eastbourne	
5-39	Nottinghamshire v Warwickshire	Worksop	
6-42	Nottinghamshire v Somerset	Nottingham	
6-41	Nottinghamshire v Somerset	Nottingham	
6-60	Nottinghamshire v Northamptonshire	Nottingham	
6-20	Nottinghamshire v Sussex	Nottingham	
6-38	Nottinghamshire v Glamorgan	Nottingham	
5-37	New Zealanders v Western Australia	Perth	1987–88
5-30	New Zealanders v Western Australia	Perth	
5-68	**New Zealand v Australia**	**Adelaide**	
5-109	**New Zealand v Australia**	**Melbourne**	
5-67	**New Zealand v Australia**	**Melbourne**	
9-55	New Zealanders v Western Zone	Rajkot	1988–89
5-65	**New Zealand v India**	**Bangalore**	
6-49	**New Zealand v India**	**Bombay**	

Hat Tricks
(2)

Canterbury v Central Districts	Nelson	1971–72
Nottinghamshire v Kent	Canterbury	1987

Centuries
(14)

101*	Nottinghamshire v Derbyshire	Nottingham	1978
103	**New Zealand v West Indies**	**Christchurch**	1979–80
103	New Zealanders v Queensland	Brisbane	1980–81
142*	Nottinghamshire v Yorkshire	Bradford	1981
131	Nottinghamshire v Surrey	The Oval	1982
100*	Nottinghamshire v Worcestershire	Worcester	1982
103	Nottinghamshire v Sussex	Hove	1983
100*	Nottinghamshire v Hampshire	Bournemouth	1984
210*	Nottinghamshire v Middlesex	Lord's	1984
105*	Nottinghamshire v Surrey	The Oval	1986
129*	Nottinghamshire v Somerset	Nottingham	1986
151*	**New Zealand v Sri Lanka**	**Colombo**	1986–87
133*	Nottinghamshire v Somerset	Taunton	1987
101	Nottinghamshire v Somerset	Nottingham	1987

ONE-DAY INTERNATIONAL CAREER RECORDS

		Batting & Fielding							Bowling						
		M	I	NO	Runs	Ave	HS	Ct	Balls	M	R	W	Ave	BB	4w	BW
1972–73	Pakistan in NZ	1	1	1	21	–	21*	–	40	0	37	0	–	–	–	–
1973	England in England	2	1	0	28	28.00	28	1	114	2	58	2	29.00	2-23	–	57
1973–74	Australia in NZ	1	1	0	3	3.00	3	–	48	0	35	0	–	–	–	–
1974–75	England in NZ	2	1	1	6	–	6*	1	64	0	25	2	12.50	2-21	–	32
1975[1]	East Africa in England	1	1	1	6	–	6*	–	72	6	10	0	–	–	–	–
	England in England	1	1	0	0	0.00	0	–	72	2	66	1	66.00	1-66	–	72
	India in England	1	1	0	15	15.00	15	1	72	2	48	2	24.00	2-48	–	36
1975–76	India in NZ	2	1	0	0	0.00	0	1	104	0	63	1	63.00	1-35	–	104
1978	England in England	2	2	0	2	1.00	1	–	132	4	92	3	30.66	2-22	–	44
1979[1]	Sri Lanka in England	1	–	–	–	–	–	–	72	3	24	1	24.00	1-24	–	72
	India in England	1	–	–	–	–	–	–	60	2	20	2	10.00	2-20	–	30
	West Indies in England	1	1	0	42	42.00	42	–	66	2	41	1	41.00	1-41	–	66
	England in England	1	1	0	15	15.00	15	–	72	4	32	1	32.00	1-32	–	72
1979–80	West Indies in NZ	1	1	0	41	41.00	41	–	60	3	28	2	14.00	2-28	–	30
1980–81[2]	Australia in Australia	9	8	1	117	16.71	39	3	511	14	323	11	29.36	5-26	1	46
	India in Australia	5	4	0	56	14.00	32	1	276	9	125	6	20.83	5-32	1	46
1980–81	India in NZ	2	2	0	45	22.50	23	1	84	4	33	3	11.00	2-27	–	28
1981–82	Australia in NZ	3	3	0	36	12.00	18	–	153	8	64	3	21.33	2-24	–	51
1982–83[2]	Australia in Australia	5	5	0	63	12.60	24	4	229	9	98	5	19.60	2-15	–	45
	England in Australia	5	4	0	139	34.75	79	–	282	7	169	7	24.14	3-15	–	40
1982–83	Sri Lanka in NZ	3	2	0	20	10.00	11	2	150	8	49	3	16.33	3-9	–	50
1982–83[3]	Australia in Australia	1	1	0	0	0.00	0	–	42	1	15	1	15.00	1-15	–	42
1983[1]	England in England	2	2	0	32	16.00	31	–	132	7	58	4	14.50	3-32	–	33
	Pakistan in England	2	2	0	24	12.00	13	–	126	3	81	4	20.25	3-20	–	31
	Sri Lanka in England	2	1	0	15	15.00	15	2	133	7	41	6	6.83	5-25	1	22
1983–84	England in NZ	3	2	0	44	22.00	23	–	180	6	114	8	14.25	5-32	1	22
1983–84	Sri Lanka in Sri Lanka	3	3	0	28	9.33	13	2	135	2	68	7	9.71	3-19	–	19
1984–85	Pakistan in NZ	4	3	2	56	56.00	34*	1	221	7	132	6	22.00	3-32	–	36
1984–85[4]	West Indies in Australia	2	1	0	11	11.00	11	–	60	4	23	3	7.66	3-23	–	20
	Sri Lanka in Australia	1	1	0	9	9.00	9	2	36	1	23	2	11.50	2-23	–	18
	India in Australia	1	1	0	3	3.00	3	–	51	3	50	1	50.00	1-50	–	51
1984–85	West Indies in West Indies	5	4	1	75	25.00	41	–	210	3	119	3	39.66	2-29	–	70
1985–86[2]	Australia in Australia	5	5	2	95	31.66	30*	–	205	3	127	9	14.11	3-14	–	22
	India in Australia	5	5	1	104	26.00	71	–	288	13	155	6	25.83	2-16	–	48
1985–86	Australia in NZ	4	4	1	79	26.33	40	–	224	10	112	9	12.44	4-15	1	24
1986	England in England	2	2	1	29	29.00	18*	–	122	1	63	2	31.50	2-29	–	61
1986–87	West Indies in NZ	3	3	0	53	17.66	24	2	138	1	96	2	48.00	2-46	–	69
1987–88[2]	Australia in Australia	5	5	1	108	27.00	34	–	256	3	163	5	32.60	3-35	–	51
	Sri Lanka in Australia	4	3	1	98	49.00	52	1	228	7	94	5	18.80	3-35	–	45
1987–88	England in NZ	1	1	1	33	–	33*	–	60	0	43	0	–	–	–	–
1987–88[5]	India in Sharjah	2	2	0	38	38.00	35*	1	120	0	103	4	25.75	3-54	–	30
	Sri Lanka in Sharjah	1	1	0	14	14.00	14	–	60	1	25	1	25.00	1-25	–	60
1988–89	Pakistan in NZ	1	–	–	–	–	–	–	60	0	38	5	7.60	5-38	1	12
	Total	**109**	**93**	**16**	**1603**	**20.81**	**79**	**26**	**5820**	**172**	**3183**	**149**	**21.36**	**5-25**	**6**	**39**

1 World Cup
2 World Series Cup
3 Bushfire Appeal Game
4 World Championship of Cricket
5 Sharjah Cup

Fifties
(3)

79	New Zealand v England	Adelaide	1982–83
71	New Zealand v India	Adelaide	1985–86
52	New Zealand v Sri Lanka	Hobart	1987–88

Four Wickets in an Innings
(6)

5-32	New Zealand v India	Perth	1980–81
5-26	New Zealand v Australia	Sydney	1980–81
5-25	New Zealand v Sri Lanka	Bristol	1983
5-32	New Zealand v England	Christchurch	1983-84
4-15	New Zealand v Australia	Dunedin	1985–86
5-38	New Zealand v Pakistan	Dunedin	1988–89

Summary

	M	I	NO	Runs	Ave	HS	Ct	Balls	M	R	W	Ave	BB	4w	BW
World Cup	13	10	1	149	16.55	42	3	877	38	421	22	19.13	5-25	1	39
World Series Cup	43	39	6	780	23.63	79	9	2275	65	1254	54	23.22	5-26	2	42
World Championship of Cricket	4	3	0	23	7.66	11	2	147	8	96	6	16.00	3-23	–	24
Sharjah	3	3	1	52	26.00	35*	1	180	1	128	5	25.60	3-54	–	36
Others	46	38	8	599	19.96	41	11	2341	60	1284	62	20.70	5-32	3	37
Total	**109**	**93**	**16**	**1603**	**20.81**	**79**	**26**	**5820**	**172**	**3183**	**149**	**21.36**	**5-25**	**6**	**39**

By Country

	M	I	NO	Runs	Ave	HS	Ct	Balls	M	R	W	Ave	BB	4w	BW
v England	21	17	3	328	23.42	79	2	1230	33	720	30	24.00	5-32	1	41
v Australia	33	32	5	501	18.55	40	7	1668	48	937	43	21.79	5-26	2	38
v West Indies	12	10	1	222	24.66	42	2	534	13	307	11	27.90	3-23	–	48
v India	19	16	2	261	18.64	71	5	1055	33	597	25	23.88	5-32	1	42
v Pakistan	8	6	3	101	33.66	34*	1	447	10	288	15	19.20	5-38	1	29
v Sri Lanka	15	11	1	184	18.40	52	9	814	29	324	25	12.96	5-25	1	32
v East Africa	1	1	1	6	–	6*	–	72	6	10	0	–	–	–	–
Total	**109**	**93**	**16**	**1603**	**20.81**	**79**	**26**	**5820**	**172**	**3183**	**149**	**21.36**	**5-25**	**6**	**39**